ALL THE LEAVES ARE BROWN

HOW THE MAMAS & THE PAPAS CAME TOGETHER AND BROKE APART

ALL THE LEAVES ARE BROWN

HOW THE MAMAS & THE PAPAS CAME TOGETHER AND BROKE APART

SCOTT G. SHEA

Backbeat
Books
ESSEX, CONNECTICUT

Backbeat Books

An imprint of Globe Pequot, the trade division of
The Rowman & Littlefield Publishing Group, Inc.
4501 Forbes Blvd., Ste. 200
Lanham, MD 20706
www.rowman.com

Distributed by NATIONAL BOOK NETWORK

British Library Cataloguing in Publication Information Available

Library of Congress Cataloging-in-Publication

Names: Shea, Scott, author.
Title: All the leaves are brown : how the Mamas & the Papas came together
    and broke apart / Scott Shea.
Identifiers: LCCN 2022060905 (print) | LCCN 2022060906 (ebook) | ISBN
    9781493072118 (cloth) | ISBN 9781493072125 (ebook)
Subjects: LCSH: Mamas and the Papas (Musical group) | Rock
    musicians—United States—Biography. | LCGFT: Biographies.
Classification: LCC ML421.M35 S54 2023 (print) | LCC ML421.M35 (ebook) |
    DDC 782.42166092/2 [B]—dc23/eng/20221220
LC record available at https://lccn.loc.gov/2022060905
LC ebook record available at https://lccn.loc.gov/2022060906

CONTENTS

ACKNOWLEDGMENTS

All praise and thanksgiving to almighty God for providing me the opportunity to tell this story. Next, I must thank my family for all their love and support in this venture and in all things. I thank my beautiful and wonderful wife Rebecca and our two darling children, Peter and Zoe. Next, my parents Marc and Teresa; my brother Marc; his wife Beverly and their three children, Josie, Marc, and Maggie; my sister Tamara; her husband Kyle; and their two children, Cinthia and Sawyer; and to Janet and Bill. I also must thank my in-laws, James and Joanne Edinger, for all their love and support and my sisters-in-law Elizabeth and Alina. I also thank Ryan Sr., Ryan Jr., Julia, Gabriel, Rich, and Pauline and my two closest friends Wyman Vintson and Ed Sinawa for their support and my extended family on both sides.

I want to thank all my colleagues at the Catholic Channel on SiriusXM for all their love and support, including Gus Lloyd, Jacklyn Resciniti, Tyler Veghte, Adam Hamway, Fr. Dave Dwyer, Christina Howard and Hallie Lord. Writing and researching would've never happened if it weren't for my former program director Liz Aiello. She recognized my passion for history and telling a story when she commissioned me to write and direct several audio documentaries that aired on the channel and for that I'm forever grateful. I also would like to thank SiriusXM colleagues and fellow music buffs, Dave Horvath and Bob Bradley, for their interest in my work on this book, and my friend Bob Olney for his consistent support and encouragement.

Getting this book into the hands of Backbeat Books wouldn't have happened if not for friends and mentors Kathryn Jean Lopez, Fr. John Devaney, Mike Aquilina, Bill Flanagan, and Gary Jansen. Thanks to you all.

I also have to thank Dick Weissman, Pat La Croix, Jill Gibson, Jeffrey Phillips, Steve Barri, Barry McGuire, Scott Fagan, and Christine Boran for taking the time to talk with me and giving me deeper insight into the members of the Mamas & the Papas, which made this book unlike any others that came before it. I also would like to thank Kette for providing me with a treasure trove of John Phillips/the Mamas & the Papas archival material and articles.

Finally, I want to thank Backbeat acquisition editor John Cerullo for his belief in my writing and editorial assistant Barbara Claire for navigating me through this process.

CHAPTER 1:
OKMULGEE

The family history of John Phillips is so fanciful that it's almost difficult to believe. It reads like a novel that strikes so many chords of the early American experience and hits all the touchstones of the 20th century. His paternal ancestry can be traced back to England through his grandfather John Andrew Phillips, whose family emigrated from there to Canada and ultimately settled in Watertown, New York, just across the border from Ontario. There, he met Anna Elizabeth Moran, an Irish immigrant who arrived in Watertown as an infant. They eventually married and had two children, Marcia, born in 1878, and Claude Andrew, born April 25, 1887. It was a devoutly Catholic home with Anna being a daily communicant.

John's grandfather was a gifted architect and engineer whose life was cut short after a fatal fall at a jobsite in Watertown. Now a single mother, Anna moved the kids into a smaller home and took a job to support them. A few years later, when Marcia graduated high school, she took a job as a school-teacher at the nearby Mullin Street School to support her mother.

With a 10-year age difference between the children, Claude became a latchkey kid, and his youth became one of fantasy and adventure. After high school graduation, he took a series of local odd jobs before finding steady employment as an ironworker. He was on course to follow his father's example when he abruptly decided to join the U.S. Marines at the age of 25. Upon signing his enlistment papers on November 29, 1913, he was shipped off to the Marine Barracks Navy Yard in Norfolk, Virginia. He chose engineering as his military occupational specialty after graduating from boot camp and spent his first three years serving on the Battleship *Virginia*, which practiced maneuvers in Guantanamo Bay, Chesapeake Bay, and Veracruz, Mexico, at the height of the Mexican Revolution.

His next assignment was serving as a drill instructor at the Marine Corps Training Depot in Parris Island, South Carolina, as World War I was raging in Europe. Claude managed to avoid overseas combat after the United States entered the war on April 4, 1917, and spent that entire time in Parris Island, where he got his first taste of drinking and gambling at the NCO club, where he'd also occasionally show off his Irish tenor. On November 18, 1918, two days before the signing of the Armistice of Compiegne, which ended the war, he was shipped off to Europe with the intention of being stationed in Germany to assist in the Allied attempt to control civil unrest as the country fell into a depression.

He arrived in Brest, France, and remained there for approximately nine months as his orders kept changing. Eventually, he received his discharge papers and was sent back to the United States with his post-military career already in mind. Over the years, Claude told his family a fanciful story of why he headed west to Oklahoma instead of settling in Watertown. He told them he won a hotel/saloon in a craps game while on board the troop transport, the USS *Siboney*. He was up, and his hot hand was draining one particular soldier. With little left to stake, the desperate soldier put up the deed to his family-run hotel and saloon in Okmulgee, Oklahoma. Claude was skeptical. He'd never heard of Okmulgee and questioned whether the deed was even legitimate. He was assured and the soldier appealed to Claude's more primordial senses by telling him the place was crawling with pretty Native women hungering for war heroes. That was enough to convince him and, with one roll of the dice, he became the proud owner of the Depot Hotel.

It's more likely that Claude heard about the oil boom going on in Oklahoma that was attracting people from all over the country and saw an opportunity to make a good living. Okmulgee was one of those cities experiencing an influx of people. In 1919, it was the fourth-largest city in the state. But Claude wasn't interesting in drilling for oil. He wanted to serve those capitalizing on the boom and purchased the hotel located on East 5th Street across from the Frisco Train Depot. After his honorable discharge in August 1919, he spent a short time reconnecting back home in Watertown and then made the long, circuitous, 1,400-mile rail trip to Oklahoma. The American West was still wild in 1919 and was fully romanticized by Wild West shows and silent cowboy movies starring Harry Carey, William S. Hart and Douglas Fairbarks in the burgeoning film industry.

When Claude stepped off the train in Okmulgee, he stepped into an environment unlike anything he'd seen at home or overseas. The flat brown prairies stretched endlessly over the horizon and stood in stark contrast to the hills and mountains of northern New York State or anything he'd seen in Europe. Okmulgee was in the midst of an oil boom that would help fuel the growing American auto industry and the old dirt roads that surrounded the city square now accommodated a booming commerce and sidled dozens of new modern buildings that lined entire blocks. The Southwest was set to become the oil capital of the world and would make millionaires and billionaires out of the descendants of prairie farmers.

By the time Claude had arrived, Okmulgee had blossomed to over 4,000 residents and featured a substantial Cherokee population, owing to former President Andrew Jackson's Indian Removal Act of 1830. Following Jackson's order, thousands of Cherokees were forcibly relocated from their homes in Virginia, North Carolina, and South Carolina by the U.S. Army and moved to settlements in Oklahoma. The 2,200-mile trek was made by foot and, along the way, 4,000 people died from disease and exposure. This became known as the Trail of Tears. Among the descendants of the survivors were Edmund Franklin Graves, his wife Zora Gertrude Hardgrave, and their 13 children.

Zora was the housekeeper at the Depot Hotel, and several times a week, she made the 15-mile journey from Henryetta with one or more of her daughters in tow to assist her. Usually, it was her eldest daughter Dene Gertrude Gaines who went by the Anglicized version of her name, Edna. Although he was twice her age, Claude was smitten and took every opportunity he could to playfully grope and paw the 16-year-old maiden when nobody was looking. It often ended with him getting walloped across the jaw by her, but, below the surface, the romantic feeling was mutual. This cat-and-mouse game ensued for several months and Claude eventually made his feelings known.

It also started to be noticed by the saloon patrons, and one regular who warned Claude of the potential consequences of his actions was the rector of St. Anthony's Church, Fr. Urban de Hasque. In addition to the sinful nature of his actions, Fr. Urban advised Claude of Edna's notorious brothers, known around town as the Gaines Boys. Hoyt, Earl, and Orby were well-known desperadoes who'd already spent considerable time in jail. If word got back to them about Claude's brazenness toward Edna, they'd waste no time coming for him. But even that wasn't enough to stop Claude. He was head-over-heels in love with Edna. Being the peacemaker, and not wanting to see Claude shot, Fr. Urban advised him to propose to her. Claude took his advice and very promptly asked for her hand in marriage. Edna didn't take to the proposal right away. Leaving her family was a big decision, especially since she was the eldest daughter.

Born February 12, 1904, in Coahuila, Mexico, home of the state-recognized Cherokee Nation of Mexico, the infant Edna survived an 800-mile journey to Okmulgee to rejoin her father, who was an oil field worker, and brothers. When Edna was five, she was kidnapped by a band of gypsies encamped on the edge of the tribal jurisdictional area. Edmund made it his mission to track them down and retrieve his daughter. He scoured through every gypsy camp that came through town and, two years later, tracked her down in Mexico and rescued her.

They were a very tight and loving family and Edna felt indebted to her parents. She played a significant role in helping her mother raise her younger siblings who looked up to her. But her parents were also dirt poor, and Claude did provide a level of security she'd never imagined. Edna marrying Claude would mean one less mouth for them to feed. It was a tough decision, but she ultimately decided to marry Claude. They had two wedding ceremonies, one in the Cherokee tradition and one in the Catholic. When Claude sent word to his mother and sister that he married a Cherokee woman, they gave their blessings on the condition that she'd convert to Catholicism and agree to raise their children in the faith. Edna acquiesced, and the two were married on January 4, 1921, at St. Anthony's Church in Okmulgee.

The newlyweds moved into the hotel Claude continued to manage, and Edna studied English and the Catholic catechism and remained about a year. The bloom had come off the rose in being a hotel and saloon proprietor, and relief came in the form of the United States Marines when they offered Claude an officer's commission. He didn't hesitate to accept it, and, very quickly, he and his new bride set off for officer training in Quantico, Virginia.

At first, Edna enjoyed being an officer's wife but eventually found life on the base unsettling because of the lingering racism against Native people that was very prevalent in white culture. It was a cold war among the other officers' wives but was displayed openly by enlisted men who'd often hurl racist insults her way whenever the opportunity presented itself. It got to be too much for Edna to bear, and she threatened to move back to Okmulgee. Seeing his young bride in distress upset Claude but he insisted she stick with it, twice giving in and supplying her with train fare home. Both times he followed her to the station and persuaded her to give it another try. In a peacekeeping effort, he took leave in order to take her back home for a visit to try and calm the waters.

While there, Claude confided in Edna's father Edmund about their situation back home, and Edmund offered him some simple, age-old advice. Get her pregnant. It made sense. Claude was pushing 35, which was fairly old for a first-time father in 1922, and it would certainly give Edna motivation to stick with him. Claude took his father-in-law's advice, and, on December 31, 1922, Edna gave birth to Rosemary Ann. A little less than two years later, they welcomed a son, Thomas Richard Moran.

As Claude and Edna settled into family life, things began leveling off and life for Edna as the wife of a Marine officer began to take hold. Claude's Marine career was also on the upswing being placed in charge of all Parris Island base construction and engineering projects. Three years later, Claude was dispatched to Haiti and his family joined him. On the surface, the U.S. mission was an effort to aid an unstable government but in actuality, it was to keep Germany out of the Caribbean.

In 1931, the Phillips' next stop was Managua, Nicaragua, another site of U.S. military occupation following the end of the Constitutionalist War that divided the country four years earlier. Only a few months into their time there, a devastating 6.0 magnitude earthquake ravaged Managua, decimating the city and taking the lives of 2,000 people. The quake triggered an enormous fire that raged through the area, and Claude helped lead a demolitions team that dynamited the central marketplace in Managua, which created a firewall that saved much of downtown. He was cited by the Marines for his heroism.

The rise of the Great Depression, which began with the stock market crash on October 29, 1929, forced the Marines to shore up their overseas operations and brought the Phillips' back to Parris Island in 1931. Despite the mass unemployment and breadlines that became commonplace across the nation during the Depression, Claude and Edna lived quite well and provided well for their two young children. Edna traipsed around town in Railene dresses and sun hats, and Claude's rank of major provided them with a houseboy, a gardener, and a chef-in-residence. At the end of 1934, Edna discovered she was pregnant again, which took Claude by surprise. With two young children, his busy schedule and sex getting lower on the priority list, he didn't recollect having relations with Edna. Claude's drinking had also escalated over the last 14 years to the point where he had become a functional alcoholic, so it's possible that's why he didn't recollect it. Nevertheless, he referred to the child in utero as a "miracle baby."

On August 31, 1935, Claude and Edna welcome their third child, a son named John Edmund Andrew Phillips. His two middle names were in tribute to his grandfathers. On the day they brought him home from the hospital, a Category 5 hurricane was bearing down on the Atlantic Coast. In spite of the driving wind and rain, a tipsy Claude drove the newborn around Parris Island, introducing him to friends and launching a three-day celebration at their home.

As joyful as the family environment John was born into was, there were chinks in the armor. Claude's alcoholism had placed a wedge between him and Edna that was widening more and more. It also negatively affected his health. In 1937, after a move to the Brooklyn Navy Yard, Claude suffered a heart attack that landed him in the Bethesda Naval Hospital, where he'd spend considerable time over the next two years. It all took its toll on his ability to work, and, in 1939, he received his second honorable discharge from the Marines. After his second heart attack, the family moved to a two-story single-family home on East Oxford Street in Alexandria, Virginia. With Claude's now-constant health issues, it allowed him to be close to Bethesda Naval Hospital.

His discharge was an embarrassment to Claude and only served to sink him deeper into his alcoholism. His military status and take-home pay were a great source of pride and had allowed him and his family to live a pampered lifestyle during the throes of the Depression. Though his pension still paid him $600/month, a considerable sum in 1940, the intangible of not having a daily Marine regimen to adhere to had a devastating effect. While on active duty, Claude served as a functional alcoholic. Now, with nothing and nobody to be beholden to, he quickly descended into dysfunctional alcoholism. Even raising bulldogs and building a workroom for himself in the basement wasn't enough to keep his alcoholic demons at bay. Instead, it just became a place for him to drink himself silly on Four Roses bourbon on a daily basis surrounded by his stinky, loyal pack.

The impact of this sudden change had an effect on the rest of the family too. In the fall of 1940, Rosemary left to attend Mary Washington College in Fredericksburg, Virginia. In December 1941, Tommy dropped out of high school to join the Army after the Japanese bombed Pearl Harbor, which thrust the United States into World War II. Edna, meanwhile, had used a considerable portion of Claude's pension to open up a dress shop, not far from their home, as a way to supplement their income and get away from the depressing and toxic atmosphere at home. Six-year-old John was the casualty of this, spending many days at home alone with his intoxicated father.

One of John's earliest memories was slipping past his father's bulldogs, who were devoted to him but hated everyone else, and sneaking down to the basement to find the pathetic sight of Claude passed out, sloppily dressed in his Marine dress blues and surrounded by empty bourbon bottles. It stirred up a range of emotions most six-year-olds rarely feel. Why couldn't he have a normal father like his friends? Their fathers took them to the racetrack and tossed the ball around in the yard. His was broken and paralyzed by alcohol.

Claude's Marine pension was enough to help keep their mortgage and debts current, but Edna's dress shop put a considerable dent in their savings and eventually went out of business. She took a job at Woodward & Lothrop's flagship department store in downtown Washington, D.C., to help make ends meet and try and rebuild their cash reserves. The pressure she felt was enormous. Not only was her failed business venture a source of financial pain and embarrassment, but her marriage was failing as well. With John getting older and starting school and working and commuting 12 hours a day, she began drinking too.

The reality of her messy situation revealed itself when young John unexpectedly showed up at work late one morning. He'd ridden his bicycle eight miles, which included crossing over the George Mason Memorial Bridge, into downtown Washington, D.C., by skitching on the back fenders of cars and buses. He explained to her that he'd rather be at work with her than stuck at home with Daddy. Edna reassured John of both of their love for him and explained that his father gets sick sometimes. With a kiss and a hug, she placed him in his bicycle in a cab and sent him back home, but she knew something had to be done. There was a glimmer of hope however.

With the United States now fully engaged in a war with both Japan and Germany, all branches of service were in desperate need of veterans under the age of 60 for training purposes and other forms of combat service support. It wasn't long into 1942 before the Marines, once again, came calling on Claude who was now 55. It shook him sober. He sensed his great comeback and he resumed his Marine PT with daily running and exercise. It was going to take getting in shape and a little bit of luck to pass that physical. He stopped drinking, ate healthier, and became reengaged in his family life. John had a functioning father again, and it lifted the mood in the home considerably. But it wasn't to be. Claude had too much to overcome and he failed his physical. His drinking had caused too much damage to his heart and even a desperate Marine Corps couldn't afford to reinvest in his services. It was another crushing blow to Claude who immediately settled back in to his alcoholic ways.

The dysfunction at home began filtering into John's school life. At the end of the spring semester, a letter included in his report card from St. Mary's Academy asked his parents not to readmit him for the fall because of his poor attendance record. Turns out, John was a serious truant, which came as a complete shock to Edna. His misbehavior wasn't limited to school. At home, young John acted out by suffocating one of his father's bulldogs and acting rudely toward strangers by swiping newspapers out of the hands of bus riders and purposely stepping on toes.

Edna knew she had to get John out of this environment and signed him up for the fall semester at Linton Hall Military Academy in Bristow, Virginia. It was a bizarre amalgam of private Catholic school and military academy run concurrently by nuns and Commandant Major Marlin S. Reichley. Here, John would be under strict supervision and be confined to the campus, which was located at the foot of the Bull Run Mountains and outskirts of Manassas. Little did Edna know that this atmosphere at Linton Hall would kindle a rebellious streak that would drive and hinder John for the rest of his life.

CHAPTER 2:
JOHN'S TALKIN' BLUES

Linton Hall Military Academy in Bristow, Virginia, located in the foothills of the Bull Run Mountains, is approximately 40 miles southwest of Alexandria. In the 1940s, it was a bizarre combination of private Catholic school and pseudo-military academy that focused on boys aged six to 16. Benedictine nuns started the institution in 1878 when they were bequeathed 120 acres by fellow sister Sarah Elliott Linton, who'd inherited the land from her wealthy family. During that period, Virginia was under the auspices of the Vicar Apostolic of North Carolina. With the bishop's permission, separate boys and girls schools, as well as a military school, were established there in 1894.

By 1932, the schools were defunct, but a handful of nuns, led by Mother Agnes Johnston, remained behind to establish a novitiate and to reestablish the military school with the help of Lt. Lawrence Scott Carson. Now, under the Diocese of Richmond, the school seemed to have gotten lost in the shuffle, which may account for the bizarre blend of nuns and military, attributed solely to Mother Agnes' complete fascination with military life and structure.

The boys attending Linton Hall typically fell into one of three categories: juvenile delinquents on the verge of going to reform school, local children who came from a family with military tradition, or parents who were stretched thin and couldn't provide the proper time needed for their child. John Phillips fell into the last category.

In September 1942, when John was enrolled as a first-grader, Linton Hall boasted approximately 150 students with an annual tuition of $315. It was another burden that stretched Claude's pension thinner and kept Edna working long hours at Woodward & Lothrop, but, in their minds, it was worth it. Both recognized John's potential as a student. Claude, particularly, had plans for his youngest child. He was going to be a Naval officer, and Linton Hall was as good a place to start that journey as any. But any grand visions they may have had of this being the launching pad for John's eventual success were dashed by the school's toxic atmosphere.

As with recruits arriving at boot camp, John was quickly stripped of his individuality and dignity by the senior cadets through ritual hazing and humiliation. In very short order, he and his fellow new recruits learned how to look like a tight military unit by marching in step and standing in formation properly. Up to this point, John's life had been fairly structureless. Now, each day, he had 30 seconds to wash his face and comb his hair, 30 seconds to brush his teeth, and 30 seconds to get dressed before morning formation followed by class.

The nuns involved themselves in the military aspect by waking the boys up with reveille at 6:00 a.m. and dispensing the discipline, which was just as brutal as the upperclassmen's hazing. Boys who wet their beds were forced to wear their soiled undergarments around their necks as a deterrent. The preferred method of punishment for rule breakers was paddling a bare bottom. John fell victim to that rite of passage in his first week on campus and became a repeat offender. The nuns also engaged in the frightening practice of observing the boys as they showered, which served as a preventive measure against horseplay, bullying, and homosexual activity.

Despite feeling displaced and lashing out every chance he could, John earned good grades at Linton Hall. He got his first exposure to music through his involvement in the Drum & Bugle Corps and joined the basketball team. Edna did her best to insert herself into John's life away from home by visiting him most weekends. Nearly every Sunday, she'd catch the train to Manassas from Union Station with a picnic basket and John's favorite meal, a stuffed potato, lovingly packed away. They'd walk the majestic school grounds, chat about their weeks, and read from one of Edna's favorite novels or poetry books. She'd also update him on the war effort, which now included both brother Tommy and new brother-in-law Bill Throckmorton. Inevitably, though, the peace was always broken by John asking her why he was there, which never ended with a satisfactory answer for the seven-year-old. Before leaving to catch the 5:00 train home, Edna would sit silently with John in prayer and meditation after mass in the Immaculate Conception chapel.

John spent four years at Linton Hall, and the main qualities he acquired while there were a dislike for authority and a newfound sense of rebellious-ness. In September 1946, he enrolled in junior high at St. Stephen Martyr School in Washington, D.C., where his height, which was approaching six feet, caused him to stand out. He was a shoo-in for the basketball team but particularly excelled at baseball. He was also active in the local Catholic Youth Organization and served as an altar boy at his parish, St. Rita's.

His faith, however, was quickly being tested by his peers and by girls. Although, through time immemorial, those two elements have always pro-vided pressure for teenage boys, by the time John had landed back in Alex-andria, U.S. culture had entered the golden era of the teenager. With World War II now over, and a booming national economy, teenagers, who'd taken over for the twentysomethings overseas during the war effort, had carved a niche in the U.S. workforce and now had money of their own to spend. The various entertainment industries were among the first to target them. In the movies, teenage boys were having their hearts captured by Elizabeth Taylor and Shirley Temple, who'd matured mightily since her days as a child star. And their emotions and desires were being put eloquently into song by a new breed of young crooners, including Frank Sinatra, Frankie Laine, and Perry Como.

In this new age of teenage-ism, sex was growing increasingly casual and disposable and virginity, mostly for boys, was now seen as something to be ashamed of; the quicker one disposed of it, the better. In the summer of 1948, John got his first taste of the opposite sex when he paid a schoolmate a quarter to sleep with his sister, which ignited an insatiable appetite for sex that would follow him the rest of his life.

The peer pressure element of John's life manifested in gangs, another growing aspect of teenage life. The neighborhood inside Alexandria that the Phillips lived in was known as Del Ray, and the gang of boys who "controlled the turf" called themselves the Del Ray Locals. They engaged in the local brand of petty terrorism: stealing cars, busting windows, slashing tires, and breaking into the Belle Haven Country Club kitchen. With John's homelife growing increasingly dysfunctional, the prospect of joining a brotherhood like this became more and more attractive.

In the years he'd been away at Linton Hall, his parents had grown further and further apart. Claude had sunk further into alcoholism and was slowly killing himself on bourbon and isolating himself in the cellar. Edna left the department store and took a job with the Navy. She began engaging in extra-marital affairs. Her drinking had also escalated and, like Claude during his Marine days, she became a functional alcoholic. This behavior caused collateral damage. With Rosemary and Tommy off with families of their own, and John growing older and more independent, the closeness that once existed between mother and son had grown increasingly distant.

Perhaps in a subconscious grab for attention, John began lashing out and became self-destructive. It started small enough with things like shoplifting, ignoring his schoolwork, and cutting class and would continue to go unnoticed by Edna until he embarrassed himself in a public way. The same summer John lost his virginity, he was also a star Little League Baseball pitcher and earned a spot on the Alexandria All-Star squad that made it to the quarterfinals in the second-ever Little League World Series. His six-foot frame gave him a distinct advantage in maximum stride and velocity, not to mention the intimidation factor he had over his opponents, who averaged about 5'4".

En route to Original Field in Williamsport, Pennsylvania, while stopping for breakfast, John shoplifted a penknife in the gift shop and was busted by his coach. He was forced to return it, and the infraction earned him a benching and a confinement to his motel room during the game. And his teammates felt his loss that day too. They were shellacked by the eventual champion, Lock Haven, 12–1.

John entered George Washington High School in the fall of 1949. He was now over six feet tall and had developed into a gawky class clown with a sarcastic wit that was always getting him in trouble. His size caught the attention of basketball coach Rasty Doran, but his grades kept him off the varsity squad until his senior year. Over the course of his high school career, more than one teacher recognized his natural aptitude and high IQ and challenged him to focus, particularly in writing. Sometimes it met with positive results but mostly it didn't. He scored particularly high on standardized tests and any sort of self-discipline could have resulted in straight As. But his lack of foundation combined with his pathetic homelife subverted all that. There was no reward for hard work and no example set.

With the incident at the Little League World Series seemingly behind him, Edna continued to be confronted with John's issues. One morning, while making John's bed, she discovered 10 brand-new penknives stuffed in his pillowcase. She confronted him when he got home, and he confessed to stealing them from a local hardware store. She immediately drove him down to it and ordered him to give them back and apologize. Going in alone, John simply just slipped them back into the display case and walked out, telling his mother the store owner was very sympathetic. He had gotten pretty good at bamboozling those closest to him.

By the time he was in high school, John was a full-fledged member of the Del Ray Locals, and although they continued to be a neighborhood nuisance, it wasn't always petty crime with them. The early 1950s was a transitional time musically, and John was becoming devoted to the radio. The diversity of popular acts and vocal stylings was growing and he and some of his Locals buddies tried their hand at re-creating the sounds made by popular acts like the Ames Brothers, the Four Lads, the Four Freshmen and the Hi-Lo's. John was at the forefront of it all and, for the first time in his life, tried his hand at vocal arrangement. He was naturally adept at finding the strongest voices, identifying the weakest and putting them in positions to contribute to an overall pleasant sound.

Cruising around in cars was also becoming a big part of the 1950s teenage experience and, in his junior year, John was able to acquire a canary-yellow 1948 Plymouth in order to get around and cruise the Alexandria-D.C. circuit. John and fellow Local Bill Cleary would throw on T-shirts and jeans, slick back their hair with Vaseline, and cruise in and out of town. The only thing missing in John's life was the requisite sweetheart, and he found that in Susie Adams, a fellow George Washington student who was a year younger than he was. She was no pushover, though. She came from a prominent family who boasted of being descendants of President John Adams. John pawed her every chance he could, which always ended in playful rejection. She made it clear, if he wanted her, he'd have to wait for marriage. It was an idle threat. Neither were ready at that point in their young lives.

Back at home, life had gotten pretty unbearable for John. His mother had become much more absent than normal and he started getting suspicious. For as long as he could remember, she was always doing something extracurricular. She'd been a member of the Officers Wives club, the VFW ladies auxiliary and several church sodalities, but she never gone to any of those gatherings as done-up as she had been lately. John suspected his mother was having an affair and attempted to express his concern to Claude but his alcoholism made him indifferent. His only response was to ask John to bring him down another bottle of bourbon.

John took matters in his own hands one evening by tailing Edna to a cheap motel where she went into a room with a man dressed in an Army officer's uniform. Not knowing how to react, he just sat and waited and cracked open a beer from a six pack he'd brought along to take the edge off. After 15 impatient minutes, he finally built up the nerve and walked up to their door. Inside, he could hear the disturbing sounds of his mother making love to a stranger and, all at once, a rush of anger that stretched back to his time at Linton Hall swelled up. He braced himself to kick open the door or bust open the window, but he couldn't. He was paralyzed. Though perhaps a little wiser and world-weary than other kids his age, he was still a child incapable of this type of confrontation. He slunk back to his car and drove away.

The thought of returning to his parents' house was too much. He moved in with his sister and her family in the Rose Hill subdivision of Alexandria. Music was becoming a bigger force in John's life and in order to alleviate the stress of his mother's infidelity, he retreated to the radio and the pop sounds coming out of WOL in Washington, D.C., and WITH in Baltimore. He continued to be fascinated by the vocalese of Clark Burroughs and the Hi-Lo's and the big sounds of the more popular hitmakers like Teresa Brewer, Vaughn Monroe, Rosemary Clooney, and Frank Sinatra. He still, however, couldn't say out of trouble and the confusion brought upon by his mother's indiscretion only amplified his rage.

John's involvement with the Del Ray Locals increased throughout his high school tenure, especially as his situation at home deteriorated. Some of the more brazen members of the gang enjoyed getting into fistfights with the servicemen who permeated the area and patronized the bars and pool halls. John wasn't one for that type of confrontation, but he enjoyed watching. One particularly disturbing activity they enjoyed was traveling over the Potomac to Lafayette Park, directly across the street from the White House, and attacking gay men looking for hook-ups. It was strictly for kicks. Because of the social stigma associated with homosexuality, most of these assaults went unreported. The police caught wind of it though and, in no time, placed undercover vice officers in the park.

One night, John and a few other Locals, including a big guy named Ronald McShea, headed out that way for some misadventure. When McShea attempted to attack a man dressed in drag, the police trap was sprung and he, John and the others were whisked off to the local precinct. While waiting to be booked, the teasing by the cops was merciless. John and the others took their lumps, but for McShea, beneath the surface, he was seething. When he was denied a cigarette, something inside him snapped. He calmly walked up to the arresting officer and sucker-punched him in the stomach. A brawl ensued. John, whose brother Tommy was a police officer in that very precinct, wanted no part of it and hid under a desk.

After the war ended, Tommy joined the D.C. Metro police and quickly established a reputation for being unstable and had already been suspended once for abusive behavior toward the city's black population. As luck would have it, he walked right into the melee and fired two warning shots to break it up. Seeing John peek up from behind a desk, he asked everyone in the room who the bastard was who hit his kid brother.

Even though he'd avoided any conflict, John pointed to the officer McShea had slugged. Tommy walked over to his fellow officer, still hunched over from the blow he'd just taken, and sent him back to the floor with a punch across the jaw. The other officers jumped Tommy and restrained him. He was suspended three months without pay. For John, though, it served him well by scaring him straight. He quit the Locals and fled back to Rosemary's house and tried to get a grasp on his rudderless life.

Edna's affair with the Army officer was no longer a secret. It had had a deleterious effect on John's life, which, in turn affected his sister and brother. Because of John's juvenile delinquency, Tommy had to figure out how to make ends meet for three months and Rosemary had inherited another mouth to feed.

They mutually decided an intervention was necessary and met up with their mother. But, getting it out in the open didn't have the desired effect. She remained steadfast in her ways, telling them she had no desire to give up her relationship with a man she identified as Col. George Lacy. She no longer loved their father but needed his pension in order to live. Edna told her children that she's as free now as she would be if she left him and saw no reason to disrupt the status quo.

That ended that. John continued to stay away and sought solace in music, but it was about to get a little deeper. Rosemary's husband Bill drummed for a jazz band who played local clubs on the weekends and began to take John along. Back at home, he introduced John to the jazz greats by playing records by Buddy Miles, Dave Brubeck, Art Blakey, Gerry Mulligan and others. Bill had some rehearsal space in their basement, and he'd allow John to play on his drums and piano, but it was mostly incoherent banging. That changed when he taught John how to play some chords on his guitar. Slowly, John started strumming G to C to G to C with Bill gently brushing his drums to show him how it all came together. John was fascinated and hooked. Right in front of him, music becoming something real and tangible. Singing along in harmony to the songs on the radio was one thing, but this was a whole other world.

Sitting in Bill and Rosemary's basement, John strummed for hours, perfecting F to C to D to F to D and getting into A minor and B-7th. The feel of the strings beneath his fingertips and the vibration of the guitar body gave John a type of kinetic energy he'd never experienced before. When he finally emerged, it was dark outside, and the house was empty. Bill had tapped into something that filled a void. He'd been electrified with a newfound sense of freedom and there was no going back.

CHAPTER 3:
IN THE NAVY

The pop music landscape had grown considerably since Reginald Fessenden played "O Holy Night" on his violin on the first audio radio broadcast to a small listening audience in Brant Rock, Massachusetts, on Christmas Eve 1906. Over the course of the next 25 years, the music industry, fueled by music publishers out of Tin Pan Alley in New York City, would rise through the combination of the phonograph and radio despite challenges presented by the Great Depression and World War II.

Throughout the 1930s and 1940s, names like Bing Crosby, Duke Ellington and Frank Sinatra were spoken on the lips of people from coast to coast paralleled by an almost underground music scene of black musicians. Performers of at least equal talent like Jelly Roll Morton, Louis Armstrong, and Ella Fitzgerald influenced the mainstream, consciously or unconsciously. By the very nature of being suppressed, black music was always on the cutting edge and pushing the boundaries of what was considered decent and acceptable in the public square, and so, for any connoisseur of jazz or blues, black artists cornered the market on originality and influence.

In postwar America, their place in the pop music scene was still held at bay although widespread acceptance was bubbling underneath the surface. In September 1952, John Phillips began his senior year at George Washington High School and, with his newfound love for making music, was much more in tune with the popular music scene than ever before. Though entertaining, it wasn't exactly the most fertile of times. In fact, the pop music scene was mostly just a refined, better-produced version of what had been dominating the airwaves since KDKA began spinning records in 1920. In fact, the top selling records of 1953 were Percy Faith's "Song from Moulin Rouge" and, more infamously, Patti Page's "How Much Is that Doggie in the Window." Not exactly cutting edge.

But, there's always good music to be found, and John remained under the tutelage of his brother-in-law, who schooled him on jazz guitar by playing records by Django Reinhart and Charlie Christian's work with the Benny Goodman Sextet. He'd also taken up dancing and, when he wasn't practicing his guitar, was swing dancing and doing the boogie-woogie with girlfriend Susie Adams, which ramped up the sexual tension. Susie wouldn't allow him to go any further than stolen kisses in dark corners, which only served to frustrate him. He found his sexual release through gangbangs with a few neighborhood trollops organized by the Del Ray Locals who he still kept in touch with even though he wasn't really running with them any longer.

As the school year wore on, John and Susie's relationship began to sour. It was a combination of the prospect of no sex and her parents' dislike of John. Susie's potential as a world-class ballerina and her family's blue-blooded lineage made him unworthy of Susie's attention in their eyes. Science and medicine are where the Adams' made their mark and there was no place for a delinquent with an alcoholic father and a Navy secretary mother. Her father, James Jr., was a scientific consultant for the Air Force and her grandfather practiced medicine along the Eastern Shore of Maryland and taught anatomy at the University of Maryland Medical College. The family had also gained a notable reputation as champion horse breeders who entered their Thorough-breds annually in the Laurel Futurity Stakes.

Susie's interest in John became too much for them, so they sent her off to a prominent school of ballet in Vienna, Austria, to focus on her talent and forget about him. John was able to move on through the help of his music and basketball season. He'd peaked at 6'5" and helped lead the GWHS Presidents to a 14–5 regular season and a spot in the state tournament where they lost in the semifinals to Lynchburg's E. C. Glass High School. But whatever elation John may have gained from his basketball team's incredible run was quickly dashed when he was expelled for purposely dropping a typewriter on his instructor's foot. His protest that the male teacher groped him from behind fell on Principal Edgar G. Pruet's deaf ears as he perused John's poor grades and attendance record. He was escorted out of the hallowed halls never to walk them again.

John's exit from GWHS was somewhat surreptitious. He wasn't very popular during his tenure there and most in the graduating class of 211 hardly noticed he was gone. Most of his friends were either younger than he was or went to other schools. Either through Rosemary's insistence or through his own motivation, he took a job driving a soda truck around town and kept his basketball skills fresh by playing in the National Industrial Basketball League, a precursor to AAU basketball. His father still had visions of his son carrying on his Marine tradition and used his rank and John's standardized test scores to get him into the Bullis School, a preparatory school for the United States Naval Academy where he enrolled for the fall 1953 semester. Like or not, John was heading back to military school.

After witnessing the lengths his drunken father went to for him following his embarrassing exit from high school, John felt compelled to move back home. The thought of Bullis, however, was a double-edged sword. It was going to be a fresh start, but he did not share in his father's military dream. He was absolutely stuck.

Whatever range of emotions John was going through that spring were further muddled when his mother dropped a bombshell on him after a terrible argument with Claude in which he hit her and threatened to burn the house down. After things died down, she came to John's room in tears and revealed to him that Claude wasn't his real father. She went further and told him that his birth father was actually a man named Roland Meeks, a Jewish Navy doctor who was stationed at Parris Island in the mid-1930s. She described him as a sensitive, poetic man with whom she fell in love against her will.

In an instant, John's world came crashing down. He couldn't believe what he was hearing. Everything he'd known was now all different. Rosemary and Tommy were demoted to half-siblings and Claude to stepfather. His own self-identity had evaporated. He thought back to stories his mother and sister had told him about how shocked his father was when he found out Edna was pregnant in the winter of 1935 and how he referred to his unborn son as a gift from heaven. That had a new meaning now. The only question John could muster was whether or not she ever saw him again.

She explained that shortly after their rendezvous in December 1934, he was transferred. They wrote each other in the ensuing years until she heard he had died in a Japanese prison camp during World War II. John couldn't wrap his mind around the story his mother had just woven and, after a little while, decided it was time again to leave. He didn't want to leave in a huff this time, however. He reassured his mother of his love for her and Claude and she left him with words that would stick with him the remainder of his life.

"John, you just have to go where you want to go, do what you want to do," she told him. "Don't let others rule your life. Please remember that."

He drove around for a long time, going up and down the radio dial, picking up hitchhikers, doing whatever he could to get his mind off his mother's revelation, but it was all in vain. His mind raced as he tried to picture who Roland Meeks was. What did he look like? Could he really be his father? After several hours cruising around Alexandria and D.C., he pulled up to his sister's house. He needed somebody to talk to about all this, and she'd always been his rock. Unreservedly, he unloaded the whole thing on Rosemary, and, to his astonishment, she didn't flinch. In fact, she'd heard it all before.

She explained that, quite often, the line between truth and fiction in their mother's stories could be blurry, especially as the years and alcoholism had worn on. She also diagnosed that perhaps Edna felt her children were against her and supported their father, especially since they'd recently confronted her about her affair. It may have been a desperate shot at discrediting Claude in John's eyes since he'd sobered up in order to get him into Bullis Prep. She also told John that, once, after a fight with their father, Edna confessed to her that her real father was a rodeo cowboy she'd met on a trip back to Okmulgee.

His talk with Rosemary did make him feel better. It was a bonding moment. They talked for hours about Edna's relatives and some of the crazy made-up stories she'd told throughout the years. Still, at the end of the night, John was still unnerved by the bombshell his mother dropped on him.

"Why should I spend the rest of my life wondering who the hell my real father is," he asked Rosemary. "I just want to know the truth!"

"In this family, that might be asking too much," she replied.

John set off for Bullis Prep in September 1953, determined more than ever to succeed to spite his mother, but, when he got there, it reminded him of his Linton Hall days, only the nuns had been replaced by more intense Navy officers and NCOs. And he encountered the same obligatory kind of hazing from the upperclassmen that he had those many years ago. Nevertheless, he forged ahead and gave it his best with his guitar helping him get through the stress.

That June, he graduated 136th out of 145 cadets, reeling in a solid D average, but he managed to pass the entrance exams for the United States Naval Academy and was admitted for the fall 1954 semester. It was mostly his father's distinguished service record that earned his appointment and, recognizing how this did change his father's self-destructive behavior, John resolved to try.

The month between graduation from Bullis and the start of Plebe Summer at the Naval Academy was bittersweet for John. He bid farewell to the Del Ray Locals, who gave him a raucous send-off with plenty of partying, dancing and one last cruise around the circuit. But more meaningful was a trip with his father to Griffith Stadium, home of the Washington Senators, to watch their losing effort against the Cleveland Indians. The two connected over beer, hot dogs, and cheering on the home team. For the first time, Claude opened up to his youngest son about his life, his health, his struggle against alcoholism, and how he knew he'd let the family down.

After the game, they caught a movie and shot a few rounds of pool at a beer hall where the deep discussion continued. He shared war stories, talked about meeting his mother back in Okmulgee, their life together there and his battle with depression over the years. It was a tender moment but a fleeting one. He and John would never experience this type of closeness again.

John entered the U.S. Naval Academy as a 4/C Plebe in late June 1954 and endured the six-week course of physical and mental training known as Plebe Summer. He was assigned to 22nd Company under the command of Marine Capt. R. D. Rosecrans. After receiving their vaccinations, the plebes were psychologically beat down by the upperclassmen and taught the basics, including formations, saluting and about-facing properly. They were also required to memorize the 11 General Orders of a Sentry, Naval leadership and history. It served as a mini boot camp that was designed to acclimate the newbies to a military environment and weed out the weak ones. John's newfound sense of obligation to his father willed him through this summer of torture. His anger toward his mother fueled him as well. He didn't want to give her the satisfaction of ending his father's Marine dream for him. As was becoming commonplace, he turned to his guitar for comfort until it was seized by the Plebe Summer cadre. The infraction earned him a demerit and, over the course of the six weeks, he'd racked up a sizable number of them. Discovering that 300 demerits results in expulsion, he saw his way out.

It was a formidable task but one that John felt he could achieve. As Plebe Summer concluded and the fall semester began, he did everything he could to rack up demerits. Over the course of two months, he racked up 297, but his plan was threatened when he learned of the Naval Academy's plan to host Queen Elizabeth II in early November as she toured the United States for the first time since her ascension to the throne in 1952. The news seemed innocuous at first until he learned that it's customary for visiting royalty and heads of state to be given the honor of erasing all demerits. The scuttlebutt around campus was that the Queen Mother would indeed keep the tradition, which excited every cadet except John.

When she arrived on campus that Monday morning, accompanied by Maryland governor Theodore McKeldin and several other dignitaries, the school pulled out all the stops, including a full-dress parade, a formal breakfast and an address before the student body. As John sat and listened to her speech, his hopes were raised when it concluded without any mention of wiping away all demerits. But, when Commandant Robert T. S. Keith and Commander Isaac C. Kidd presented her with a photo album documenting her visit, she uttered those dreaded words.

"It's my honor and privilege . . ."

John tuned out and sunk in his chair. All his demerits were erased. As she was whisked away to a state dinner in her honor in Washington, D.C., John was the only sad cadet on campus. It was back to square one. He'd have to devise a new plan. His disappointment, however, was short-lived when he learned his father suffered another serious heart attack and was hospitalized. He was granted temporary leave and rushed to Bethesda Naval Hospital's ICU to find Claude enshrouded in an oxygen tent and heavily medicated. The sight of John in his service dress whites did lift his spirits as he clasped his hand and mumbled incoherently. John was able to make out his father's sense of pride.

The tender moment was interrupted by Edna's arrival with the colonel in tow. It was the first time John was able to get a good look at him, and he wasn't impressed. He could tell he was inebriated and, outside of Claude's room, he tried to explain to John his love for his mother, which ended up in a tussle.

"You can't take care of anybody, you rotten bastard," John screamed as him.

He straightened up his uniform and left. With his father dying, his mother completely disengaged and being stuck in the Naval Academy out of a sense of guilt, his life seemed to be in a downward spiral.

The family did reunite later, without Colonel Lacy, and shared their grief and told family stories. Edna reminisced about John's childhood and made a comment about a neighbor of theirs tossing him up when he was an infant and dropping him on his head, which ended up in a minor skull fracture. They only took him to the hospital a couple of days later after he began blacking out and vomiting. He was kept in the hospital for a week for monitoring and was sent home with the assurance of the doctor that, because he was a baby, it would heal on its own because his bones were still soft. The entire incident was eventually forgotten.

When John returned to Annapolis, he began studiously researching skull fractures and head injuries and began imitating many of the various symptoms associated with them. During the spring semester he became a regular at sick bay. It caught the Navy's attention, especially upon closer examination of his medical history, which did document the incident. The Navy couldn't afford to commission an academy cadet who could become a liability. In March 1955, John received his discharge papers. Mission accomplished.

John feigned disappointment so as not to arouse suspicion from his father, who was recovering at home. Although saddened his son wouldn't continue the Marine tradition, he understood the Navy's decision. He was now at another crossroads. Like his 1948 Plymouth, John's time at the Naval Academy was nothing more than a glossy paint job over a rusty surface, and the rust bubbled through. Though he didn't realize it yet, he was a musical artist in the making and, now that he had no superiors or structure to adhere to, was free to pluck his guitar strings and while away the time. But he couldn't sit idle for long. Nobody in his family was going to pay his way. He'd exhausted all their support. In the meantime, he felt the instinct to pursue his future through higher education and began looking around for schools to attend. He didn't know it but an unexpected reunion was just around the corner.

CHAPTER 4:
SUSIE

After his exit from the Naval Academy, John enrolled in American University in Washington, D.C., and moved into the Devonshire Apartments located only a few blocks from campus. His time there was rather unremarkable and quite short. In what was becoming a pattern, John only lasted one semester and spent most of the time entertaining the brothers of Alpha Sigma Phi with his guitar.

Though stuck in neutral academically, he did graduate musically by quickly going from learning the guitar in his sister's basement to informally entertaining his fellow plebes at Annapolis to entertaining strangers in a collegiate setting. And, while John was bouncing from one learning institution to another, the musical landscape was in the middle of an earthquake. The influence of the black music community, which had gotten red hot in the years following the end of World War II, through performers like Louis Jordan, Bullmoose Jackson and Wynonie Harris, had crossed over to the white music world. As John was enduring the rigors of Plebe Summer at the Naval Academy, the Decca record label issued the single "Rock Around the Clock" by Bill Haley & His Comets. It didn't make a seismic impact at first but thanks to its presence in the 1955 feature film *The Blackboard Jungle* starring Glenn Ford, Vic Morrow and Sidney Poitier, it shot to #1 that summer. The movie perfectly encapsulated the restless, raucous rock and roll spirit and the conflict it created between teenagers and adults.

At the same time, a young singer named Elvis Presley was shaking things up in Memphis, putting out singles on the local Sun label and appearing regularly on the Louisiana Hayride. With each performance, the teenage presence at the Shreveport Municipal Memorial Auditorium grew bigger and louder, causing emcee Horace Logan to first utter that now-famous phrase, "Elvis has left the building," in order to restore order. While John was entertaining the Alpha Sigs, Elvis had already moved to RCA Victor Records and issued four number one singles in a row.

Black artists like Chuck Berry, Fats Domino and Little Richard were crossing into the Billboard and Cash Box Top 40s with regularity and ease, issuing fresh-sounding songs like "Johnny B. Goode," "Ain't that a Shame" and "Tutti Frutti," respectively. A revolutionary cultural milieu was underway, and John was right in the middle of it with the notable instrument of change, the guitar, in hand. He didn't take to it though. He still preferred slick, jazzy group harmony and quartets like Four Aces and the Hi-Lo's over the Spaniels and the Penguins and the more sanitized versions of black songs performed by safer artists like Pat Boone and Georgia Gibbs.

After another spring and summer sitting home and working various jobs in order to pay rent, John accepted a basketball scholarship from Hampden Sydney College. The tiny men's liberal arts college, founded in 1775, located in the middle of Virginia was very rural and nothing like he'd ever seen before. It was the alma mater of President William Henry Harrison and was a legacy school for the sons of many wealthy businessmen and politicians. It was tough from the start, especially considering John was a 21-year-old freshman who had to endure the traditional hazing from the blue-blooded upperclassmen.

With a spirit of rebelliousness firmly entrenched, John was resistant to any form of peer discipline. When his antiauthoritarianism became too much for its dispensers to bear, a few sophomores paid him a visit and beat him down in his dorm room. Their efforts didn't end a battle, however. It started a war.

John wasn't going to take this lying down. He identified the chief instigator of the hazing as a sophomore named Chuck. He galvanized his classmates and sprung a plan into action immediately. After talking approximately 140 classmates into contributing a dollar, he purchased a one-way airline ticket to Miami, Florida, and, along with two cohorts, kidnapped Chuck, drove four hours to National Airport in Washington, D.C., and put him on the plane minus his shoes. They did loan him a dime so he could call for help upon his arrival. To add insult to injury, John and some of his buddies printed up signs with Chuck's face emblazoned upon them under a caption that read, "Where's Chuck?" and posted them all over campus.

Chuck, however, wasn't amused and, when he returned to Hampden Sydney a few days later, issued a formal complaint against John. He was summoned to Dean Thomas Edward Gilmer's office and was promptly expelled. John had now been through three colleges in less than a year and a half and it was becoming pretty clear that higher education wasn't his calling.

By the time he returned to Alexandria in October 1957, his parents had separated, so he moved into an apartment in downtown Alexandria. In order to pay for rent and make ends meet, he took on a series of sales jobs that went about as well as his college experience. In a matter of months, he went from selling encyclopedias door-to-door to sewing machines to Kinney shoes until finding steady employment selling graveyard plots. Each time he told a friend or girl what he did for a living, he was met with the same tired old jokes. "Are people just dying to do business with you?" "You must work with a bunch of stiffs." His comeback was always, "It's quite an undertaking."

He spent many nights in the lounge of the Huntington Towers apartment complex near National Airport trying to pick up stewardesses bunking there for an overnight stop. On one particular night, a face he recognized came strolling through the door. He spotted her in the mirror behind the bar. It was old high school sweetheart Susie Adams, and, boy, did she ever grow up.

In the nearly four years since he'd last seen her, she had developed into quite a young woman and, having trained as a ballerina, was in great physical shape. She stood about 5'4" and was rather petite. Thoroughly modern, she wore slacks and sported a modern pageboy hairstyle, made popular recently by Grace Kelly and Lauren Bacall.

She wasn't alone though. A young man escorted her into the bar. Watching them steadily, he waited until the gentleman stepped away, then he made his move and casually walked up to her table. Recognizing him almost immediately, she spoke right up and playfully feigned played dumb.

"You can't be Johnny Phillips, can you?" she asked.

"No one can be Johnny Phillips," he quipped back. "Believe me, I've tried."

She kicked her head back and laughed like it was the funniest thing she'd ever heard in her familiar hoarse laugh. They slipped right back into their friendship like nothing had ever separated it and caught up with each other over screwdrivers. John told her all about Bullis and the Naval Academy and what happened at Hampden-Sydney. She told him about her experience at the Vienna State Opera Ballet School where she stayed at the home of the late composer Franz Lehar and then moved on to study in London. When John inquired about her date, who'd, by now, gone missing, she informed him that he was her brother. In fact, Susie hadn't been back very long and was staying with her sister at her apartment about three blocks away.

John moved in closer now. They continued to drink and talk and eventually ended at the Alpha Sig Quonset hut, where he still had some friends, and danced until the wee hours. He started to take her home but ended up parked in the parking lot of the Old Dominion Boat Club off Ramsey Alley where they made out until being broken up by a Metro police officer tapping his flashlight on his window. He took her back home and, from then on, they saw each other steadily.

Though John's love life was thriving, his family life was in shambles. With his parents separated, there was nobody willing to take care of his ailing father and, with a mostly empty apartment, that responsibility fell to him. He still harbored plenty of guilt for how things ended at the Naval Academy so he put him up, but it didn't last for very long. Claude's drinking and everything that came along with it quickly proved too much to handle. Every day, John came home to his house in disarray and empty beer cans everywhere.

John's job woes continued to haunt him too. Right before Christmas, he was fired from his graveyard plot sales job for fraud after a family accused him of pocketing their initial premium. When pressed by his bosses, John confessed to that and two other swindles. He did it in order to wine, dine and impress Susie. He agreed to pay back the company and was escorted out of the building.

He bounced back quickly though, taking a job as a sales rep at a Chevrolet dealership that specialized in Corvettes. It wasn't uncommon to see John cruising around D.C. and Alexandria in a brand-new Corvette with a prospective buyer.

Come spring 1957, Susie discovered she was pregnant with John's baby, and the two decided to get married in May by a justice of the peace. They spent their honeymoon in a cheap motel and dined on deli sandwiches and champagne.

Susie's parents were against the marriage and made no secret about it. They considered it hasty and impulsive and urged her to leave John and continue her studies abroad. They'd invested quite a bit of money in her education and were disappointed to see her with a Naval Academy dropout. Dr. and Mrs. Adams forbade John from setting foot on their 400-acre horse farm near Catonsville, Maryland.

John's family had quite the opposite reaction. They lovingly took to Susie and her presence brought them closer to John. At a small family gathering after the wedding, Edna toasted the newlyweds, telling her son that he found himself a real lady. But, deep down, John was unsure about his new circumstances. There was part of him that loved Susie, but things had moved very quickly, and he wondered how far his love went. After all, he only married her out of a sense of obligation. For now, though, he suppressed any questions and feelings of wanderlust and was determined to give it his best try. His first move was trying to establish more steady, gainful employment by taking the civil service exam, which he passed.

The newlyweds moved into an apartment on Ramsey Alley, and John started his new job at the post office. Susie, ever the socialite, put her famous last name and heritage to use and got a job at the *Washington Evening Star* as a weekly contributor to their society page. Their married life together was starting off nicely, but how long would it last?

CHAPTER 5:
ABSTRACTS

By the summer of 1957, the Phillips' apartment in Ramsey Alley became party central. It was reminiscent of how John's parents entertained when he was a child before retirement and alcohol completely incapacitated Claude. In an effort to numb himself from his stressful work and home life, John surrounded himself with old friends and complete strangers and hosted parties that lasted for days with his wife being several months pregnant. The companionship and booze helped take the edge off, but it also served as a vehicle for him to perform musically in front of an audience. He'd begun writing his own songs and would often use these gatherings as time to try them out.

John kept in touch with many of his old Del Ray Locals buddies, and their presence often dominated these parties. On one particular evening, a young man about four years his junior approached John and introduced himself as Phillip Blondheim. He told him he was a recent high school graduate and was playing around town in a group. As he eagerly spoke, John coolly strummed his guitar. John didn't think much of Phillip at first, but when he sat down and began harmonizing as John sang, it aroused his attention. The kid could really sing. Phil had a beautiful lilting tenor that was easy on the ears and beautifully conveyed melancholy and lovesickness.

Phil visited the Phillips' apartment a few more times and joined in on some of John's informal vocal rehearsals. For the first time, John was considering forming a group, and it gave him a renewed sense of hope. He needed it because his job at the post office wasn't going so well. It bored the hell out of him and, after only a few weeks there, he was fired for hoarding the mail. He managed to get his job back at the Chevrolet dealership and, even though it brought back a steady income, it opened the door to temptation and John began having affairs with young girls who came into the dealership. Susie discovered a bunch of scribbled-down phone numbers and put it together. The betrayal was additional stress added to John's shaky career ambitions and, at eight months pregnant, Susie left their apartment and moved back with her sister.

John was embarrassed and ashamed. Around the same time, his father was put into a nursing home. One afternoon, while visiting Claude, John ran into his mother and confided his troubles to her. Edna believed that Susie was good for John and she urged him to win her back. To help give Susie some sense of stability, she told John they could move in with her at her apartment in University Heights. John was getting increasingly good at smooth talking, and he managed to convince Susie to move back with him and his mother. On December 13, 1957, they welcomed their son Jeffrey to the world. Shortly afterward, they moved into an apartment of their own.

But the new baby and environment were just a band-aid. If John felt trapped before, his new set of circumstances made him feel downright imprisoned. He rebelled by continuing to have affairs, including one with Susie's former assistant at the *Evening Star*. The vicious cycle only continued to repeat itself. John would apologize, Susie would take him back, they'd have intense makeup sex, and then he'd feel trapped and start sleeping around again. In the meantime, they were struggling mightily financially, even with the help of Edna. Susie finally swallowed her pride and asked her parents for money. They agreed on the condition that she leave John and come back home. She refused. Despite all the heartache he'd caused her, she still believed in him. In order to help make ends meet, she took a job with an aerial photography firm.

John wasn't nearly as dedicated. The new year brought a new job at an Austin Healey dealership, but, come summer 1958, that old feeling began to tug at him again and, this time, he planned a doozy. He'd already exhausted his mother's and Susie's patience, so this time he decided he was going to get as far away as he could and quite possibly never return. One evening, after coming home from work to a fancy dinner prepared by Susie and Edna, John acted agitated and went out of his way to make it known. When Susie finally asked him what was wrong, he told a sad story about how his co-worker Mike's father just passed away and needed a ride to the airport so he could get to his funeral. It seemed innocent enough and, when Mike showed up a little while later, nobody thought anything of it. He and John went into the bedroom and, after a few minutes, emerged with two suitcases in hand. John kissed Susie and his mother goodbye and left for the airport.

Hours passed and John hadn't returned home. Susie was getting worried. In the middle of the night, the phone rang. It was John. He told her he was in Havana, Cuba, and that he and Mike had been inspired to join Fidel Castro's band of rebels who were fighting against President Fulgencio Batista's Army for control of the island nation.

"Goddamn you, John Phillips!" Susie screamed into the phone. "This is the most disgusting stunt you have ever pulled in your life!"

It was as far-fetched as she possibly could've imagined but nevertheless true. The story of Cuba had been dominating the news lately, and John, indeed, was there but it wasn't to fight in any rebel army. In fact, they never made it out of Havana. The allure of Sans Souchi Nightclub & Casino, the Tropicana, and the Hotel Capri completely distracted them. John did bring his guitar, and it came in handy. He and Mike busked around town for tips. They even caught the attention of a local television variety program and were invited to perform.

For two weeks, John and Mike existed in an inebriated, sweaty haze. Every day they resolved to go meet up with Castro's band of soldiers but always ended up getting drunk and watching stag films. John's sexual appetite was getting increasingly insatiable, and those films only stirred up his passions and desire for female companionship. He found it in a Cuban American hooker named Rita who worked at the motel in which they were staying. Her sexual prowess certainly impressed him but the biggest thing she did was introduce him to marijuana. Before sex, she'd light up a joint and then finish it afterward. She offered it to John, who thought it was a Cuban cigar. After basic instruction on how to ingest it, he was hooked. John told her why they were there, and she warned him about Castro. She told him he was a vicious communist who wanted to oppress his people and isolate the island nation. She advised him to get back to the United States as soon as possible and gave him his $10 back.

John may have missed the revolution, but his time there caused him to develop an affinity for the Caribbean that would last the rest of his life.

Expecting to face a firing squad when he got home, John instead encountered a seemingly indifferent Susie. The mistrust he'd sowed since getting married was overwhelming and she didn't have the energy to fight it. Come fall, John was again on the move. This time, he set his sights on Los Angeles and hopped on a plane, once again leaving his wife and son.

When he arrived, he stayed in cheap motels with hourly rates and got a job at a Chevrolet dealership. After getting his bearings, he made his way to the Sunset Strip, where legendary nightclubs bedecked the mile-and-half boulevard that cut through West Hollywood. As impressive as this sight was to a stranger from the East Coast, the Strip was in a period of transition. The cool cats like Frank Sinatra, Dean Martin, and Sammy Davis Jr., who'd inhabited the scene in the late 1940s and early 1950s, had moved on to Las Vegas. The many clubs they frequented, like Ciro's Le Disc and Slapsy Maxie's, had either gone out of business or were a shell of their former selves. Since most of the clubs catered to seasoned jazz musicians, John made his way down to Pandora's Box, located on a concrete island at the intersection of Sunset and Crescent Heights Boulevard. Its purple paint job and gold stripes served as a beacon to under-21 L.A. youth.

It was one of the first clubs to cater to rock and roll and the growing folk music scene and welcomed newcomers with amateur nights. The first time John's number was called, he was loud and energetic and not very good but, over the course of a month, he improved and gained confidence on stage. He even caught the attention of Austrian American folk singer and Elektra recording artist Theodore Bikel, who was friends with club owner Bill Tilden and happened to be in the audience one night. He saw something in John and, after getting to know him, told him he'd put in a word with Tilden. John was overjoyed. It was his first paying gig as a performer. For a month, he shared the stage with bongo player Preston Epps and sharpened his act.

When John wasn't on stage, he was rubbing elbows with the regulars, including many smitten young girls who were quite taken with his confidence and charm. During his time there, several ended up leaving the club with him and providing him with free food, shelter, and sex. But after about a month of this, he began to grow weary and homesick. Even though he felt empowered onstage and had taken a big step in his music career, he couldn't sustain this type of living and he couldn't overcome the feeling of guilt that was eating away at him for abandoning his wife and infant son.

He was stuck though. He had little money and no way of getting back home until he overheard two customers at Pandora's Box talking about a road trip to Florida. It was closer to Alexandria than L.A., so he busted into their conversation and, over a few drinks, talked his way into joining them. A few hours later, they set off in an old Studebaker, taking turns driving and splitting gasoline expenses. They had gotten as far as the outskirts of New Orleans when the fuel pump went. They got a tow for the car but didn't have money for repairs. Walking around town, they noticed a help wanted sign for the Baton Rouge Shrine Club's 10th Annual Circus at Memorial Stadium and were able to land temporary work as peanut vendors. During a break, John phoned Susie and told her he wanted to come home. Understandably hurt and tired of his antics, she refused him and hung up the phone.

After the circus moved on, John and his two friends decided to abandon the car and wrote bad checks for airline tickets to Miami, Florida. When they landed, they went their separate ways. John stayed in town and got a job as a bellhop and trampoline instructor at a hotel on South Beach even though he'd never been on a trampoline in his life. In return, he received free room and board from the hotel. Things were going fairly well for a few weeks until John slept with a married Cuban woman. When he discovered that her jealous husband had found out and was coming for him, he phoned Susie, and this time told her he was coming home whether she wanted him to or not. He abruptly packed up and caught the first plane to D.C.

It took a while, but as 1958 turned into 1959, John and Susie were able to function again as a married couple, but it wasn't necessarily because John was ready to be a good husband and father. He became preoccupied with figuring out his entrance into the music business and needed time. His month at Pandora's Box really lit a fire, and he wanted to put a singing group together as quickly as possible. Though rock and roll was all around him, he was devoted to the sound of the Hi-Lo's and the Four Freshmen, which was still pretty popular among his demographic. The Hi-Lo's were his chief source of inspiration. Even though only ever had one chart hit, 1954's "My Baby Just Cares for Me," they built up quite a reputation among college kids and sophisticated record buyers of the mid-1950s who were now young professionals. He hadn't seen many of his friends since living in Ramsey Alley, but he knew who he wanted and sought them out.

Bill Cleary was an old friend from the Del Ray neighborhood. He was a couple years younger than John, but they played in the same CYO basketball leagues and sang together quite often. Bill was a natural tenor but had a crippling shyness that didn't allow him to sing lead. When John found him, he was still in the old neighborhood, singing in front of Gibson's Drug Store on the corner of King Street and Alfred Street.

Another kid John knew who could sing was his GWHS classmate Edgar Boran's younger brother Michael. John hung out at their house a lot during his high school days and was familiar with Michael's musical prowess. Michael became a bit of a local celebrity when he put together a makeshift band to fill in for the popular Parkside Band who pulled a no-show at a dance at the Lyon Park Community Center in Arlington. The called themselves the Spotlighters and rocked the house with Michael particularly standing out for his ability to channel his inner Little Richard. The group eventually morphed into the Capitol City All-Stars and gained a good reputation playing the Alexandria/D.C. party and fraternity circuit.

John invited a few other of his old GWHS buddies to join in and began rehearsing throughout the winter at the Boran house and at the recreation center near Mount Vernon Elementary School. Attrition took its toll, and, after a few weeks, it was back down to John, Bill, and Michael. John was bound and determined to get his group up to the standard of the Hi-Lo's, and he knew he needed another strong voice, and the strongest one he knew belonged to Phil Blondheim, the kid he had met a year earlier at one of his Ramsey Alley parties. But he lost touch. As it turned out, John and Phil had some friends in common, and so he went in search.

Like John, Phil grew up under less than ideal familial circumstances. He was born in Jacksonville, Florida, in 1939 and his father died before he'd turned two. His mother Dorothy moved to Washington, D.C., when Phil was three and left him behind with her parents in North Carolina. After the war ended, Phil moved back with his mother, who'd found steady employment as one of Gen. George Marshall's secretaries and was living in a town house in Falls Church, Virginia. By the time he entered St. Stephen's Episcopal High School for Boys in Alexandria, he and his mother had moved to Arlington. Upon graduation, Philheim, as his high school buddies referred to him, did a six-month hitch in the Army as part of President Eisenhower's Reserve Forces Act of 1955, which fulfilled his obligation to his country.

When he returned to Arlington, he took a job as a bank teller and performed for a while with the Singing Strings, which included former high
school classmate Buck Hunnicut and neighborhood friend Tim Rose. It was
through these connections that John was able to track Phil down. He was
singing at the Silver Dollar, a popular club in Georgetown. One evening he
and Bill Cleary took a ride and watch him perform a set. After closing with
Johnny Mathis' "Chances Are," the two approached Phil about joining their
new group. He accepted. John could now make four-part harmony, and his
dream of being in a professional singing quartet got one step closer to reality.
They called themselves the Abstracts.

Back at home, things weren't going as well. Since returning from his forays
in Los Angeles and Miami, John had not found work, which left Susie as the
sole provider. When she found out she was pregnant in March, the pressure
mounted. John tried talking her into getting an abortion, but she wouldn't
hear of it.

Around the same time, John's father suffered another heart attack. It had
been quite a while since John last saw him, and he went to Bethesda to visit
him, along with his mother and sister. Sitting by his bedside alone, he pondered their relationship and how it didn't really start until Claude got him
enrolled at Bullis Prep. He thought of how he let his father down with his
Naval Academy exit, and how his mother told him Claude wasn't his real
father; he was still unsure whether it was a truthful admission or an inebriated response to a domestic argument. The thought still enraged him, but he
allowed that feeling to be tempered by the moment. For now, all he saw was
his father and all he felt was love. When Claude's condition improved, he was
transferred to the VA Hospital in Martinsburg, West Virginia.

John buried his emotions in his work with the Abstracts. They pooled their
money and bought matching cardigans with an embroidered letter "A" over
the left pocket and had publicity photos taken. John also met with George
Wilkins, co-owner of Edgewood Studios in Washington, D.C., and set up
some studio time to record a demo record. John was as serious as ever, and
his energy and excitement transferred over to his bandmates. Wilkins was
impressed and passed along a copy of their songs to his former manager
Charles V. Ryan, who ran an artist management firm in New York City. Ryan
offered them an audition that John wasted no time in accepting.

It was a no-brainer. New York was the home of Tin Pan Alley, and every major record label was either headquartered there or had some kind of presence. John set up a date with Ryan and, the day before, he, Phil, Bill and Michael hopped in John's station wagon and headed up I-95 to New York City. As they got closer to the Manhattan skyline, the excitement in the car was palpable. They entered the Holland Tunnel and exited into Lower Manhattan and did their best to follow the confusing signs and maze of roads that inevitably get first timers lost. Making their way through Greenwich Village, John set his sights for Midtown and the office of Charles V. Ryan. It was time to let the music world known that John Phillips had arrived.

CHAPTER 6:
AN OLD SMOOTHIE

The pop music scene that John Phillips and the Abstracts entered in 1959 was undergoing a change. Rock and roll was still hot, but its main players were essentially beaten into submission or fell victim to their own bad judgment. Elvis Presley, who perfectly encapsulated the rebellious rock and roll zeitgeist, was drafted into the Army in March 1958. Little Richard, whose energetic blues shouting probably frightened parents the most, turned away from rock and roll after encountering heavy turbulence on an airplane while flying over Australia in 1957. He saw it as a sign from God to leave secular music and become a gospel artist. Texas rock and roll singer Buddy Holly wasn't as fortunate. Along with fellow singer Ritchie Valens and the Big Bopper, he was killed on February 3, 1959, when his twin-engine Beechcraft Bonanza crashed in a cornfield outside of Mason City, Iowa, shortly after takeoff. Jerry Lee Lewis' records became untouchable for radio stations, theaters, and retailers after it was revealed he had married 13-year-old Myra Gale Brown, who was nine years younger than he was. To compound the situation, it was further discovered that she was his first cousin once removed. Chuck Berry, who reeled off five Top 10 hits after his debut "Maybelline" hit the Top 5 in the summer of 1955, was struggling to regain his chart footing. By the end of the year, he would be accused of the statutory rape of 14-year-old Janice Escalante and for transporting her over state lines for immoral purposes. He would eventually serve a year and a half in a Missouri jail.

There were other artists who carried the torch, like Fats Domino, Gene Vincent, Ricky Nelson, and Eddie Cochran, but much of the bare-bones edge had been taken off their music through slick production, pleasant strings, and background singers. A major part of the next phase of rock and roll was being fashioned in office buildings in Midtown Manhattan. The transfer of hit songwriting power had begun its move from Tin Pan Alley in Lower Manhattan to 1650 and 1619 Broadway, also known as the Brill Building. Together, they housed several prolific music publishing companies like Hill and Range, Robert Mellin Music and Aldon Music who cranked out hits for Elvis Presley, Bobby Darin, the Drifters, and dozens of others with great regularity. The era of the teen idol was warming up and the songwriters who inhabited these office buildings, including Otis Blackwell, Jerry Leiber and Mike Stoller, Doc Pomus, and Mort Shuman, wrote guaranteed hits for Elvis, the Everly Brothers, Brook Benton, and Neil Sedaka and were priming the pumps for soon-to-be hit artists like Bobby Vee, the Shirelles, and Dionne Warwick. Leiber and Stoller, in particular, intensified the Brill Building's success by grooming a younger set of hit songwriting teams like Burt Bacharach and Hal David, Gerry Goffin and Carole King, and Barry Mann and Cynthia Weil.

This was the state of the music business that John Phillips and the Abstracts drove into that summer day in 1959. Charles Ryan's office wasn't in either 1619 or 1650 but it was only eight blocks away, and like many others was attempting to feed off their success. Ryan was thoroughly impressed with the Abstracts and offered to manage them if they dropped their name and took on the moniker the Smoothies instead. It was the name of Ryan's old vocal group, which he fronted in the 1930s and 1940s and had moderate success. They recorded for Bluebird, His Master's Voice, and Apollo, and appeared regularly on Fred Waring's NBC radio program under the Smoothies name and as Babs & Her Brothers.

Ryan wanted to revive the act with John and his group and encouraged them to move up to New York City. He offered them a contract and, after a short return trip home, they moved into the Albert Hotel in Greenwich Village. It wasn't all glitz and glam, especially in the beginning. Gigs were hard to come by, and Ryan wasn't necessarily coming through for them. When the money ran out, they spent a few nights in John's station wagon, where personalities and lifestyles began to clash. John would often go days without showering and think nothing of it whereas Bill Cleary would take as many as three showers a day. It didn't take long for John's stink to bother the other three, who often threatened to stuff him in the trunk.

Eventually, Ryan got the Smoothies on the road, where they played clubs in the Poconos, in Atlantic City, the Memphis Cotton Carnival, and a little closer to home at the Blue Mirror in Washington, D.C. It allowed them to move back into the Albert and enjoy a slightly more civilized existence. Just as they were getting their touring legs beneath them, John got a call from Susie that she was going into labor. He got home in time for his daughter Laura Mackenzie's birth on November 10, 1959. Now that he had an extra mouth to feed, the pressure to make it big mounted. Shortly after getting home from the hospital, John received a call from Charles Ryan. He'd booked their biggest gig yet, a month-long stand at the Elmwood Casino, across the river from Detroit in Windsor, Ontario. It was Christmas season, one of their peak seasons, and they'd be sharing the bill with Jimmy Durante, Sophie Tucker, and Sammy Davis Jr. Things were looking pretty good for a bunch of newbies who hadn't recorded yet.

The Elmwood was one of several Las Vegas–style motels and supper club combinations that sprouted up in smaller cities across the country after the war. Though it was called a casino, no gambling was permitted. The aim was to bring the glitter and glam of Las Vegas to densely populated regions in North America. The Smoothies and the other acts performed in the swanky, smoke-filled Ambassador Room where the patrons were stuffed in like sardines and could dine, dance, and be entertained until the wee hours of the morning. Each night they'd perform in front of an amalgam of tourists, traveling salesmen, auto industry workers, politicians, business executives, and mobsters. The gig seemed almost too good to be true and it did have one catch. After their initial excitement wore off, Ryan informed them that they'd have to perform dressed as Canadian Mounties and elves in three Christmas-themed productions per night. But it was a small price to pay for this eager band of unknowns. They were allowed their own nightly 20-minute set and John was able to show off his vocal arrangement skills to a packed house. John also showed off his charm and wit to many of the females who populated the Elmwood, and his wandering eye and raging libido began to get the better of him. Even the notion of a brand-new baby daughter back home couldn't keep him from bedding a few of the showgirls.

It was during this month-long gig that John decided to rename his lead tenor. Phil Blondheim wasn't exactly on the same level as Elvis Presley, Johnny Cash, or Frank Sinatra and he wanted his lead vocalist's name to ring with a little more pizzazz when introducing him. It came together pretty quickly. The Smoothies were often fodder for many of the comedians who traveled through and one evening Jackie Curtiss told a packed crowd that Phil resembled a Scottish terrier with his chippy ears and bushy eyebrows. That, along with his newborn daughter's middle name, inspired John to rechristen him "Scott McKenzie."

Shortly after the name change, Michael Boran's parents made the 530-mile drive to see their son perform with his group. Afterward, the Smoothies met up with them in the lobby surrounded by dozens of adoring fans asking for their autographs. It was quite a sight for the proud parents to see. Breaking away, Phil approached Charlotte Boran and pulled her aside.

"Mrs. Boran," he said quite seriously. "I know how to spell Scott, but how do you spell McKenzie?"

John's time in New York City exposed his strengths and his weaknesses. He wasn't tethered to anything. He couldn't be contained when he was at home with wife and children and, being away in New York City, was downright amoral. He caroused and partied without any regard to consequences. But he was driven and determined to make it in show business and worked relentlessly. With his group, he made it clear that he was in charge. He determined how they comported themselves onstage and off and what they sang and how they sang it. When he wasn't on the road, he could be found in the Brill Building and 1650 Broadway going from office to office pitching his songs and getting summarily rejected, but he didn't allow it to deject him. On the contrary, it only served to make his songwriting stronger.

His ambitions were put on hold when he received word on February 23 that his father had passed away. During one of his last visits with Claude, he told his son that he kept himself alive by envisioning his heart still beating. But a series of strokes was too much, and he finally succumbed that cold winter morning. Maj. Claude Andrew Phillips was laid to rest a few days later in Arlington National Cemetery with full honors. At a gathering at Edna's apartment afterward, the family sat around and reminisced. Though their lives with Claude were complicated and shrouded by his alcoholism, the good outweighed the bad as everyone recollected him lovingly. Unfortunately for John, his memories were limited. After a few days of mourning and catching up, he returned to New York.

In March, he received the best news any aspiring songwriter could get. Charles Ryan got the Smoothies a contract with Decca Records and secured a session date for them to record their first single. This was John's big opportunity to press his arranging and songwriting abilities into wax and, with a little luck, onto the radio. But it wasn't going to be so easy. When they made their way to Pythian Temple studio on the Upper West Side, they were placed under the direction of producer Milt Gabler and arranger Jack Pleis, who'd collaborated recently on recordings by Bobby Darin, Domenico Modugno and Al Hibbler. John wasted no time in getting on Jack Pleis' nerves with suggestions to his arrangements, which included an 18-piece orchestra.

John was either persuasive or forceful enough to get one of his compositions, "Softly," recorded, and the decision-makers at Decca were convinced to put it as the A-side. The other song, "Joanie," was composed by the songwriting team of Alan Hood and Richard Loring, who'd written songs for the Four Freshmen and the Four Preps. But, for someone who emulated the Hi-Lo's and the rubber band vocal stylings of Clark Burroughs and Bob Flanigan, John's song sounded more like a Paul Anka record.

As the record was being pressed and prepared for release, the Smoothies continued with a moderate tour schedule, fulfilling dates at the Town Casino in Buffalo, the Town 'n' Country in Winnipeg and several USO shows. They were also invited back for a spring engagement at the Elmwood Casino. Ryan also put them on a weekly dole that wasn't much, but it kept them from being homeless and starving when they weren't on the road. To supplement their income, he also got them modeling jobs making $25 to $60 per session for the trashy pulp magazines *True Detective* and *Personal Romances*.

During this period, John and Scott grew closer. In their downtime, the two would frequent the various clubs in Greenwich Village that mostly catered to folk artists like Ed McCurdy, the Clancy Brothers, Brother John Sellers, and Sonny Terry & Brownie McGhee. John even got to catch up with Theodore Bikel, who came into town to play the Fifth Peg. The folk bug was spreading rapidly, and John and Scott were right in the thick of it.

The single was released in July, and John and the Smoothies got their biggest break yet when they were invited to lip-synch to "Softly" on Dick Clark's

American Bandstand. Their nationally syndicated appearance on the ABC program was a reinforcement of their talents and belief in themselves, especially for John. It was also the first chance for all their family members and friends to see what their group looked and sounded like.

They made the drive to WFIL's studios in West Philadelphia on July 25 and were the first act up. They were understandably nervous as it was the first time any of them stood in front of network cameras, and, dressed in matching flannel blazers, they looked more like a high school glee club than a pop act. Scott's nerves were particularly on display as he lip-synched with his eyes closed almost the entire time. But, the biggest influence on John that day wasn't the cameras or Dick Clark's big introduction. Rather, it was the impression the main act, Conway Twitty, left on him. He walked into the studios, surrounded by a throng of young girls, looking like a million bucks in his sunglasses and big pompadour and entourage trailing behind him. It was John's first up-close look at the trappings of wealth and fame, and he wanted it badly.

But they weren't there yet, and that reality hit John a few days later after a performance back in D.C. on the locally televised *Milt Grant Show*. A group of kids came up to them and one young boy asked Scott for his autograph. When he handed it to him, the kid groaned in disappointment.

"I thought you were Dion," he told Scott.

Despite all their promotional efforts, "Softly" lived up to its name. Its impact was hardly felt. Nevertheless, Decca believed in them enough to schedule sessions for a follow-up single and an album. On the production side, it was the same cast of characters with Milt Gabler and Jack Pleis and a moderate sized orchestra. This time, however, they didn't come with a song prepared. Instead, they did two John Phillips originals. The first, "Lonely Boy and Pretty Girl," co-written with Scott, fit alongside their first two songs. It was a haunting mid-tempo ballad with schmaltzy lyrics about two would-be lovers who couldn't overcome their shyness. But the arrangement made the Smoothies sound like background singers to a lead singer who went missing.

The other song, which ended up being the A-side, "Ride, Ride, Ride," was, quite frankly, cutting edge for its time and hinted at the direction John was going in his songwriting. It hit along the up-and-coming folk sounds that were beginning to trend in the Top 40 by artists like the Kingston Trio and the

CHAPTER 7:
JOURNEYMEN

Greenwich Village in Lower Manhattan has been a gathering place for political activists and musicians for decades and, oftentimes, the lines between the two get blurred. In the 1940s, native son Pete Seeger formed the Weavers, who specialized in mixing old-timey Appalachian ballads with political and social commentary. They were communists who played at union halls and strike gatherings and weren't necessarily in it for the money. Because of this, they were often targeted and harassed by the government. Greenwich Village was a safe place for them to disappear into the shadows and be among similar nonconformists who held an equal mistrust of authority.

That part of Manhattan was inherently contrary. When the city began reconfiguring itself in 1807 to become a much more navigable grid system, the citizens of the tiny village on the Lower East Side successfully resisted. Around the turn of the century, while many of the immigrants passing through Ellis Island eagerly shed their former identities to become uniquely American, the people of Greenwich Village clung to their European roots. Over time, that spirit attracted artists and writers and by 1915, Greenwich Village could count notables like Robert Louis Stevenson, Mark Twain, Henry James, and Walt Whitman among its past and present inhabitants.

As the 20th century rolled along, the Village became a hotbed of nonconformity. The atmosphere created by the numerous starving and established artists roving about gave it a pretty paint job, as did the growth of New York

University, which snaked right through it. It gave the neighborhood a collegiate exuberance that contrasted starkly to the buttoned-up financial excess and greed of its Wall Street neighbors. Though jazz was still king, by the early 1950s, the legacies of Leadbelly and the Woody Guthrie were proudly embraced. Folk music began to billow out of the ever-growing number of nightclubs filling up Bleecker and MacDougall Streets that were being patronized by NYU students and regional young adults. Word began to spread that this was the place to be entertained and younger folk singers like Bob Gibson, Dave Van Ronk and Ramblin' Jack Elliott crossed the river from Brooklyn to make Greenwich Village their home base. Following closely behind them were exports from other parts of the country who'd convene for informal picking sessions at the crown jewel of the Village, Washington Square Park.

With rock and roll being embraced by the major labels as well as on radio and TV, breaking into it became increasingly difficult. The sheen of Frankie Avalon, Fabian and Bobby Rydell became off-putting to many of the kids who were inspired to pick up a guitar after seeing Elvis on *The Ed Sullivan Show*. The spirit that had lifted rock and roll a mere five years earlier had moved over to folk music and Greenwich Village was the heart of it all. Dejected Brill Building songwriter Fred Neil moved downtown in 1960 and became the king of MacDougall Street and the folk singer's folk singer. After an infinitesimally short stint in Bobby Vee's touring band, recent University of Minnesota dropout Robert Zimmerman headed to Greenwich Village in January 1961 and renamed himself Bob Dylan. Greenwich Village became a place where an aspiring musician not pretty enough to make it in rock and roll could reinvent himself. Over the next two years, they started coming from around the world.

In January 1961, Greenwich Village transplant John Phillips was looking to shed his Smoothies skin and refashion himself as a serious folk musician. His transformation was strategic and deliberate. He found a kindred spirit in Izzy Young, the proprietor of the Folk Center at 110 MacDougall Street. His store specialized in sheet music and musical instruments but, more importantly, became a meeting center for the growing Greenwich Village folk community. John became a regular and picked Izzy's brain on folk songs and arrangements. In fact, it was at Izzy's that John first encountered Dick Weissman and invited him to be on the second Smoothies session. In the months following, a friendship began to emerge.

When they met, Dick was a graduate student at Columbia University. He'd moved to New York from Philadelphia in 1957 after exhausting the folk music limits of his native city, which pretty much consisted of the Gilded Cage and an ever-changing number of coffeehouses in Rittenhouse Square. His musical acumen was head and shoulders above that of his peers as a result of his parents signing him up for piano lessons at age seven. In his teen years, he devoted his passion to ping pong and, in his freshman year at Goddard College, won the 1953 Vermont State Table Tennis Championship. When China began allowing sponge paddles in competition, Dick hung up his wooden pads and devoted himself exclusively to folk music. He'd switched from piano to stringed instruments and bought a cheap banjo and Pete Seeger's instructional book *How to Play the 5-String Banjo*.

Dick first experienced the kinetic energy of Greenwich Village during his junior year at Goddard while on a work study program that landed him at the New School for Social Research on 12th Street. He immersed himself in the local music culture and hung out with Lead Belly's niece Tiny Ledbetter and gospel blues guitarist Gary Davis. After leaving the New School, he did a semester at the University of New Mexico and studied under folklorist Stu Jamieson who, after returning home from World War II, traveled throughout Appalachia in order to record and preserve the folk traditions still present.

With all this accumulated knowledge along with his prolific musical ability, Dick became not only a scholar of folk music but an implementer as well. Not long after moving to New York City in 1957, he teamed up with Eric Weissberg and Billy Faier and recorded the album *Banjos, Banjos and More Banjos!* for Judson Records. By the time he met John, he'd released two more LPs with fellow folk musician Pat Foster. More recently, he was part of a folk group organized by Brill Building songwriters Sid Jacobson and Lou Stallman called the Citizens who issued the album *Sing About a City of People* on Laurie Records.

Dick's musical reputation preceded him, and he was the same age as John and exhibited a level of maturity absent in his younger bandmates, which was attractive. John wanted to collaborate with him badly and proposed forming a band together. Dick recognized John's musical genius at the Smoothies session and eagerly accepted his invitation if his girlfriend, Karen Dalton, could be involved. John was skeptical but, if that's what it took to get Dick, he could compromise. Eventually John left his room at the Albert and moved in with

Dick and Karen Dalton at their oversized apartment on the Upper West Side. Scott, however, remained in Greenwich Village. He'd been with John long enough to know he couldn't live with him and, though he didn't realize it at the time, he was struggling with depression. They convened daily at the apartment and practiced up to 10 hours per day, six days a week. It didn't take long for John and Karen to clash over arrangements and after only a couple rehearsals, she quit and left Dick.

Undeterred, the new trio forged ahead. Dick taught them the basic folk chord progressions of I-IV-V-I and variations like II, III, VI and VII chords. Once those were mastered, they worked on their repertoire with Dick constructing the instrumental arrangement and John arranging vocals. They went over standards like "Pallet on the Floor," "In the Pines" and "Fenario" and then got into deeper songs like "Dunya" and "Whiskey in the Jar." They also worked up a few originals, including John's "Soft Blow the Summer Winds," a revamped three-part harmony version of "Ride, Ride, Ride" and Dick's "Chase the Rising Sun."

John and Dick's musicianship sped things along quite rapidly, and, around March, they decided it was time to court record labels. No label was too big or too small, except Decca. They didn't want to go back to that well and record again for Milt Gabler and Jack Pleis. Laurie was out of the question too. Dick wasn't sure whether he was still under contract or not. Their biggest problem was that in 1961, the live audition had gone the way of the dinosaur. Record companies wanted demos. It was a major time-saver and gave them an idea of how this group would sound on wax. Before pooling their resources and committing to that type of investment, they decided to go the old-fashioned way. They thumbed through the Schwann record catalog and began cold-calling with John handling the pitch. Only one label, MGM, offered a live audition.

They set up a date and made their way to their offices in Midtown and auditioned for a few A&R reps who, though impressed, hemmed and hawed in terms of an offer because they didn't hear anything with hit potential. But they understood folk music was starting to make waves and didn't want to let them slip away completely. They asked the trio to come back in a few days and work with a few professional songwriters.

With a potential offer from MGM looming, Dick felt they had enough cachet to expedite professional representation and picked up a recent edition of *Billboard Magazine*. They began skimming through the ads until they came upon one for International Talent Agency. It sounded good. John made the call and set up an audition at their Madison Avenue office. ITA was ahead of the folk trend in 1961. They held management contracts with the Kingston Trio, the Brothers Four, and Odetta and were very eager to see what John, Scott and Dick had to offer. And they didn't disappoint. As they got into their first number, their exquisite harmonies filtered through the corridors of ITA and, one by one, secretaries and executives emerged from their desks to listen to them up close.

When they finished, they were met with rousing applause. One of those clapping was a well-connected independent talent agent named Rene Cardenas who just so happened to be visiting from San Francisco. He shared a partnership with Frank Werber, the charismatic manager of the red-hot Kingston Trio, who had sent him on a mission to the East Coast to mine for talent. ITA was one of their partners. Without hesitation, he approached John, Scott, and Dick and offered them a contract, which they eagerly accepted. Under Werber's auspices, the sky was the limit. But, for now, getting signed to a label was the top priority.

After going over their current situations, Cardenas realized John and Scott were still under contract to Decca and that could pose a potential problem. John, who by now had mastered the art of bamboozling, had a solution. He arranged a meeting with Milt Gabler to discuss his next project and went to see him with Scott and Dick. On the "Ride, Ride, Ride" session, Gabler had made it clear that he was no fan of banjo music. In Gabler's office, John put Dick front and center. It didn't take long for the clanging of the banjo strings to make Gabler cut the session short. Moments later, John and Scott walked out of the Decca offices free men.

Cardenas came along with them at their next meeting with MGM a few days later and handled the negotiations. In a room full of executives, including veteran producers Danny Davis and Jim Vinneau, he told them his clients wanted a two-album deal and a $5,000 promotional guarantee for the first record. It completely shocked the team of executives and put them immediately on the defensive. They were trapped. Folk music was getting hot, and they didn't want to lose this trio, but they also knew that these three musicians in front of them had little to no status in the industry. Davis maintained his charm and cool, telling him that MGM would never approve a deal like that for a group of unknowns. Vinneau was much blunter.

"You'll never get a deal like that in the record business," he scoffed.

It was clear they had reached an impasse, and all agreed that MGM wasn't the label for them. Cardenas gathered the three of them and left. John, Scott, and Dick were disappointed and perplexed over their brand-new agent's aggressive tactics, but they soon found out why. Cardenas was shrewd and understood that MGM wasn't serious about getting into the folk music field. They mostly specialized in soundtracks for their Hollywood films and had only made a cautious foray into pop music. At the time, their major acts were Connie Francis and, following at a distant second, Conway Twitty. If they made the mistake of signing with MGM, there'd be little label support and they would most likely disappear along with all their other acts.

Cardenas had an ace up his sleeve. What he didn't tell his new clients is that he'd set up a second audition that day with Capitol Records. They shuffled over to their offices on 55th and Broadway and played for East Coast A&R man Andy Wiswell. It didn't take long to convince him. He loved what he heard and asked Cardena for their terms. They were the same ones he gave MGM. Wiswell placed a call to Voyle Gilmore, Capitol's A&R man out in Los Angeles, and by the time he hung up the phone, John, Scott, and Dick were Capitol Records recording artists.

After celebrating, they realized they didn't have a name. In 1961, folk music was moving forward, and the new acts had names that were reflective of that sentiment. There were plenty of "trios" and "brothers" and "singers" already out there, but they were looking for something a little fresher sounding like the Limeliters or the Highwaymen. Years later, when reflecting on the name they eventually chose, Scott McKenzie would say they picked it because they felt it represented a craftsman who is not yet a master of his trade but accomplished enough to bear his profession's name. Dick Weismann offered a little more honest assessment.

"An agent picked the name out of a dictionary."

Regardless of how it came about, the trio of John Phillips, Scott McKenzie, and Dick Weissman were henceforward known as the Journeymen.

CHAPTER 8:
JOHN & MITCHIE

Back in Washington, D.C., while John was away pursuing his music career, Susie Phillips was eking out a living and raising their two children. She took on a full-time job at the Pentagon while John's family helped as much as they could watching Jeffrey and Laura. Considering Susie's presidential family roots and status, it was quite a fall from grace. She was still outside of her parents' good graces and couldn't rely on them for any type of support as long as she remained with John. But that devotion only went one way. The gap was widening between John and his family life. His success was growing, but he didn't want to share it.

With the Journeymen now signed to Capitol Records, getting into the studio to record their debut LP was crucial, and they did that a few weeks after signing their contracts. But, their first sessions weren't exactly what they had in mind as they only recorded several radio spots for Canada Dry. Promoting a soft drink may have been the antithesis of authentic folk music, but the payday did help pay off a few bills, and the sessions served as a warmup. Come late March, they were in Capitol's studios in Times Square working on their album.

The sessions convened on March 21 and lasted about three weeks. The initial tracks they laid down consisted mostly of the songs they'd spent a couple of months rehearsing in Dick's apartment, so getting through them was a breeze. The newer stuff came afterward and took a little more fine-tuning. "In the Pines" was rewritten as "Black Girl" and featured a stunning duet between John and Scott. Dick showed off his banjo chops in "Cumberland Mountain Deer Chase" and John's skillful vocal arrangements stood out in "River, She Come Down" and "500 Miles." The latter was a song with roots that date back at least to 1924, when Fiddlin' John Carson released a song called "I'm Nine Hundred Miles from Home" on the Okeh label that featured many of the same lyrics. Thirty-five years later, it was adapted and rewritten by Georgia native Hedy West who played it in many of the folk clubs in Greenwich Village while John was living there. The Journeymen's version was the first recorded one in its more contemporary arrangement and featured John as a co-writer.

After the sessions were completed on April 12, Dick and studio musician Arnold Fishkin overdubbed all lead guitar and bass parts, giving the songs a richer, fuller sound. Much to their consternation, however, the tracks were shelved for a few months. Capitol was too focused on the Kingston Trio, who, in addition to recording and releasing their new *Goin' Places* album, were facing a crisis. Founding member and chief arranger Dave Guard was leaving. His leadership, musicianship, and presence were invaluable, and Frank Werber and Rene Cardenas did their best to minimize the damage and buy time to find a suitable replacement. Frank had his eye on John, which also contributed to the Journeymen's album delay. Nevertheless, Werber and Cardenas knew it was important to build up their brand through live performances and they kicked that off in big way with a week-long stand at Gerde's Folk City in Greenwich Village. It was one of the biggest folk venues in the country and the gig of a lifetime.

May 2, 1961: The spring thaw was in bloom. The days were noticeably longer, jackets were a little lighter and the growing optimism of warmer days ahead was contagious. It was an ideal day, topping off at 60 degrees. As John Phillips and Dick Weissman boarded the 1 train at 103rd and Broadway to get to Washington Square, there was a range of emotions stirring within each of them over the course of their half-hour ride. For John, it was validation of his professional musical career, which had its fair share of doubters. He'd been steadily climbing the ladder of success and this was another rung. Inside, his excitement billowed, and he walked proudly. He'd played plenty of live gigs but nothing like Gerde's Folk City. This was big-time.

For Dick, the emotions were a little more mixed. He loved playing with John and Scott and admired what they'd accomplished in a very short period, but this was a little more commercial than he'd ever been and a little out of his comfort zone. He'd built up a solid reputation as a folk purist, and now he was playing with a couple of guys who, up to a few months ago, probably had never even heard of Woody Guthrie or Pete Seeger. Who would be at Gerde's tonight? What would his friends think? Selling out was a mortal sin in the folk world. However, he made a commitment with his bandmates and he was going to see it through, and he soldiered through his apprehension with a smile. Dick had a strong work ethic, and confidence was not a problem for him. He could play with the best of them. It was now time to see what Greenwich Village thought of the Journeymen.

As they exited the train and walked down the platform in their matching two-button suits, starched white shirts and thin black ties, they most certainly stood out. It had nothing to do with their outfits but more their exaggerated difference in height and instruments strapped over their shoulders. John had Dick's small-bodied Martin and Dick carried his Vega Tubaphone Special Deluxe banjo. Journeymen indeed. And the journey had only begun. Scott McKenzie had a much shorter trip to Gerde's. He left the Albert and walked the seven blocks north carrying Dick's Martin 0042.

Gerde's was on a recent uptick as John Lee Hooker had just headlined a couple weeks earlier. His performances proved so popular the he and his opening act, 20-year-old Bob Dylan, were held over for an additional week. Also, Village folk fans were under fire from New York City Police Commissioner Newbold Morris, who had recently banned performing in Washington Square Park. It pushed many fans toward the clubs, which guaranteed larger audiences for them. The place was packed.

The opening act was folk singer Logan English, who also served as the club's emcee. The Journeymen did two shows, with the first starting at 9:00 p.m. and the second starting at midnight. They got through them with ease, mostly performing songs they'd recorded for their album. Even though they were a big-label folk group and a bit more commercial than the audience was used to, the crowds were warm. The rest of the week went smoothly and, after they finished their week, they hung around for a few days to watch performances by Brother John Sellers and Peter Yarrow. Afterward, it was on to the 2nd Fret in Philadelphia followed by an appearance on the *Herb Shriner Show* in Boston and on the *World of Folk Music* program in Toronto, where they performed "River, She Come Down."

The Journeymen performed regularly throughout June 1961 and were building up a good reputation. Cardenas lined up a solid slate of bookings that took them across the country and ended at the Hungry "i" in San Francisco, where they'd be paid $1,500 for a week's worth of performances. But, before heading out for the West Coast, John's conscience began getting the better of him. While he was out fulfilling his dream, his wife and kids were struggling back home. Susie had sacrificed so much standing by her man and all he'd done is made her look foolish in the eyes of family and friends with his philandering, absenteeism, and lack of income. His last trip to California traumatized her and almost sunk the marriage completely. His recent success renewed him, and he was determined to make his marriage work. He asked Susie to move out west with him. It was a bold move, as she'd be nearly 3,000 miles away from her support system, but she was all in on the marriage too and accepted. They dropped everything, grabbed the kids, and split for the West Coast and a fresh start.

If there was an entire city that resembled the spirit of Greenwich Village, it was San Francisco. The second-oldest city on the West Coast of the United States has always been a bit on the edgy, progressive side particularly in the worlds of politics and the arts and ripe for the folk movement of the early 1960s. However, it was very different from its eastern counterpart. In Greenwich Village, the folk scene was tight-knit and fraternal. San Francisco's scene was much more spread out and unorganized. Clubs weren't on top of one another and there was no central gathering place. Like Greenwich Village, it provided safe haven for socialists, communists, radicals, and homosexuals, but it was intermingled between Chinese restaurants, topless bars, cable cars, and the Coexistence Bagel Shop. The Beat Generation poets like Kerouac, Ginsberg, and Burroughs, who, less than 10 years earlier, had defined the counterculture in Greenwich Village, fled to San Francisco in the late 1950s when jazz clubs in New York City began being overrun by folkies.

The two most popular clubs in San Francisco, the Purple Onion and the Hungry "i," weren't exclusively folk, but artists of that genre were beginning to dominate their bills. The stand-up comedy scene was electric in San Francisco as well and, oftentimes, the two commingled. It wasn't uncommon to see the Kingston Trio perform following a stand-up set by Bob Newhart, Mort Sahl, or Bill Dana performing as José Jiménez.

The Hungry "i" was beginning to garner national attention among folkies thanks to live albums issued by both the Kingston Trio and the Gateway Singers. It was opened in 1950 by German poet Eric "Big Daddy" Nord in the basement of the Sentinel Building in the financial district. Its bizarre name and location evoked a natural curiosity among club goers, and its coziness attracted many a young banker looking to unwind at the end of a workday. Though still shrouded in mystery, it's widely believe that the "i" was short for "id," as in the Freudian term for the part of the human psyche most in tune with repressed, antisocial desires. It was becoming a common term in early 1950s bohemian culture. Nord sold the club after only one year to local impresario Enrico Banducci, who moved it to the basement of International Hotel in Manilatown, where its golden era began.

Throughout the 1950s, on any given night, patrons would be in stitches enjoying a range of comedic stylings from Lenny Bruce to Dick Cavett to Bill Cosby to Professor Irwin Corey. They all stood in front of that legendary red brick wall, which later inspired the Hollywood Improv. In addition to the Kingston Trio, folk singers like Judy Henske, the Limeliters and Rod McKuen would entertain audiences regularly, and all worked comedy into their sets.

This is the scene that 17-year-old Michelle Gilliam walked into in the summer of 1961. The recent high school dropout would frequent the Hungry "i," dressed to kill, along with her best friend Tamar Hodel. The blonde bombshell had recently moved to San Francisco from Los Angeles to pursue a modeling career. She found mentorship and a place to stay in her friend Tamar, who was nine years her senior and the daughter of the demented Dr. George Hodel, the prime suspect in the Black Dahlia murder in 1947.

Born Holly Michelle Gilliam in Long Beach, California, on June 4, 1944, Michelle's life was uprooted at the age of five when her mother Joyce died from a brain aneurysm shortly after putting her daughters to bed. It left a noticeable gap in her and her older sister Russell Ann's lives and sent her father, Gardner Burnett Gilliam, on an existential journey. Gardner, who went by Gil, was a bit of a vagabond. Tall, sturdy, and strong, he enlisted in the Merchant Marines but, after marrying Joyce, moved over to Hollywood where he worked as a production assistant. When Joyce was pregnant with Russell, Gil purchased a liquor store in hopes of securing a steadier income.

The family settled in Lynwood, in south Los Angeles, after Michelle's birth a year later.

The marriage was fraught with infidelity and mistrust. Nevertheless, Joyce's death was traumatic and sent Gil into a tailspin. In the span of two years, he and his daughters went from Los Angeles to Buffalo, New York, and down to Mexico City, where Gil decided to pursue a degree in sociology and psychology at Mexico City College.

They settled in the Colonia Cuauhtémoc neighborhood and stayed at the home of Gil's friend Fabian Andre, the co-writer of the standard "Dream a Little Dream of Me." Gil's beefy, square-jawed American looks made him stand out among his Mexican neighbors and he looked more like a stand-in for leading men like Jeff Chandler or Rod Taylor than a student. He captivated many local and university women, and his bedroom became a revolving door of sex partners. But Gil got bored easily, and, just as Rusty and Michelle would get used to his latest girlfriend, she'd be replaced by a new one.

Gil's romantic dalliances notwithstanding, Michelle's time in Mexico City was fundamental. She learned to speak Spanish so fluently that, for a little while, English became her second language. Her fierce independent nature was forged with Gil being away at school and work much of the time. She and Rusty often skipped school to go gallivanting around town. Upon Gil's graduation in 1956, they returned to Los Angeles, where he took a job as a juvenile probation officer. They moved into a multifamily home in the residential Silver Lake neighborhood, and the Gilliam girls attended Thomas Starr King Junior High School followed by John Marshall High School. Over the course of their teenage years, both developed into high school beauty queens and became the objects of many a teenage boy's desire.

But their personalities couldn't be more disparate. Whereas Rusty was more grounded and responsible, Michelle was wild and unpredictable and became Gil's prodigal daughter. The picture of the quintessential 1950s California blonde, she engaged in many of the common teen hijinks, including sneaking out past curfew, cutting class, and hanging out with ne'er-do-wells. In her case, it was the local car club, the Diabolics.

Those were childish idiosyncrasies that Gil could look past. What was more concerning was Michelle's friendship with Tamar Hodel. They first met in 1957 when she, her husband, folk singer Stan Wilson, and their young daughter Debbie moved into their neighborhood. Rusty was dating Tamar's half-brother Kelly, who hadn't seen his sister since childhood. When he learned she lived close to Rusty, the Gilliam girls took him to see her and provide moral support. Nobody was prepared for the pretty in lavender, petite force of nature who answered the door. The meeting brought two lost siblings together, but it was Michelle and Tamar who connected the strongest despite their nine-year age difference. They quickly became inseparable.

Tamar's childhood was hellish. She was the eldest daughter of Dr. George Hodel and his first child with his second wife Dorothy Anthony. Dr. Hodel was one of the LAPD's prime suspects in the gruesome 1947 murder of 22-year-old aspiring actress Elizabeth Short, who later became dubbed the Black Dahlia. He was a trained surgeon and perfectly capable of making the skilled cut that severed Short's body at the waist. His hedonistic lifestyle, however, was more incriminating. The wealthy doctor was fixated on sex, and the more depraved, the more exciting it was. Hodel routinely held parties at his Sowden House mansion that featured Hollywood movie stars and producers as well as a variety of artists of all denominations. These gatherings always degraded into bacchanalias, and he supplemented them with wannabe actresses and prostitutes.

Though Hodel wasn't named publicly as a suspect in the Black Dahlia murder, he became infamous nonetheless in 1949 after he was arrested when Tamar accused him of sexually molesting and impregnating her. Despite her testimony, which was corroborated by three witnesses, Hodel's leverage as a venereal doctor in 1940s Hollywood was far-reaching. He was acquitted of all charges based on character witnesses. Tamar was thrown into juvenile hall and blackballed in L.A. high society, but it didn't last long. In April 1950, when Hodel caught wind that the LAPD was closing in on him in connection with Short's murder, he split for the Philippines, where he remained for the next 40 years. Free from her father's long shadow, Tamar maintained a low profile and cut off contact with her family. Moving to Silver Lake was almost as good as moving across country.

Tamar took to Michelle, and their friendship became a welcome distraction from her failing marriage. She schooled Michelle in glamour and fashion and groomed her to be the picture of late 1950s beauty. For Michelle, Tamar filled the void left by her mother's death, and she idolized her. Tamar taught her style, makeup, and color coordination and that it was important to match everything, from the paint job on her Nash Rambler right down to the ashtrays in her living room complementing the lavender curtains. She also introduced Michelle to her inner circle, which included folk and blues luminaries like Josh White and Odetta and comedian Dick Gregory.

There was a dark side, though. Although Tamar despised her father, she inherited his penchant for contributing to the delinquency of a minor. Over time, she introduced Michelle to alcohol and amphetamines, provided fake IDs, and took her along parties where drugs and booze flowed freely. At an after-party following a Josh White concert at UCLA, the two were arrested for trespassing after exiting his hotel room. It was a vintage case of racial profiling, as the police were immediately suspicious seeing two pretty young white girls coming out of a black man's hotel room in the wee hours of the morning. They were taken down to the Hollywood Division and questioned about what they were up to but were let off with only a warning when they learned Michelle's father was a probation officer. To smooth things over with Gil, Tamar slept with him.

As her relationship with Tamar grew, Michelle's teenage problems escalated. She got kicked out of John Marshall High School her junior year for forging her father's signature on absentee excuses and transferred to Eagle Rock in northeast Los Angeles. She also became the quintessential party girl, and, with Gil working overnight three nights a week, she often transformed his home into party central. The only guidance and discipline she received was from her godmother Marika Sail, who was an old friend of her mother's.

Things were topsy-turvy in Tamar's life too. She ended her marriage to Stan Wilson when she learned of his unsuccessful attempt at seducing Michelle. After Tamar filed for divorce, she and Debbie moved to San Francisco. Michelle was devastated. Not only did she feel like she was the cause of Tamar's divorce but now she was without her best friend. Tamar didn't harbor any ill will toward her, though, and the two regularly talked for hours by phone. Michelle soldiered through the rest of her junior year, pining away for her best friend and making everyone around her know it. When summer break finally arrived, she convinced her father to let her spend it in San Francisco with Tamar as long as she promised to keep clean and stay out of trouble.

When she arrived in June, their tight friendship resumed, but Tamar took on an additional role as Michelle's benefactor. She knew Michelle had the looks and the body to be a professional model, so she enrolled her at Nerice Fugate's House of Charm to learn how to pose, apply makeup, coordinate outfits, and get a better understanding of the business. And she put what she learned to good use regularly. She and Tamar became denizens of the San Francisco nightlife and frequented the Purple Onion and the Hungry "i." Michelle would prepare with a light foundation to cover her freckles and eyeliner to highlight her baby blues. She got her hair done regularly at Tamar's hairdresser, and twice a week, rinsed it with lemon juice to make it look richer and fuller. She certainly stood out in a crowd.

Tuesday, July 11, 1961, seemed like any other night in San Francisco. The two girls made their way to the Hungry "i." Comedian Dick Gregory was the headliner, and Tamar had her sights set on him. When they walked in, the Journeymen were in the middle of their set. They were the opening act and would be for the next month. They were a dapper-looking trio, and their short time on the road had fine-tuned their act. Scott's natural position as lead vocalist and his youthful good looks commanded the most attention. His confident guitar playing onstage betrayed the fact that he was the least musical of the three. Dick was totally into the music, looking entranced as he bobbed his head back and forth to his banjo picking. John gave off the confident vibe of a bandleader and nodded rhythmically during the up-tempo songs and beautifully enhanced Scott's lead with his delicate harmonies. Between numbers, it was easy to see that John was in charge as he benevolently commanded the other two.

Michelle noticed it too and found it attractive. Tamar made it known that she had her sights set on Scott and made a play for him the first chance she got. So much for Dick Gregory. She knew club owner Enrico Banducci through her estranged husband, and he happily arranged for the Journeymen to come over and meet them after their set. The exchange was modest and perfunctory. Pleasantries and compliments were paid and didn't go beyond small talk.

John was attracted to Michelle too but, with moving Susie and the kids out to San Francisco, was on a short leash and minding his manners. He told himself that both girls were interested in Scott and asked to be excused so he could go call home. With his marriage announcement, Michelle mentally crossed him off her list. The gathering broke up shortly after that and Michelle and Tamar mingled a while. They eventually left to have dinner at Enrico's Coffee House on Broadway. After they were seated, they noticed Scott eating alone and invited him to join them. Over steak tartare and coffee, a spark erupted between him and Tamar and he ended up leaving the restaurant with her and spending the night.

In fact, he spent many nights. It got so serious that Scott lost track of everything, and John would have to come to their apartment to get him ready and drive him to the club. While Scott would scramble around, looking for his socks and tie, John and Michelle would make small talk. Over the next couple of weeks, they got to know each other better. She was very worldly for her age and made quite an impression on the husband and father of two. He was captivated by her youthful beauty and free spirit. Michelle found him quite charming and began having feelings for him.

She began attending the Journeymen's shows nightly and hanging out backstage with John. It didn't take long for her attention to reignite his old habits. Soon, his phone calls to Susie would be lies about why he couldn't come home right away. The only thing he wanted to do was spend time with Michelle. A few weeks later, before their stand at the Hungry "i" ended, the Journeymen were invited to a party at the Yacht Dock in Sausalito given by Frank Werber in the Kingston Trio's honor. Scott brought Tamar and Michelle along, much to John's delight. They escaped to a private table to chat and take in one another. As the night progressed, they fell madly for each other and slipped away the first chance they got. Since Scott and Tamar were enjoying themselves at the party, they headed straight for Michelle's apartment, where John carried her across the threshold and into her bed and made love for hours.

John was totally hooked on Michelle and began to dread the end of the Journeymen's stand at the Hungry "i." He'd made San Francisco his home, so there was reason for optimism, but when he was there, he led a double life. When he was away, he yearned for her and gave little thought to Susie and the kids. All he knew was that he wanted Michelle around him all the time, and he had put himself in quite a jam. Michelle wanted him too and willfully became the other woman. There was no going back for either of them. Though they didn't know it at the time, half of the Mamas & the Papas were now in place.

CHAPTER 9:
DON'T YOU WORK AS HARD AS YOU PLAY

The month-long stand at the Hungry "i" served as a springboard for the Journeymen professionally, but it was also where the first fissures of their personal relationship started to show. Scott and Dick could only watch as John juggled his relationship with 17-year-old Michelle Gilliam and his family. They were aware of his attempt at rehabilitating his marriage to Susie and were now unwilling conscripts in his game of deception.

Dick didn't have much of a history with either John or Scott, so he didn't socialize too much with them offstage. He didn't feel it was his place to moralize to either one, but essentially did just that by actively keeping away from their soap operas. Rather than join them for drinks or carousing, he spent much of his free time picking with other folk and bluegrass players at the Fox and the Hound on Grant Avenue.

Scott's love life was also complicated. His relationship with Tamar was dampening his musical aspirations. It was his first serious relationship and every day with her was a new adventure. She introduced him to marijuana and the combination of that and sex was killing his stage energy and fracturing his relationship with his bandmates. John would have to pry him away from her and onto stage. He finally laid it on the line and made Scott choose between Tamar and the Journeymen. The group won out. When Scott broke the news to her, she went into a tailspin.

Beneath Tamar's cool, Kim Novak–like façade was an emotionally fragile little girl. The sexual abuse she had suffered at the hands of her father and the fallout from his trial caused her incredible emotional trauma. Scott's rejection of her aggravated it and added stress to her contentious divorce from Stan Wilson. She decided the only way to stop all her suffering was to end her life and told Michelle about her plans. Michelle did her best to try and talk Tamar out of it and reminded her about her daughter Debbie, who depended on her, but it was no use. She'd already made up her mind and wrote a holographic will that granted Michelle custody of Debbie.

Two nights later, Tamar made herself up, put on a nice dress, and downed 48 tablets of the barbiturate Seconal. Moments later, she collapsed into Michelle's arms and began convulsing. Suddenly, it all became very real, and Michelle began to panic. After trying in vain to reach John by phone, she dragged Tamar to her bed, surrendered to the inevitable, and fell asleep beside her still body. A little while later, she was awakened by John tickling the bottom of her feet. En route to a gig at the Joker in San Jose, Scott told him about Tamar's suicide plans. John was dumbstruck by what he'd heard and raced back to their Sausalito apartment.

Michelle was groggy and half-asleep as John questioned her about what had happened. When Scott spotted the empty bottle of Seconal, she confessed that she'd helped Tamar consume the entire thing. They flushed every legal drug they could find down the toilet and called for an ambulance. John gathered Michelle and Scott and made sure they got their stories straight. He told them that if anyone asked, they had all returned from an evening out and found Tamar unresponsive on her bed. Then he coached them on how to respond in case certain incriminating questions were asked so that no suspicion could be placed on Michelle.

Though they pulled it off, John was shaken, and the entire incident provided him with some clarity about his current situation. He began to wonder what exactly he'd gotten himself into and if it was worth it. For now, the best thing to do was to send Michelle home. He put her and Debbie on a flight back to Los Angeles and got back on the road with Scott to meet up with Dick in San Jose. Their residence at the Joker was for six weeks, which got him out of San Francisco and away from this nightmare for a good deal of time.

She may not have known it, but Michelle needed a reset too. When she arrived home, Gil was aghast at the sight of her. She'd only been away two months but was noticeably skinnier and pale and the stress of what she'd endured over the last 24 hours was visible. It triggered Gil to start acting fatherly and he began laying down rules. Going back to San Francisco and Tamar was out of the question. She was going to go back to school in September and get her life back on track. Though he meant well, his new tight ship undermined any sort of respite she was seeking and, as soon as Tamar began calling her from the hospital, the urge to return began to grow.

But it was out of the question as far as Gil was concerned. The only things he asked her to do were keep clean and stay out of trouble, and she had clearly violated those rules. His trust evaporated, but whether he knew it or not, Gil's lifestyle had sowed a sense of independence in his youngest daughter long ago, and nothing he could say or do would keep her from leaving. It only took a day for Gil's tough façade to crumble. Michelle picked up Tamar's daughter and took a train back to San Francisco.

It had only been less than a week since the incident back at the apartment, but John had left Michelle no forwarding information. Everything had happened so quickly, and she couldn't remember what club they were playing or what town they were in. Nobody at the Hungry "i" seemed to know either. There was nothing else Michelle could do except bide her time. John would have to come home to his wife and kids eventually. A few weeks later, while thumbing through the newspaper, she spotted an ad for the Journeymen's stand at the Joker Coffeehouse in San Jose. She and Tamar wasted no time in getting dolled up and made the 60-mile drive.

Much like they had done over a month earlier, the girls walked into the club in the middle of the Journeymen's set. This time, they walked boldly up to the stage and made their presence known. For Scott, absence didn't make his heart grow fonder for Tamar. As soon as he saw her, he set his guitar down, walked outside, hopped in his car, and sped away. John and Dick waited in vain for his return and soldiered through the remainder of the set without him.

John's reaction was much warmer. He was excited to see Michelle, and, when they finished their set, sat down with her and caught up. From this moment on, they made every attempt to be near each other. Michelle even moved out of Tamar's apartment and into a rental home with Scott and Dick so they could be together freely. John had crossed that threshold of marriage infidelity yet again, but this time was different. The other girls he cheated with were a means to an end of his frustration and boredom. With Michelle, he was in love and envisioned spending his life with her. He mentally divorced Susie. Now, he just had to figure out a graceful exit and wondered whether that was even possible.

John's increasingly peculiar behavior wasn't lost on Susie. Because of his history, she had every reason to suspect the cause of it was another woman. It got out in the open when Susie asked John for his V-neck sweater that he wore onstage so she could wash it. Realizing he left it at Michelle's apartment, he brushed it off by telling her that he left it in the car. When she went to retrieve it, she instead found one of Michelle's silk scarves that reeked of her perfume. She burst back in the apartment and threw it at him.

"I'll bet you look terrific on stage in this, darling," she screamed.

John attempted to lighten the mood by joking about how chilly it gets in San Jose. Things became pretty uncomfortable, but that didn't spur Susie into leaving him. The next time the Journeymen played locally, Susie went to investigate. Looking around the club, she noticed Michelle in a pink angora sweater and tight black slacks lovingly gazing at John from her table. Her rival was more than she bargained for. This wasn't going to be easy. Susie didn't know it yet, but she was being investigated too.

John kept much of his home life hidden from Michelle, and it stirred a natural curiosity within her. She was madly in love with him and the notion that he couldn't be hers exclusively became an obsession. Their nine-year age difference and John's commanding presence were intimidating, which made her too timid to ask him directly. When the Journeymen headed to Spokane, Washington, for a two-week gig in late summer, Michelle decided to do some snooping. She knew John and his wife lived in an apartment complex owned by Kingston Trio singer Nick Reynolds in Mill Valley. She found out the name of it was Strawberry Manor and, along with a male friend, took a drive up to scout it out. It was quaint little community on Richardson Bay and a long way from the San Francisco nightlife.

The two pulled up close to John and Susie's unit and sat idle for a while. Eventually, they saw two little faces peeking at them through the curtains in the front window. It was John and Susie's kids. Suddenly, John's other life became very real to Michelle. There were other innocent people involved, and she wondered whether he could truly ever leave this.

They sat there for what seemed like forever when Michelle's friend decided he was going to knock on their door and pose as an encyclopedia salesman.

It caught her off guard and, before she could stop him, he was out of the car and beelining straight to the Phillips' front door. Michelle slumped down in the passenger's seat and slowly peeked over the dashboard. She couldn't resist observing their interaction. When he returned, he jumped in the driver's seat and quickly sped away. As they were pulling out of Strawberry Manor, he confessed that he didn't pose as an encyclopedia salesman. Instead, he told Susie the truth about what he was doing there, and that Michelle was hiding in his parked car. When Susie asked him to bring her over, he panicked and split. Michelle was stunned, but his confession only emboldened her. She sat up, composed herself and told him to take her back to John and Susie's apartment. She coolly walked up to the front door and knocked. A moment later, an unruffled Susie opened it.

"I'm Michelle."

"I'm Susie."

Susie was skilled in the art of colonial hospitality and invited Michelle inside. They stood in silence for several long seconds, looking each other over without cracking their façades. Susie broke the ice by offering Michelle a tuna fish sandwich she'd just made for the kids and then got down to business.

"You must realize there's a Michelle in every city," Susie said, referring to John's penchant for infidelity. "We've been married a long time. I don't want you to feel bad about John. That's the way he is."

Michelle didn't flinch, but inside she was shattered. She hadn't considered the idea that John was just using her and that she might not be his only mistress.

"But they're not like me," Michelle replied. "He's only going to have one when I'm around."

Susie scoffed but did agree that she was unique. None of John's previous girlfriends had had the nerve to introduce themselves. There wasn't much left to say after that, so Michelle excused herself and Susie politely walked her to the door. After closing it behind her, Susie broke down. She'd noticed Michelle at the club, but seeing her up close, in all her youthful beauty, shook her. Michelle was right. She wasn't like any of the others. John's musical profile was rising and so was his level of groupies. When John got back from Spokane, Susie let him have it.

"Your pretty blonde teenager came over to tell me how happy the two of you are," she screamed as he walked through the door.

Susie reached her breaking point and told John to lay it all on the line. He acquiesced and told her he was deeply in love with Michelle. It was the first time he'd ever said it out loud, and he shocked even himself. There was no turning back now. A few days later, Susie packed up her things and took the kids back east. She moved in with her parents on their Glen Wilde Estate in Catonsville, Maryland, finally giving in to their demand to leave John. Their divorce was finalized in April 1962.

Losing his wife and kids didn't crush John. His love for Susie was never deep, and, though he loved his children, they were products of a marriage he never took seriously. He was elated at his newfound freedom and ran to Michelle. The problem was, she was nowhere to be found. She took to heart what Susie said about girls in other cities and didn't want to be played for a fool. With the Journeymen out of town, she moved out of Scott and Dick's house unnoticed and into an apartment with her sister Rusty, who'd just moved up to San Francisco. She took a job at an insurance agency and left no forwarding address. It was time to move on from John Phillips.

It took John a few weeks to track Michelle down, and, when he did, he was puzzled and asked her why she disappeared. She told him what Susie had said about other women. John denied the accusation and told her that he and Susie were over and that she'd headed back east to begin divorce proceedings. He assured Michelle that she was the only one and apologized profusely about not being open about his marriage. Michelle surrendered to her emotions and fell into John's arms. They made love and moved in together. John and Michelle were now a couple.

Things were looking up for John both personally and professionally. He was with the woman he loved, and the Journeymen were in full bloom. They were playing steadily and making good money. After playing the Steak House in Phoenix in early fall, they went on a college tour and were playing to packed auditoriums. The recordings they made back in March showed signs of life when their debut single "500 Miles" backed by "River, She Come Down" was released in September. Both sides got four-star reviews by *Billboard* but didn't get much airplay outside of college radio stations. John and Scott also experienced a financial windfall when their old Smoothies song "Lonely Boy and Pretty Girl" was recorded by British artist Anthony Newley and placed as the B side of his Top 10 UK hit "And the Heavens Cried."

John's songwriting skills were improving too. He usually wrote alone but had forged a tight friendship with fellow folk musician John Stewart of the Cumberland Three. They were another product of the Werber-Cardenas-ITA partnership who called San Francisco their home. When they weren't out on tour, the two Johns often got together to fish, drink beer, and pick their guitars. Over their short time together on the West Coast, they wrote "Don't Turn Around," "Oh Miss Mary," and "Chilly Winds," with the latter two being covered by a multitude of artists over the next few years.

The friendship of John Phillips and John Stewart was coincidental as, unbeknownst to them, both were being looked at by Frank Werber, Nick Reynolds and Bob Shane as a replacement for the Kingston Trio's Dave Guard. The founding member had come to terms with Reynolds and Shane and agreed to fulfill six months of group commitments. On a creative level, they were neck and neck, but, for Frank Werber, it came down to character. He flat-out hated John. The Journeymen were far less successful and commercial than the Kingston Trio, and John was already a pain in the ass. He was demanding and difficult and was constantly borrowing money from them to pay rent and bills. He even had Rene Cardenas arrange for an abortion for Susie when, shortly after John's profession of love for Michelle, Susie found out she was pregnant with his third child. He couldn't imagine how much worse he'd be as part of a major act. John also couldn't play banjo. John Stewart could, and so, in August, he was invited to be Dave Guard's replacement. The official announcement was made in late September.

John had only heard whispers about his Kingston Trio potential. When the announcement was made, he fell back into the Journeymen and played another stand at the Hungry "i" in October. One night, during the engagement, a tall, good-looking, middle-aged man approached him before the show and introduced himself as a Los Angeles juvenile probation officer. John was alarmed but played it cool with thoughts of Michelle running through his mind. The stranger asked him to join him at the bar for a drink and told him he was Gardner Gilliam, Michelle's father. John wasn't sure whether to be relieved or not, but Gil put him at ease when he began making small talk. He eventually got down to brass tacks and asked John if he was sleeping with his daughter. It caught him off guard, but he didn't let it show. He told him that he was and that he loved her.

"Do you know how old she is?" Gil asked.

"Yup, seventeen," John answered.

"You'd better be good to her then," Gil replied.

"I guess I better," John told him coolly.

The irony was that Gil had recently married one of Michelle's former classmates, and John knew it. He could point it out if provoked, but Gil kept it friendly. If anything, his camaraderie with John assuaged any guilty feelings he might be having about his current relationship and, despite John's shortcomings, he appeared more responsible and less bombastic than Tamar Hodel. They had another drink, and John left to prepare for the show. Michelle was pleased her dad and her lover got along so well and could now go on tour with John with greater peace of mind.

On October 31, 1961, the Journeymen's album was finally released. It was simply called *The Journeymen* and it went over with a whimper, but it wasn't because of the quality of the material. It had more to do with the Kingston Trio's new album, which had been released in mid-September and was climbing the charts. Of more concern to Werber was that their debut single with John Stewart, "Coming from the Mountains," was going nowhere. It made the Journeymen a much lower priority to their management and, by default, their label. The snubbing only got worse.

As the promotional machine for the new lineup of the Kingston Trio got up to speed, it became clear to John, Scott, and Dick that their deal with Frank Werber and Rene Cardenas was merely an insurance policy in case the Kingston Trio broke up or failed without Dave Guard. In the case of the former, the Journeymen could become their main focus. If it was the latter, and Stewart didn't work out, they could simply replace him with John and put Dick in the background as their instrumentalist and musicologist. It left a bad taste in their mouths.

To add insult to injury, Werber got into an undisclosed disagreement with ITA, which afterward exercised an option to pull the Journeymen out of their deal with him. It had a profoundly negative effect on their touring schedule. They went from playing main college campuses to satellite campuses and, eventually, those began to dry up. Since Werber was contractually responsible for keeping the band working, he would give them menial tasks like sending Dick down to UCLA to do copyright research for the Kingston Trio.

The situation wreaked havoc on their income. In no time, they went from raking in around $1,500 a week to next to nothing. It got so bad that Scott and Dick moved out of a rental house and into a seedy motel located above a Chinese restaurant. When it got to the point where they had to share about $3 a day for meals, they mutually agreed that their best option was to get out of their deal with Werber-Cardenas. They appealed to ITA for help and were advised to file suit, which they did.

The Journeymen starved through the holidays as their lawsuit wended its way through the legal system. In the new year, they settled out of court. The Journeymen could buy out of their contract with Werber-Cardenas and sign with a new agency if the group agreed to pay back all monies owed to them. Most of the debt belonged to John. Part of it was paid immediately, and the balance would be garnished from future earnings. It was all rather peaceful but showed that Werber and Cardenas saw no real future value in the Journeymen.

They signed with ITA and Stan Greeson was assigned as their manager. He quickly got them on a tour of New England, which put some money back in their pockets. On January 6, 1962, their second single, "Kumbaya," was released with John's "Soft Blow the Summer Winds" placed on the B side. Like its predecessor, it stiffed but continued to garner favorable reviews from the trade publications.

Now that John and the Journeymen were no longer under the management of Werber-Cardenas, they moved back to New York to be closer to their family and their agency. John asked Michelle to move back east with him. It was a much bigger decision for her, but she was in love with John and wanted to be with him, so she agreed. They took an apartment on the Upper East Side and got a poodle puppy as a housewarming gift. Michelle didn't want to be idle, though, so John put her in touch with his old Smoothies manager, Charlie Ryan, who helped get her signed with the Frances Gill Model Agency on 5th Avenue. It added a nice supplemental income to what John was bringing in.

Greeson quickly got the Journeymen back up and running. They were touring steadily, and he also booked sessions for their next single. In late February, they flew out to Capitol's Hollywood studios, where they cut a John Phillips–John Stewart original, "Don't Turn Around," as well as "Hush Now Sally," co-written by John and Dick. "Don't Turn Around" was their most commercial song yet and exhibited similar characteristics to the Kingston Trio's latest singles. It featured a beautiful guitar intro accompanied by some soft banjo picking from Dick, and the beautiful harmonizing between Scott and John showed considerable growth in John's vocal arranging skills. Unfortunately, it wasn't enough to convince disc jockeys to spin it or the public to buy it. Nevertheless, it was time to record their second LP but, with a fully booked touring schedule, there simply wasn't enough time to get into the studio and record 10 or 12 tracks. They all agreed their best option was a live album, and they arranged for it to be recorded at their appearance at the Padded Cell in Minneapolis in May.

The performance was spirited and comical. Dick's background as a folk-lorist shone brightly in the eclectic choice of songs like turn-of-the-century Appalachian ballads "The Waggoner's Lad" and "Old Joe Clarke's Blues" and retitled versions of older English folk classics "The Rambling Boy" and "Jack the Jolly Tar." They also tapped into much more recent folk and bluegrass standards "I Never Will Marry" and "Dark as a Dungeon." There was also a John Phillips original called "Johnny Booker" and another Hedy West cover in "Cotton Mill Girls" and four other songs.

Many of the numbers were interspersed with the comedy bits, which had become quite popular among most touring folk acts, and it was particularly on display in their unique cover of Sheldon Harnick's "Metamorphosis." It told a silly tale of a caterpillar's story of changing into a butterfly and featured John and Scott playfully attempting to outdo each other vocally. The LP, which was subsequently released as "Coming Attraction!" on September 4, 1962, perfectly encapsulated a live Journeymen performance, which, once again, didn't resonate on the charts although it received good reviews. John, Scott, and Dick, however, were unimpressed with what they heard. Although the audience seemed engaging at the time, on record they sounded flat and nowhere near as raucous as the ones on recent live albums by the Chad Mitchell Trio and the Kingston Trio. It neatly summarized the Journeymen's struggle with mainstream acclaim.

Perhaps the best thing to come out of their stand at the Padded Cell was befriending another folk group called the Highland Three, which featured prolific guitarist Eric Hord. He was a musician's musician and attracted John's attention right away. The two bonded back at their hotel, where they talked about chord progressions and exchanged contact information. They would routinely keep in touch, and John filed his name away for potential future collaborations.

After their engagement at the Padded Cell, the Journeymen stayed in Minneapolis and played a popular supper club called Freddie's. On their opening night, everything seemed normal but, as Scott went to sing the opening verse to "Old Joe Clarke's Blues," nothing came out but a whisper. He'd been out the night before partying and drinking, but that wasn't unusual. Nothing like this had ever happened. Something was terribly wrong. They had no choice but to cancel the gig and fly Scott to San Francisco to see a specialist recommended to them by his vocal coach Judy Davis. The diagnosis was precancerous nodes on his throat. He went into surgery immediately, and his rest and recuperation put the Journeymen on a six-week hiatus.

The Journeymen's hectic tour schedule was bringing in money but was also keeping John and Michelle apart, which was driving them both crazy. Because of her age, John didn't bring Michelle out with him as it could lead to trouble. Chuck Berry was sitting in a Missouri jail for transporting a minor across state lines for immoral purposes. Though John and Michelle were in a consensual relationship, it could still cause trouble and sink the Journeymen if anything scandalous ever happened. Traveling musicians were often in the crosshairs of law enforcement in many smaller towns throughout the country.

When they were on the road, John would check Michelle into the Rehearsal Club, a girls-only boardinghouse for theater performers located in Times Square. Though he told her it was for her safety, in his mind, it also kept her away from any sexual temptation. To remedy this, John proposed to Michelle. Being legally married would wipe away any legal issues and allow them to be together on the road. Michelle eagerly accepted, and the two were wed on December 31, 1962, at the First Baptist Church in Rockville, Maryland. Scott and Dick served as witnesses.

After the ceremony, they celebrated at a reception thrown by Bob Cavallo at his new Georgetown folk club called the Shadows. The Journeymen were his featured act that week. Scott and Dick gifted the newlyweds with a brand-new Lady Martin guitar. It was a musical symbol of their marriage. At the end of their gig, as they were packing up and getting ready to head up to New York, John propped the guitar up against the building so as to put it in last to prevent damaging it and promptly drove away without it. When they arrived in New York City, Stan Greeson greeted them with some exciting news. WNEW-FM, an automated MOR station in New York City, had added "River, She Come Down" to their playlist, and it was growing in popularity and increasing album sales. He believed it was enough for them to renegotiate their contract with Capitol. The Journeymen's journey was heading toward a new horizon.

CHAPTER 10:
THREE SONGS

In May 1963, the folk music movement gained new momentum with the release of 22-year-old Bob Dylan's second album, *The Freewheelin' Bob Dylan*. It featured a cover photo of Dylan walking down a snowy Greenwich Village street with his girlfriend, Suze Rotolo. *Freewheelin'* contained 13 songs, 11 of which were Dylan originals. "Blowin' in the Wind" would become an anthem of the Civil Rights Movement. "Oxford Town" was a biting satire of the violence around the desegregation of the University of Mississippi. "Masters of War" indicted the military-industrial complex. There were also love songs, comedy songs and in "A Hard Rain's Gonna Fall," a lyric that played with surrealism. It was all a long way from "Michael, Row the Boat Ashore."

Freewheelin' was one more enticement for the young-but-daily-growing throng of folk musicians flocking to Greenwich Village. The peaceful Italian American neighborhood had a long history as a sanctuary for artists and freethinkers. Now Washington Square, the central plaza, was overrun with young folk singers, joining the usual poets, playwrights and hustlers. On weekends tourists filled the streets looking for beatniks. The antiauthoritarians were becoming a fad.

A new breed of personal manager wanted to get in on the action. The Village was ripe with talent. Among the young folk musicians playing the coffeehouses were Phil Ochs, Judy Collins, Buffy Sainte-Marie, and Fred Neil. They all needed professional representation. Albert Grossman was the top manager in the folk field. His clients included Dylan, Joan Baez, and Odetta. Grossman had flirted with signing the Journeymen in 1961, but rejected them over a dinner in Denver. He saw more potential in Dylan and perhaps too much pugnaciousness in John.

Grossman was looking for a folk group who would follow his vision without question. Not being able to find one he liked, he created his own. The manager combined the striking blonde singer Mary Travers with Peter Yarrow and Noel Stookey, two goateed young men who looked like twins. He renamed Noel "Paul" to give "Peter, Paul and Mary" a sprinkle of New Testament virtue. Through their sweet harmonies, Grossman introduced Dylan's songs to the mainstream.

Peter, Paul and Mary's covers of "Blowin' in the Wind" and "Don't Think Twice, It's All Right" both went Top 10 on the pop charts in 1963. From Trini Lopez to the Rooftop Singers, Top 40 radio was filled with folk-inspired hits. Dylan's growing influence fell on the next wave of musicians carrying acoustic guitars down Bleecker Street, including Jim McGuinn, John Sebastian, Peter Tork, and Jesse Colin Young.

John Phillips had watched the pop music scene grow and develop since his days at George Washington High School in the early 1950s. Ten years in, he finally found himself part of a major musical movement. The Journeymen, however, were in danger of being written off. Their polite, necktie-wearing, singalong style of folk music was being replaced by the biting, rough edged sound made by Dylan, Ochs, and Dave Van Ronk. "Entertainment" was out. "Authenticity" was in.

Whatever misgivings John had entertained about making his mark in folk music were put aside. This was his best opportunity to find success, and he was not going to miss his shot. In the next year John would leap forward as a songwriter, composing three songs that would change his life. But it would be a few years between the writing and the success. John Phillips was not by nature a patient man, but he would learn that dreams don't come true on the dreamer's schedule.

The Greenwich Village folk movement was the most exciting musical scene in America, and nobody networked it better than John. He and Michelle moved into a suite at the Earle Hotel, opposite the northwest corner of Washington Square. John had become a regular marijuana smoker and was using

Benzedrine, a powerful amphetamine. Michelle had experience with the drug from her modeling days in San Francisco. Benzedrine was designed to fill one with energy and confidence. It was used by long-haul truck drivers, soldiers in combat, and touring musicians.

Did speed help John Phillips' songwriting? It's unprovable either way. Drugs can't make a mediocre artist great, but they might keep a talented artist awake and focused long enough to finish something good. It's a temporary trade-off that often ends in addiction and disintegration. In the short term, Benzedrine John was bursting with ideas. When not onstage, he could be seen noodling on his guitar, coming up with new melodies, and scribbling lyrics.

He was generous with credit, listing as co-writers friends who made lyrical suggestions or even just wrote down the words John spun out. Like Dylan, John had begun writing from a contemporary perspective. Out in middle America, folk music might still mean songs about poling down the Erie Canal and missing Darling Clementine, but around Washington Square they were writing and singing about what it felt like to be alive and aware in the 1960s.

The winter months of 1963 were bitterly cold in New York with the last week of January and first half of February being particularly frigid. Michelle, who had grown up in Mexico and Los Angeles, was unprepared for this kind of weather and reminisced about the warm temperatures back home. John empathized. One freezing February night, after being up for a couple of days, addled on speed, he sat in their cold living room, the heater on the fritz, working on a new song.

The somber melody was not unlike numbers previously played by the Journeymen, but it was the words, inspired by personal events, that made it different and new: *All the leaves are brown and the sky is gray/I've been for a walk on a winter's day/I'd be safe and warm if I was in L.A./California dreamin' on such a winter's day.*

The lyrics recounted a stroll through Greenwich Village that he and Michelle had taken that afternoon. The first snowfall of the season had blanketed New York. Michelle had not seen snow since her childhood, and she liked the romantic notion of strolling about town through it with her husband. The only problem was that she didn't know how to dress for the New York winter. She threw an overcoat over a tank top, jeans and sneakers. Walking through Washington Square Park, the reality of the northeast February set in, and she and John reminisced about California sunshine.

The scene ran through John's memory after Michelle went to bed. As the night progressed and the temperature dropped to two below zero, he knew he was on to something special. Since first being drawn to poetry at Linton Hall, he had written many songs, but this was something altogether different. None of his other songs had sounded as fluid and natural as this. John didn't want to lose this one. He went into the dark bedroom where Michelle was asleep.

"Help me write this," he whispered.

"I want to sleep. Tomorrow," she replied groggily.

"No! Now," he insisted.

Michelle could tell he was high on bennies and took the path of least resistance. John assured her, "You'll thank me for this someday."

She climbed out of bed and made her way to the living room, still half asleep.

She grabbed a notepad and wrote down the words as John sang them to her. They immediately conjured up memories of their walk together. She thought of a detail John had left out. To get out of the cold, they had gone inside St. Patrick's Old Cathedral on Mott Street, the venerable seat of the Archdiocese of New York from 1815 to 1879.

The Romanesque church had served as refuge from the cold, a place they could warm up without being pressured to buy something. Although irreligious, Michelle had a soft spot for Catholic churches stemming from her childhood in Mexico. She admired the architecture and artwork. The flowers and the smell of incense brought back memories of Saturday night sleepovers at the homes of school friends, which almost always included mass the following morning.

John had the opposite reaction. Churches made him uneasy, mostly because of the trauma he endured at Linton Hall. After only a few minutes, he retreated outside while Michelle meditated and warmed up inside a little longer. Back in their apartment, Michelle proposed these lyrics: *I stopped into a church I saw along the way/I got down on my knees and I pretend to pray.*

John wasn't enamored but accepted them as a placeholder to be rewritten later. Michelle, on a roll, came up with the next line. *You know the preacher loves the cold, he knows I'm gonna stay.* Which rhymed with John's refrain, *California dreamin' on such a winter's day.*

Happy with the results, John stowed the song away in his notepad of potentials. He debuted it a few nights later, at a party at Judy Collins' apartment, to a small audience of fellow musicians. It went over well but didn't leave anybody breathless. The folk song arrangement was a far cry from the clarion call it would eventually become with the Mamas & the Papas. Still, "California Dreamin'" was unlike anything John Phillips had written before. He thought he might take it uptown and pitch it to the music publishers at the Brill Building. Maybe somebody would want to record it.

Two other future John Phillips classics, "Go Where You Wanna Go" and "Monday, Monday" began their genesis later that year under much more stressful circumstances as his band and his young marriage were falling apart. In September, the third Journeymen album, *New Directions*, was released, and it met with the same tepid sales as the others but favorable reviews. Nevertheless, a tour ensued.

Back in August, with the folk boom still in effect, the Journeymen signed on to a fall Hootenanny Tour Package, an extension of the ABC television program that presented folk artists in an *American Bandstand*–type setting on college campuses. It was a tense time in the country, particularly the South, where the Civil Rights Movement caused the most furor. Ground zero was often college campuses, where most of their concerts took place, and performers were often thrown into the fray, enduring jeers and objects being thrown at them.

At a tour stop in Jackson, Mississippi, leaders from the Tougaloo College Student Non-Violent Coordinating Committee approached John and the others and urged them not to perform that night at the Jackson City Auditorium as a show of solidarity with civil rights groups. Reluctant at first, all agreed and instead performed for free on the Tougaloo campus ending the night in an arm-in-arm group singalong of "We Shall Overcome" and then got out of there as quickly and quietly as possible. A stop the next day in Baton Rouge didn't go quite as well. Their bus was greeted with KKK members rocking their bus and hitting it with baseball bats. No outreach was attempted this time and they just left town.

The tour ultimately fell apart later in Cleveland after the assassination of President John F. Kennedy on November 22. In one fell swoop, venues abruptly canceled concerts, and many performers simply lost the desire to play with a nation in crisis. Despite these awful circumstances, John, who'd been touring without Michelle, anticipated their reunion that very day.

Michelle had been visiting her aunt and uncle in Kansas City when President Kennedy was killed. The events that transpired that dreadful November day had been the capper to a very stressful time for her. Her Kansas City respite was prompted after being attacked early on in the tour at a stop in Washington, D.C. She and John had been staying at the Potomac Bridge Marriott Hotel when an unknown assailant, assuming she was alone, followed her into her room. In her state of confusion, the well-dressed stranger slammed the door shut and lunged at her throat. Pressed between his body weight and the floor, she felt her life slipping away, when John emerged from the bathroom where he'd been showering. Beholding the surreal spectacle that lay before him, he reacted instantly and tackled the stranger and began beating him mercilessly.

He opened the door and tossed the attacker out, pummeling him further in the hallway even though his towel slipped away and he was completely naked. A crowd began to grow around the melee, believing John to be the assailant, especially since Michelle began pleading with him to leave the man alone. As the 50 or so onlookers began to grumble, the attacker wriggled free and escaped into the night never to be seen again.

This event, her whirlwind romance and marriage to John and enduring the rigors that come with being the wife of a professional musician took their toll on the 19-year-old. She needed to extend her break and, shortly after their reunion in Cleveland, Michelle headed back to Los Angeles to reconnect with her family and a degree of normalcy. The warmth and familiarity was refreshing and, only a short time into her hiatus, she met a young man her age named Russ Titleman at a welcome-home party thrown by her sister. After their initial introduction, they began seeing each other regularly.

Like John, Russ was also a musician and involved in the music business but in a more behind-the-scenes capacity. Phil Spector was a rising producer in pop music in 1963 and Russ had known him since he was 14. His older sister Susan dated Marshall Leib, a vocalist in Spector's trio the Teddy Bears who'd recorded the number one hit "To Know Him Is to Love Him" and appeared on *American Bandstand* and the *Perry Como Show*. Before making it big, they'd often rehearse in the Titlemans' living room, and over the next few years Russ would work with Spector in a variety of capacities as the emerging music mogul split time between L.A. and New York.

Unlike John, Russ came from wealth. His family had emigrated to Altoona, Pennsylvania, from Russia and made their fortune in textiles, manufacturing

Ban-Lon shirts and other apparel so he potentially offered a level of security that she had never experienced. When the two met, Russ was a theater major at Los Angeles College and was working as a staff songwriter for Spector's business partner Lester Sill at Screen Gems-Columbia Music. Before long, he was dazzling her with trips to Gold Star Studios, where hits were beginning to be cranked out regularly. The bustle of session musicians, producers and recording artists she'd heard on the radio mingling about the hallways and control rooms was an exciting sight to behold. But, perhaps more rewarding was the quiet time they spent together listening to records and getting to know one another. Before they knew it, they'd fallen in love.

In fact, they fell so deeply that Michelle felt compelled to call John and tell him that she'd met someone new and began sleeping with him. He was blindsided.

"Who is he? I'll tear his fucking head off," he shouted over the phone.

Michelle just giggled. It was her coping mechanism in times of stress, but it only served to anger John further. But anger soon gave way to desperation. He didn't want to lose Michelle, and he tried several different persuasive tactics. He attempted to guilt her by reminding her of their upcoming wedding anniversary. That didn't break her, but when he told her how disappointed in her and how inappropriate her behavior was, something in her flipped, and she agreed to come back to New York. But all was not as it would seem. Michelle's compromise had a dubious nature.

After hanging up, the shock began to settle in, and John was facing the prospect of losing the woman for whom he'd completely uprooted his personal life. The period of time between the phone call and Michelle's return was agonizing. In order to get through it, he resorted to his own coping mechanism, which was his music. He began noodling around and tapping into his emotions. He'd grown as a musician since the formation of the Journeymen and was coming into his own as a romantic songwriter, which was increasingly evident in some of the group's singles releases. Eventually, these words came to him: *Oh Monday morning, you gave me no warning of what was to be/Monday, Monday, how could you leave and not take me?*

It was just a fragment of what was eventually to become his biggest hit and, although incomplete, he filed it away with "California Dreamin'."

A few days later, Michelle arrived back at their new apartment on Charles Street, and John tried to his best to resume normal married life. His typical chauvinistic answer to any marital problems was always hot sex but, in this case, it only served to confuse Michelle and push her away even more. But whatever front she was putting on at home was not completely genuine. Little did John know that Michelle's new lover had followed her from California at her behest. And it wasn't difficult for Russ. He had family on the East Coast and a job waiting at Aldon Music, located in the Brill Building in Midtown Manhattan. Songwriter Jeff Barry, whom he'd met a few months earlier at Screen Gems, had been courting him to come to New York and work for him so making the move was both convenient and exciting.

Their plan on rendezvousing, however, betrayed their youthful age. Michelle would stay with John at their apartment while Russ would rent a room at the Earle a few blocks away. But only a couple weeks in it was too much to bear for Michelle. She told John she was going back to Los Angeles to think things through. John told her he wanted to come with her but she insisted he remain in New York. After all, he had his group and career to consider.

But, Michelle wasn't going anywhere. She rented a room on Second Avenue in the East Village so she could see Russ much more freely. And to keep up the scam, she sent John prepurchased postcards that she'd mail routinely.

John's heart once again went through the wringer and he turned to his music in order to soothe it. He recollected advice his mother had given him years ago when she confessed her affair with Roland Meeks to him. Locked in a loveless marriage to an alcoholic, she urged him to not repeat her mistakes and go where you want to go, do what you want to do. He'd certainly followed that rule many times, but this time, that free-spirit notion was coming back to haunt him. In his melancholy, he crafted the lyrics and melody. *You don't understand that a girl like me can love just one man/Three thousand miles, that's how far you'll go/And you said to me, please don't follow.*

Unbeknownst to John at the time, Michelle was becoming an incredible songwriting muse. What he did know was that his world was falling apart before him and he couldn't do more than sit home and pine away for his wayward bride through songwriting. He received her phony postcards regularly, but whenever he tried to connect with her on the phone, his attempts were was unsuccessful. Eventually, he managed to get her sister Rusty on the line and pressed her for information. Cracking under the unwanted pressure her sister had placed on her, Rusty broke and confessed to John that she was playing him for a fool and that Michelle, in fact, had never left New York. He couldn't believe what he was hearing. How could this be? He was receiving her postcards. Whatever skepticism he had about Rusty's omission, however, was quickly vanquished when their surrogate mother, Marika Sail, confirmed it. This entire time, she'd only been seven blocks away.

Michelle, on the other hand, forged ahead in her new life without a care in the world. She regularly went uptown to the Brill Building with Russ and hung out with the gang at Aldon Music, which included Barry Mann and his songwriting partner and wife Cynthia Weil, Gerry Goffin and Carole King, another married hit-songwriting duo, their mentors Jerry Leiber and Mike Stoller, singer and songwriter Neil Sedaka, and Aldon co-founder Don Kirshner.

In very short order, Russ put a deposit down on an apartment in Brooklyn Heights that they could move into together, but, when news of this reached Russ' family, the boom was lowered on their relationship. Suddenly, with patriarchs and outraged aunts bearing down on him, Russ became shaky and noncommittal. It agitated Michelle tremendously. She was used to take-charge adult male figures like John who never let anyone get in his way when he wanted something. He'd proven that when he left his wife and kids for her. Russ' youth was now a liability.

As their relationship was crumbling, John was able to track Michelle down with the help from her family. He surprised her one day outside her new apartment and urged her to come back home. Though she put on a good front, it was just the ticket out she needed. Later that day, there was a knock at John's door. When he opened it, there stood Michelle with bags in hand.

"John, I made a mistake," was all she said.

He invited her in and played it cool. He told her that he was getting ready to go out on the road with the Journeymen and asked if she was ready to join him. She said yes. As usual, a night of makeup sex ensued, and the subject of Russ Titleman was never brought up again. But a new, unhealthy precedent had now been set in their marriage.

Although John's marriage was now mended, his relationship with bandmate Scott McKenzie was falling apart. The two always enjoyed a brotherly relationship but, over the course of their time together as bandmates, it had deteriorated. Scott had grown to resent John's control over the group, of which he had little to no say. His view of John as a big brother had morphed into considering him a nosy, overbearing father, especially with John's constant interference in his personal life. It got so bad that, offstage, the two wouldn't even speak to one another. Dick Weismann had become the arbiter of their relationship.

"Dick, tell Scott his right sock doesn't match his left sock," John would tell him.

John's solution was a band vacation to Mazatlan, Mexico. He, Scott, and Michelle, along with Michelle's sister Rusty, traveled together while Dick and his fiancé Diane Deschanel opted to go instead to the Rocky Mountains. The combination of sun, sand, fishing, Brandy Alexanders, and marijuana put a band-aid on things, but it didn't heal the wound. Come fall, the Journeymen endured the tumultuous Hootenanny tour. After regrouping in late November, they played the tour finale at Carnegie Hall, which culminated in Scott smashing a cheap prop guitar onstage to John's complete astonishment.

Even Capitol Records had lost faith in the Journeymen. When their third LP, *New Directions*, bombed, no sessions were scheduled for a follow-up single or album. They played a string of dates in January 1964 and made one final television appearance on the Canadian folk music–oriented program *Let's Sing Out!* in April. After that, they called it quits and each went their separate ways.

John bummed around New York, often heading uptown to pitch his songs to various publishers in the Brill Building but got blown off. They told him nobody wants to hear a song about a state or a day of the week. But his heart still lay in Greenwich Village and its wilting folk scene. He hung out and played informally with younger musicians like Jim McGuinn, David Crosby, John Sebastian, and others. To him, it seemed almost criminal that such a hotbed of youthful talent was going unrecognized. It seemed there was no room in the public consciousness for serious folk music beyond Bob Dylan and Joan Baez and even their success was limited mostly to college campuses and *Time Magazine* articles. Pleasant harmonies from Peter, Paul and Mary and the Kingston Trio seemed to be all radio and TV would tolerate. The common thread that ran through many of these aspiring folk stars was they were children of rock and roll who grew up watching Elvis Presley, Buddy Holly, and Bo Diddley play *The Ed Sullivan Show* and Ricky Nelson crooning at the end of *The Adventures of Ozzie and Harriet*. Whether they knew it or not, folk music was simply a placeholder.

That all changed on February 9, 1964, when Ed Sullivan invited four young men from England, known as the Beatles, on his program, which was required viewing in most American households. Their single "I Want to Hold Your Hand" had reached the #1 spot on *Billboard* a week earlier, and Sullivan allowed them to perform five songs. Seventy-three million people tuned in to hear the quartet crank into "All My Loving," which sounded unlike anything anybody had ever heard before. It was vibrant, fresh and invigorating and it was rock and roll. Reborn!

To say the performance had a profound impact on American culture is an understatement. It was revolutionary and caught the music industry and music lovers off guard. All of a sudden, teen idols were out, and bands were in, especially self-sustaining ones who could write their own hits and record filler like Lennon and McCartney. Their musicianship, folk-styled electric arrangements, fashion, harmonies, and enthusiasm shook many a folk musician back to his rock and roll roots. Martins and Gibsons were traded in for Gretsches and Rickenbackers and hair was summarily left simply to grow.

It seemed the only folk musician in Greenwich Village who wasn't impressed by their performance was John Phillips. In fact, he paid them no attention at all. Although still unsure of what his next move should be, he was dug in on folk music and was determined to make a go of it even though the scene was evaporating all around him.

Elsewhere in Greenwich Village, another folk musician, Denny Doherty, was feeling the effects of the Beatles' impact. His folk group, the Halifax Three, had also recently broken up, and he and their old accompanist, Zal Yanovsky, were bumming around town trying to figure out their next move too. But, unlike John, he was open to ditching folk for rock. Very open. Unknown to them at the time, their stars were about to cross again, and it would be up to Denny to show John the light.

CHAPTER 11:
MUGWUMPS, HIGH JUMPS,
LOW SLUMPS, BIG BUMPS

In the summer of 1964, with the ashes of the Journeymen scattered before him, John Phillips attempted to raise up a new folk trio, but it would not include Scott McKenzie or Dick Weissman, and the feeling was mutual. They all needed a break from each other. Scott was in therapy, and Dick was about to get married. The break gave John a newfound sense of freedom and, even though folk music was on its way out, he was determined to revive it. His trouble was that the Beatles and electric were in fashion, and finding young musicians willing to continue with folk music was getting increasingly difficult.

That notion wasn't lost on John, and the pickings for tenors and accompanists were getting slim. His first choice couldn't be any closer to home. It was his wife, Michelle. She wasn't a particularly good singer, but she wasn't bad either, and her beauty was enough to garner plenty of male attention. Peter, Paul and Mary had proven that pretty blondes were very much in style in folk. Even though Mary Travers could sing circles around Michelle, that didn't matter to John. Michelle had the look.

It wasn't an easy decision for Michelle. She'd been modeling steadily since arriving in New York and had recently been contracted by Kayser-Roth, appearing regularly in JCPenney circulars modeling their hosiery in the Misses section. It brought in $700 a week and provided her with plenty of discretionary income. But John had his mind made up and insisted she drop it and go along with him. He could be difficult in these types of situations, and Michelle wasn't up for a fight, so she relented. He attempted to soften his hard stance by telling her she'd make more money singing with him, and soon his excitement became contagious. But there was a dual motive. The wound from Michelle's affair with Russ Titleman was still fairly fresh for John, and her being on the road with him meant he could keep a closer eye on her. Nevertheless, the two couldn't contain their excitement over their potential success and fruits of their labor.

But dreams are one thing, reality is another. After the breakup of the Journeymen, John had no steady income, and their finances began drying up. They left their apartment on Charles Street and moved into a cheaper one in the East Village on the corner of East 7th Street and Avenue D, directly across the street from the Riis Housing Project. It was only a short walk from Greenwich Village, but it seemed like a world away as it lacked the vibrancy and the sense of community they were used to.

But John didn't allow his misfortune to bring him down. It was onward and upward, and his next move was to find his third member. One of the strengths of the Journeymen's sound was Dick Weissman's banjo and he wanted to replicate that as best he could. Through his folk network, he was able to find what he needed in Marshall Brickman, a 24-year-old banjoist from Brooklyn. He'd most recently played in the popular Greenwich Village folk group the Tarriers and had recorded an album with Eric Weissberg in 1963 called *New Dimensions in Banjo and Bluegrass* for Elektra. He accepted John's offer and began rehearsing with him and Michelle at their apartment.

They settled on the name the New Journeymen, and John pitched his new group to ITA. Since John was still under contract and had a pedigree, they fully backed him as long as the New Journeymen picked up the already scheduled Journeymen dates. They agreed, and ITA issued all three members American Express cards for expenses. For John, it was free money, and it gave him an idea. After a couple of weeks of rehearsal, he'd decided they needed to get out of Greenwich Village. Even though the arrival of the Beatles had effectively pushed most of the younger musicians back to rock and roll, it was still a major tourist destination for fans and for the curious. The streets were still packed regularly, and getting in and out of clubs for a dress rehearsal was difficult. They settled on San Francisco and rented a house in Sausalito with their ITA credit cards covering most of their day-to-day expenses.

Over the course of their West Coast rehearsals, the one thing that was painfully obvious was that Michelle needed singing lessons. John signed her up with renowned vocal coach Judy Davis who'd been Scott McKenzie's instructor during the Journeymen's San Francisco days. She taught Michelle how to breathe properly, project, enunciate and strengthen her vocal cords, which would help her considerably on stage. After a couple months, the New Journeymen were ready to go on tour. They all went and purchased new formal stage attire and had a series of publicity photos taken, and on November 6, the New Journeymen made their debut performance at the University of South Carolina's homecoming concert at Township Auditorium. Their set contained several Journeymen numbers, and Marshall held his own on banjo-driven tunes like "Chase the Rising Sun" and "I Am Poor and Ramblin' Boy." New numbers like "Guantanamera" and "One Morning in May" were incorporated, and they got downright cutting-edge with performances of Bob Dylan's "Mr. Tambourine Man" and Len Chandler's "Roll, Spin, Turn."

They got through their gigs with relative ease, but it was clear that neither John nor Marshall were tenors. Both had pleasant enough voices, but they weren't good enough to handle lead vocal duties on a regular basis, and continuing this way would put considerable strain on their vocal cords. With gigs drying up and the negative ripple effect of the British Invasion on hootenannies, they needed somebody who could captivate audiences, and they needed him fast. John had only one person in mind.

Dennis Gerard Stephen Doherty was one of many successful singers imported to the United States from Canada during the 1960s and one of a handful who hailed from Nova Scotia. He was born the youngest child of five to Dennis and Mary Doherty on November 29, 1940, in Halifax and grew up in a public housing complex near Rockhead Prison in the city's North End. His family called him Denny, and though his looks favored his father, his heart was formed like his mother's. She was a gentle soul who, even though she didn't have much to give, offered many a passerby down on his luck food, water, or just a sympathetic ear.

His love of music came from his father. Denny Sr. was a tuba player for the Princess Louis Fusiliers Marching Band during his time in the Canadian Armed Forces Reserves. When he was discharged, he tried becoming a professional musician by forming his own dance band, but it didn't take him long to realize that wasn't his calling. He got into the local steamfitter union and became a plumber and pipefitter. It was an in-demand profession in a major port city and allowed him to better support his growing family.

Denny Sr. didn't actively pass along his love for music to his youngest son in hopes that Denny Jr. wouldn't go through the same heartbreak he did. Even as Denny sung in the shower, in the kitchen or at his mother's behest to the insurance man, his father's bitterness toward his failed musical venture blinded him to the fact that his son possessed a powerful tenor. When he was 15 years old, Denny took a job at a local pawnshop called the Barrington Exchange. It was a hot spot for young Navy seamen who pawned and purchased musical instruments there daily and helped rock and roll find its way to Nova Scotia. Denny caught the bug and often sang along with any decent sailor testing out a guitar.

His singing ability wasn't lost on his friends either. Denny was always singing along to the AM radio while riding along in their cars, almost to the point that some people got annoyed. One particularly irritated friend dared him to take his talents to the Halifax Forum, a 5,600-seat arena not far from Denny's home that hosted dances and amateur singing contests in the hockey off-season. Denny was never one to back down and accepted his friend's challenge. He told his family about his plans and his father, who'd always avoided any positive affirmations of his son's singing ability, fully supported Denny in this and even offered to help him make a big impression. When Denny made his way down to the next amateur night, he was accompanied by his father's old fusilier buddy Peter Power and his 15-piece orchestra, and they performed Pat Boone's current hit "Love Letters in the Sand" to a captivated audience of about 600. He impressed the sponsors so much that they asked him to come back for the remainder of the season.

But it was the reaction of the girls when he sang that stirred Denny's senses the most and made him keep coming back. The breadth of his popularity was confirmed one afternoon at the Barrington Exchange when a local musician named Richard Sheehan came in to pawn his drum kit and recognized Denny from the forum. They spoke for a while and eventually Richard invited Denny to sing with his band the Hepsters at a wedding in Indian Harbour the following weekend. It was a tall task on such short notice, but Denny accepted, and this one-off gig turned into a two-year foray into the music business. The Hepsters gigged mostly around Halifax, playing rock and roll covers at high school dances, weddings and gatherings at their local Knights of Columbus hall. During their time together, they built up a pretty steady following and even managed to make an appearance on *Burt's Bandstand*, a CBC dance program shot locally in Halifax. But the hard-knock life of the music industry eventually caught up with Denny's bandmates, and the Hepsters broke up in 1959.

Denny went back to the Barrington Exchange with his tail between his legs but determined to somehow continue with his music career. He forged ahead alone, exploiting his role as lead singer of the Hepsters, and managed to land a couple of solo gigs. He spent most of his nights singing at the ratty BYOB Halifax Jazz Club on Barrington Street. There he befriended Buddy Burke, the club's janitor and jack-of-all-trades, who, in exchange for cleaning up the place, changing light bulbs, and fixing anything that broke, was granted access to the apartment above the club. Quite often, after the club closed, the party continued upstairs.

On New Year's Eve 1960, Buddy hosted a party at the apartment and invited Denny and several other local musician friends, including Pat LaCroix and Dick Byrne. Pat was a bit of a local celebrity, and Denny recognized him right away. He hosted the *Pat LaCroix Show*, a 15-minute CBC dance show that had recently been canceled. Pat grew up in Victoria, British Columbia, and was a such a promising musician that he was accepted into the Westlake College of Music in Hollywood, California. He cut his teeth in the music business there by singing in the Four Winds with fellow Canadian student Gordon Lightfoot. Dick Byrne also had some stage experience in the Montreal nightclub scene, but it was as a stage performer where, most recently, his specialty was knocking a lit cigarette out of his wife Bobbie's mouth with a bullwhip. But he could play the guitar and he brought it along to the party, which attracted Denny's attention.

By that time, the folk music craze had reached Halifax and after talking shop with Pat and Dick for a while, Dick started strumming his guitar and the three launched into an impromptu version of the Kingston Trio's "Tom Dooley." Those in attendance were enraptured by their harmony and greeted their song's end with rousing applause. After the ball dropped, the three made plans to get together in few days to see how they sounded after a little bit of rehearsal. Their next meeting confirmed that they did have something. They agreed to give it a try and named themselves the Colonials.

They managed themselves initially and sang for free at fraternity parties at Dalhousie University in Halifax's West End. It got their feet wet but didn't build much of a following. They were also able to find audiences down at the Halifax waterfront. After receiving permission from the officer on deck, they'd sing for crews of freighters and commercial fishing boats in between departures. It was an old-fashioned form of entertainment, but the crews enjoyed them, and they were almost never turned away. After a couple months of building up their repertoire and nearly starving to death, Pat reached out to his old CBC producer Glenn Sarty and pitched a show idea featuring the Colonials. His timing couldn't have been better. Sarty and the management at CBC Nova Scotia recognized the folk boom that was sweeping across North America and offered the Colonials a 16-week variety series called *Travelling on Home*. It aired Wednesday nights from 8:30 to 8:45 and featured music performed by the Colonials and other local and international artists.

The show did wonders for their live gigs, and they quickly became the most happening thing around Halifax. They even got to record a single released by local record label Rodeo Records. They chose the traditional Bahamian lullaby "All My Trials" backed by the Lerner & Loewe standard "They Call the Wind Maria" from their 1951 musical *Paint Your Wagon*. They also recorded several spots for the IGA grocery chain, which put some extra money in their pockets. The single stiffed, but it got them some studio experience and whetted their appetite for something bigger.

By early 1962, they'd conquered Nova Scotia, but they wanted something greater. They all felt they'd outgrown the province and, on Dick's advice, agreed to head for Montreal, which had a bustling nightclub scene that was clamoring for folk music performers. This time, Dick used his connections and got them a short stand at the Embers followed by three weeks at the Venus de Milo Room, where they'd make $75 a night opening for pop singer Tommy Desmond. They loaded their bags and instruments into Dick's station wagon and made the nearly 800-mile drive westward. The strange and vibrant nightlife attracted many big name acts from the United States who played the bigger venues. There were also dozens of smaller clubs up and down Saint-Denis Street that featured a hodgepodge of homegrown acts like the Steele Bandits, Frank Motley & His Motley Crew, and Dino Vale, many of whom were first rate but didn't attract much interest from any major record labels. The most successful artist to come out of Montreal was reclusive

Nashville-born transgender soul singer Jackie Shane who could be found regularly entertaining patrons at the Esquire Show Bar.

The Colonials honed their act over the spring playing a variety of clubs and eventually moving to the upscale Lou Black's Living Room where they played for a crowd of 400 opening for local folk singer Iris Paul. It was the pièce de résistance of Montreal nightclubs. Lou Black was a veteran of the Manhattan club scene and he decorated his Living Room with red velvet couches with matching curtains and gold and brass fixtures filling every open space. Black's clubs attracted out-of-town mobsters often trying to extort the impresario, and they were a rude and intimidating bunch. They talked loudly and laughed during numbers and nobody, not even Lou Black, was brave enough to tell them to shut up. That was, until the Colonials showed up. Over their short time together, the Colonials' personalities emerged. Denny was the witty one, and Pat was congenial, and both preferred to avoid confrontation. Dick was much more assertive, so when a loud group of mobsters were disrupting his group's show, he casually walked up to their table with his microphone and asked them who shines their suits. None of them found it amusing, and one pulled him down by his tie and told him to "take a fucking walk."

That was the end of the Colonials' time in Montreal. They headed southwest to Toronto, Ontario, which had the most genuine folk scene in all of Canada. Its central hub was an area in downtown Toronto called Gerrard Village that encapsulated several blocks along Gerrard Street West and was filled with coffeehouses that catered to the artist culture. But genuine wasn't what any of them were used to. There were a few promising clubs there like the Toronto version of the Purple Onion, the Village Corner, and the Bohemian Embassy but they didn't pay anything. In fact, most performers relied solely on tips. They did manage to befriend a few young folk duos like Ian & Sylvia and Malka & Joso, but their short time there was mostly a letdown. They decided to try their local again with the CBC and their Toronto affiliate but, this time, they were turned down. Name acts only.

The Colonials had made it pretty far managing themselves, but now they were running on fumes, and the CBC rejection made them realize that. If they wanted to get any sort of recognition, they needed professional management. In Toronto, the most famous talent agent and promotor was Colonel Harold Kudlets who'd made quite a name for himself in the 1940s managing the 4,500-seat Hamilton Forum and booking big-time acts like the Glenn Miller

Orchestra, Tommy Dorsey, and Duke Ellington. As of late, his biggest clients were Conway Twitty and Ronnie Hawkins & the Hawks. The Colonials decided to shoot for the stars and approach him.

Kudlets liked what he saw in the Colonials, but he wasn't 100 percent convinced that they were a sure thing, but because of the folk music boom, he agreed to take them on, if only on a temporary basis. He got them booked in the popular Seaway Motel in Toronto for a week followed by a stand at the Fifth Peg on Church Street opening for comedian Bill Cosby. On the plus side, they were under the auspices of a first-rate agent whose gigs put money in their wallets. On the negative side, the up and downs of their time together started to bring up tensions within the group, particularly with Dick Byrne. While Pat and Denny got along quite well, Dick was a classic type A personality who was prone to outbursts and tirades. He also suffered from a degree of paranoia and often thought his bandmates were out to screw him. It got so bad that Denny and Pat were getting ready to kick him out of the group when fate intervened.

In April 1962 Kudlets got them booked in the Fallsway Hotel in Niagara Falls. When it ended, the Colonials ventured over to Buffalo, New York, and did a cold audition for the Town Casino, the so-called largest nightclub between New and Chicago. Co-owner Harry Altman turned them down. It was the old dreaded "name act" excuse again, but there was something about them he liked and decided to do them a favor. He was impressed enough with their harmony and offered to hook them up with Bert Block, president of International Talent Associates in New York City, and they happily took him up on his offer. Block agreed to an audition, but only on the condition that it be at 9:00 the next morning. They had no choice. It gave them 14 hours to get back to their hotel rooms, get what they needed, and make the eight-hour drive to New York City. There was no way Denny and Pat could sack Dick now, especially since they needed the use of his station wagon.

They arrived with a few hours to spare and got themselves prepared as best they could. After rehearsing in the car, they combed their hair and straightened themselves up and made their way to ITA's offices on Madison Avenue. When they got in front of Block, they played three of their best numbers. Their harmony soared through the corridors and impressed Block enough that he offered to sign them to a two-year contract on the spot and set them up with manager Larry Bell. They were elated. Next Block sent them for an audition with Columbia A&R chief David Kapralik, who also liked what he heard and offered them a two-year, two-LP deal on their Epic subsidiary.

The only thing Bert Block wasn't crazy about was their name. It sounded outdated, and he figured it wouldn't go over well in the United States. They began brainstorming and throwing ideas out there, but couldn't come up with anything catchy. Block was a veteran and had named groups before so he started a question-and-answer routine with his new trio.

"Where are you boys from?" he asked.

"Nova Scotia," they all replied in unison.

Since Nova Scotia was mostly surrounded by the Atlantic Ocean, he tossed around some nautical-themed ideas like the Dorymen and the Oarlocks but those sounded hokey. Block dug a little deeper.

"Say, what town are you boys from?" he asked.

"Halifax!" they all replied again in unison.

"Great! You're the Halifax Three!" he exclaimed.

It all happened so fast. In less than 24 hours, they had a record deal and a new name. After a night at the Plaza Hotel in Midtown, courtesy of Columbia Records, the boys rented an apartment at the Hotel Albert in Greenwich Village and got to know their surroundings. The folk scene had exploded since the Journeymen left town a year earlier. By the spring of 1962, there were approximately 37 coffeehouses cluttering up the famous streets, and many of them were fly-by-night basket houses. They were different from full-fledged clubs in that they didn't have cabaret licenses, which meant they couldn't hire entertainment. In order to get around that, they allowed musicians and groups to come in for free and play a 20-30-minute set and pass the hat around for donations from patrons. The Halifax Three did this in the interim to help pay rent and held their own among a cavalcade of talented contemporaries like David Crosby, John Sebastian, and Bob Gibson.

On May 28, Denny, Pat, and Dick made their way uptown to Columbia Records Studio A on 7th Avenue and 52nd Street to begin work on their debut album. They were assigned veteran producer Bob Morgan, who'd been producing records on Columbia subsidiary labels since the early 1950s. By the time he was hooked up with the Halifax Three, he was riding a hit streak with Bobby Vinton. It seemed that Morgan had the golden touch since being named the A&R chief for both Epic and Okeh three years earlier. Under his guidance, he turned Epic into a cash cow with 1962 sales already up

300 percent over the previous year and had considerable experience working with folk artists. He'd produced the self-titled debut album from the Brothers Four on Columbia in 1960 and was currently working with the Clancy Brothers & Tommy Makem. He was also patient and helpful and had a solid reputation as a hands-on producer.

They recorded three songs at their inaugural session and finished eight more over the next two weeks, including the two that would make up their debut single, "Bull Train" and "Come on By." As they were hard at work in the studio, their manager Larry Bell got them booked on a summer tour package. The start date cut into their sessions, and it forced them to leave the studio one song shy of a full 12-song album. After a summer on the road, honing their act, they returned to the studio at the end of September, and the final track was a real doozy. It was an Eamonn O'Shea novelty number called "Come Down the Mountain, Katie Daly," where Denny and Pat were able to put their impish Irish brogue impressions to good use.

Their first single was released in November with the self-titled LP following in January, and they returned to the road to build up as much promotion as they could but neither charted. It wasn't completely unexpected but a disappointment, nonetheless. However, their hopes were raised after playing Farrington's in Cleveland and the Padded Cell in Minneapolis when they received a phone call from Larry Bell who told them about a surefire hit he'd just gotten his hands on called "The Man Who Wouldn't Sing Along with Mitch."

In January 1963, NBC's *Sing Along with Mitch* was one of the hottest shows on TV. It was hosted by veteran bandleader and Columbia Records A&R head Mitch Miller. Each week the goateed host led viewers at home through old favorites with closed-captioned lyrics that featured an illustrated bouncing ball guiding the rhythm above them. He was popular with the over-30 demographic but couldn't be more out of step with young people. Though he was cheerful on the air, behind the scenes, Miller ruled Columbia Records with an iron fist and refused to capitulate to teen music, and nobody at Columbia questioned his judgment. He had a legacy and friends in high places. Over the years, he'd worked with some of the best in the business, including George Gershwin, Charlie Parker, and Frank Sinatra and then became the director of A&R at Mercury Records in 1948. He moved to Columbia in 1956 when his old Eastman School of Music buddy Goddard Lieberson became president of CBS Music Group. But it wasn't solely nepotism that got him hired at the major label. Miller had an ear for popular music and was responsible for the label's acquisition of hitmakers Frankie Laine, Patti Page, Tony Bennett, and Johnny Mathis.

When rock and roll hit the culture like a freight train around the same time Miller started running things at Columbia, his response was simply to ignore it. In his own words, he would not give in to the "worship of mediocrity" and referred to it as musical baby food. He passed over Elvis Presley and Buddy Holly and, although he had redeemed himself with Johnny Cash, by the early 1960s, Miller's choices were leaving Columbia in the dust. In 1963, he was the picture of squareness to teenagers, the demographic who spent the most money on music, and gave Columbia the reputation as being their parents' label. Miller's director of publicity, Lloyd Leipzig, thought that the best way to overcome this was through a little self-deprecation that could also serve as a show promo. He commissioned composers Charles Randolph Grean and Fred Hertz to write a song lampooning his boss. They drew inspiration from the Kingston Trio's 1959 hit "M.T.A.," a novelty folk tune that told the absurd story of a man named Charlie who got stuck in Boston's subway system because he couldn't afford the new exit fares that went into effect in the middle of his train ride.

"The Man Who Wouldn't Sing Along with Mitch" was equally absurd in that it told a tale of a Washington bureaucrat who refused to sing along with Mitch Miller and the Gang, thus making himself a national pariah. His last resort is to flee to the moon where, much to his dismay, even there they sing along with Mitch. The finished product was tailored to suit a folk ensemble and was given to Bob Morgan, who had the duty of assigning it to one of his acts. There was no way the Clancy Brothers & Tommy Makem were going to sing something so hokey, so it naturally fell to the Halifax Three, who hadn't yet earned the right to be choosey.

Denny, Pat, and Dick arrived at Columbia Studios in Midtown Manhattan on January 21, 1963, to record the song. None of them particularly liked it but they trusted in Larry Bell and Bob Morgan's judgment, and really had no choice but to go along with it. It was fast-tracked to release and was issued on February 8. The trio made the rounds, promoting it on *Mike Douglas Show* and *Merv Griffin Show,* and the song got heavy airplay on several New York stations. The real clincher would've been an appearance on *The Ed Sullivan*

Show, which was in the works until the CBC torpedoed the whole deal. The only date offered by the Sullivan people conflicted with a contractual appearance on CBC Toronto, which wouldn't release them from their obligation. It was a missed opportunity, but the trip to Toronto did have a silver lining. In order to perform "The Man Who Wouldn't Sing Along with Mitch" live, the Halifax Three needed a banjoist, as the banjo featured prominently throughout the entire song. None of the them knew how to play a banjo, so they hired a 19-year-old Toronto native named Zalman Yanovsky, who completely blew them away with his multi-instrumentalism and stayed on with them..

Despite all the promotion, "The Man Who Wouldn't Sing Along with Mitch" barely cracked the Top 100. Disheartened, they resumed their tour and headed down South for more tour dates before heading back to New York in April to record their second album. Afterward, the group did manage to get a little downtime, and Denny spent his days and nights hanging out in Greenwich Village at the peak of the folk boom. The streets were teeming with music lovers, tourists, and pretty girls, and Denny was happy to be in the thick of it.

It was on a Tuesday night during this time that his life changed forever. Being a recording artist, Denny gravitated to the higher-end folk clubs like Gerde's Folk City and the Bitter End where the top talent coalesced. On Tuesday nights, the Bitter End held an open mic night, which attracted newcomers trying to make their mark and where established acts sang along with their peers on stage. As Denny got closer to the Bitter End, he heard a big, booming female voice belting out "I Know You Rider" from inside of it. The sound filtered out into the ether and it was like ear candy to Denny and he couldn't help but be drawn inside to see who was making this beautiful sound. On stage were two good-looking young men playing guitar and banjo and in between them stood a heavyset woman singing her heart out, and everybody in the club had their eyes on her. It was Cass Elliot and her bandmates Tim Rose and Jim Hendricks, who called themselves the Big 3. They had just arrived after a failed audition at the Shadows in D.C. It wasn't only Cass' singing that impressed Denny but also her command of the stage. In between numbers, she dazzled the audience with her charm and wit, which bought Tim and Jim time to retune their instruments.

Cass noticed Denny too. The 23-year-old tenor had all the good looks of a lead singer and stood out in a room. He had plenty of female admirers, and

Cass quickly jumped to the top of the list. She could spot a fellow musician and, in the ensuing weeks, kept her eye out for him. She finally spotted him one night at the Dugout, the bar right next to the Bitter End, which served as its unofficial greenroom and after-party center for performers. She kept her eye on him and when a seat next to him opened up, she seized her opportunity and introduced herself. Denny recognized her immediately and began complimenting her vocal range. They exchanged pleasantries and flirtatiously witty repartee and ordered drink after drink.

"We're going to drink each other under the table," Cass said. "I have an idea! Why don't we drink under the table?"

He and Cass were immediately on the same wavelength, and Denny understood exactly was she was proposing. They both crawled underneath their table and continued the conversation and drinking on the dirty marble terrazzo floor. As the evening progressed a true friendship was born, but Cass was hopeful it would develop into something more. As the summer wore on, the Halifax Three and the Big 3 both got back on tour, and seeing each other in person became increasingly sporadic. Cass was determined to stay in touch and did so by copying the Halifax Three's itinerary and calling around at local hotels near their tour stops until she found him.

The Halifax Three's second album, *San Francisco Bay Blues and the Rest of Our Best*, was released in July and the results were the same. Sales were paltry despite heavy touring and long stands at Grossinger's Resort in the Catskills and the Shadows in Washington, D.C. It didn't seem like the Halifax Three was going anywhere, and the group was starting to feel glum about their future. But Denny had a real advocate in his new friend Cass Elliot and their long phone calls in hotel rooms and handwritten notes from her passed along to him by motel clerks lifted his spirits.

In late October, the Halifax Three was added to the Hootenanny Tour that also featured Glenn Yarbrough, the Geezinslaw Brothers, Jo Mapes and the Journeymen. It's the first time Denny set his eyes on John Phillips and his beautiful California bride, Michelle. The tour wound its way through 15 southern states in 30 days, They formed a fast friendship and the camaraderie couldn't have come at a better time. They toured through the heart of the Civil Rights Movement, and tensions were at their highest. Only five months earlier, Bull Connor had used fire hoses and police dogs on underage demonstrators in Birmingham, and less than one month before the same city had experienced the 16th Street Baptist Church bombing that killed four young girls and injured dozens. It wasn't a far-fetched fear that a tour bus could be mistaken for Freedom Riders who were often greeted with jeering, peltings, or even worse and many times the Hootenanny Tour bus encountered hostility.

John Phillips was excellent at taking charge and putting everybody at ease, and Denny felt a real kinship with him. The conversation and singalongs were always going, and John would help everyone pass the time by inventing brainteaser games that kept their minds racing for hours. One was called "Name that Fruit or Vegetable" where John would yell out a clue like "an Italian begging for his life," which initially left everyone involved completely perplexed. An hour later, someone would yell out, "I got it! Asparagus! Ah-spare-a-Gus!" Next up, John would yell, "A homosexual dog." The answer: "Collie flower!"

John took to Denny too, and he was especially impressed by how girls reacted to Denny when he sang onstage. John particularly noticed how several girls in the balcony of the Memphis Auditorium, the home of Elvis Presley, the original rock and roll sex symbol, screamed in ecstasy. On the tour bus, John and Denny were as thick as thieves, singing, chatting, and sneaking away at rest stops to smoke a joint. A new friendship was born but, as the Hootenanny Tour winded down, another friendship was coming to its end.

While on tour, the Halifax Three got friendly with Glenn Yarbrough's manager Bert Zell, who convinced them to drop Larry Bell and take him on as their manager. He promised that he could change their fortunes by breaking them on the West Coast, where their type of folk pop was more acceptable and thriving. They agreed, and, after finishing a gig at the Royal York Hotel in Toronto, headed west by way of a car delivery service out of Detroit that hired them to deliver a Cadillac to its owner in Los Angeles. Upon their arrival, they checked into the Sunset Colonial Motel on the Sunset Strip and waited for Bert's call. But it never arrived. It was a metaphor for their career. Frustrated and sick of each other, the Halifax Three decided to call it quits and go their separate ways. Dick and Pat headed back to Canada, and Denny and Zal headed back east.

Denny and Zal weren't sure what they wanted to do, but they knew it wasn't in folk music. They went first to D.C. and got jobs bartending and waiting tables at Olde Mac's Pipe and Drum in Georgetown. The bar had a stage, and the owner allowed them to play if they wanted to. It was the perfect vehicle for them to shed their folk skin and do something a little more rock and roll. Denny had only cursory guitar skills, so he took on the electric bass, and Zal's proficiency on guitar covered for any mistakes he might have made. They recruited local drummer Ted Hamm and played mostly surf instrumentals. This lasted a few months until Denny and Zal gave Ted his first taste of marijuana and he had a bad reaction to it. When he confessed to his father who gave it to him, the heir to the Hamm's Brewery fortune used his pull to boot Denny and Zal out of town. It was back to Greenwich Village.

It was now spring 1964, and Denny and Zal reconnected with Cass Elliot and Jim Hendricks and another folk refugee, Erik Jacobsen, formerly of the bluegrass group the Knob Lick Upper 10,000. Cass and Jim sensed the end of the Big 3 was near and hooked up with Erik, who'd just returned from Chicago after his group's demise. The three would often listen to the Beatles together in secret and commiserate about the dying folk scene. Erik was looking to move on from performing and into production and found two willing conscripts in Denny and Zal. In May, the three of them along with trombonist Tony Studd recorded a demo of a novelty dance song they called "The Slurp." Tony produced a strange effect on his trombone that was supposed to be the sound of the slurp but sounded more like somebody passing gas. The no-named group wasn't rewarded with a release but, more importantly for Denny and Zal, it was their first foray into rock and roll and a harbinger of things to come.

In June, the Big 3 broke up, much to all their relief, and Cass and Jim, who were aware of Denny and Zal's recording with Erik Jacobson, decided to form a rock and roll group. They initially called themselves Cass Elliot & the Big 3 and began rehearsing with Cass and Denny sharing lead vocals with added harmony from Jim and Zal. They fancied themselves as a Doolittle's Raiders–type response to the British Invasion. By June 1964, it wasn't just the Beatles cluttering the Top 40 of *Billboard* and *Cash Box* but also Peter & Gordon, Gerry & the Pacemakers, the Dave Clark Five, and others. Within a month, they added drummer Art Stokes and Erik's neighbor John Sebastian, formerly of the Even Dozen Jug Band, on harmonica and changed their name to the more British-sounding Mugwumps.

Cass and Jim brought their old manager Roy Silver aboard, and he got the word out on them quickly. In less than no time, he got them booked in Bob Cavallo's new club the Shadows in July. The 24-year-old entrepreneur had opened the club three years earlier with business partner Frank Weis and catered to folk artists with an emphasis on breaking new talent. But the folk crowd there wasn't impressed by a bunch of ex-folkies playing electrified versions of Tim Hardin and Fred Neil songs. Appreciation came from something they hadn't considered.

Word soon spread about this combo who played Beatles-like rock and roll around Georgetown University, and soon college students began filling up the club. It even filtered down to high schools and junior highs, and large groups of teenagers would come and stand outside the Shadows just to listen to the muffled sounds filter through the walls. Sensing an opportunity for growth, the Mugwumps and Cavallo agreed to open Saturday mornings, when alcohol couldn't be served, so the underage crowd could see them play. Cavallo was always looking for the next big thing, and he liked what he saw in the Mugwumps and the teenage reaction. He convinced the group to take him on as their manager and used the Shadows as their base. One of his first acts as manager was to kick John Sebastian out of the group for being a negative influence and got them booked at the Bitter End in Greenwich Village followed by gigs at the Village Corner in Toronto and opening for the Beach Boys at a roller rink in Alexandria, Virginia. Things were moving fast.

Cavallo moved quickly and got the Mugwumps signed to Warner Brothers and booked into Bell Studios in New York, where they recorded nine songs in August. Two of them, "I Don't Wanna Know" and "I'll Remember Tonight," saw release as a single in September, but it went nowhere, and that's when the bloom of the Mugwumps' rose began to fade. They were all used to singles flopping but, after it did, they started to run out of gas. Being the answer to the Beatles was going to be an enormous task and one that none of them were ready for yet. In November, Cavallo got them booked in the once-trendy Peppermint Lounge in Midtown Manhattan. The legendary club where the twist was born four years earlier, and regularly hosted popular acts like Joey Dee & the Starlighters and the Ronettes, had fallen on hard times. Unbeknownst to anyone outside of Peppermint Lounge management, the Mugwumps would be the club's final act ever. When they returned the next night to find the club permanently closed, they decided this experiment was too. Rock and roll crowds wanted rowdy, mindless entertainment, and the Mugwumps sounded more like the Springfields trying to play rock and roll. Theirs was a much softer, electrified folk sound, which, in time, would catch on. It just wasn't time yet.

Back to the New Journeymen. At the same time, over in the East Village, John Phillips knew he needed a showstopping lead singer for the New Journeymen,and the first person he thought of was his new friend Denny Doherty. If anyone could breathe life and sex appeal into their performances and take a little stress of him and Marshall, it was him. The problem was tracking him down. They'd lost touch since the end of the Hootenanny Tour and John had heard about the Halifax Three's breakup.

But he did finally find him through his network of folk friends. Denny was staying at Cass Elliot's apartment at the Hotel Albert, which had become party central since the breakup of the Mugwumps. He rang him up immediately and invited him to join his folk group. Denny was torn. He really wanted to break away from the whole folk thing but was barely eking out a living. The position in the New Journeymen paid modestly well and it could at least go toward rent. He agreed and took on the tall task of memorizing 40 songs in three days. He shaved off the goatee he'd acquired since the start of the Mugwumps and took his Brooks Brothers suit out of the closet. He left the apartment and walked over to John and Michelle's apartment in the East Village. Surely, he must've thought he was taking a step backward. Little did he know he was about a mile and a half from the ride of his lifetime.

Brothers Four and in saga ballads like "El Paso" by Marty Robbins and "North to Alaska" by Johnny Horton. It tells the story of a weary young gunfighter on the run to see his sweetheart and escape to the Mexican border with the sheriff's posse hot on his trail. The song's frenetic pace jumps out of the gate and matches the intensity of the lyrics with help from New York folk musicians Dick Weissman on banjo and Eric Weissberg on mandolin.

The single was issued in November and was even less successful than their first one. Things weren't going so smoothly for the Smoothies. The bookings began drying up. They returned to the Elmwood Casino for another Christmas season, this time featuring Scott's old Singing Strings bandmate Tim Rose on banjo to supplement the folk element now present in their repertoire. John began to recognize that his singing quartet suddenly seemed out of date. Even their name was passé and prone to excite the parents of teenagers and not the teenagers themselves. The scene was changing rapidly. Folk music was in and Greenwich Village was the epicenter and he wanted to be part of it. After their engagement at the Yule Show on December 18, the Smoothies called it quits.

Mike and Tim Rose returned to D.C. and formed a folk duo called Michael & Timothy. Eventually Mike would leave the music business entirely. He got his master's degree in education and became a fixture in the Fairfax County public school system for 25 years. He and John never crossed paths again. Bill Cleary also returned to the D.C. area and entered the nightclub business. He and John would maintain an on-again, off-again friendship over the next 40 years.

John and Scott stayed on in Greenwich Village to figure out their entrée into folk. The number of musicians in town was growing daily, and the cream began rising to the top. John knew he was in that cream. The two rededicated their efforts and joined the growing masses of young musicians playing informally in Washington Square Park. Success was just around the corner. He could feel it.

CHAPTER 12:
BIRDS IN A CAGE

By 1964, John Phillips was a full-fledged drug addict. Marijuana and amphetamines were his drugs of choice and he kept them in a little green Gucci medicine bag buried underneath guitar strings and picks. Marijuana was illegal, so he needed to travel with it discreetly and it became an inside joke known only to close friends who shared in his secret. Since being introduced to it almost five years earlier in Cuba, John had become a connoisseur. When he became a professional touring musician, the rigors of playing two or three shows a night took their toll and, like many musicians of that era, he got turned on to amphetamines, a stimulant that greatly increases energy and awareness whose affects can last for up to 12 hours. By the time he'd formed the New Journeymen, he'd worked out a system with the pharmacist next to his apartment that provided him a steady stream of Eskatrol, Dexedrine, and Biphetamine.

Drugs and music had become the two most important things in John's life and everything else took a back seat, even his children. Jeffrey was now seven and Laura was five, and he hadn't seen either since leaving Susie two years earlier. It would've remained that way if Susie hadn't reached out to John in the spring of 1964, shortly after the breakup of the Journeymen. The kids missed their father and were constantly asking for him. Contrary to her ex-husband, they were the most important thing in Susie's life, so she put her pride aside and invited John and Michelle to come down and stay at her home in Alexandria. The timing couldn't have been any better for John. He was idle for the first time since forming the Smoothies and needed a respite while he figured out his next move, so he and Michelle accepted and drove down. The trip also gave him an opportunity to visit his mother and his sister, from whom he'd been somewhat estranged since the divorce. They sided with Susie and were appalled at John's actions, but two years apart had softened everybody's heart, and they were all just happy to reunite. Although Michelle seemed like a marked woman, Edna, Rosemary, and even Susie found her quite charming and held nothing against her.

John was especially happy seeing his kids again. He didn't intend to be an absentee father. It just worked out that way. Remaining on the opposite end of the country after Susie left him, he got used to them not being around, and understanding they were in better hands with her got him through his days. Over time, checking in with them became less and less of a priority. His drug use also hampered him. With his ever-increasing level of consumption, getting that next high was more important than following traditional familial and social norms. Before they returned home, John pledged to be a more involved father and check in with them more often but hitting it big in music was still his primary focus.

The New Journeymen got back on the road in December, opening for Bill Cosby at the Blue Room in the Shoreham Hotel in Washington, D.C. Denny did well, despite having to cram, and got more comfortable with every performance. His lead vocals raised their profile considerably. He and John quickly became best friends and pill-popping, weed-smoking buddies. It got so gratuitous that, at the end of January, Marshall Brickman decided to leave because of it. He held no ill will toward John and Denny for their drug use. He was just uncomfortable being around two friends who were fast becoming junkies. Besides, his first love was writing, and he landed a job writing for Allen Funt's *Candid Camera*, which eventually led to becoming the lead writer for *The Tonight Show*.

Not long after Marshall's departure, the New Journeymen made some professional recordings to pitch around to record labels. When they were completed, John got in touch with Dick Weissman to play him the recordings in hopes that he might be interested in replacing Marshall. He also played him a new song he wrote called "Me and My Uncle," a Marty Robbins-type western ballad of a Colorado man and his uncle cheating at cards and stealing gold with a twist ending. Dick praised the song but wasn't as complimentary about the New Journeymen demos. John's arrangements were well done but somewhat outdated, and the vocal blend between him and Denny was fine. It was Michelle. Her vocals weren't as strong, and she tended to warble in lower octaves, making them sound like a poor man's Peter, Paul and Mary.

John was aware of Michelle's weakness but forged ahead despite Dick's criticism. He was determined to make this work and invited his friend Eric Hord to be the New Journeymen's instrumentalist. He jumped at the chance and joined them for their last few remaining shows and two television tapings for CTV's *Let's Sing Out* filmed at Ryerson University in Toronto. After that, they were dead in the water. They had no scheduled live appearances, and no record label had expressed interest in signing them. The four headed back to New York and with a mounting debt and no clue what to do next, sat around and made good use of John's medicine bag. But uppers weren't as necessary when there was no schedule to keep, and marijuana wasn't as exciting as it used to be. John and Denny wanted to go further and, in 1965, the next step was LSD.

Drug use had grown substantially among young people in post–World War II Western culture and new and more innovative methods were always being developed. The drug of choice was still marijuana, but there was growing interest in lysergic acid diethylamide, better known as LSD. It had been around for nearly 30 years when it was first synthesized by Swiss chemist Dr. Albert Hofmann, who'd been trying to develop a stimulant for human respiratory and circulatory systems through the synthesis of squill and ergot fungi. When he accidentally absorbed a small amount through his fingertips, he discovered he'd instead created a powerful mind-altering stimulant. His research was disrupted by World War II but in 1943, after a second, controlled experiment on himself, he experienced the full effect of the drug in vivid hallucinations, hyper anxiety, and delusions.

In 1947, Sandoz marketed LSD as a psychiatric drug under the trade name Delysid, and its effects on human beings were studied by independent labs and the U.S. government. By the end of the 1950s, those studies made their way to the university level, and that's where the psychedelic was introduced to the two men most responsible for bringing it to the masses. Dr. Timothy Leary was a clinical psychologist and researcher at Harvard University when

LSD arrived on campus in 1960. He'd already been testing other mind-altering effects of Mexican psilocybin mushrooms, and after experimenting on himself, he became a regular user. The effects influenced him greatly, and he became a great believer in LSD's effectiveness on human psychosis and sought to prove that criminal recidivism and alcoholism could be reduced through measured doses of LSD and regular psychotherapy. He not only experimented on consenting men and women but also preached to his subjects that LSD had therapeutic and spiritual benefits and could lift them to a higher level of consciousness. Harvard fired him in 1963 when it was discovered he was doing controlled experiments of LSD on university students. But Leary would not be silenced. He privatized his experiments in order to maintain his supply and keep the party going. In 1966, he coined the phrase "turn on, tune in, drop out" that spread throughout the university counterculture like wildfire.

A year before Dr. Leary's discovery of LSD, Bay Area Renaissance man and aspiring novelist Ken Kesey volunteered to be part of a Stanford University human study of the effects of psychedelics secretly funded by the CIA. The former wrestling champion with a large personality was enamored with his state of consciousness under LSD and it inspired him to write his 1962 novel *One Flew Over the Cuckoo's Nest* and to form a group of like-minded users called the Merry Pranksters, a traveling group who initially went around the state dressed in outrageous costumes telling young people about the good news of LSD. They took it even further by organizing carnival-like gatherings called "acid tests" where they'd give any willing participant his or her first taste of the drug in a controlled environment, except the environment was controlled mostly by people already under the influence. There was even a soundtrack provided by a newly formed San Francisco rock and roll band called the Warlocks, who, in 1966, would change their name to the Grateful Dead.

As the pop music scene was going through its metamorphosis of teen idols to folk music to the resurgence of rock and roll through the British Invasion, the Merry Pranksters took their show on the road, going from coast to coast. By the middle of the decade, the mixture of the drugs and the music created a movement that was scary, dangerous, and inspirational. In 1965, dabbling in LSD was still only whispered about in dark corners by the general public, but for musicians, it was the next level of drug experimentation, and the notion that psychedelics enhanced the creative process began to spread. New Journeymen lead singer Denny Doherty had already experimented with LSD when he was in the Mugwumps. John and Michelle had not yet tried it but had recently witnessed Michelle's sister Rusty and her boyfriend Peter Pilafian's first trip shortly after they moved into an apartment in Greenwich Village. John heard all the rumors, good and bad, and decided he had to try it.

He got in touch with Stewart Reed, his marijuana dealer, and asked him to bring along some LSD the next time he made his marijuana delivery. A few days later, Stewart arrived with the merchandise and charged John $10 per piece. He bought a handful and invited Denny, who'd already dabbled, to come on over and join in the experiment. When Denny arrived, the three sat around the living room table and unwrapped the goods. Seeing the LSD in cube form intrigued John as they all sat and examined them. Michelle, ready to get started, eagerly grabbed at one, but John, always the leader of this group, stopped her and gently took it from her grasp. He held it up, analyzed it and sniffed it like a cigar.

"I think I'd better try it first, darling," he told Michelle.

After his cube dissolved on his tongue, Michelle and Denny took theirs and waited for it to kick in but after 10, 15, 20 minutes, nothing seemed to be happening. While they were sitting around, a knock came at the door. Denny casually mentioned that he had invited Cass Elliot over to join them, but when Michelle opened it, there stood Rusty and Peter instead. She invited them in and told them about how they were now trying LSD for the first time, but nobody had gotten high yet. Still sober, she decided that, now that there was a party underway, she was going to run to the pharmacy next door to get some drinks and necessities. Still nothing.

As the rest of them sat in the living room anxiously waiting for something happen, Denny lightened the mood by putting on some music. He brought over some records with him, but there was only one he wanted to play, and he dropped the needle on *Meet the Beatles*. He'd been waiting for this moment to play it and seized the moment. John was still dismissive of the number one British group that was rapidly changing the music scene and the culture. As "I Want to Hold Your Hand" played in the background, Denny lit up a joint and passed it around. As they ingested the marijuana smoke, everybody except John nodded to the rhythm, and a debate about the Beatles ensued between him and Denny.

"It's too simple, Dennis! It's three chords!" John exclaimed. "It's 'Guanta-namera' with a beat!"

Denny protested. John was listening with his brain and not his ears. Sure, he'd developed into a first-class music arranger but, for somebody who, only years earlier, preferred Pat Boone's version of "Tutti Frutti" to Little Richard's, he'd become an incorrigible music snob. Like many folk purists, John preferred acoustic music to electric and wouldn't condescend to listen to four guys from England caterwaul about love. But Denny was patient. He knew John would be a tough nut to crack. As the back-and-forth continued, Michelle returned from the store and began putting her groceries away.

"I don't know about you guys, but this drug does nothing for me," she stated.

As she continued to question what was so special about LSD, a knock came at the door. The four of them in the living room watched as Michelle went to open it and, as she turned the knob, her acid kicked in and she couldn't have beheld a more surreal sight. In front of her stood a 5'5" 300-pound woman in a pink angora sweater, a white pleated skirt, and untrimmed false eyelashes with her hair in a flip. Michelle couldn't decide if she was hallucinating or if what she was seeing was indeed real. Nevertheless, she remained a gracious hostess.

"You must be Cass," she said. "I'm Michelle. We've just taken some LSD. Would you like some?"

"Sure!" Cass replied excitedly.

Michelle had no idea an acid-taking veteran was in her presence, and Cass charmed them all immediately. She was loud and her personality was bub-bly and she made everybody laugh by poking fun at her weight. In no time, joyousness filled the air, and LSD filled their brains. Everybody got along as if they were old friends. It turned out that Cass knew John by reputation, and it wasn't only from his time with the Journeymen. It turns out both shared an alma mater, George Washington High School in Alexandria, Virginia, and some of John's antics there had become legendary. They also shared the distinction of never graduating from there.

Later that evening, only John, Michelle, Cass, and Denny remained. They were all very much under the influence, sharing pleasant hallucinations with visions of large, amorphous colors jumping, flashing, and pouring out at them and they were giggling uncontrollably at every little thing. Things got a little more serious when Cass shared a story with Michelle about being raped at knifepoint by a large black man in Florida. She told her that rather than fight him she submitted and while on top of her, the rapist was so overcome by her passion that he died. Their talk then transitioned into Cass confiding to Michelle about her love for Denny, who had just emerged from the kitchen with John. Both were giggling like schoolboys, because John had stuffed Red Devil ham in his nose and ears and was struggling trying to get it out.

The night rolled on and things took a turn for the surreal when John lit a candle in Michelle's decorative wrought-iron filigree birdcage and hung it from the living room ceiling. It created a long flickering shadow when John turned out the lights and, in their inebriated state, it looked lifelike. When they all stood beside it, it looked like their shadows were trapped in a cage, and they all began making bird noises. John then became the cat who was trying to eat the birds. It almost resembled a scene out of a Fellini film. When they grew tired of that, Denny continued to try and convince John about the merits of the Beatles in his inebriated state, which led to the most profound event of the evening. As the LSD continued to circulate through their bodies, John slouched down on the couch and began slowly sliding off the edge of the cushions. Denny, who was right beside him, gently eased him onto the floor and placed him in the center of the living room and then placed John's two large stereo speakers beside each of his ears, put the Beatles record back on, and looked him right in the eyes.

"OK man, I want you to listen to these guys once and for all," Denny said. "I know you think they're jive but you're wrong. I want you to listen and just keep listening."

John laid back in a wild Technicolor dream. As the Beatles launched into "I Want to Hold Your Hand," he became awash in an acid-fueled musical ecstasy. Colors sprang out of the ether and flowed in and around the birdcage and through him. The music of the Beatles thumped along like a heartbeat, and the pulsating sensation made the ceiling and walls seem to come alive. Most of the songs were two years old, but John was hearing them for the first time and in a psychedelic haze. One by one the electrifying new sounds streamed through his brain. Denny knelt down over John's body and leaned in toward him until they were nose to nose and softly, but firmly, gave him the following instructions.

"I want you to write songs. Songs that sound like these songs. No more folk. Folk is dead."

John nodded obediently and continued to listen to the music as the seeds of his rock and roll consciousness were sown. As dawn arrived, the effects of the LSD began wearing off, and they all came crashing down. Denny staggered around the living room and tripped over the birdcage that was now on the floor with the candle still lit, and he and John scrambled to put out the small fire. Michelle put on a pot of coffee to help everybody shake the hangover then everybody slunk away to sleep it off. When they all woke up a day or so later, a new day had arrived for John, Michelle, and Denny. The LSD experience drew them closer together, and Denny really felt he had a breakthrough with John. Over the ensuing weeks, John began writing songs with a new sense of purpose and took several more acid trips, hoping it would stir his senses. It was time to hit the reset button.

The pop music scene had changed considerably since John had unplugged from it four years earlier when he formed the Journeymen. Gone from the charts were Little Richard, Buddy Holly, Chuck Berry, Bill Haley & the Comets, the Everly Brothers, Rick Nelson, and most of the first generation of rock and rollers. And the king of them all, Elvis Presley, was busier being an actor, cranking out one hokey movie after another, all accompanied by insipid soundtracks. They'd been replaced by the Beatles, the Rolling Stones, the Kinks, the Dave Clark Five, Gerry & the Pacemakers, Peter & Gordon, and several other imports from England. And there were newer American artists too like the Beach Boys, the Four Seasons, and Jan & Dean, but they all faced uphill battles for chart position after the onslaught of the British Invasion, which forced them to redefine their musical directions.

Black music was also crossing over into the *Billboard* and *Cash Box* Top 40s like never before and reaching young listeners who otherwise would never have heard them. After the successes of black artists like Chuck Berry, Little Richard, and Fats Domino the bigger record labels got involved, signing black artists in numbers. It put them in top-notch studios, which greatly increased the quality of their records and put them on par with their white counterparts. Roy Hamilton and the Platters were among the first to benefit from slicker production and promotion. Countless others followed but none more influential than Chicago native Sam Cooke, who'd left gospel behind him in 1957 with his number one hit "You Send Me." Over the next seven years, he became a chart regular with his sophisticated version of rhythm and blues, and his refined, soulful blend set off a chain reaction among contemporaries like Clyde McPhatter and Jackie Wilson who shed their rawer blues and doo-wop based sound behind for something more refined.

In 1959, Jackie Wilson's hit songwriter Berry Gordy Jr. decided to form his own label with the intention of reinventing rhythm and blues as a form of tailor-made pop made by black artists that reached young Americans of all cultures. Over the first half of the 1960s, they unleashed a stable of homegrown hitmakers in Mary Wells, the Miracles, the Temptations, the Supremes, the Four Tops, Martha & the Vandellas, Marvin Gaye, and the Marvelettes who in turn had a profound influence on the British artists who were now dominating mid-1960s American culture.

On the outside looking in were the folk refugees who traded in their acoustic guitars for electric ones after the Beatles landed and were trying to find a place in this new landscape, but it was difficult. American record labels didn't even want to look at artists who weren't British. But, little by little, they began to make an impact. On the West Coast, former Greenwich Village regulars Jim McGuinn and David Crosby joined forces with ex-New Christy Minstrel Gene Clark and called themselves the Jet Set. After recruiting a rhythm section in bassist Chris Hillman and drummer Michael Clarke, Elektra Records did an experiment with them in a one-off single deal. The label christened them the British-sounding Beefeaters and released two band-written originals that went nowhere. With that, Elektra dropped them, but manager Jim Dickson was undeterred and, with a helpful recommendation from jazz legend Miles Davis, got them a deal with Columbia Records. On January 20, 1965, they entered Columbia Studios in Hollywood and laid down a hair-raising rock and roll arrangement of Bob Dylan's "Mr. Tambourine Man."

Dylan himself entered Columbia's Studio A in New York City a week earlier with several session musicians and ex-Mugwump John Sebastian and laid down his first full-band, electric recording since his debut single "Mixed Up Confusion" over two years earlier. Over two days, he recorded seven electric songs that would fill up the A-side of his album *Bringing It All Back Home*. This time, he applied his profound poetic meanderings over a rambunctious rock and roll beat, and his completely original approach pushed the music to a level of maturity that it had never seen before. When it was released in March, with one side fully electric and one side fully acoustic, it split his fan base right down the middle but set him on the pathway to mainstream acceptance and superstardom.

Much like his friend Bob Dylan, John Sebastian wanted to amplify his sound too. He and Zal Yanovsky sought to rebuild the shattered remains of the Mugwumps by holding informal jam sessions in the basement of the Hotel Albert. Their vision was a rock and roll version of the type of loose and zany but cohesive sound he'd help create in the Even Dozen Jug Band, but with a bit of Beatles-esque sophistication. When they learned that Trude Heller's was hosting the first rock and roll band to play Greenwich Village, their curiosity was piqued. The band was fittingly named the Sellouts, and it was made up of several young guys from Long Island who had previously dabbled in folk music. But it seemed that not too many locals shared the same interest as John and Zal. Night after they night, they were two of only a few people in the entire place, but it gave them a chance to connect with the band, and they became friendly with drummer Joe Butler and guitarist Skip Boone. After jamming with the two of them at the Albert, John and Zal invited both to join their new unnamed group. They were flattered, but they had to turn them down. The Sellouts were professionally managed and had a record deal in place, but they liked John and Zal and recommended to them Skip's bass-playing brother Steve and Long Island drummer Jan Buchner.

After a few weeks of rehearsal with Steve and Jan, they felt ready to get in front of an audience and got a spot at the tiny Night Owl Café in Greenwich Village and called themselves the Lovin' Spoonful after a line in blues singer Mississippi John's Hurt's song "Coffee Blues." After a rough start with over-modulated amps, they went back to the drawing board. They knew they had something, but there was still some tweaking that needed to be done. John, Zal, and Steve agreed that Jan's drumming was too conventional for their style of playing, so they dumped him and persuaded Joe Butler to play with them at their next Night Owl gig. In February, they returned to the stage and blew everybody away. All the pieces seemed to be in place now, and John began writing original material. They made a serious run and pitched his "Do You Believe in Magic" to every record label who had an office in New York but ran into a steady stream of rejections simply because they weren't British. Eventually, Koppelman & Rubin Associates, a newly founded publishing and production company, got behind them and convinced them to sign with Artie Ripp's Kama Sutra label. It was a completely mobbed-up deal that the

Lovin' Spoonful would later come to regret, but, for now, they had a label and studio time.

While Bob Dylan was going electric, the Byrds were recording his "Mr. Tambourine Man" and the Lovin' Spoonful were rocking the Night Owl Café, John Phillips was spinning his wheels. It was getting harder for him to ignore what was going on right in front of him, but he still had his heart set on a career in folk music. Michelle decided they needed a vacation away from the music business, and John agreed. When none of them could decide on where to go, John and Denny went to a projection map they had hung on the wall, blindfolded Michelle, spun her around a couple times, and had her point to a spot on the map and it landed on the U.S. Virgin Islands. It was perfect. John had already gone tropical twice when he needed to clear his head, so why not a third time? He had about $9,000 in cash stashed away from Journeymen gigs, so getting there and having a good time wouldn't be a problem.

In January 1965, John, Michelle, and Denny spent 10 majestic days at the Villa Fairview in Charlotte Amalie, St. Thomas, doing nothing but resting, smoking grass and dropping acid. Drugs notwithstanding, the Caribbean sun, salt air, sand and crystal blue waters did wonders for their spirits and, when it was time to go, nobody wanted to leave. They all agreed to come back as soon as possible, and they were serious. They had one final New Journeymen commitment to honor and, once that was finished, they would head back but this time bring a host of friends along with them. John's cash reserves took a slight hit with this vacation, but his ace in the hole was his still-valid American Express card from ITA with a large, open balance. John, Michelle, and Denny couldn't have imagined it at the time, but this was all part of a big investment into their future that would lead to them finding their missing piece. And she couldn't have been any closer.

CHAPTER 13:
CASS ELLIOT

Cass Elliot was born Ellen Naomi Cohen on September 19, 1941, to second-generation Russian-Jewish immigrants Philip and Bess Cohen (née Levine) whose families settled in the Baltimore area in the 1890s. Her parents were singers, and both briefly dabbled in the music industry. Her mother sang for bandleader Fred Waring for a very short time and her father was skilled enough to have ambitions of being an opera singer. After appearing in *Aida* as a spear-carrier for one night at the Lyric Opera House in Baltimore, he inexplicably gave up the dream and found his way into the catering business to which he would devote the rest of his life.

After becoming a father, Philip initiated several food services, all of which seemed destined to fail. He opened a kosher catering service in Alexandria, which had a very small Jewish community. When that closed, he opened a small delicatessen in Washington, D.C., diagonally across the street from the Library of Congress, where a teenage John Phillips unknowingly first laid eyes on his future contralto, but that didn't last very long either. It went on this way for years. Bess worked part-time for a railroad company, and the couple had two more children, Leah Rachel, born seven years after Ellen, and Joseph William in 1951. The Cohens settled into a Washington, D.C. row home on Allison Street where they lived through Ellen's sophomore year in high school.

Ellen favored her mother's looks and, although Bess was a robust woman, she didn't struggle with weight issues like her eldest daughter. Oftentimes the subject of scorn and derision because of her size, young Ellen countered her self-consciousness with a witty and bubbly personality that was aided quite substantially by an IQ of 165. Throughout her childhood, her parents were more concerned than she was about her weight and put her through a steady diet of psychoanalysis and Dexedrine, an oft-prescribed amphetamine marketed as a diet pill. Despite her idiosyncrasies, Ellen was always able to engage and, from the time of her youth, was confident enough to converse with adults on myriad subjects. Social issues and politics were spoken about quite freely in her home and openly by her socialist parents, and young Ellen never shied away from asking questions. The Cohens liked to sing too, and they did it well. Ellen's mother preferred the more contemporary artists like Frank Sinatra and Perry Como and contemporary interpretations of Yiddish folk songs. Her father remained true to his opera and schooled young Ellen on the wonders of Puccini's *La bohème* and Verdi's *Rigoletto*. Because of this, singing came naturally to young Ellen, and she was always entertaining family and friends from a young age.

In 1956, as Cass was entering high school, Philip developed a mobile food service after purchasing an old bus for a few hundred dollars at auction. The postwar suburban Baltimore/D.C. landscape was growing rapidly, which included the increased development of shopping malls and plazas. Philip fed the entire construction crew of the Mondawmin Mall project in 1955–1956, which allowed him to purchase two more buses and hire a staff that included his kids, who worked only out of a sense of obligation. And as if high school life wasn't tough enough for her, Ellen was forced to work weekday mornings before heading off to class at George Washington High in Alexandria.

At school, Ellen had ambition and wanted to make good use of her studies. She'd seen her parents struggle to make ends meet all her life and figured medicine must be her calling. It did run in her family after all. Three of her uncles on her father's side were successful doctors, but whatever innate talent they all had for medicine didn't rub off on her. She struggled mightily in the courses that required high aptitude for students wishing to go on to medical school and didn't have much in common with fellow classmates who also belonged to the pre-med Caduceus Club. In fact, Ellen struggled finding many friends at all. Her offbeat personality and her weight brought out the worst in some of her GWHS classmates. She did have at least one friend though. Her name was Priscilla Lainoff, and she had all the tangible teenage qualities Ellen didn't. She was strikingly beautiful, popular, and made friends easily. She also cared deeply for Ellen and, whenever she went out with a boy, insisted her date bring along a friend for Ellen, which almost always meant spending an evening out with a sheepish conscript.

In 1958, her family moved to Baltimore where she enrolled at Forest Park High School and if life at GW was difficult because of her weight and quirkiness, it was downright hellish at Forest Park. At GW, Jews were a minority, which tended to build up sense of community and camaraderie, but at Forest Park, most of the student body was Jewish, and it caused greater scrutiny among peers. Their cliquish fraternity and sorority system could make or break a high schooler's class standing not to mention spirit. But it was at Forest Park where the first inklings of Ellen's Cass Elliot persona began to show. Where many of her peers dressed in petticoats, gathered skirts, and cardigans with bobby socks, Ellen wore Bermuda shorts and heels and covered up in the warmer months with heavy stockings and long sleeves. Her hair was almost always a mess for having to get up early to work in her father's food bus, and she also cursed like a sailor, no doubt helped in part by spending mornings surrounded by construction workers.

The rock and roll revolution occurred in the middle of Ellen's high school career, and, although she enjoyed the music, her first love was Broadway and the Tin Pan Alley tunes of the 1920s, 1930s, and 1940s. While Elvis, Chuck Berry, Little Richard, Bill Haley, and others were giving the music of the 1950s a sense of sonic sexuality and enchanting her peers, Ellen was more into the music of Rodgers & Hammerstein and the Gershwin Brothers. Her favorite musical was Jule Styne and Stephen Sondheim's *Gypsy,* and she preferred singing along to "Small World" or "Everything's Coming Up Roses" on her long player over an Elvis or Little Richard 45. Her best friend at Forest Park, Sharon Paige, shared her love of show tunes, and, in the summer of 1959, at Ellen's urging, successfully tried out for summer stock at Don Swann's New Hilltop Theater in Owings Mills. The 11-year-old country theater produced two to three musicals each summer and debuted their 1959 season with Jule Styne, Betty Comden and Adolph Green's relatively new musical *Bells Are Ringing,* which ran through mid-July. Ellen was still too shy and self-conscious to try out herself, but Sharon's entry into the world of musicals meant a free pass for Ellen to hang around like-minded and talented young people, and she discovered a more accepting crowd who adored her and allowed her to be herself.

The second summer musical New Hilltop produced was Sandy Wilson's *The Boy Friend*, which ran through August and was so successful that it was extended into September. That's when opportunity knocked for Ellen. The extension caused problems for the girl playing the role of Hortense the maid. She had a previous commitment that she couldn't break and since there wasn't time to audition somebody new, the role was offered to the newly confident Ellen, who'd hung around the theater all summer and gotten to know the actors and production staff. *The Boy Friend* took place on the French Riviera during the roaring twenties and gaily portrays the exploits of three women of various ages all in pursuit of a respective boyfriend, a plot that surely must've resonated with the overweight teenager. The role also allowed her to display her singing chops for the first time as part of the opening ensemble number, "Perfect Young Ladies," and in a mostly solo spot on "It's Nicer in Nice" in Act II. At the end of that run, she was cast right away as a clown in a September production called *Prior to Broadway* where she would come onstage, playfully placing placards on an easel that introduced each scene, which allowed the hammy side of her personality to shine.

With this new world opening to her, and no longer willing to deal with the drudgery of life at Forest Hills, Ellen dropped out a couple of months before graduation in order to pursue a career on Broadway. Her parents, however, were not as enthusiastic over her showbiz ambitions. Before permitting her to move 200 miles away to New York City, they insisted she get her GED. She agreed and started night school. It was a blessing in disguise because it forced her to bide her time and map out her plans more strategically. She took a job at the *Baltimore Jewish Times*, which allowed her to finance singing lessons with local vocal coach Shirley Richmond. She supplemented her income with a part-time job at the *Baltimore Sun* newspaper, which she eventually lost for spending most of her time gabbing with friends on the outside line. Richmond recognized Ellen's pure talent and helped her control and refine it. She told her gifted student that she had what it took to sing on Broadway, which only fueled Ellen's desire to move to New York.

Opportunity knocked for Ellen when Sharon told her she was going up to New York following graduation with her friend Shelley Spector and asked if she wanted to come. Summer stock at New Hilltop permanently closed following the 1959 season, and they figured it was their moment to take a shot at the big time. Ellen pleaded with her parents, but her father was dead set against it and wanted her to go to college instead. Her mother, who was far more liberated woman than many in those days, wanted Ellen to follow her dream, but was more worried about her oldest child living so far away in a rough city and trying to break into a notoriously cutthroat business. But Ellen wouldn't let it go until they relented. A compromise was reached when her mother arranged for her to stay with her sister Lillian and her husband Martin Finn in their New York City apartment.

As Sharon and Shelley's school year wrapped up, Ellen dreamed of what life on Broadway would be like. She decided to continue a tradition perpetuated by many legendary actors and actresses of the Great White Way by adopting a stage name. Ellen Cohen wasn't going to cut it, and she looked at Broadway as an opportunity to establish a new identity. Although she never actually revealed how exactly she came up with the name Cass Elliot, friends who were around her at the time almost universally agree that she took the name Cass from 1930s/40s comedienne and singer Cass Daley, who had an uproarious, slapstick stage demeanor and a great singing voice. Her dad also used to jokingly nicknamed her "the mad Greek Cassandra" as a child because of her boisterous nature. Her choice of "Elliot" is a little less clear as some friends believe it came from British writer T. S. Eliot while others say she took it from a young man named Jesse Elliot whose girlfriend acted alongside Ellen in *Prior to Broadway*. Whatever the source, Ellen Cohen was now Cass Elliot and New York–bound.

Cass' New York experience was overall unspectacular, but it had its peaks and valleys and in very short order. It started out badly. As she parked her car outside her aunt and uncle's apartment in West Harlem, most of her possessions were stolen while she was inside being welcomed. Initially devastated and chagrined at herself for being so naïve, she got over it quickly and her luck turned for the better when she landed her first job as a hatcheck girl at the Greenwich Village cabaret Upstairs-at-the-Duplex and later at the Showplace, located a few blocks away on West 4th Street. Here, she witnessed firsthand many of the rising singers and comedians of the day, including Joan Rivers, Liza Minnelli, Woody Allen, and Barbra Streisand.

Over the course of the next year, Cass auditioned regularly for plays on Broadway, off-Broadway, and anything and everything that would help her get her foot in the door but had no luck. In November 1961, along with hundreds of others, she auditioned for the role of Miss Marmelstein in the

Broadway premiere of Harold Rome's *I Can Get It for You Wholesale*, a comedy set in the Jewish garment district, but lost out to Barbra Streisand. The role seemed tailor-made for Cass and she got pretty far along in the audition process before the producers ultimately chose Brooklyn native Streisand, whose talent was immense and self-promotion relentless. She'd already performed on *The Jack Paar Show* a couple of times, had played the Caucus Club in Detroit and was singing at the Duplex and the Showplace while Cass was checking hats. In fact, Streisand's performance as Miss Marmelstein was so powerful that Rome eventually expanded her role.

It was a blow to Cass for sure, as she'd come so close. Losing out to a thinner, unconventionally pretty peer must've stirred some doubt within her, but she also couldn't deny Streisand's talent. She carried on with auditions, and it didn't take long before her first break finally arrived. Shortly after the New Year, she was cast in the national touring company of Meredith Willson's the *Music Man* starring veteran stage actor, and future *F Troop* star Forrest Tucker as Professor Harold Hill. Come March, Cass had settled into her small role and was doing quite well when the unthinkable happened. Her father was killed in a car accident. She took a hiatus to return to Baltimore and help her mother with Leah and Joseph and returned to finish out the last few weeks of the season. When the tour ended, Cass accepted that her family needed her more than the stage, and perhaps she needed them too, so she put her career ambitions on hiatus. She moved into the basement of her mother's new house in Alexandria and took a part-time job at a drugstore.

With her Broadway dream on hold, Cass didn't want to sit around and mope, so she began working on her plan B by enrolling at American University in Washington, D.C., and majoring in speech arts. She practically applied her studies by putting her gift of gab to use in a jazz program at the school radio station, where she spun a mix of contemporary and classic jazz vocalists and developed a solid banter between songs. Cass also made the rounds of the open mic nights at many of the local D.C. clubs where she'd sing a mixture of show tunes and folk songs. Unfortunately, her physical appearance often superseded her performances and her incredible vocals often passed unnoticed by patrons. Rival singers and musicians took notice, however, including a Georgetown senior named John Keats who was immediately taken with her powerful contralto and quickly befriended her.

John grew up in the D.C. area and had played alongside Scott McKenzie and Tim Rose in their many various iterations of the Singing Strings. Afterward, he and Tim formed a bluegrass duo called the Kentucky Colonels (*Note: Not to be confused with the L.A.-based Kentucky Colonels featuring Clarence White.*), but that ended when Tim joined the Air Force after graduation. When Tim was discharged in 1961, he decided to pursue a career in folk music and got in to it fairly quickly when Scott McKenzie got in touch with him to play electric guitar on one of the Smoothies sessions and play banjo with them on tour. After they broke up, he and ex-Smoothie Michael Boran tried to get something going as the folk duo Michael & Timothy. That had only lasted a few months when he and John reconnected at a Georgetown party in December 1962. Cass Elliot was also in attendance and Tim wasn't exactly bowled over when John raved to him about the 300-pound female singer over in the corner. She didn't exactly fit Tim's Mary Travers vision, and his initial reaction was, "No way! I don't care how good she sings." John laughed it off and insisted he go talk to her.

Despite his trepidation, Tim walked up to Cass, struck up a conversation, and was immediately taken with her friendly personality. The two ended up talking all night, then headed home to his parents' house to listen to some blues records, which, though she feigned knowledge, was all new to her. After listening and talking for a while, Tim finally asked her to sing for him. He had an original idea of how he wanted his trio to sound and gave her some parts to sing. She was perfect from the start. Not only was her voice powerful and sweet, but she also sung on key and took instruction. When Tim asked her to sing a C against a C sharp, she could, which was rare in her relatively novice capacity. Tim began reconsidering his initial thoughts about Cass. She also had something else Tim needed: a viable means of transportation in an old VW Bug she'd recently purchased. He asked her to form a trio with him, and she instantly accepted. Then he convinced her to go with him to Chicago and join up with their third member, a singer named John Brown. It was a hasty decision, but Cass felt good about it and drove home to tell her mother and start packing. A couple days later, they set out on the 700-mile drive and in subzero temperatures met John at his apartment in the Old Town section of North Chicago where he lived with his wife and three children. He'd recently given up his newspaper job to try and make it as a folk singer and met Tim earlier in the year on a Midwest folk circuit. Tim and John struck up a friendship and, with an idea that his duo with Michael Boran wasn't going anywhere, made plans to try and form a new duo with the Chicago native.

Cass was a surprise to John. Tim didn't have time to get word to him about her and, once again, her physique aroused John's prejudice but, like everyone else, he quickly changed his mind once she sang. With Peter, Paul and Mary blowing up the charts with songs like "Lemon Tree" and "If I Had a Hammer," John was keen on Tim's trio idea and already lined up their first gig. He'd been booked as a solo act at the Fred A. Niles Film Studio employee Christmas party and had no problem convincing the company that a trio would give them more bang for their buck. They began rehearsing mornings and afternoons at Tim and Cass' room at the Hotel Lincoln, putting a repertoire together that included the traditional folk ballads "Delia's Gone," "All the Pretty Little Horses," and "I Know You Rider." Tim played banjo, John manned the six-string, and Cass lifted both their vocals. At night, Tim and Cass would venture out to Chicago's thriving club scene, particularly at basket houses like the Bear, the Fickle Pickle, the Rising Moon, and the marquee spot for every Midwest folk singer, the Gate of Horn, co-owned and operated by folk music impresario and new Bob Dylan manager Albert Grossman.

They called themselves the Triumvirate and played an open mic night at a local club before the big Niles Studio Christmas party, which included approximately 100 employees and their families. The boys arrived in matching brown blazers, and Cass wore a black dress. They played a seven-song set and had their onstage patter finely rehearsed in a relatively short period of time. In addition to her voice, Cass' other strength was entertaining the audience in between songs or whenever Tim or John had to retune or change strings. It went over well, even though they didn't know enough songs for an encore. Shortly after the party, they were booked for two weeks at the Old Town North Club in Chicago. From there, they went on to tour the Midwest and Northeast, but it was at the Cleveland folk club La Cave where things began to take off for the Triumvirate.

While the trio was generating good buzz at La Cave, the local ABC affiliate invited them to perform on their daytime talk show, the 1 O'Clock Club, hosted by Bill Gordon and Dorothy Fuldheim. After the Triumverate performed two numbers, the producer offered them a chance to perform on the program daily for six months. It was completely unexpected and the biggest offer of their very young career and a lucrative deal that would pay them $750 a week divided three ways. It was more money than they could conceive, and, in addition, the network would allow them to play anywhere, anytime after their daily taping was completed. The local gigs would be endless, as they'd be the hottest thing in Cleveland. It was a dream come true in a very short period of time.

John was elated and suddenly had overwhelming peace of mind. He was several years older than both Tim and Cass and had a lot more financial responsibility. In his mind, he imagined relocating his family to Cleveland and forever putting away the days of worrying about how he was going to feed his family. But it wasn't meant to be. Tim was totally against the idea. He wanted to be big nationwide, not just in Cleveland. John didn't see it that way. To him, it was more of a launching pad. Both men were very strong-willed and reached an impasse trying to make their respective cases. It was up to Cass to cast the deciding vote and it put her in the uncomfortable position of having to choose one bandmate over another. She sided with Tim—not because he made the most sense but rather because she felt indebted to him for breaking her into the music business. Also, in what would become a common theme for Cass, she'd fallen in love with him. The word "triumvirate" means a coalition of three people holding equal power. John Brown found out that in this group it would always be two against one on important decisions.

They moved on to a gig in Omaha, Nebraska, in early spring 1963 where they shared a bill with a tall and lanky, Chuck Connors–looking singing schoolteacher named Jim Hendricks. He was ruggedly handsome, extremely talented, and engaging, and Cass flipped for him. With Tim and John's relationship on the rocks, she urged her banjoist to come check him out and he was suitably impressed. They immediately considered the prospect of Jim replacing John and set about getting to know him better. After the show, the three hung out and sang together for several hours and Cass and Tim apprised him of their situation. Jim had been impressed with what he'd heard out of them, particularly Cass' singing, and liked the way Tim's voice blended with Cass'. Noticing their talent, he was also honored and excited that they wanted him to join them but was hesitant to say yes right away. Before committing, he consulted with the club manager Ray Valerio, who was his mentor, about it. He saw a tremendous upside to Tim and Cass and advised Jim to take it. Even better, he offered to finance a trip for them to Fort Lauderdale, Florida, to rehearse properly and put together a professional act. Initially skeptical of

Valerio's offer, Tim and Cass agreed and broke the news to John. He took it pretty poorly but had no choice but to slink back to Chicago.

The re-formed Triumvirate and Ray all had business to settle in their respective hometowns and agreed to meet in Washington, D.C., in a month's time and drive down to Fort Lauderdale together. Come May, they spent about a week getting a feel for each other while rehearsing along the white sandy beaches of southeastern Florida. Through some old contacts, Tim was able to arrange for a rehearsal for Shadows owner Bob Cavallo in D.C., and off they went in Jim's Pontiac Tempest. But the pressure of the situation and not playing live with the new lineup got to all three of them, and they crashed and burned in front of Cavallo. They sang poorly, and Cavallo was put off by Cass' obesity. But, when this door of opportunity slammed shut, a window quickly flew open. Bill Cosby's manager, Roy Silver, just so happened to be hanging out in the club during the audition and saw their potential. Silver had worked under Albert Grossman and was currently partners with Fred Weintraub in the Bitter End club in Greenwich Village. With the folk boom at its crest, Silver was always on the lookout for talented new acts and approached Tim about managing them the following day. Tim was keenly aware that his group needed professional management if they were to succeed and easily convinced the others to sign on with him. The first thing Silver did was change their name from the difficult-to-spit-out and hard-to-spell Triumvirate to the Big 3. The second thing he did was get them booked at the Bitter End.

In New York, their fortunes changed considerably. Fred Weintraub was so impressed by what he'd heard that, for much of the summer of 1963, the Big 3 were the house band for the Bitter End, and, with the new lineup firmly up to speed, they were one of the tightest and hottest folk groups in the Village. Their repertoire expanded as did their friendships and connections. Cass made the most of the former by forging lifelong friendships with Denny Doherty, Zal Yanovsky, and just about every other starving up-and-comer in the Village. The Big 3 made use of their Bitter End residency by signing a record deal with the tiny local FM label run by former Weavers manager Pete Kameron. Over the summer they recorded their debut album, which saw release in October and included their debut single, and signature tune, "The Banjo Song," a remarkable souped-up arrangement of "Oh Susannah" that highlighted Tim and Cass' remarkable vocal chemistry.

From there, they made the familiar rounds of TV shows, including appearances on *Hootenanny* and *Merv Griffin's Talent Scouts*. And they truly were the envy of their contemporaries when they were invited to perform on the fresh and hip *Tonight Show Starring Johnny Carson* in September. In December, they performed two songs on the *Danny Kaye Show*, where the veteran comedian/host recounted personally seeing them perform at the Bitter End and being blown away. Before that, however, they joined up for the November Hootenanny Tour, but on a different leg than the Journeymen and Halifax Three. They toured with Les Baxter's Balladeers, featuring a 22-year-old David Crosby, black folk duo Joe & Eddie, and Philadelphia folk chanteuse Raun McKinnon. Their tour was slightly less traumatic than John, Denny, and Michelle's experience but still came face-to-face with the ugliness of segregation and the bravery of civil rights activists and was similarly disrupted by JFK's assassination. Despite this, things seemed to be looking up for the Big 3. The only thing they lacked was a hit.

There were chinks in the armor, however, and they began showing themselves on that tour. In a short period of time, Cass had become the group's rabble-rouser. Along with David Crosby, she spent most of her downtime playing pranks, being a jokester, and smoking pot. Crosby was young and brash, even during his pre-fame days, and could easily rub people the wrong way, particularly an equally confident and headstrong colleague in Tim Rose. Also, in a very short period of time, Tim, like many young folk musicians, became a folk elitist, and his bandmates were not exempt from his snootiness. He also struggled mightily with Cass being the most popular in the group even though she was truly gifted. Tim's change in attitude drew Cass closer to the much quieter and confident Jim, who could often be found on the tour bus sitting quietly and reading a book. Their friendship grew deeper after Jim's military draft deferment expired when the draft board was notified that he'd quit his teaching job. Being the ultimate team player, Cass married him civilly so that he could renew the deferment, but their relationship remained strictly platonic.

Come spring 1964, the Big 3 recorded their second, and final, album at Gotham Studios, in the heart of Midtown Manhattan, which, at the time, predominantly served as the New York studio for Elektra Records. Tensions were high from the get-go. Cass acted completely like a diva and rubbed everybody from Tim to Roy Silver to the studio musicians and staff the wrong way. She'd typically arrive over an hour late every day and couldn't sing until she finished eating and only until she no longer felt full. Then the bickering would begin between her and Tim over arrangements and who would sing which part. By the time the album was issued in June, the Big 3 were no more, breaking up backstage after finishing a gig in Fall River, Massachusetts, in April. The writing was on the wall for folk following the arrival of the Beatles back in February, and nobody welcomed it more than Cass. She'd been ready to move on and was more interested in hanging out with her folk expatriate friends in Greenwich Village. She bought in to the group from the beginning and when they debuted on the *The Ed Sullivan Show* in February, she threw a big viewing party at her apartment, where her guests included Denny Doherty, Jim Hendricks, and Zal Yanovsky. Cass was the first to really vocalize forming a rock and roll group with her talented friends and kickstarted the Mugwumps experiment that had a promising start but ultimately fizzled out at the Peppermint Lounge.

As Denny went off to join John and Michelle Phillips in the New Journeymen and John Sebastian and Zal formed the Lovin' Spoonful, Cass got together Jim, drummer Sticks Evans, and ex–Modern Folk Quartet members Jerry Yester and Henry Diltz and kept her rock and roll dream alive. With the help of Erik Jacobson, they recorded several electrified demos, including a version of "The Banjo Song" but were unsatisfied with the results. She was in limbo when Denny introduced her to John and Michelle at their first acid experiment and the foundation of the Mamas & the Papas was unknowingly laid.

After their first get-together at John and Michelle's apartment, Cass had no reason to believe that this was anything more than an introduction to Denny's friends and that there'd be some familiarity if they bumped into each other on the road. As Denny and his new friends were laying down vacation plans, and with no invitation from them forthcoming, Cass wasn't letting any grass grow under her feet. She knew she had the talent and had a voice that could fill a cathedral. Shadows manager Bob Cavallo, who had his heart changed about Cass when he booked the Mugwumps, now believed in her talents and invited her to come down and kick off her career as a jazz soloist at his club. With no other prospects in sight, and being a lover of jazz, Cass headed back home to Washington, D.C., to start over again.

CHAPTER 14:
CREEQUE ALLEY

After a 10-day sojourn to St. Thomas in the U.S. Virgin Islands in January 1965, where John, Michelle, and Denny spent a resplendent vacation in a mountainside hotel, sunning, swimming, and getting high, the trio were keen on returning but this time with a feast of friends and to stay for as long as possible. They returned to cold New York to honor an appearance on Oscar Brand's Canadian folk variety program *Let's Sing Out*, and a few other dates, but it served more as a time to regroup, recruit, and repack for an indefinite stay in the Virgin Islands beginning in a couple weeks.

While in Charlotte Amalie, the largest city in St. Thomas, John scouted out the best place for them to stay for an extended period of time and get the most bang for their buck. The answer lay on the neighboring island of St. John, where 60 percent of the protected, undeveloped land is composed of Laurence Rockefeller's Virgin Islands National Park. Camping is only permitted at the northern part of the island on Cinnamon Bay Campground, which offered tents, cottages, tent-covered platforms, or bare sites for about $30 a month. In this tropical campground, John and his coterie could rent snorkeling equipment, kayaks, and sailboats, walk the numerous hiking trails and admire the beautiful landscape and breathtaking views of the bay and its neighboring waters.

Back in New York, John, Michelle, and Denny were making their plans and only had a couple weeks to get everything organized. Michelle and Denny headed to a military surplus store on 3rd Avenue and purchased tents, cots, blankets, portable Coleman stoves, and any other creature comfort they could think of that might make living outdoors for several months a little more bearable. The biggest items purchased were two Yamaha 125 YA-6 Santa Barbara motorcycles, with the new "Autolube" feature, that retailed about $350 each so they could scoot about the island freely. They also procured enough drugs to get them through the vacation, including lots of marijuana and 50 hits of acid, which John stowed away in his green Gucci medicine bag.

They invited some of their closest friends to join them, which included New Journeymen accompanist Eric Hord, now known as "the Doctor" because of his meticulously skilled handling of their instruments, and his girlfriend Davine. Michelle reached out to her sister Rusty and her boyfriend Peter Pilafian, who had given up on New York City and retreated to L.A. They were up for it but only had four days to drive coast-to-coast, which they did in a Philadelphia-bound Driveaway car that they delivered the day of the flight. Denny was sent to meet them at the car depot and bring them to JFK International Airport in New York where they arrived a couple hours before takeoff. John also financed a large shipping container, through the airline, that held all their camping equipment, the two Yamahas, and myriad instruments, as they planned on making use of this time away developing a new sound.

Before heading off to the airport, John and Michelle handed the keys to their apartment on East 7th and Avenue D to Scott McKenzie and his girlfriend, who had agreed to sublet it for as long as they were away. Scott's debut solo single on Capitol, a cover of British singer Mike Hurst's "Look in Your Eyes," had just been released but was going nowhere. A couple hours later, John, Michelle, Denny, Eric, Davine, Peter, Rusty, and Michelle's poodle Maud boarded a Pan Am flight at JFK. Their money was abundant and flowing freely. Peter arrived with a newly purchased upright bass and, since their container had already been loaded, John kindly purchased an additional plane ticket for his instrument. They flew to Philadelphia International Airport, where they caught a connection to St. Thomas. During the layover, John was reunited with his five-year-old daughter, Laura, who flew up by herself from Washington National. Only the night before, on a whim, he called Susie and asked if their youngest child could join them, to which she consented even though John was routinely late with child support and hadn't lived up to his commitment of being more involved.

After a five-hour flight, the group landed at Harry S. Truman Airport
in West Charlotte Amalie to pleasant mid-80s tropical temperatures, surrounded by sun, sand, surf, and palm trees. They were as good as a million
miles away from cold, gloomy Greenwich Village, where all their musical
dreams appeared to be dying before them. They made their way down to the
waterfront and boarded the public ferry to St. John, which disembarked at the
Cruz Bay ferry dock where they most likely took taxis to the Cinnamon Bay
Campgrounds, about a 15-minute drive through the dry forests that made up
most of the island. They arrived none too soon, as all the prime camping sites
had already been rented, and they were forced to take a bare site way down on
the opposite end of the beach close to a mosquito bog. For $30 a month, the
entire group was able to come and go as they pleased in their own makeshift
home on the beach, and, in no particular order, began getting high, unpack-
ing, setting up, swimming, and relaxing.

John and Michelle had the largest tent, which was an embryonic hippie
pad in which they were shielded from the sand and dirt by an Oriental rug,
along with a couple of cots, and several candles strategically strewn about by
Michelle to provide a stylishly peaceful atmosphere and keep the bugs away.
Laura was situated close by in a pup tent that had considerably less ambiance.
In fact, she was being constantly bitten by bugs and getting freaked out by
large spiders and ended up most nights with John and Michelle.

Although they were in an idyllic setting, there were plenty of negatives,
which almost seemed to outweigh the benefits at times. Mosquitoes were
plentiful and much larger than those found in the United States. In addition
to living with sand everywhere and dealing with the tropical humidity, they
had to share the beach, and surrounding woods, with tarantulas, scorpions,
snakes, frogs, iguanas, lizards, mongoose, wild donkeys, and several other
indigenous and imported species that were uncommon sights in most of
North America. But, the mosquitoes were no doubt the worst and nobody
suffered worse than Davine, who was allergic to mosquito bites. On the beach,
Laura came close to suffering a scorpion's sting as one crawled toward her
bare foot, but the scorpion's life was snuffed out by the accurate downward
thrust of a piece of driftwood yielded by Denny. And then there was the heat.
St. John averages pleasant temperatures in the high 80s and low 90s all year
round, but it can make countless days without air-conditioning and nights
sleeping outside very uncomfortable, especially after the new wears off. All

these idiosyncrasies, which nobody had anticipated, earned their campground the nickname Camp Torture.

But it wasn't all bad. It hardly ever rained, and the gang spent their days
waking up to coconut daiquiris, barbecuing, snorkeling, hiking, skinny-
dipping, and admiring the beautiful tropical sunsets that only a Caribbean
island could provide. And, of course, there was also singing. John was
constantly noodling on his guitar and coming up with new songs and new
arrangements to ones already written like "California Dreamin'" and "Go
Where You Wanna Go" and assigning parts and leading singalongs on the
beach. To really get in the island spirit, they'd rent a catamaran or trimaran,
multihulled passenger boats designed for safe sailing for novices, and drift
around St. John through the night, close to shore, stargazing on acid.

In this tropical paradise, Michelle's beauty shone brightly, and fellow
campers surely must've taken notice of her moving about in bathing suits,
T-shirts, and jean cutoffs. But the one who took the most notice was Denny
and his infatuation with his friend's wife soon found him wading into dangerous waters. He'd been taken by Michelle's waifish, youthful beauty since
the first time he saw her aboard the Hootenanny tour bus nearly two years
earlier, but on St. John, he saw a lot more of her than he'd ever dreamed and
got to know her on a deeper level. He couldn't help but admire her fair skin
glistening in the azure blue waters of Cinnamon Bay and how the sun shone
on her long blonde hair. The feeling was mutual. Michelle, who'd never really
looked at Denny in a sexual way, was getting a new perspective on the handsome 24-year-old tenor, who she now saw more as a young Errol Flynn. As
she watched the fit, young singer frolic on the beach athletically and often
shirtless, the words of Cass Elliot began ringing in her head.

"Isn't he the grooviest?"

Soon, soft glances between the two turned into meaningful exchanges of
something more carnal, all under John's unwitting nose. As the days and
weeks wore on, their silent, unconsummated love affair intensified and
the two got bolder, playing footsie underneath the picnic tables even with
John and others present. Their physicality got ratcheted up even further
when Michelle began casually sitting on Denny's lap or lying next to him
on a hammock, getting comfortable with the touch of each other's skin.
And whenever the coast was clear, small kisses were often stolen. Under
ordinary circumstances this type of flirtation could be dangerous, but

along the shores of the Caribbean, among the LSD and marijuana, it passed unnoticed.

With John completely wrapped up in figuring out ways to adapt his music to fit 1965 standards, and with everybody in state of perpetual psychedelic haze, Denny and Michelle stole away on their Yamahas to nearby Caneel Bay. It was the only place on the island where campers could get a dose of civilization and enjoy North American amenities, provided by Laurance Rockefeller's Rock Resorts. The picturesque beaches included plenty of fine dining and tiki bars where they imbibed rum and Coke and LSD and ventured into the warm waters, where they imbibed each other. Under the guise of snorkeling one afternoon, the would-be lovebirds got more acquainted with one another until, overcome by the seriousness of what they were attempting, they came to their senses and retreated, albeit temporarily.

While Michelle was drifting back into unhealthy extramarital habits, John was in another world working on songs and arrangements and coming up with three-part harmonies better suited to a pop audience. And for the first time in his musical career he had to consider arrangements for bass, guitar, and drums, which caused him to be even more meticulous and easily frustrated. But, as immersed as he was, John was still in vacation mode, and the practical application of his new musical approach wouldn't take place until desperation kicked in. Around April, the money had just about run out. Over the period they'd been in St. John, a few more friends had joined them, which drove expenses up. Feeding everybody daily, plus paying for campground and boat rentals, gasoline for the motorcycles, and the money spent on supplies, airfare, a shipping container, and daily odds and ends, had substantially drained the coffers. Perhaps even worse for all those involved was that the acid and grass had nearly run out. The 50 hits they packed didn't last very long.

John, the leader of this assorted gaggle of family, friends, and acidheads, knew they needed income and figured the best way was through music. One afternoon, he hopped the ferry back to Charlotte Amalie, St. Thomas, and headed down to the waterfront, where there was a small music scene. The main clubs and bars were on Main Street in the center of town, and included long-established clubs like Trader Dan's, Rocky's Waterfront Bar, the Sand Box, Upchucks, and the most popular, Sparky's Waterfront Saloon. Although the landscape may not have been as vast and crowded as Greenwich Village, the laid-back sun-bleached atmosphere rivaled the Village's sense of bohe-mia. A variety of locals, tourists, mainland transplants, priests, prostitutes, and general ne'er-do-wells populated these establishments and intertwined within this whole scene were old alleyways that connected the waterfront to Main Street that were originally designed to carry ship cargo and pirate booty to warehouses located farther inland. Entrenched in these alleys were other shops and side entrances for many of the taverns that dominated Main Street.

On this particular day, John happened down Creque Alley, which con-nected the waterfront to Sparky's Waterfront Tavern's Main Street entrance. Above it was a club called Duffy's, which was owned by New York native Hugh Duffy. It was situated in a vast upstairs loft that included three bars, a discotheque, and an 11-room boardinghouse. Duffy, an island denizen, got to know the U.S. Virgin Islands, and many of its Caribbean neighbors, during his 13-year tenure as a merchant marine, during which he mostly sailed from New York to Cuba and back. He'd also worked in the restaurant and bar scene in New York in various capacities before settling in St. Thomas, where he opened his first bar. Inspired by Bar Dos Hermanos in Havana, which had a wildly eclectic mix of patrons, Duffy jumped into the Charlotte Amalie club scene and rented the space above Sparky's in 1964. Although John Phillips claims he inspired Duffy to feature live music, Duffy came up with that idea on his own. Only the summer before, Duffy's featured live music nightly courtesy of a local band called the Urchins, which featured 17-year-old Scott Fagan, who'd go on to record the cult classic solo LP *South Atlantic Blues* in 1968.

John wandered up to Duffy's, which was virtually dead inside, particularly compared to what was going on below at Sparky's, where a pretty tight rock and roll band from New Jersey had the crowd jumping nightly with Beatles, Beach Boys, and Motown covers. Scanning around the empty bars and guest rooms in the fledgling club, and sensing Duffy's frustration, he seized the opportunity and offered him his band from New York who were just across the bay at St. John and could play rock and roll. It was a bold offer for John, as his group hadn't formally rehearsed in months and didn't have all the neces-sary instruments required to play rock and roll, but he persisted, nonetheless. All Duffy heard was "a band from New York" and "rock and roll music," and he said yes immediately and, since it was the off-season, agreed to put John and his group up in his rooms as part of their compensation in addition to

$165 a week. On the surface, everybody got something out of this deal, but now John had to get to work.

He arrived back at Camp Torture later that night and filled everybody in on their financial situation and laid out the change of plans. The next morning, they packed everything up and moved into Duffy's boardinghouse on St. Thomas. In the atmosphere that surrounded Creeque Alley, John knew a folk rehash wouldn't bring anybody in and, in his mind, he acquiesced to the electric band he promised Duffy. He still held rock and roll in contempt but was desperate. Denny, a true rock fan with Mugwumps experience under his belt, did his best to guide him. They needed instruments. Electric instruments. Although they'd packed plenty of acoustic guitars and Denny's electric bass, they had nothing else: no electric guitars, no amplifiers, no drums and no drummer. Peter Pilafian offered that he had played drums in a jazz combo in college for two weeks and got the job. Duffy helped by giving John his son's 1962 Fender Musicmaster. The Doctor was given the role of lead guitarist and scrounger. He combed the entire island in search of the missing pieces and managed to bring back a drum set and two Silvertone guitars from a music shop run by local musician Bill La Motta.

They began rehearsing in Duffy's, in late April or early May, where they started from scratch. John was in uncharted waters. Rock and roll tempo was completely foreign to him, and getting everything in sync was arduous, especially given the fact that Denny was not a very proficient musician and Peter was hardly one at all. Eric was the best musician out of all of them but, since his specialty was guitar, all he could do was advise the rhythm section. Also, John still considered rock and roll vastly inferior to folk, so he was initially involved only under duress. They rehearsed a few standards like "Searchin'," "Twist and Shout," and "Walk Don't Run," and new arrangements of some old Journeymen songs, as well as the arrangement of "Mr. Tambourine Man" that they'd recorded as a demo back in January, but John's arrangement was already outdated.

"It's got to have a backbeat. We've got to slow it down and give it a backbeat," Denny offered.

"What does that even mean?" a frustrated John asked in reply.

Nobody was really having any fun, and not one of them could've possibly imagined anything fruitful coming from this until Denny visited Duffy's jukebox one afternoon. Duffy always kept it well-stocked and up-to-date, and his latest shipment included a new Columbia Records release that was shooting up the charts in the United States. It was their old friend Jim McGuinn and his new band, the Byrds, with their sophisticated arrangement of "Mr. Tambourine Man." It was the first significant American response to the British Invasion, and the timing couldn't have been more serendipitous. They brought John over, turned the jukebox up as loud as it could go, and put a dime in it. He recognized his old friend's vocals blaring out of the speaker and couldn't believe his ears. He was hypnotized.

"Ahh . . . so that's it," was all he could muster as the light of his imagination finally clicked on.

Walking around St. Thomas, John, Michelle, Denny, and their companions got the full experience of the U.S. Virgin Islands and took in its unique blend of West Indian culture and Old-World European resplendence. The passage of time had barely touched the 32 square miles that were first inhabited by the Ciboney people in 1500 BCE who were followed by the Arawaks and later the Caribs. After Christopher Columbus discovered it in the name of the Western World in 1493, it become a haven for pirates and remained untouched by European influence for nearly two more centuries until a post was established by the Dutch West India Company in 1657. Nine years later, it was overtaken by the Dutch. Under their rule, the culture flourished and the seaside capital, Charlotte Amalie, the name of King Christian V's wife, was established. The Danes declared it a free port and, soon thereafter, Danish, American, British, German, French, Italian, and Sephardic travelers and inhabitants all melted into one society. When slavery was abolished in 1848, African and black Caribbean influence permeated the island's culture more freely.

Although the island was a progressive melting pot, symbols of its past lingered majestically, becoming a cornerstone of its fabric. Just a stone's throw away from Duffy's stands St. Thomas' oldest structure, the Old Danish settlement Fort Christian, which overlooks the harbor, and, in 1965, it served as the police station and prison. To the north, along the rolling hills that ornamented the small island, rested Blackbeard's Castle and its imposing 40-foot tower, where it's believed the ruthless pirate searched for targets along the horizon and easily spotted enemy ships entering the harbor. Moving about town, they walked up and down the charming cobblestone alleyways that snaked between the main thoroughfares and still went by their original Danish names. Duffy's was located on Dronningens Gade.

In 1917, the United States purchased St. Thomas, St. John, and St. Croix for $25 million and officially made them U.S. territories in 1954. Although it had become a vacation spot with the increase of leisure travel around the turn of the century, tourism to St. Thomas received a boon when the United States enacted an embargo against Cuba in 1960 after Fidel Castro took over several U.S.-owned oil refineries without compensation thus severing itself from its Caribbean counterparts. By the time John, Michelle, and Denny arrived in the spring of 1965, Charlotte Amalie was growing in terms of hotels and resorts but managed to maintain a very small, hometown feel to it, like what one might encounter in the United States but with a heavy dose of Caribbean flamboyance and color. In the mid-1960s, the locals referred to Charlotte Amalie as "town" because it was indeed the only real municipality on the island and resembled any small town in North America. There were two drugstores, several restaurants, two butcher shops, and a bakery right on Main Street. The only movie theater in town, the Center Theater, debuted the movie of the week on Sunday afternoons, and kids played safely and freely in Emancipation Gardens diagonally across the street from Fort Christian. And most shopping by the locals was done at one of three department stores: La Gracia, Lockhart's, or Hays. For simple groceries, the only game in town was Chinnery's Food-o-Mat unless you wanted fresh fare, like seafood and produce, and went to the outdoor Market Square. In fact, everything was so close-knit that most inhabitants had no need for a car.

John, Michelle, Denny, and their companions seemed to fit right into Charlotte Amalie's eclectic environment. The laid-back tropical milieu combined with their circumstances contributed to what would become the Mamas & the Papas look. Money was tight and getting tighter every day, which led to five o'clock shadows on the men, long, straight, untouched hair on the women, and dirty clothes on all. But it seemed to go unnoticed when they first arrived in town, where the gaggle of unkempt twentysomethings were just brushed off as mainland tourists. As everybody settled into Duffy's loft, the excitement was buzzing. Not only did they have a place to sleep indoors and shower, they were going to ply their trade and entertain a new audience in a tropical setting.

Because of the excitement and confusion that surrounded the new sound, John hardly put in any time thinking of a new group name, so they still went by the New Journeymen. They spent the early days of June rehearsing new material and helping Duffy build a suitable stage and do a little redecorating, covering the tables in burlap and sackcloth topped with candles to create a more intimate mood. John was really buzzing now that he had some sense of direction and was putting a solid set list together. He now happily added Beatles songs to their repertoire, including both sides of their latest hit single, "Ticket to Ride." This renewed sense of dedication to his music and his quest to perfect it consumed most of his time while in St. Thomas, and his focus became singular. The times when Michelle was able to pull him away from it were spent on catamaran rentals and hanging out on the public beaches, all while tripping, but he still had his guitar with him. Drugs and money were getting tight, though, and these carefree days of boating and tripping were nearing their end when one unnamed member of the group came up with the idea of growing marijuana in a few of the waterfront planters that decked the shoreline just outside of Creeque Alley. The plant blended well with the hibiscus and bougainvillea that splashed the island with color and helped keep them self-medicated.

One early afternoon while taking a break, John, Denny, Michelle, and a few others were relaxing on the beach, sustaining their highs as best they could when, off in the distance, two figures ventured closer and closer. One was male and the other a female and the nearer they came the more Denny took notice. The female looked incredibly familiar. She stood about 5'5" and was portly and round. Suddenly, Denny jumped up and shouted.

"I don't believe my fucking eyes! It's Cass!"

They all rans toward her and gathered around her like she'd just touched home plate after hitting a game-winning homerun. It was a grand reunion on the beaches of St. Thomas. Cass was her usual effervescent self despite having had her pockets picked at some point between the airport and the beach. Her companion was none other than John's nephew Billy Throckmorton Jr., who had gotten to know Cass back in D.C. They joined forces and came together to St. Thomas. The circumstances were incredibly unbelievable, and spirits got even higher was Cass presented them with a vial filled with liquid Sandoz LSD. One drop on the tongue did the trick, and they had enough to sustain them for months. Denny told Cass about what they'd been up to at Duffy's and invited her to bunk with him for as long she stayed.

Cass was thrilled simply being in Denny's presence. The last two months had only managed to intensify her unrequited love for him. As Denny, John, and Michelle had prepared for a vacation back in January, Cass had gone back to the Shadows in D.C. with owner Bob Cavallo acting as her manager. She put together a nightly supper club act with pianist Martin Siegel and, when she wasn't onstage, answered phones in the club's back office and helped with books. She'd also pushed her pride aside and moved back into her mother's basement. Although her act was mature and well-received, it was a personal low point for her, and her main source of solace, Denny, was incommunicado. Cavallo pressed on and went next level when he booked her in the swanky Bon Soir cabaret in Greenwich Village where Barbra Streisand had launched her career several years earlier. He sent Cass to a vocal coach in New York and invited the who's who of New York music press, but her performance was a disaster. She was visibly nervous, off-key, and behind on just about every note. She went home devastated and less certain of her future than ever despite Cavallo's reassurances. All she could think about was Denny and wanted to be near him as quickly as possible. She thought back to winter when he paid her a visit before heading off to St. Thomas, along with John and Michelle, and all she could think about was him being on an island with a beautiful blonde. Even 1,600 miles away, Cass' sixth sense could sense something simmering between the two of them. She decided to catch the first plane to Charlotte Amalie and went to talk to her friend, and Shadows office manager Stephen Sanders, who'd recently come into a big inheritance. He gave her the money for a round-trip ticket, and off she went with Billy Throckmorton in tow.

After hugs and a little chat, they headed back to Duffy's where Cass ingratiated herself to the owner by asking him to stick out his tongue. Duffy was a pretty loose cat, so he chuckled and obliged. She placed a drop of acid on it and, a short while later, he was tripping. John's five-year-old daughter, Laura, followed after Duffy and reassured him that the sun would indeed rise tomorrow. Cass doled out acid to everybody each morning as if it were their daily bread. There was hardly a day when the entire group, save Rusty, who was pregnant, wasn't tripping.

Over the next few days, the rehearsals continued, but there was no invitation for Cass to jump in from John. He'd had a vision in his head of where this was going and what it was going to look like, and she wasn't part of it. Michelle was to be the centerpiece, and, in his mind, Cass was too fat to even be considered. He never gave a second thought to the fact that her voice could stop traffic. Cass was excited by what she'd heard even with the limitations caused by Silvertone guitars and Peter Pilafian's drumming. The Journeymen were beloved by the heady and intellectual folk set and she knew that, if John Phillips was involved, it would be, at worst, well done and, at best, a smash success. Everyone involved tried reasoning with John about including Cass, but he wouldn't hear of it. Cass, who was never shy, pitched John constantly about how valuable her contribution would be, but it was no use. He gave professional excuses, saying that he didn't want to rewrite his arrangements to suit a quartet and that her contralto didn't fit the sound he had in his mind, but, below the surface, her dominant personality and outward appearance really got under his skin. Not even Denny could change his mind.

"Her eyes are too close together," John confided to him. "And she smells!"

John wanted a group that not only sounded like an electrified Peter, Paul and Mary, but also looked like them and would attract the attention of labels and promoters. Cass threatened that. In the face of mounting pressure from Denny and Michelle, John was steadfast in his decision. As long as he was the musical brains behind this project, she was out, but she wouldn't take no for an answer. She joined them at rehearsals at Duffy's and on the beach when they'd sing around a campfire and offered plenty of criticism and critique, which further grated on John's nerves. As the debut at Duffy's drew ever closer, Cass and Rusty got jobs waiting tables to bring in some much-needed income and, for Cass, to be closer to the action onstage.

With the relocation to St. Thomas, the rehearsals at Duffy's and Cass' surprise arrival all occurring in relatively short order, one might think the silent love affair brewing between Michelle and Denny would have been stifled, but it only served to make it more thrilling and erotic. It reached its boiling point on the island one afternoon when all four ventured out to the harbor docks on the waterfront that ran alongside Veterans Drive to take their daily dose of

CHAPTER 14: CREEQUE ALLEY

LSD. To everyone's shock, Denny suddenly jumped into the filthy, oil-slicked waters of the harbor.

"Come on in! The water's fine!" he shouted to the others.

Only Michelle followed. Fully clothed and soaking wet, they waded next to one another, grinning from ear to ear, urging the other two to join them. Clearly unamused and uninterested in swimming in dirty water, Cass and John picked up and went home. Denny and Michelle were alone and together for the first time since St. John, so they spent the afternoon flirting and hanging out on the docks with some locals Denny had befriended. It was later in the evening when they decided to head back to Duffy's. Walking slowly down Creeque Alley, Denny found a quiet, isolated spot and seductively pressed Michelle up against the rustic brick wall and landed a long, wet kiss right on her lips. She didn't necessarily escalate the passion by kissing back, but she didn't resist either. It just sort of happened, and both enjoyed it. After a longing gaze, they both understood that's as far as it was going tonight and walked back to their rooms at Duffy's. Both knew full well where this was heading.

Michelle had been down this road before, and it didn't go so well. John was very intelligent, and she understood he'd only remain clueless for so long. Although she was enticed and excited by Denny's kiss, she felt uneasy enough about it to confide in John about her feelings. She was either seeking his counsel or subconsciously priming him for the inevitable. A couple days later, she finally worked up the courage to tell him while they were alone in their room. John was preoccupied writing a song and noodling on his guitar when she approached him.

"John, I feel a strong attraction to Denny, and I think it's unhealthy for us to all live together," she said.

"What are you talking about?" John asked sharply. "You're my wife, he's my best friend!"

Sensing that he was getting agitated, she did her best to quell any tension.

"Oh, we didn't do anything. Don't be angry. I'm just trying to be honest. We sat on the rocks and the water came rushing up and the sun went down, and the night fell and it was all so . . ."

"Romantic?" John finished.

Although he felt like he'd been punched in the stomach, as he was with the Russ Titleman revelation, he didn't let on.

"Don't be ridiculous. Denny has no interest in you, Mitch."

Conversation over. Michelle let it go but inside she was incensed over John's attempt to minimize her concerns. In her mind, she made a valiant attempt to stop a problem before it started, although she conveniently omitted the kiss part. John hadn't taken it seriously, which, to her, symbolized a green light to continue tempting fate with Denny and reopened the chasm that once existed between her and John.

As the summer grew late, the big debut at Duffy's finally arrived. Other than being the first time John, Michelle, Denny, and Cass sang together, there wasn't anything monumental about their performance of mostly Beatles covers. And, even though all four were together, Cass still hadn't been invited. She and Rusty had taken waitressing jobs to provide some much-needed income, and she'd sing along from the floor in between orders. The audience grew larger as Naval seamen and Marines arrived on liberty from fleet oilers like the USS *Mississinewa* and USS *Truckee*. They had their biggest audience when the USS *Boxer*, an aircraft carrier that doubled as a troop transporter, came into port carrying troops back from Vietnam. Young, battle-weary, and crass, many of the patrons blew off energy ridiculing Cass.

"Hey fatty! You forgot our orders, or did you eat them all yourselves?"

"Hey fatty, get the hell over here!"

Cass took it in stride and never let them see her sweat, but Rusty let them have it whenever she heard them. Cass had heard it all her life, but it was humiliating nevertheless, especially with the beautiful Michelle onstage next to the love of her life. Still, she kept singing and could be heard over the other three's amplified voices, but that's as far as it would go until fate intervened. One afternoon before showtime, Duffy was having his ice machine removed in order to make more room for patrons. He and a couple men disconnected the copper coil from the back and one of them tossed it down a stairwell that led up from the alleyway just as Cass was walking up it. It hit her square on the head and knocked her out cold. Someone called an ambulance, and Cass was carried off in front of a large group of curious onlookers. A worried Denny escorted her to the hospital. When she came to, all fears were dashed, as she immediately tried to get him to crawl in bed with her. From this incident, John and the others invented the apocryphal story that somehow getting hit on the head increased Cass' octave range, which eventually caused John to put her in the band.

Eventually though, John did relent and allowed her to come on the stage a couple times, but it was all short-lived. Even though there was a sense of growing camaraderie and excitement in the music for the New Journeymen, for Duffy, the whole situation was a complete disaster. The entire clan was seriously draining his finances, and he could no longer afford to house them, especially with tourism season around the corner. The stress caused him to have a minor heart attack, so, in July, John relocated everybody to a rental house at the foot of Bunker Hill, where they lived for the remainder of their stay. Their tenure at Duffy's came to an unceremonious end in early August when the local fire marshal dropped by for a surprise inspection and deemed the tablecloths and candles to be a fire hazard and shut it down immediately.

Around that time, John received a frantic correspondence from his ex-wife Susie inquiring about Laura's welfare. Apparently, in all the time he was there getting high, working on music, and forgetting about time, he never once checked in to update her. Laura was five and had to fend for herself because everybody was too busy tripping or concerned about their own affairs to mind her. She took to panhandling servicemen to pay for her meals and even convinced one to buy her a new pair of shoes. So, even with the money drying up, John put Laura on a one-way flight back to D.C. The writing was on the wall. The money had run out, and John knew full well he wouldn't be able to pay rent or, for that matter, fly everybody back home. One afternoon, John took the ferry to St. John to try and get a $500 cash advance from the American Express office on Caneel Bay but had his card confiscated and destroyed due to an extremely large unpaid balance. Things were really looking dire. They had open tabs at the pharmacies, the grocery store, and even a local seamstress John and Michelle had commissioned to put together stage outfits for the group. He took Michelle and Denny to the Mermaid Café and laid it all out plainly to all of them.

"We cannot stay," he said. "This is the end of paradise. It's over. We have to get back and get to work."

They went back to the house and broke the news to everyone else. Cass took it so poorly that she put her fist through a plate glass window, which required stitches and racked up two more bills. A couple of days later, she and Billy Throckmorton put their round-trip tickets to use and flew home. And just in time. The local authorities were beginning to have their fill of these interloping tourists, and things took a turn for the worse when Michelle got arrested after speeding around town on a Yamaha with no plates. The officer, a Sgt. Hershey, initially was going to let Michelle off with a warning but, when she kept insisting it was a case of mistaken identity, Michelle lost her temper and ended up in a cell in Fort Christian for disturbing the peace. John bailed her out, but she was fined for the plates and received a notice to appear in court in two weeks for pleading not guilty to the disturbing the peace charge. Another bill.

"We have to get out of here," he told her as they were leaving. "Things are somehow catching up with us."

Just like that, paradise became a nightmare from which they needed to escape as quickly and as stealthily as possible. They began selling off all their camping gear and instruments with the exception of the Fender. One Yamaha was impounded, and whatever became of the other one has been lost to history, so they couldn't benefit from their sale, which would've brought in enough to get everybody home. Instead, all they had from the proceeds of their rummage sale was $150, not enough for 10 airfares. Things got hotter for them when a nephew of St. Thomas' governor, Ralph Moses Paiewonsky, who'd been hanging out with John and company returned home in the middle of a bad LSD trip, causing his parents to think he'd gone insane. When the drug finally wore off, he quickly pointed the finger at his now-former friends and Gov. Paiewonsky gave them 24 hours to get off the island, unaware of the massive debts they'd accrued.

Since John was in charge, he laid out the plan. First, they would catch the earliest flight they could, and, second, they'd travel to the airport in small groups so as not to attract attention. More importantly, the airline would be unable to do a credit check on John at that time of day. He caught a break when one unsuspecting Caribair attendant accepted a check and issued everybody tickets. The only problem was the farthest they could get was Puerto Rico, but it was off St. Thomas and good enough. As they headed toward the terminal, they bumped into Sgt. Hershey. Michelle thought for sure they'd be busted for skipping town with unpaid bills, but he inexplicably let them pass. As the plane lifted off the runway, headed for San Juan, everybody breathed a sigh of relief, but it was only temporary. They still had to figure out how to get home.

Upon landing at Puerto Rico National Airport 30 minutes later, John headed to the Pan Am counter and attempted to get them to accept a personal check for another round of 10 one-way tickets to New York and was denied. Despite his efforts to sound important by talking to manager after manager and then the supervisor, he was laughed away. He gathered the group and told them they were stuck. They had less than $50. The idea of calling parents and asking for the fare crossed more than one mind but John presented another, albeit more desperate, option.

"There's only one thing we can do with this money that makes any kind of sense. We have to go to the tables," he told everyone.

Nobody could believe what he said. They were stuck on a distant island with hardly any money, nothing to eat and nowhere to sleep, and he was proposing they gamble away what little capital they had.

"We can't even eat out on $20," he continued. "We have nothing now so we're going to go to the casino and see what happens."

He was right. He couldn't feed 10 people with only $20, and even if he had stretched it, it would only afford them each one measly meal. John and Denny had packed their New Journeymen Brooks Brothers suits, and Michelle had her slinky red onstage dress. Unbathed and stinky, they went to the restrooms and cleaned themselves up as best they could and headed to the casino inside the Caribe Hilton. Denny was too nervous and waited outside. John and Michelle made a beeline for the craps table, an exciting game with the smallest house edge, and waited for a new round.

When it started, it's no surprise the stickman handed the dice to the very fetching Michelle. John put his minimum bet down on the pass line and urged her to roll. She had no idea what she was doing but let them rip and, just like that, John doubled his money on the "come out roll." He breathed a sigh of relief and urged Michelle on her next roll. Michelle had no idea what she was doing but kept rolling the dice with John leaving his money on the Pass Line. And she kept winning. And winning. And winning. The table got louder and louder. It got so loud that Denny came in to see what all the commotion was and came to the table where he observed everybody jumping up and down in excitement, cheering on Michelle.

"Go blondie!" shouted the more serious gamblers who staggered their bets between the Pass, Don't Pass, Field, Come, and all the other lines on the complicated craps board.

In just under an hour, Michelle rolled 17 straight passes and the trio walked away with over $2,000 and a pair of monogramed dice courtesy of the casino. It was enough to fly everybody back to New York first class. As they boarded the plane, the worry and uncertainty melted into relief.

When they got back to Greenwich Village, it was like a ghost town. The once fervent, overcrowded streets were now empty. The young people who flocked in from everywhere to be part of the bustling music scene and the musicians who provided the show were nowhere to be found. Stalwarts like Dave Van Ronk, Phil Ochs, Tim Hardin, and Ramblin' Jack Elliot still lingered but gone were their former bandmates and contemporaries, Jim Hendricks, Zal Yanovsky, John Sebastian, David Crosby, Jim McGuinn, and everybody else. Even Cass was missing in action.

When John and Michelle got back to their apartment, no one was happier to see them than Scott McKenzie, who'd been subletting it since April. He and his girlfriend were in the middle of a terrible fight, and Scott was packing up just as they walked in. Depressed and confused, John and Michelle settled back in after dropping their poodle Maud off at the Animal Medical Center in Manhattan. She'd begun hemorrhaging not long after landing, and they drove straight there. The following morning, they were notified that Maud had died. Michelle took it hard and blamed John.

Listening to the radio over the course of the next week only added to John's frustration and despair but also answered a lot of questions. It seems all their friends had split for California and were having tremendous success. John Sebastian and Zal Yanovsky's new group, the Lovin' Spoonful, had just issued their debut single, "Do You Believe in Magic," which was racing up the charts. It sent John's mind racing back to winter when Sebastian played it for him in their apartment, which ended with a friendly argument over which notes were C-major and C-major 7th. It would hit the Top 10 in a month's time. A week later, another contemporary, Barry McGuire, issued "Eve of Destruction," his first single on the L.A.–based Dunhill label. That would hit number one in September. After hitting number one in both the United States and the United Kingdom with "Mr. Tambourine Man," Jim McGuinn and David Crosby's Byrds issued their follow-up single, another Bob Dylan tune, "All I Really Want to Do." It peaked at a disappointing number 40 but kept them in the charts and on TV. Dylan himself was blowing everybody's minds with his six-minute-plus single "Like a Rolling Stone," which defied all odds and hit number two. But, perhaps most galling of all was former manager Frank

Werber's new group, the We Five, whose debut single, an electrified cover of Ian & Sylvia's "You Were on My Mind," was on its way to peaking at number three. This new music had been dubbed folk-rock by the music press. It got John's blood flowing and heart racing. Had he been away too long? Was it too late to jump aboard this bandwagon? Had he blown his big opportunity? There was only one way to find out. They had to get to L.A. fast.

CHAPTER 15:
CALIFORNIA DREAMIN'
BECOMES A REALITY

In the late summer of 1965, time was running out for John Phillips. He was long on talent but equally long on bullshit, and the latter seemed to be overriding the former. Since launching his professional career in 1959, he'd had a pretty good sense of what was hot musically. He'd anticipated the folk music trend and took advantage of it admirably with the Journeymen, but now he was behind his younger contemporaries. Folk-rock was passing him by and, in retrospect, was one of the most important musical movements of the 20th century. Admittedly, he was late to the party. He tried ignoring the British Invasion. When that didn't work, he belittled it but found himself in the minority. Finally, after witnessing many of his ex-folk brethren embrace and adapt to the new sounds from England, and successfully respond to them, he got on board. He was too remarkable a talent not to be a part of the phenomenon, but he needed time. Much like the early months of 1961, holed up with Scott McKenzie and Dick Weissman, in their Upper West Side apartment, learning folk music, he adjusted in a self-imposed exile and got his folk-rock repertoire together. The Virgin Islands experience served as the beginning of that process, and it continued after getting back to New York.

John had a tremendous backlog of first-rate original songs that fit perfectly into the folk-rock idiom and, over the course of the upcoming weeks and months, would put the finishing touches on them in order to pitch them to prospective labels and compose new ones. Of equal importance was the recognition that the one element that would change his group from average to extraordinary was Cass Elliot. It was becoming ridiculously obvious she wasn't going away.

On returning from St. Thomas, Cass arrived at the same empty Greenwich Village that John, Denny and Michelle did, only a week or so earlier. She wasted no time in getting a line on what was happening. She had a pretty good networking system, which dated back to her days at the *Baltimore Sun*, and through a series of phone calls, was able to locate her former Mugwumps bandmate, and legal husband, Jim Hendricks all the way in Los Angeles. He told her everybody had moved out there. He and his girlfriend Vanessa Ware split for the West Coast back in February in hopes of launching a duet act together and succeeded in getting signed to tiny L.A.-based Chattahoochee label where they released one single in May. It went nowhere but was produced by freelancer and Hollywood hipster Kim Fowley, who'd ingratiated himself to the couple and introduced them to the thriving Sunset Strip music scene. Jim told Cass to come out and stay with them in their one-bedroom apartment off Sunset, and she wasted no time. There was nothing back east for her now. Even her manager Bob Cavallo had moved to L.A. after selling the Shadows to his former bartender Charles Fichman. (*Note: Fichman renamed the club the Cellar Door, and it operated from 1965 to 1981.*) Upset over Denny's rejection in the hospital in Charlotte Amalie, and sick of John's arrogance and Michelle's beauty, Cass took the first flight out and left no forwarding address.

Following the dramatic return from the Caribbean with John and Michelle, it didn't take long for Denny to track Jim down either. As he did with Cass, he filled Denny in on the L.A. scene and invited him out to stay with them too. Denny got excited. Michelle was certainly up for going home to L.A. and it didn't take much for them to convince John. They wasted no time either but since they were broke, they needed a strategy, and, once again, turned to a car delivery service as the best mode of transportation. John and Michelle cleaned themselves up and signed on with a local agency who hooked them up with a barely used Cadillac Fleetwood Series limousine bound for San Francisco. They put down the required $25 deposit and were given seven days and a few hundred dollars to get it there. There was ample room in the limo, so John put out another invitation to whichever friends were left in New York, but only his nephew Billy Throckmorton took advantage. Michelle's sister Rusty had already headed out to L.A. after Peter went to Europe to work in the sound department for the Conrad Rooks film *Chappaqua*. Eric Hord was set to join them but, a couple days before leaving, got arrested for drug possession. On Monday morning, August 9, John, Denny, Michelle and Billy piled into the limousine and set out for San Francisco. In order to make the 3,000-mile trip on the cheap and as quickly as they could, they drove in shifts nonstop and packed only the necessities, which included LSD, Lebanese hash, marijuana, speed, and a few guitars.

All four tripped madly throughout the entire journey, even while driving, which completely enhanced the good vibes. John drove first. Early into his shift he accidentally turned on the windshield wipers, which, under the influence of acid, acted like a Technicolor paintbrush, splashing the most brilliant transparent colors and psychedelic ribbons across the horizon, making everybody giddier. Every 100 miles or so, Denny would remind them that it wasn't even raining but nobody cared. As Michelle and Denny placed flowers in the air vents, the nascent hippie ethos was on full display.

And then there was the music. The various AM Top 40 formats served as their soundtrack and testing grounds for John, Denny, and Michelle as they harmonized joyfully over the amazing batch of songs that made their debut in the summer of 1965. During the drive, Herman's Hermits' second number one hit, the dreadful novelty number "I'm Henry VIII, I Am," was replaced by Sonny & Cher's chart debut, the folk-rockish "I Got You Babe." The musically ambitious, Spectorian arrangement bore all the hallmarks of the current folk-rock trend right down to emulating Jim McGuinn's 12-string Rickenbacker in order to give it a Byrds-ian sound. As Sonny & Cher were as far from being folkies as two could possibly be, it proved just how widespread this musical phenomenon had gotten in a short period of time.

That AM Top 40 on that trip played a significant part in John's continuing conversion process. Blasting out of the speakers were the Rolling Stones' signature tune "(I Can't Get No) Satisfaction" and Dylan's "Like a Rolling Stone." The Beach Boys' chart dominance continued with "California Girls," and DJs kept Phil Spector's Wall of Sound in vogue by flipping over the Righteous Brothers' "Hung on You" and playing their version of the 1950s standard "Unchained Melody" instead. Motown artists were all over the place with the Temptations' "Since I Lost My Baby" and the Supremes' "Nothing but Heartaches" both in the Top 30 and rising. The Four Tops had two songs in the Top 35, "It's the Same Old Song" at number seven and "I Can't Help Myself (Sugar Pie Honey Bunch)" on its way down from two nonconsecutive weeks at number one and the Miracles' monster hit "The Tracks of My Tears" was moving quickly. The Beatles' "Help!" arrived at number 41 with a bullet, on its way to number one, and the Lovin' Spoonful's debut "Do You Believe in Magic" was bubbling just outside of the Top 100.

The music was so contagious, and, in the advent of folk-rock, John had completely bought into it. When the We Five's debut, "You Were On My Mind," came on as the number 33 hit of the week, he thought of the song's producer, and his old Journeymen manager, Frank Werber. His San Francisco office would be their first destination after they dropped the limo off. Surely, he'd appreciate his new songs. But, for now, there was plenty of highway between them and San Francisco. Since they drove nonstop, the time they saved allowed for a few pit stops along the way. They drove through the Rocky Mountains in Colorado, took a stoned-out hike to the bottom of Bryce Canyon in Utah, and tried to repeat their San Juan luck in Las Vegas, but no such luck this time. Whenever John was feeling carnal, which was often, the back of the limo allowed for conjugal visits for him and Michelle, with a bedsheet blocking the partition for some privacy, thus complicating her unspoken love triangle even more. The open space also allowed John to concentrate on writing new songs and arrangements. Along the way, he composed "Straight Shooter," which lyrically proved he was aware, on some level, that there was something going on between Michelle and Denny. Their growing closeness was getting harder to deny.

They made it to San Francisco on Friday, August 13, flat broke. John was forced to phone his mother and ask her to wire him $100 for meals and a room at the International Hotel in Manilatown. He also managed to swipe Scott McKenzie's American Express back in New York and used it to rent a car after dropping off the limo. After getting settled, they walked a short distance to Columbus Tower, home of Frank Werber's offices, and waited for the moody ex-manager in the lobby. Their time together back in 1961 had been difficult and, since Frank held grudges, this was by no means a slam dunk. While waiting, John bumped into his old songwriting buddy the Kingston Trio veteran John Stewart, who was excited to see him. John filled him in on why they were there and what had happened the past few months and the musical awakening he was currently undergoing. He even let him in on the new batch of songs he was getting ready to pitch for Werber and even sang "California Dreamin'" and a few others for him. Stewart was blown away and brought in Don Graham, Werber's chief records promotion man, to hear it, who was also impressed. Even though the songs were gems, Stewart knew John would be a tough sell to Werber, but perhaps he'd be more swayed by Graham's endorsement. Finally, after waiting around for about an hour, it became clear Werber wasn't coming. His old manager was one of the few people who intimidated John, and he hadn't the gumption to walk into his penthouse office demanding he listen to him. Seeing the writing on the wall, John, Michelle, and Denny started packing it in.

"Frank doesn't like me very much," he told Stewart.

Stewart told him that was nonsense. Even if Werber didn't like him, he had an ear for music and knew a hit when he heard one. So, they put John, Denny, and Michelle in a conference room and went to his office to campaign for them. Inside, Werber was hard at work. The Kingston Trio hadn't cracked the Top 40 since "Desert Pete" two years earlier, and he was transitioning into another successful venture, Trident Productions, which was off to a resounding start with his new group the We Five's debut single up 11 spots to number 22 and climbing. Though he still maintained a 1950s beatnik hepster coolness about him, there was nothing cool in his demeanor when they told him John Phillips was on the premises with some new songs.

"Get John Phillips out of this building," he told Stewart and Graham firmly.

"But the songs . . ." Stewart pleaded.

"Frank, this is going to be huge," Graham interrupted.

Werber wouldn't hear it. He had no time for John Phillips.

"Get that drug-addled psychopath out of here right away! I'll call the cops on him!" Werber shouted.

John's reputation preceded him, but, amid all the tension, Stewart and Graham managed to convince Werber to at least say hello, or so they thought. He headed to the conference room, but it was to personally tell John to leave his building. Werber burst in and found him, long-haired and dirty, looking much different than the last time he saw him in a Brooks Brothers suit and an Ivy League haircut. Obviously feigning graciousness, he told John it was good to see him and that John Stewart was pitching him on his new songs but that he wasn't interested. (*Note: In Werber's own words, he said*

*John Stewart presented him with a demo tape of John's new songs, although
that remains unclear especially considering they would've had precious little
time to record them between returning from the Virgin Islands and leaving for
San Francisco.)*

"I believe you're a most talented individual and that's why we took you on
in the first place," he told John. "But I also believe you are also a drag to work
with. A pain in the ass. So I'll tell you what. Before whatever you have sways
me, I'm going to say we're not interested."

Door shut. Time to move on. John, Denny, and Michelle got back in their
rented Ford LTD and headed to L.A. the next day. Since Michelle was the
only one who'd ever made the six-hour drive, she got tapped for it. They had
a lot to talk about. The Werber rejection surely stung, but it wasn't completely
unexpected. They probably had a better chance in L.A. anyway, especially
since the axis of the rock and roll world was rotating from New York to there.
Capitol Records, the American home of the Beatles and the Beach Boys, was
headquartered in L.A., as was Warner Brothers. All the other major labels
had offices there too. And there were countless independent labels with
many experiencing overnight success. The two biggest were Imperial and
Liberty, both of which were artist-friendly and had myriad successful artists.
Bobby Vee, Jackie DeShannon, Jan & Dean and Gary Lewis & the Playboys
all recorded for Liberty while Imperial boasted Johnny Rivers, Sandy Nelson
and Cher and was the American home of Billy J. Kramer & the Dakotas, the
Searchers and the Hollies. Autumn was hitting with the Beau Brummels, Del-
Fi had the Bobby Fuller Four, and a new label, White Whale, had success right
out of the gate with the Turtles' folk-rock take on Bob Dylan's "It Ain't Me
Babe." There seemed to be a new success story every day.

That was the fresh and exciting atmosphere to which John, Michelle and
Denny arrived on Saturday, August 14, but label shopping would have to wait
for the time being. First, they needed a place to stay and get organized, but,
as they came down I-5 and onto the Harbor Freeway, they entered the outer
perimeter of the Watts Riots, a racially charged uprising that exploded after a
traffic stop in the predominantly black L.A. suburb several days earlier escalated
into a fistfight between reckless driving suspect Marquette Frye and his family and arresting officers. By the time John, Michelle and Denny arrived, three
days in, Watts resembled a war zone with widespread looting, destruction,
and arson. John, Michelle, and Denny drove past police blockades, California

National Guard tanks, and snipers positioned along the freeway. When the unrest finally concluded on Monday, August 16, 34 people were dead.

For their first couple of days in L.A., the trio stayed at Michelle's surrogate mother Marika Sail's house. John was focused and immediately got to work honing his arrangements and rehearsed everybody for auditions. His song-writing creativity was ascending rapidly as he quickly wrote "Got a Feelin'" with Denny while there. After the riots died down, they were able to go into Hollywood and explore the club scene. It was like nothing they'd ever seen before and a far cry from the Sunset Strip John had visited back in the late 1950s, although Pandora's Box was still there. They borrowed more money and got a room at the Landmark Hotel on Franklin Avenue and ventured down to Sunset Boulevard. What they saw was otherworldly. The streets of Greenwich Village had nothing on the colorful, vibrant, rock and roll–infused landscape of downtown Hollywood. It made Greenwich Village look old-fashioned by comparison, and the streets and sidewalks were wider and fuller than those in Lower Manhattan. The inhabitants who lined the boulevard wore bright, modern space age fashions in polyester and PVC. Miniskirts, go-go boots, drainpipe jeans, Nehru jackets, and swing coats could be spotted up and down the strip. And thick bold stripes were in, thanks to Sonny & Cher.

As they walked up and down a packed Sunset, each club appeared bigger and better as the scene unfolded before them. Past Ciro's, Ben Frank's, the Sea Witch, the Whisky a Go Go, the Trip, the London Fog, and Gazzari's, the music filtered onto the street and the world of rock and roll possibilities was as bright as their marquees. This indulgent scene was kicked off by the underage club the Cinnamon Cinder in Studio City, opened by KRLA DJ Bob Eubanks in 1962 and quickly franchised into locations in Long Branch, San Diego, Fresno, and San Bernadino. When the more traditional jazz clubs that catered to the middle-aged set moved to Las Vegas in the early to mid-1960s, vacant Sunset Strip clubs were renamed, reopened, and geared to the under-21 set. They were the demographic purchasing the most music, and the rebirth gave any hot band who recorded in L.A. places to play to their fans. The rock and roll billowing out of these clubs was easily a far cry from folk, but also didn't resemble anything on AM radio. Inside each club were mostly L.A.-based bands who saturated the air around them with fuzztone guitars and hypnotic rhythms courtesy of Love, the Seeds, the Leaves and the Rising Sons. The lead vocals provided by Arthur Lee, Sky Saxon, Jim Pons, and

Taj Mahal, respectively, were frightening to many in 1965 and often dancing behind or suspended above these groups were young, shapely go-go dancers, in miniskirts and high boots. They twisted, hully-gullyed, and ponied along with the music and balanced their ominousness rock band counterparts with sex appeal. At the Whisky a Go Go, when Johnny Rivers wasn't electrifying the crowd with his white-hot live show, female DJs spun the hottest 45s from a booth suspended above the stage that featured a $35,000 sound system, giving rise to the discotheque, which defined the club scene in the ensuing decades.

It was a lot to take in so, when John, Michelle, and Denny stumbled on to the Troubadour, a folk club on Santa Monica Boulevard, they felt a little more in their element and took in old friend Hoyt Axton's show. This new direction they were taking was a lot to process. When folk musicians began migrating to L.A. in 1964/65, they were eager to put their fingerprint on the L.A.-based rock music scene in hopes of getting signed. While John, Denny, and Michelle were bumming around in the Virgin Islands, old friends Jim McGuinn and David Crosby and their new band, the Byrds, made their debut at the revamped Ciro's Le Disc a month before the release of "Mr. Tambourine Man." Along with ex–New Christy Minstrel Gene Clark and two California musicians, Chris Hillman and Michael Clarke, they unleashed their rock and roll version of folk music to an unsuspecting public. They were the first new American group signed to a major label in the wake of the Beatles and the music they played was different. It bore the fruit of their experience as folk musicians but was accentuated by Crosby's lilting harmonies, McGuinn's 12-string Rickenbacker guitar, and a rhythm section. Leading up to their big Ciro's debut, they were given rehearsal space at sculptor, and hippie guru, Vito Paulekas' art studios in Los Angeles. In fair trade, the Byrds allowed his and Carl Franzoni's avant-garde dance troupe to infiltrate Ciro's dance floor. After the Byrds hit it big and toured the United States, other East Coast ex-folk acts, like the Lovin' Spoonful and the Modern Folk Quartet, took their place and perpetuated the completely unorthodox scene of 1965. By the time John, Michelle, and Denny hit the scene, the groundwork had been laid. All they could do was put their fingerprint on it.

After their evening on the Sunset Strip, John, Michelle, and Denny went back to the Landmark to soak it in and sleep it off. When they awoke the next day, their rental car had been stolen with most of their belongings still inside it. Things looked dire now. They rode down to L.A. on fumes and now they didn't even have a change of clothes and were broker and dirtier than ever. John's hair was now down below his ears, and Denny's coiffure was longer than ever, resembling John Lennon's in *Help!* Michelle's hair was long and straight, and she wore no makeup, a look she'd later exploit. In retrospect, they fit the era but, in the moment, they looked borderline homeless.

They weren't completely out of luck though. Denny remembered his conversation with Jim Hendricks before leaving New York. His apartment was just a couple blocks down the street from the Whisky a Go Go, and they went off in search of it. When they tracked it down on North San Vicente Boulevard, an eviction notice from the local sheriff was posted on the door, but they took a chance and knocked anyway. To their surprise, Cass opened the door and, once again, the quartet was reunited and excitement filled the air. After catching up, she told them she'd been devoting her short time in town learning everything she could about the L.A. music business from Kim Fowley and pitching the Mugwumps to every local record label who'd let her in the door, but there were no takers. The apartment was tiny and already crowded, but Jim and his girlfriend Vanessa invited the weary trio to stay with them until the police removed them. It was another serendipitous moment between John and Cass and perhaps another sign that their union was meant to be.

Between the six of them, they hardly had two nickels to rub together, but they made do. The electricity and water had already been shut off so handy Denny converted their wall oven into a hot plate so they could at least cook their meals of hot dogs and beans. During the days, John and Denny would go to various supermarkets and steal cold cuts. Times were getting hard, but, within the poverty-stricken set of circumstances in which they found themselves, there was a silver lining. The lack of electricity meant more time devoted to singing and playing, and being in such close quarters didn't allow for separation from Cass for John. She was able to get in nice and tight with Denny and Michelle's harmony. Under these conditions, the clouds that were blinding John to Cass' amazing contribution began to lift. There was no getting around the fact that she made them better, and, soon, John began giving her direction and was pleased with her understanding. Her powerful contralto created an incredible synergy, but John's pride was still strong, and he just couldn't let go of her outward appearance. But that was all about to change.

Although he was four years younger than John, Kim Fowley had built up a much more solid all-around reputation in the music industry by the time the two met in September 1965. The tall, lanky, steely-eyed promoter had already arranged and produced a couple of hit songs, including "Cherry Pie" by Skip & Flip, "Like, Long Hair" by Paul Revere & the Raiders, and "Nut Rocker" by B. Bumble & the Stingers. He'd even sung on the 1960 number one hit "Alley Oop," by the Hollywood Argyles, along with fellow musician/producer extraordinaire Gary S. Paxton. He was Motown's West Coast promotion man for a short time and produced P. J. Proby records in England while rubbing elbows with the Beatles and Stones at the Ad Lib Club. His most recent success was producing the number three hit for the Murmaids "Popsicles and Icicles," which showed he had an ear for vocal harmony. It further cemented his reputation as an independent producer, and he'd recently started as a talent scout at Gene Norman's GNP Crescendo label. Growing up in postwar L.A., he'd established relationships with fellow up-and-comers Phil Spector, Lou Adler, Herb Alpert, Bruce Johnston, Jan Berry, Dean Torrence, Sandy Nelson, and original Beach Boys producer Nick Venet. Cass was fascinated with his résumé after being introduced to him by Jim Hendricks, and would barrage him with questions about breaking into the L.A. music industry to the point of annoyance.

But he did have an ear for talent and recognized it in Cass, so when she called him one day in early September to tell him about her three musician friends just in from the East Coast who were label-shopping, he took it seriously. In fact, he made a house call as a representative of GNP Crescendo. After singing "California Dreamin'," "Straight Shooter" and a reworking of his torch song for Michelle, "Monday, Monday," for him, sans Cass, he'd heard enough. He asked them how much they wanted in advance. John replied, "$250 a month." Fowley phoned Gene Norman.

"Where are you?" Norman asked Fowley suspiciously. "Are you working?"

Fowley told him he'd just discovered a great unsigned group with great original songs.

"What do they want?" Norman fired back.

"$250 a month," Fowley replied. There was silence. Sensing Norman's trepidation, Fowley offered, "Plus, the guys will do janitor work and the girl will do accounting work."

"Nobody's worth $250 a month, not even you," Norman replied and hung up the phone.

Fowley didn't blink. He knew he had a sure thing and still had plenty of options at his disposal. He called up his old buddy Nick Venet, the head A&R man at Capitol Records, and a producer at several other smaller labels, including Mira Records, and did his best cold sales pitch. Knowing Fowley's ear for talent, Venet agreed to audition them the following day at his home. In fact, Fowley was so sure of John's songwriting prowess that he made a side deal with Venet that, if things worked out, he'd get the publishing and Venet would produce.

The next day, Cass made the fortuitous decision to drive John, Denny, and Michelle to Venet's house. When the producer, who discovered the Beach Boys, saw the four of them at his doorstep, he was captivated by their image. They stood in stark contrast to one another and their scraggy appearance was nothing he'd ever seen before in this setting. John was extremely tall, thin and gangly. Cass, at 300 pounds, was short and squat. Denny was a good-looking young guy sporting a Beatles haircut, and Michelle was the picture of modern beauty.

"What a great image the four of you have!" Venet exclaimed as he welcomed them into his house.

John still had not verbally removed the embargo on Cass' involvement, so Denny sheepishly informed Venet that Cass wasn't part of the group, but Nick wouldn't hear of it. He was completely sold on the quartet image and asked Cass if she could sing.

"Yeah, I know all the parts," she responded.

Since John was at Venet's mercy, he acquiesced, and they proceeded to blow his socks off with the same songs they'd sung for Kim Fowley.

"The *four* of you are remarkable," he stressed. "I don't care what the three of you are like, and I don't care to know."

He asked them if they needed money and John quickly affirmed. In fact, he wanted a lot of money. All Venet could scrounge on the spot was $150, but promised he'd get them the rest in about a week's time and muttered something about selling his car. He wanted them on Mira Records but couldn't completely seal the deal without label owner Randy Wood's blessing. He scribbled down an address on a piece of paper and handed it to John.

"Here's the deal," he told them. "Tomorrow you'll go to this address at 3:00 and sing for Randy Wood. If all goes well, you'll get a contract with Mira Records. We'll put out a single and hopefully it'll be a hit. What do you say?"

It sounded promising to them, and they left feeling pretty excited. But, on the trip home, something deep down just didn't feel right. Mira Records wasn't exactly Capitol or Columbia, the labels on which the Journeymen and the Halifax Three had recorded, respectively. It would do if there were no other offers, but this was only their first one, and perhaps they were selling themselves a little short. Sure, Venet had made them $150 richer but how lucrative was Mira Records if he had to sell his car in order to pay their advance? If Nick Venet, a big label executive with the Beach Boys to his credit, was excited, wouldn't others be also? John was circumspect, and everybody else was jittery.

When they got back to Jim and Vanessa's, the mood was more somber than excited. Cass decided they needed some grass to calm their nerves. Unfortunately, they were out, so Cass called another singer friend, Barry McGuire, who was known for always having potent weed. They had met a year earlier when his former group, the New Christy Minstrels, shared the bill with the Big 3 on an episode of *Hootenanny*. He'd picked up the habit of smoking marijuana a couple years earlier to better cope with the New Christy Minstrels' rigorous touring schedule and, by 1965, had become a connoisseur. After talking for a few minutes with Cass, he gathered enough weed for a small group and jumped on his brand-new Royal Enfield motorcycle and arrived at Jim and Vanessa's apartment a short while later.

Barry was a scrappy self-starter with a no-bullshit blue-collar demeanor. Despite his limited vocal range, he'd carved out a successful recording career, which began with his debut single on the Mosaic label in late 1961. Before that, he'd lived a hardscrabble life. Born in Oklahoma in 1935, his parents divorced when he was two and he was periodically uprooted during his developmental years, as his stepfather jumped around to different construction jobs around L.A. By age 14, he worked on a fishing boat and by 16 he'd joined the navy but was kicked out 10 months later when it was discovered he was underage. He became a drifter, taking on a variety on manual labor jobs, but the muscular blond extrovert always had a penchant for music. During the folk boom, he teamed up with singer Barry Kane, and the duo released an LP on Dave Hubert's Horizon label in 1962. Both would join Randy Myers'

New Christy Minstrels later that year and, in 1963, Barry issued his first solo LP, also on Horizon (*Note: The album featured a cover of John Phillips and John Stewart's "Oh Miss Mary."*). Though McGuire co-wrote the New Christy Minstrels' biggest hit, "Green, Green," he arrived in L.A. flat broke when he left the group to go solo in January 1965 and he eked out a living for the first several months.

Summer found him at the Sunset Strip club Ciro's, supporting his old folk buddy Jim McGuinn's new band, the Byrds, who'd begun their residency at the recently relaunched club in March. The ever-charismatic Barry had been leading a conga line with the Paulekas/Franzoni dancers one night in June when young music mogul Lou Adler noticed him. Lou was up on every artist and every move made in the music industry, and he recognized the ex–New Christy Minstrel. After the conga line dispersed, he introduced himself and brought him over to the table that he was sharing with Bob Dylan. He told him he'd just launched the Dunhill label, and, after some chitchat, invited him to come down to their offices on South Beverly Drive and listen to some publishing demos. With Dunhill yet to jump into the folk-rock fray, Barry had folk cachet and could possibly prove profitable as their first attempt. He made it down a few days later but nothing Lou played for him clicked. Barry was very particular and, since he had a folk singer's temperament, Lou sent him down to staff songwriter and producer Phil Sloan's office to listen to some more folky, topical songs he'd recently written, which included a very provocative one called "Eve of Destruction."

Composed by Phil one night in mid-1964, around the time of the Gulf of Tonkin incident, which ignited the Vietnam War, it reflected his fearful disposition and was part of a series of angst-ridden, topical songs, written under what he described as a spiritual interior locution. Five poems were spoken to him by what he claimed was a voice of divine origin, and "Eve of Destruction," in particular, placed his parents' generation, blind patriotism, the voting age, and segregation under scrutiny. A day later, he pitched them all to Lou Adler, who promptly rejected each one, calling them "unpublishable." Barry wasn't crazy about it either when Phil first played it for him. In fact, he rejected every song he played for him until they got to one called "What Exactly's the Matter with Me," an angry declaration of independence that criticized the status quo. It was just what Barry was looking for, and the two excitedly went to Lou's office, made a deal, and arranged for a session on Thursday, July 15. Along with it, they recorded a P. F. Sloan/Steve Barri tune called "Ain't No Way I'm Gonna Change My Mind" and squeezed "Eve of Destruction" in the last 30 minutes. The wrinkled, handwritten lyrics were pulled out from underneath a bucket of fried chicken with the grease stains making them difficult to read. Barry grunted through the words he couldn't decipher, which gave the illusion of angst and frustration, and inadvertently gave the song its sizzle.

The rough mix was dubbed onto a reel so that Barry could take it home, learn and rerecord it during his next session. Another copy was given to Jay Lasker, who, through Dunhill promotions director Barry Gross, made its way to pop station KFWB over the weekend and debuted as a "Pick Hit" on Wink Martindale's show Monday morning. Even though response from listeners was ecstatic, Lou was pissed that it was given to them without his approval and that they were playing the rough mix. He had Sloan and Barri quickly overdub the background voices and give it a more professional mix, which they passed along to KFWB, who replaced it in their rotation. Despite initial fears over the potential negative reaction to the song's in-your-face political rant, Lou and his partners agreed to press it as a single and it began breaking in Chicago, causing a chain reaction that spread throughout the Midwest and into the bigger markets. Many stations in the major cities banned it from their playlists but even that couldn't stop its organic growth. Barry McGuire became an overnight sensation, loved by teenagers, scorned by their patriotic parents, and Dunhill had its first major hit.

A month later, when Barry walked into Jim and Vanessa's apartment in jeans and motorcycle boots worn over his pants and bags of grass, he certainly didn't look like a singer who had the number two song in the country. But success hadn't spoiled him. He made himself at home, making small talk and rolling joints. He'd already met Jim and Denny but hadn't yet formally met John and Michelle. For whatever reason, their meeting with Nick Venet was never mentioned, but Cass told him that they'd recently joined forces as a group and were looking for a label.

Then they sang for him and, like they had done with everybody else, their harmony and songs blew him away. Cass sang with ease, ironing clothes, as her vibrato caused the windows to rattle. He'd heard her sing before, but in a larger setting, and her blend with the others was lethal and John's songs made them downright hitmakers. He loved what he was hearing, and ideas for his next single began racing in his head. In the thick of the marijuana clouds, Barry sat up and got serious.

"You guys should meet Lou Adler," he said.

"Who's that?" they asked.

Barry explained that he was the head of Dunhill Records, his current label, and he ran it like a family and had a great ear for marketable music. And he wasn't just blowing marijuana smoke. Lou had written some well-known hits, worked with some legendary artists and, in the pop music world of 1965, was on an upward trend with Barry's "Eve of Destruction" about to hit number one even though the song's lyrics were drawing conservative ire and igniting a national discussion. Barry was under a lot of pressure and wanted a less controversial folk-rock follow-up, and he loved John's songs. It was an opportune time to get these two together. After getting sufficiently high, the group made the four-mile trek east to Western Recorders.

Whether or not Lou signed them was really of no consequence to Barry. The most important thing was John's songs and getting a follow-up single that would garner the same type of response as "Eve of Destruction" had. He was in the crosshairs of plenty of angry radio programmers and his next single would most likely be dead on arrival, but Barry wasn't one to give up. Lou wasn't in when they arrived, so Barry had them sing to the Dunhill songwriting/production team of Phil Sloan and Steve Barri, with just John's guitar accompanying them. Sloan and Barri, who were just hitting their stride writing and producing hits for Jan & Dean, Herman's Hermits and the Turtles, were also impressed and immediately recognized their hit potential. They took them to Lou's office and asked his secretary Julie Weinberg to track him down and get him here as quickly as possible.

When Lou finally arrived, he found a group of dirty-looking kids all over his office and he was unimpressed with their appearance and their odor. Barry recognized Lou's consternation and told him that John had written some songs that he was interested in for his next single, which brought back into focus their being there. He told Barry to take them down to Studio A in the rear of the building and he'd be with them as soon as he finished up in Studio 3. Although John, Michelle, Denny, and Cass had all recorded in first-rate recording studios, Western felt different. It was looser. They made themselves as comfortable as they could and did some vocal warm-ups and waited an eternity for Lou, who hadn't really lived up to Barry's billing. He seemed like just another middle-aged music executive with a stick up his ass.

Lou Adler was only 34 when he met John Phillips and company. He was a late bloomer to the music industry, getting involved in 1957, aged 26, when he sold his girlfriend's girlfriend's boyfriend, aspiring musician Herb Alpert, an insurance policy. He grew up in Boyle Heights, a mostly Jewish suburb of East L.A., surrounded by Chicano families who filled the ether with their magnificent, brass-laden blend of R&B and jazz. His young ears soaked up its grandeur, enticing him to take trumpet lessons at age eight and, throughout his tenure at Fairfax High School, played in several local bands.

He was attending Los Angeles City College when he and Herb, a musician and aspiring songwriter, hooked up. They hit it off quickly and made plans to write some songs together. After a few sit-down sessions, they put three or four together they really believed in and made a demo record to shop around to labels. All the major ones slammed their doors on them but they finally found a sympathetic ear when they hit the tiny black label Keen Records and their A&R head Robert "Bumps" Blackwell, who'd co-written several of Little Richard's hits and produced Sam Cooke's 1957 breakthrough "You Send Me." He thought Lou and Herb's songs were garbage but was impressed by their production. He hired them as A&R reps and put them to work grading a pile of demos gathering dust on his desk. Several months later, they made their debut as professional songwriters with the Salmas Brothers' spring 1958 Keen release "Circle Rock."

A year later, after being introduced to new singing duo Jan & Dean by their former high school classmate Kim Fowley, Lou and Herb produced their first hit, "Baby Talk," which peaked at number 10 on the Dore label. They left Keen and became independent producers crafting hits for Sam Cooke, Dante & the Evergreens and the Everly Brothers. But their breadwinner was Jan & Dean, who, under their guidance, racked up a dozen Top 40 singles, until Jan Berry's near-fatal car accident in April 1966. Herb couldn't shake performing and left the team to focus on his act, eventually forming the popular easy listening group the Tijuana Brass and co-founding A&M Records with promotions man Jerry Moss. Lou stayed behind the scenes and partnered with Don Kirshner, opening up Screen Gems, Aldon Music's L.A. branch, and established a pipeline of Brill Building songs to Snuff Garrett's Liberty Records artists. He left a couple of years later after realizing that Kirshner and his partner, Al Nevins, had little interest in his contributions and that Screen Gems was nothing more than a dead letter office.

In 1964, he partnered with the well-connected and wealthy Hollywood magnates Al Bennett, Pierre Cossette and Bobby Roberts and formed Dunhill Productions and Trousdale Publishing. Shortly afterward, they brought in Roberts' brother-in-law Jay Lasker, a brusque veteran label executive with a law degree, to run Dunhill Productions and hired songwriting team Phil Sloan and Steve Barri away from Screen Gems. They hit the ground running, producing veteran local singing sensation Johnny Rivers, who'd been electrifying crowds at the Whisky a Go Go with his stripped-down renditions of early rock and roll chestnuts. They broke him nationally in May 1964, on Imperial Records, with his cover of Chuck Berry's "Memphis, Tennessee," which hit number two, the first of a dozen Top 40 hits over the next three years. He launched Dunhill as a label a year later with a single by Ray Whitley, a Jay Lasker discovery, that kicked off a series of duds. Three months and 11 singles later, Dunhill had its first number one hit with "Eve of Destruction."

Though Barry McGuire had brought Dunhill to the fore with "Eve of Destruction," it brought Lou unwanted attention from his conservative contemporaries across a wide spectrum. It made it to number one through no payola of any kind and broke an unwritten industry rule that topical songs would receive no airplay. "Eve of Destruction" committed the sin of having a catchy rock and roll melody, and *Billboard, Cash Box,* and *Record World* were losing advertisers for merely charting the record. Hundreds of radio stations omitted it from their playlists even though it was number one. It also put its songwriter, Phil Sloan, under the spotlight and made Lou fearful of losing him to performance, which was a gamble and could make him potentially less profitable and put more strain on their already tenuous relationship. Furthermore, it angered politicians, parents, and war veterans and launched a nationwide debate over the temerity of the lyrics and the state of modern youth. Right-wingers called the song "subversive," and it prompted several response songs, including "The Dawn of Correction" by the Spokesmen, which peaked at number 36. CBS radio's Mike Wallace devoted an entire episode of *Mike Wallace at Large* to analyze both songs and question foreign policy by way of the jukebox. Though Lou defended his artist and song to the trade publications and glad-handed Barry every time he saw him, behind the scenes he was anxious and doing his best to keep the lions at bay, which included some of his partners. When they launched Dunhill, this was the last thing they'd anticipated. They desired a traditional label that made a profit exploiting artists and trends that were safe, and it was evident in their earliest releases: "My Prayer" by Lou's then-wife, singer/actress Shelley Fabares, and "The Surfing Songbook" by the Rincon Surf Band. There was talk among the partners of dropping Barry altogether and, now, here he was in his office with a bunch of weirdo friends.

After breaking in Studio 3, he made his way down to Studio A, along with P. F. Sloan, Steve Barri, and engineer Dayton "Bones" Howe, where Barry was sitting with John, Denny, Michelle, and Cass. Though Lou would eventually become the epitome of cool California music exec, he was all business this day, although he did dress rather casually for a label executive: jeans, sneakers and loose-fitting sweaters. His marriage with Shelley Fabares, less than two years in, was already on the rocks and, refocusing on the quartet, the one who caught his eye the most was Michelle.

"Who's the blonde?" he asked Barry in the control room.

"That's John's wife," Barry replied.

With eight years of judging talent and producing hits under his belt, Lou felt it was probably best not to look at them as they sang. He turned on the control room talkback and told them to go ahead when they were ready and turned his chair around, not expecting to hear anything more than a decent song or two for Barry. He couldn't possibly have been prepared for what he heard next. The four had impressed Nick Venet and Barry McGuire in rooms with no acoustics but, in the confines of Studio A, their voices shone as if they were singing in an opera house. "California Dreamin'" was the starter, still bearing John's original arrangement, beginning in A minor and moving into G minor, and without its legendary introduction or the call-and-response by Cass and Michelle, but nevertheless a powerful song. "Go Where You Wanna Go" was more impressive stylistically as it featured John's complex vocal arrangements. They also sang new songs "Straight Shooter," "Got a Feelin'," "Monday, Monday," and a jazzy little vocalese exercise John recently wrote called "Once Was a Time I Thought," each one stirring the rising music mogul's senses more and more as his tepidness boiled into excitement. The serendipity couldn't be scripted. How could four dirty kids straight off the street sound like that? This unknown group had serious hitmaking potential and were self-sustaining with John's magnificent songs and, even better, were unsigned! Welcome to Trousdale Publishing!

Though he believed he may have found a one-way ticket out of "Eve of Destruction" hell, Lou managed to keep his poker face and not show his hand. One thing was certain, however. He wanted them on Dunhill Records yesterday and wasn't going to let them walk out of there without a deal in place. He turned his chair around, cozied up to the board, and pressed down on the talkback button.

"What else you got?" Lou coolly asked.

"That's all we got," Cass replied. "What do you think?"

He turned to Bones Howe.

"What do you think?" he asked.

"If you don't take them, I will," Bones answered without hesitation. (*Note: Bones had recently started producing the Turtles on White Whale.*)

After a short pause, which must've seemed like a lifetime to them, Lou replied, "I think we can do business."

A collective gasp of silent excitement could be felt by everyone in the studio. He walked in to take another look at this motley crew who sang like angels and get to know them a little better.

"What do you guys want?" Lou asked.

Straight-faced, and in full business mode, John responded, "It's not what we want. It's what we need and what we need is a steady stream of cash from your office to our house . . . but we don't have a house yet."

Lou peeled them off $1,500 right there to go find a place to live and agreed to arrange for a car for them in a couple of days, which must've seemed more impressive than Nick Venet hawking his.

"Don't meet with anyone else. You're on Dunhill Records now," Lou said as he headed back down to Studio 3, still masking his excitement.

The newly signed quartet's excitement was much more obvious, and nobody had reason to celebrate more than John. He was a hustler, a bullshitter, a leader, but, above all, a talented musician who had finally turned his music into a moneymaking product with Denny, Michelle, and, above all, Cass' help. His songwriting prowess was heading toward its apex, where he would eventually be granted "genius" status by critics, contemporaries, and fans, but even a genius songwriter and arranger needs help sometimes. John was more on board with pop music than ever but still needed direction and, though he didn't know it yet, his muse was about to return. He never could've imagined on that mild mid-September afternoon just how quickly and dramatically both would manifest themselves in a very short period.

And they never did keep that 3:00 appointment with Mira Records.

CHAPTER 16:
IF YOU CAN BELIEVE YOUR EYES AND EARS

As August 1965 was rolling into September, a couple of weeks before their fateful Dunhill audition and still very much broke, John Phillips took his wife Michelle and their friends Denny Doherty and Cass Elliot to the northern rim of Los Angeles, up to the Hollywood Hills, and parked in a spot with a clear view of the legendary Hollywood Bowl seated in the valley below. The Beatles were making their second-ever appearance at the amphitheater in a two-night stand, August 29 and 30, exciting not only the paying crowd, of mostly L.A. teens, but also the many, like John and his companions, who'd camped around the venue to listen for free. As the music filtered into the night air, feeling very confident and high on LSD, John made a promise to his bandmates. Within a year's time, they'd be on that very Hollywood Bowl stage, entertaining their fans in the same way the Beatles were entertaining and inspiring them. It was a bold prediction but one that seemed slightly more plausible after their meeting less than three weeks later with Lou Adler. Still, even with a legitimate record deal in place a couple of weeks later, the Hollywood Bowl seemed out of reach. Some breaks were needed and in short order and, little did they know, they were just around the corner.

Now that they were officially a quartet and had some money in their pockets for the first time since their folk days, John, Michelle, Denny, and Cass agreed to continue to live communally but had to get out of Jim Hendricks

169

and Vanessa Ware's apartment before the sheriff made good on his eviction notice. It would take time to locate the right rental house so, in the meantime, they returned to the Landmark Hotel and rented a suite. A day after meeting with Lou, on Cass' 24th birthday, they celebrated back at the hotel with her favorite dish, duck à l'orange, which she prepared, while John provided the drugs, namely Seconals. Liquor was also in abundance with John and Cass particularly nipping the brandy used in the duck recipe.

As the night passed and the effects of the speed, the brandy, and the tryptophan took hold of John and Cass, Denny seized his opportunity in the wee hours of the morning. He and Michelle were still up celebrating until Denny crept over to the sliding door that led to the balcony and, with a devilish grin, beckoned Michelle to follow him. She knew what was on his mind and followed willingly. Although there was a short lull, their desire for one another was bubbling under the surface. Weeks earlier, during their stay in San Francisco, while John and his nephew Billy Throckmorton were asleep in their room at the International Hotel, Michelle and Denny slipped away and engaged in some heavy petting. They were getting bolder, and now they were both eagerly heading for the big moment.

The room next door was vacant so the two stepped over the railing of its adjacent balcony and slid in through the unlocked sliding door, which Denny had reconnoitered earlier. After some passionate kissing and foreplay, they ripped off their clothes and made love on the carpet, only feet away from their two counterparts with just a thin wall separating them. Their lust was finally consummated and, as they laid in each other's arms, in love for the moment, there was some sense of relief that would soon be replaced by intense feelings of guilt. What had they just done and where do they go from here? With their internal clocks ticking away, they made their way back into the suite and into their respective beds. They didn't think much of it at the time, but they had just put their collective opportunity of a lifetime in jeopardy. If John and Cass found out, it would surely spell the end of their newly signed, unnamed band.

After a couple days at the Landmark, they answered an ad in the newspaper for a house for rent in the 400 block of North Flores Street, between Rosewood and Oakwood Avenues, a two-story, three-bedroom, green stucco-fronted house that suited them perfectly. They dubbed it "The Green House," setting the practice of the quartet christening things near and dear to them.

The two upstairs bedrooms were split between Cass and John and Michelle. Denny took the downstairs bachelor pad and spent most nights sleeping on a mattress on the porch. Their communal living arrangement certainly must've stood out in a traditional West Hollywood suburb decorated with palm trees, tall hedges, and tile roofs, but it was a sign of things to come as the era of the hippie unfolded and Los Angeles became one of its major hubs. Nevertheless, it would all be a very short-lived stay for the group.

Shortly after their arrival, the car Lou Adler promised them was delivered. It was a 1959 Buick convertible he obtained from a used car dealer associate in East L.A. To match the Green House, they dubbed it "Harold the Bleak," and, as they were christening inanimate objects, it suddenly dawned on them that they hadn't yet given themselves a group name. It was a formidable task. The landscape of band names had changed considerably since the folk era, and the New Journeymen just wasn't going to cut it in the era of the Beatles, the Rolling Stones and the Byrds. They'd been calling themselves the Magic Circle, which, at first, sounded OK but ultimately didn't sit well with all of them. They needed something catchier, something contemporary that suited the group dynamic, but nothing hokey.

Inspiration came in the form of the Hells Angels motorcycle club and, in particular, its roughneck co-founder Ralph "Sonny" Barger who appeared as a guest on the September 28 broadcast of *ABC's Nightlife* hosted by Les Crane, an innovative talk show host whose ballsy, aggressive interview style predated Geraldo Rivera and Phil Donahue. He made a name for himself interviewing people like Lee Harvey Oswald's mother and Malcolm X, and he was also the first U.S. host to broadcast the Rolling Stones. In this episode, he was pressing Barger about the outlaw biker lifestyle, particularly their treatment of the women who cohabitated with them. With the implication from Crane that they were sluts, Barger got very defensive stating that "some people call our women cheap, but we just call them our 'mamas.'" As soon as Cass heard that, she jumped up with excitement.

"We are the Mamas!" she exclaimed. "I don't know who you guys are, but Michelle and I are the Mamas."

Smiling, Michelle agreed. "Yes, we are the Mamas."

John liked it and thought about it for a second.

"Hmmm. . . . Yes, the Papas and the Mamas," he said. "That sounds pretty good."

"You asshole!" Cass shouted at him. "You don't say 'the Papas and the Mamas,' you say, 'the Mamas and the Papas'!"

It was a transformative moment that not only gave the group its iconic name, but also presaged the constant headbutting that would soon take place regularly between John and Cass. Now that he needed her, Cass had a renewed sense of self confidence and had no problems calling John an asshole whereas before when she was lobbying for inclusion, she would've been hesitant. Nevertheless, from here on they were known as the Mamas & the Papas, and the party continued.

Shortly after moving into the Green House, the quartet headed to Ensenada, Baja California, for a bit of relaxation before getting into the thick of things. It continued John's trend of exiling himself to prepare for the journey ahead and conjure up good vibes within the group dynamic but, for the latter, it wasn't as successful this time around. Now that Denny and Michelle had consummated their relationship, there was noticeable tension between them and not exclusively of the sexual kind as they tried to keep their feelings for one another at bay in such a romantic setting.

In keeping with tradition, they maintained a constant LSD high throughout the short vacation and went down with the sole purpose of getting sloppy drunk, but it wasn't as pleasurable as it had been in times past. On their way, they stopped in Tijuana and made their way into the Chicago Club, a raunchy strip club filled with Marines and Navy seamen, where strippers were free to be handy with the patrons. After some heavy drinking Michelle excused herself to go to the ladies' room to vomit but managed to get herself together and hold it in. As she exited and made her way back to their table, she saw a stripper grab Denny by his ears, thrust his face into her crotch and began grinding and thrusting, much to his amusement. She zipped right back into the bathroom and this time let it all out.

The next day found them on a beach in Ensenada trying to shake off their hangovers. While the others were sitting on the sand, bleary-eyed and achy, Denny decided to take a swim. He swam out a short distance and plunged himself underwater, emerging a few seconds later with half a glass beer bottle protruding from his left pectoral with blood trickling down. Once again, a day at the beach turned into a trip to the hospital. Nevertheless, the party and the drinking continued when he returned.

They stayed at a cheap hotel where the walls were paper thin and, at night, Denny could hear John and Michelle making love, which ate away at him terribly. He needed to get out of there. Cass heard him leave his room and followed him to the car. As they drove through the early autumn Mexican night, Denny had to vent and, still feeling the effects of the alcohol, laid it all out to Cass with no thought that she had strong feelings for him. He told her everything that had happened back at the Landmark and, worst of all, confessed that he loved Michelle. In one fell swoop, Cass was crushed beneath the weight of Denny's admission. Although she witnessed their flirtation firsthand, she never saw this coming.

"Stop the car," Cass said.

Denny was caught off-guard as she burst into tears. While Denny was driving well over the speed limit, Cass deliriously began crawling over the bench into the back seat, with the top open, trying to get out of the car. Denny was forced to slam on the brakes, bringing Harold the Bleak to a dead stop in the middle of the highway. With as much composure as she could muster, she let Denny have it.

"You're an asshole!" she screamed. "Stop thinking with your dick! Think with the big head for a change! She doesn't really like either of you! She loves herself more than anyone in the fucking world anyway! Michelle will never leave John for you!"

Denny was stunned by such an emotional outburst from his close friend. Although Cass practically beat him over the head with it, he never made the connection that she was in love with him. Her reaction made it obvious and now Denny was in the position of trying to console her. With that, they drove back to the hotel in stone silence. Although Cass agreed to keep her mouth shut, on the drive back to L.A. the next day she sobbed the entire way and wasted no opportunity shooting daggers at Michelle every chance she could.

On September 13, 1965, John, Michelle, Denny, and Cass officially signed with Dunhill Records and signed a separate publishing deal with Trousdale on October 4. In the long run, only John really benefited from the latter as he was the only writer in the group, but it made him the wealthiest of all. And, although it was a dream come true, it put him under pressure to deliver, and the contract was a pretty bad deal. The group brought in no representation and agreed to 5 percent on 90 percent of retail sales, good for the Dunhill execs, bad for the Mamas & the Papas. Dunhill even managed to keep the management in-house by naming partner Bobby Roberts their manager. On the more generous side, Lou opened charge accounts for them all over town, allowing them to dress in the latest fashions and keep their pantry filled.

On October 7, they headed to Western Recorders to cut their first single, a full band version of "Go Where You Wanna Go." The sessions overseen by Bones Howe, Phil Sloan and Steve Barri featured notable musicians Hal Blaine, on drums, Larry Knechtel, on piano, and Joe Osborn on bass, part of a collective group of session players later known as "the Wrecking Crew." John's lament to Michelle, penned over two years earlier and suddenly timely again, was transformed into a swirling, upbeat folk-rock shuffle featuring John's ambitious vocal interplay with Cass' contralto soaring high above the others, implementing their signature sound from the start. It was an ambitious pop number that sounded like nothing ever heard on the charts and marked the beginning of Lou Adler's multilayered approach to overdubbing that was unique to him but didn't bear an identifiable fingerprint like Phil Spector or Brian Wilson. They also recorded the single's flip side, "Somebody Groovy," which was a newer John Phillips number filled with banal lyrics that seemed specifically designed to capitalize on the new "in" word, "groovy." The single was slated for a November release.

Their next studio session didn't take place until nearly a month later when they went in to lay down backing vocals for songs for Barry McGuire's potential next single and subsequent album. "Child of Our Times," had just been issued as a single by Dunhill but, as many predicted, didn't crack the Top 40. The centerpiece of this sessions was John's "California Dreamin'," which gave everyone involved high hopes of getting him back on the charts. Since it was John's song, he was brought in as a musician and for consultation on the its arrangement. The sessions were engineered by Bones Howe and directed mostly by Steve Barri and Phil Sloan, who went over the song with John. Phil was 10 years younger than he was, but was equally as talented, and not at all intimidated by his 6'5" frame or his musical acumen. John played him the song, which was mostly in the key of G minor, but Phil thought it was all wrong. The lyrics were great, but it sounded like a folk song, which was now about as passé as the twist. It was simply not going to work in this arrangement and Barry needed a real zinger if he was going to get back on the charts.

The song started off in the key of A minor, which caught Phil's attention. He thought on it for a moment and came back to John.

"Have you ever heard 'Walk, Don't Run' by the Ventures?" he asked.

John was indignant. How dare you ask a folk musician if he listened to surf music?

"Surf doesn't break on MacDougall Street," he replied with a slight degree of contempt.

Phil didn't budge. He didn't care if John thought the song was shit. To him, it was an energetic number that was an influential pop hit in 1960 for the Tacoma, Washington, instrumental group the Ventures. Phil played a little bit for him and incorporated the opening verse to "California Dreamin'." He then asked John if he'd ever heard of a suspended chord. He hadn't, at least not by name. He explained that it was a chord in which the major or minor third is omitted and replaced with either a perfect fourth or a major second, creating a much more open sound. Phil told him that examples of this can be heard in "Hey Girl" by Freddie Scott, "Don't Worry Baby" by the Beach Boys, and the intro to "A Hard Day's Night" by the Beatles. Phil played them throughout "California Dreamin'," using it as an effective bridge to go back and forth from the verse to the chorus. John was impressed as new life was given to his song, transforming it from a folk song to rock and roll, and he loved it.

The next thing it needed was an intro. All the big folk-rock songs of the day had one. "Mr. Tambourine Man," "Do You Believe in Magic," and "Like a Rolling Stone" all had memorable intros and if "California Dreamin'" was going to follow in that ilk, it needed a great one too, and it came pretty quickly. Inspired by the song's original arrangement, Phil told John to hold on to the A minor chord as he riffed over top it, and the result was the suspended E that's heard on the record, quickly making the song instantly recognizable. John became much more relaxed and began enjoying the process and stepped closer to manning the controls. The rhythm section of Hal Blaine and Joe Osborn, complete with tambourine played by either Phil or Steve Barri, gave his song wheels. After completing the basic track, Barry laid down his vocals with Phil developing the call-and-response from the Mamas & the Papas that fully displayed the quartet's harmony and turned the song into a complete diamond. Later, Barry overdubbed a harmonica solo. They went on to record three more tracks in the three-hour session, all of which ended up on Barry's second Dunhill LP *This Precious Time*.

When they went into the control room to listen to the playback, John got to hear how his group sounded on tape for the first time, and it took his breath away. Suddenly, Barry sounded like a croaking bullfrog singing over an angelic choir. He began having second thoughts about giving such a song away, especially when he considered how much better of a singer Denny was, and he knew how well his tenor could sing it after rehearsing it dozens of times. The question now was, how does an unproven songwriter wrestle a song away from Dunhill's feature artist? The best thing to do was to talk to Barry man-to-man and he cornered him in the hallway outside Studio 3, not long after the recording session. He told him that he thought it might make more sense for "California Dreamin'" to be the Mamas & the Papas' debut single. Barry was the original hippie and, despite his intense aura, was nonconfrontational and believed in sharing, and his reaction surely must've taken John by surprise.

"Sure man, it's your tune. You wrote it," he replied. Knowing the song's hit potential, he added, "You can buy the grass next month."

Barry's vocals were scrubbed from the multitrack, and replaced with Denny's, and the result was heavenly. (*Note: All but a second of Barry's vocals were erased with his voice still audible at "All the leaves are brown . . ." and Cass and Michelle's call-and-response at "Stopped into a church" lyric were omitted.*) Now all John had to do was confront Lou about it, which he did fairly quickly. After listening to Denny's vocals compared to Barry's, Lou also realized the commercial possibilities of the Mamas & the Papas, and suggested a small change. Not believing Barry's harmonica solo fit Denny's lead, he sent Bones Howe to fetch veteran jazz flautist Bud Shank out of a neighboring studio to perform a new solo. He recorded two takes over the backing track, following Phil Sloan's guitar lead to remain in firm pitch since the harmonica solo had been omitted. To compensate, Shank also had to pull the head joint of his alto flute out half an inch and play it up half a step, which caused it to sound slightly out of tune but good enough for rock and roll.

Although several hundred promo copies of the "Go Where You Wanna Go" single were pressed, Lou put a halt on them and replaced the A-side with "California Dreamin'." From this point on, John and Lou grew closer, first as associates and then as friends. The future was as bright as could be for the group, but as they sat back and waited for the results, they didn't come as quickly as they'd expected.

Back at the Green House, despite Cass' knowledge, things were still red hot between Denny and Michelle. John, entrenched in his role as group leader and arranger, spent most nights away at Western Recorders working on songs for their debut album and was either oblivious to or outright ignored the goings-on at home. It put him on a different schedule than his wife, and put a damper on their sex life, but something stirred his senses and made him suspicious. One late morning, shortly before the release of "California Dreamin'," John woke up and began looking for Michelle. He peeked in Cass' room, but she wasn't in there. He made his way to the living room and she wasn't there either. He slowly crept downstairs, where the kitchen was located, and from the bottom step, looking across the room and through the sliding glass door, he saw Michelle sitting on top of Denny's mattress out on the porch. He had just woken up and was still under his sheets when she had brought him orange juice and the two were in the middle of making out when John spotted them. Denny noticed him out of the corner of his eye.

"All right! What the fuck is going on with you two?" John shouted, surprising Michelle.

She jumped up, heart in throat, fled the porch, and made her way to the street. She ran until she was a safe distance away and stayed there for about two hours. Denny was left to fend for himself and braced for a fight with his best friend. Lying in a compromising position, with a fuming John above him, he didn't know what to say. Finally, clearing his throat, he managed to eke out a few words to try and explain himself.

"Well, as you see, there is something happening here between me and Michelle," he stammered to John. "I'm sorry. I tried hard to . . ."

"I can imagine," John said, cutting him off.

As intimidating as John could be, he didn't like confrontation with his friends, and nobody was closer to him than Denny. He also understood his value to the band and didn't want to harm him and risk losing such a strong tenor even though he was completely justified. This also wasn't Michelle's first dalliance, and he understood Denny's weakness. Later on, as Michelle slowly crept toward the porch and hid behind a hedge, she overheard the two in deep, chauvinistic conversation.

"I couldn't help it, John," Denny confessed.

"I understand, Denny. I understand what a little temptress she is," John replied.

Over the course of Michelle's absence, Denny was able to calm John down by pretty much blaming Michelle for everything. When she finally came back to confront the situation, things got a little more serious as the three gathered near the scene of the incident.

"We'd better sort this shit out now," John said.

Denny and Michelle fessed up, telling him how it all started back on St. John, but that it didn't get serious until a few weeks ago when they were all staying at the Landmark. John's blood began to boil all over again. He glared at Michelle.

"I thought you said nothing really happened back then, Mitch," he said accusingly. "I can't believe it's been going on that long!"

"It hasn't really," Denny chimed in, hoping to quell John's anger toward her. "Just a couple of weeks really, if that. Since we got to L.A."

It didn't work. John only got angrier, and the place of healing he and Denny had come to only minutes earlier completely crumbled.

"I just wish I had known when we signed the contracts! Who the hell signs a five-year deal to work together when the other guy in the group's got a thing going on with your wife?" John exclaimed.

He went back upstairs, still stinging from what he just witnessed, muttering to himself about the contract. Within a couple hours, John had his bags packed and was ready to move out of the house. In between, Cass had finally awoken and learned from Denny about all that had gone down over the last few hours. She wasted no time lighting into Michelle.

"How could you do this to me?" she angrily asked Michelle. "You can have any man you want! Why the one I wanted?"

Michelle had no answer. When John came down with bags in hands, he drew the line in the sand for his wife. He needed to know, in no uncertain terms, whether she was coming with him or staying with Denny, and they could both see how hurt he was.

"I'm clearing the hell out of this house today," John told Michelle. "If you want to stay here, stay. Fine. It's over. If you're coming with me, then let's forget this whole thing and get our own place."

Conflicted, Michelle looked at Denny and then back to John. Denny, uncomfortable being under such a spotlight, helped her make a decision.

"Go with John," he said.

John grabbed her by the hand and out the door they went. Less than two months after coming together, and only days short of their first release on

Dunhill, the Mamas & the Papas were on the verge of collapse. John and Michelle moved into a small house on Lookout Mountain Avenue in Laurel Canyon and a couple of days later, Cass, also disgusted with Denny, moved to Laurel Canyon as well in a house on on Kirkwood Drive. Denny, unable to bear to linger around in the Green House alone, eventually moved into his own Laurel Canyon home on Woods Drive. It seemed that paradise was lost.

"California Dreamin'" was released as a single on December 8, 1965, and it didn't instantly catch fire like "Eve of Destruction" had, which baffled many at Dunhill. There was strong belief that this could have a similar trajectory, going so far as taking out a full-page ad in the December 18 edition of *Billboard* (*Note: The ad included the first use of Adler's now-legendary remark about them and the title of their first LP "If You Can Believe Your Eyes and Ears."*), but its rise was more traditional, getting its first airplay on radio stations in the much colder East Coast of the United States. The song's sentiment of leaving the cold for sunny California struck a chord with disk jockeys and listeners. On Christmas Day, the Mamas & the Papas received perhaps their best gift to date when "California Dreamin'" debuted on the *Billboard* charts at number 116.

It was the highest any of John's songs had ever charted, and he was elated. As they tracked its upward progress over the coming weeks, success got the better of him. Upon receiving their weekly copy of *Billboard*, he and Denny made sure to circle the song's place on the charts and mail it to Frank Werber, rubbing in his face that he let this one get away. The slow boil of "California Dreamin'" over the early months of 1966 was just what this fractured group of friends needed and probably saved them from breaking up. The Werber thing brought John and Denny back together, and Cass knew this would most likely mean live dates and TV appearances, so she eagerly began putting her stage act together, borne out of her earlier failures as a soloist back at the Bon Soir Club and the Shadows. Michelle kept her distance but, as long as John was happy and Cass was busy, the spotlight was off her, for now.

Although the song charted relatively quickly following its release, its climb up the charts was steady but slow. It hung out in the bottom half of the Top 50 for most of January and first caught fire in Boston, getting into heavy rotation on the two leading Top 40 AM stations, WBZ and WMEX. By January 15, it cracked the Top 10 in that market, and a week later, it hit number 10 in Seattle. On January 29, "California Dreamin'" broke the Top 30 in San Francisco,

which surely must've given John and Denny added pleasure circling that listing and mailing it to Werber. It also made it to number one in Boston that
week and, on February 5, cracked the Top 40 nationally, hitting number 33.

As the song began its ascent up the Top 40, network TV came calling,
requesting the Mamas & the Papas perform, or lip sync, "California Dreamin'" to their massive audiences. They'd already gotten their beaks wet, performing locally on the L.A. dance show *Shivaree* and got their first national
exposure on *Shindig!* back in December, where they nervously backed Barry
McGuire on four numbers and performed both sides of their newly released
single plus an acoustic version of the Beatles' "I Call Your Name." As the
song spent the month of February breaking into the Top 10, the Mamas &
the Papas performed on the *Hollywood Palace* and *American Bandstand*, now
filmed in Hollywood. March was even busier for them, as the song reached
its peak of number four on March 12, and they made appearances on the
national teen dance shows *Hullaballoo, the Lloyd Thaxton Show* and two
appearances on *Where the Action Is.*

When the world got their first look at the intriguingly bizarre-looking four-
some, they were enchanted, especially with Cass, whose unique and powerful
contralto matched her size and wit, not to mention her colorful muumuus.
Over time, her popularity would confound John to no end, but, in those early
days as they were getting their sea legs, she took on the role of group spokesperson with only John chiming in and the audience ate it up. But, perhaps
more importantly, it was the nation's first collective look at the burgeoning
hippie culture and, for the most part, the Mamas & the Papas put a good face
on it. It was new and disturbing to many a middle-aged parent and the group
proved, at least publicly, that they could they sing, laugh and engage in witty
banter with their elder counterparts. On their episode of *Hollywood Palace*,
hosted that week by pioneering radio/TV broadcaster Arthur Godfrey, they
acted as the backing chorus to his latest single, "Be My Valentine." After some
clever back-and-forth between Godfrey and John and Cass, the group sang
along to the record, which they practiced over lunch at the Brown Derby with
Richard Wolfe, the song's co-writer and *Hollywood Palace* arranger.

As most of their appearances in the first half of 1966 didn't include any
banter with the respective hosts, they could only be judged by their spirited
performances, which featured all four happily bouncing along with John's
jaunty rhythms in casual clothing and a charming, youthful look. John's hair,

now longer than ever, and scrawny build hid the fact that he just passed age 30, violating leftist activist Jack Weinberg's recent credo, "Don't trust anyone over 30," soon to be adopted by the counterculture movement. It was a profound moment in pop culture. In the ensuing months following its release, the underlying message of "California Dreamin'" inspired many teenagers to transform from closet beatniks to open hippies. John and Michelle's simple song about getting out of the cold and home to the sunshine turned the Mamas & the Papas into, urging kids across the nation to go west, and many did.

Like every group of that era with a hit song, the days and weeks became packed with radio and television promotion, live appearances, photo shoots and, most importantly, recording sessions. The bulk of their debut LP was recorded over the months of December, January, and February and consisted of several covers, including a dreamy version of the one-off Jerry Leiber/Phil Spector collaboration "Spanish Harlem," Billy Page's "The 'In' Crowd" and John's brilliant reworking of Bobby Freeman's frenetic 1958 Top 5 hit "Do You Wanna Dance." He flipped the tune on its ear, turning it into a slow torch song with Denny's achingly vulnerable tenor atop a sparse acoustic intro that quickly built into a crescendo of Cass and Michelle's backing vocals over a luscious string arrangement. When the violin ensemble bursts into a solo in the middle of the song, it almost serves as an invitation to all the young listeners to follow them on this journey they're about to undertake. They also gave a nod to P. F. Sloan and Steve Barri with a recording of their song "You Baby" and to their main inspiration, the Beatles, recording Lennon/McCartney's "I Call Your Name." (*Note: They also took a stab at their "We Can Work It Out" and "Michelle" in December 1965 but both remain unreleased.*)

To round out the album, and follow in the example set by the Beatles and the Byrds, John brought in the fresh original "Hey Girl," co-written with Michelle, and older songs "Got a Feelin'," "Straight Shooter" and, perhaps his crown jewel, "Monday, Monday," which was grossly underappreciated by his bandmates at the time. Cass and Michelle were astounded that anyone would write a song about the worst day of the week. Lou Adler, on the other hand, was shrewd enough to understand the universal dislike of Monday and recognized the song's potential to bring about a common source of respite for working stiffs. Though they'd been working out the song with John prior to signing with Dunhill, Cass and Michelle both told John that the song was pretentious and did not want to sing his corny opening of "Ba da, ba da da-da!" Lou, always very keen on songs with hit potential, used this opportunity to assert his authority and let the two unsupportive Mamas, who were talking themselves out of a hit and potentially shaking his hit songwriter's confidence, know it.

"You two do the singing!" he barked. "I'll do the releasing."

"Monday, Monday" was recorded at a late-night session at Western on December 16, 1965. John went back to the well one more time with Phil Sloan, who was on hand to play any additional guitar parts that may be needed. Not long before that session, John had played guitar on one of Phil's sessions for a song called "City Women" that would be released under his moniker P. F. Sloan. He liked the sounds of the song's drum and guitar riffs and asked him if he could help construct a similar sound to complement his contrapuntal vocal arrangement, which they did within the first three hours of the session, going the extra mile by giving the song a false ending.

After all the sessions were concluded, Lou went to work stacking vocals and arrangements, layering them on top of one another in an Ampex 8-track recorder, which gave the Mamas & the Papas their rich sound. The vocal mix, which usually consisted of three takes, would then be mixed down into one track and then synched with the original backing track, supplied by Hal Blaine on drums, Larry Knechtel on piano and Joe Osborn on bass with John on guitar. Lou overdubbed and layered so much that it's impossible to accurately say who played on what, but the results came off beautifully over the listener's hi-fi or car radio speakers.

While the record was being mixed, the Mamas & the Papas were able to deescalate and get back to normal life, which included copious drug use and figuring out how their interpersonal relationships were going to work from here on out. The success of "California Dreamin'" and the subsequent album sessions served to reinvigorate and refocus the quartet but now they were faced with a little bit of downtime, and the shadows of Michelle and Denny's affair still loomed in the background.

In the middle of all this, at John and Michelle's quaint-but-small home, one winter afternoon, the photo sessions for the album cover convened. Twenty-seven-year-old photographer Guy Webster was commissioned by

Lou to handle the duties and shoot something unique that adequately summed up the group to the unsuspecting public. Though young, Guy had made a name for himself shooting the Rolling Stones' cover for their U.K. edition of *Aftermath* and their U.S. greatest hits compilation *Big Hits (High Tide and Green Grass)* and, a little closer to home, Barry McGuire's *Eve of Destruction* cover, where the singer appears peering out just below the surface of an open manhole.

After entering their house, Guy was brought into the living room where John was preparing to light a large bowl of high-grade marijuana and invited the young shutterbug into the fold. As they closed all the windows, the potent weed began taking effect, and the normally sober photographer was quickly stoned out of his mind. Simple tasks like holding the viewfinder to his eye and pressing the shutter button became exceedingly difficult. But, being the professional he was, he composed himself as best he could and pressed on. To make things even more complicated, the four bandmates took advantage of his unfamiliar condition by playing an impromptu game of hide-and-seek with him. In his dizzy state, Guy searched and searched, and in no time yells for them turned into pleas. The house was only about 700 square feet, so, even stoned, he eventually managed to find them hiding out in the bathroom upstairs. Inadvertently, they had placed themselves in an iconic location. Guy moved them all into the Spanish California tub as best they could, with John, Cass and Denny all scrunched up next to each other and Michelle provocatively reclining across all three of their laps, ironically ending up cheek to cheek with Denny. Guy took dozens of shots in that setting and one of them ended up gracing the cover, perfectly capturing the essence of the Mamas & the Papas before the insidiousness of the music industry began taking its toll. Also, innocently making it into the picture and onto the cover was the toilet, which was a major faux pas in 1966. When Sears and other retailers refused to carry the album because of the unsightly commode, Dunhill countered by covering it up with a scroll that read, "Includes California Dreamin'."

The album was released February 28 and was titled *If You Can Believe Your Eyes and Ears*, Lou's maxim that summed them up that September day they auditioned for him at Western Recorders. It kicked off in grandiose style with "Monday, Monday" and ran the gamut of their recent repertoire, in true original folk-rock fashion with four-part harmony, closing with "The 'In' Crowd," a fitting end that highlighted Cass' incredible lead vocal. It was an auspicious debut and perhaps their finest group effort. The album remained uncharted for a very short time as the promotional wheels began turning, and on March 26 debuted on the *Billboard* LP charts at number 118. By April 23, it hit the Top 30 and began its rapid ascent alongside their follow-up single, "Monday, Monday." The two ran neck and neck, bolstering one another on their way up, crossing into the Top 10 on April 30 with the single hitting the number one spot on May 7. The LP scraped and clawed its way up to number four with the Rolling Stones' *High Tide (and Green Grass)* above it at number three and two Herb Alpert & the Tijuana Brass LPs occupying the top two spots. Lou's old partner was the only thing standing between his new act and the number one record in the country. On May 21, *If You Can Believe Your Eyes and Ears* finally hit number one with "Monday, Monday" holding steady as the number one single for its third consecutive week. It was sweet victory for the Mamas & the Papas and complete validation for John Phillips as a songwriter/arranger extraordinaire. He and the band pitched headlong into Mamas & Papas fever, taking advantage of every opportunity and spoil of fame that came their way.

As the group's stock was rising, Lou approached them with a new contract on April 28 that extended their agreement another two years. It seemed like a perfectly natural move that seemingly rewarded everybody's hard work, and all involved walked away with a newfound feeling of security. But whatever goodwill that gesture built up was offset one month later when it was announced that the entertainment conglomerate American Broadcasting-Paramount Theaters had purchased Dunhill Records and Trousdale Publishing from its three principal partners, Lou Adler, Jay Lasker, and Bobby Roberts. It was disturbing news, but whatever fears John and company may have felt were somewhat squelched a few paragraphs in with the statement that Lou would continue to stay on as creative director for the label and his role as the producer of the Mamas & the Papas and Barry McGuire would remain unchanged. Jay Lasker would be appointed president of the new ABC/Dunhill label. Though not mentioned in the trades, the latter part of the deal was for the next five years. Also not announced was the purchase price, which amounted to $3 million split three ways. Lou walked away from the deal $1 million richer thanks in part to the Mamas & the Papas who were heating up nationally. The group couldn't help but be somewhat rankled by the announcement. They didn't benefit in any way from it and all they came away with was a little more cynicism toward the business side of music.

In the midst of their amazing chart run on both the singles and LPs charts, the Mamas & the Papas were invited to perform at the Sonny & Cher Appreciation Concert at the Hollywood Bowl on Saturday, April 2, sponsored by Los Angeles' top radio station KHJ, which was riding high on its new "Boss Radio" format. Even though the group was one of eight opening performers, and near the bottom of the marquee, John had made good on the promise he'd made back in August and he did it with four months to spare. In the face of overwhelming internal tension, the Mamas & the Papas were able to put their personal problems aside and ride their first wave of success, offering a fresh, original rock and roll sound in the face of such daunting musical competition. If they could only somehow get past the emotional unrest that comes along with a love triangle, the possibilities seemed limitless. John went back to work and sought healing through songwriting and began writing a classic that would shed light on the problem and perhaps lend a bit of levity to it. Little did he know that more trouble was lurking just around the corner.

Early modeling head shot of
Michelle Gilliam, circa 1960.
Michael Ochs Archives/Getty Images

The Halifax Three, 1963. From left to right, Denny Doherty, Pat LaCroix, and Richard Byrne.
Michael Ochs Archives/Getty Images

The Journeymen, 1961. From left: Dick Weissman, John Phillips, and Scott McKenzie.
Michael Ochs Archives/Getty Images

The Big 3. From left: Tim Rose,
Cass Elliot, and James Hendricks.
Photofest

The Mugwumps, 1964. From left: Zal Yanovsky, Jim Hendricks, Cass Elliot, and Denny Doherty.
Warner Bros./Photofest ©Warner Bros.

The Mamas & the Papas with Barry McGuire, 1965.
Michael Ochs Archives/Getty Images

The Mamas & the Papas featuring a bandaged Denny following his swimming accident in Mexico.
Photofest

The Mamas & the Papas with Lou Adler, 1966.
Michael Ochs Archives/Getty Images

The Mamas & the Papas at L'Etoile in NYC with Michelle's temporary replacement Jill Gibson.
Michael Ochs Archives/Getty Images

The Mamas and the Papas performing on *The Ed Sullivan Show*, 1967.
From Original Negative/Alamy Stock Photo

John Phillips consoling Michelle on the docks of Southampton, England, following Cass's arrest. *Mirrorpix*

John Phillips standing outside his and Michelle's Bel Air mansion.
Trinity Mirror/Mirrorpix/Alamy Stock Photo

The Mamas & the Papas on stage at the Monterey Pop Festival, June 18, 1967.
Author's collection

The Mamas &
the Papas 1971
reunion album
cover.
*Vinyls/Alamy
Stock Photo*

CHAPTER 17:
I'LL BURY YOU ALL!

"Fools rush in where angels fear to tread." The opening line to the 1936 Johnny Mercer and Rube Bloom standard had come to sum up John Phillips' relationship with his wayward wife Michelle. In their three-and-a-half-year marriage, she had already had two extramarital affairs, including one with his closest friend and tenor, and karma was coming back to bite him in the ass. John himself was a serial philanderer during his first marriage and took a big social gamble when he left Susie for this gorgeous blonde model nearly 10 years younger than him. Perhaps some friends warned him at the time and it's more than likely that many thought it but never expressed it openly. Perhaps John also felt it but was too busy thinking carnally at the time, even though their relationship did expand to being more than just sex. As a moderately successful folk singer, he took great pride in his trophy wife and eagerly took her along with him to gigs and appearances, eventually incorporating her into the band. On the Hootenanny Tour, back in 1963, he relished the moments when his young California bride showed him public affection, telling Denny and others, "Isn't she great? Got to go do it," as the two rushed off the bus for a conjugal visit.

Ironically, during this period, John was faithful. He hadn't cheated on Michelle thus far and was devoted to having a traditional marriage, or as much as they could have in the world of modern entertainment, where swinging wasn't extraordinary. When Michelle's infidelity hit him in the face, his reaction was to not talk about it. In his mind, his mere displeasure and anger should be enough to overcome the problem and prevent future affairs, but it only served to exacerbate the problem. His solution was always for them to make a fresh start and never mention it again but both times, she relapsed. For Michelle, infidelity was a by-product of marriage. She grew up witnessing it in her parents' example. Both had had extramarital affairs, and, after her mother's death, her father was married and divorced multiple times. Being bandmates in the Mamas & the Papas only complicated their relationship. John, normally happy-go-lucky and optimistic in day-to-day life, was a relentless taskmaster in the studio. He was constantly striving for the sound in his mind and his vocal arrangements required countless rehearsals and retakes. Unlike her counterparts, Michelle was not a trained or a natural singer and she struggled mightily during the sessions for the first album and built up a resentment.

Outside the studio, their latest fresh start wasn't going well. After moving into their tiny house at 8671 Lookout Mountain Avenue in Laurel Canyon, the two fought like cats and dogs, causing their sex life to dry up. Michelle's affair with Denny still hung over their marriage like a specter. She was still noticeably conflicted, and it poured salt on John's wounds. The tension was so palpable that John elected to move in with Denny at his new pad on Woods Drive, which served a twofold purpose. John too could engage in meaningless sex, with a host of Canyon groupies who made the rounds, and he could keep a watchful eye on Denny to make sure he wasn't sneaking off to see Michelle. John would be a cuckold no longer. Fidelity had gone out the window. The sprawling bachelor pad, which sat atop a ridge in the Hollywood Hills, overlooking Sunset Boulevard, made an impressive site for rock star bacchanalia. There was a constant cloud of marijuana smoke billowing, and LSD was always handy. There was a large swimming pool in the back and a sunken living room, a site of frequent orgies and one-on-one sexual encounters, which they dubbed the "fuck pit." Shortly after John moved in, Dr. Eric Hord joined them. Part of the Mamas & the Papas' agreement with Dunhill Records was to clear up their accompanist's legal problems stemming from his drug bust back in New York, and he made himself right at home, enhancing the party atmosphere and rejoining them as a side player.

Although John was in concupiscent heaven, having sex with young groupies in order to fulfill his insatiable sexual desires, he did crave relationships and started seeing Israeli photographer Nurit Wilde and L.A. socialite and model Ann Marshall, the daughter of notable stage and film actor Herbert Marshall and salesgirl at the trendy Los Angeles boutique Paraphernalia. Michelle was taking advantage of her newfound marital freedom too. She could be seen nightly on the Sunset Strip with a host of new Canyon friends, and it drove John nuts, even though he gave the appearance of having moved on. When Michelle would come to Denny's house for rehearsal or to talk band business, she was pleasant, but, if they'd run into each other on the Strip, she'd be coy and oftentimes dismissive of him. Even with so many beautiful Los Angeles women at his disposal, it was Michelle John still desired, and if he couldn't have her, no one could. In their network of friends, he let it be known that she was off-limits, and anyone who crossed him would suffer his wrath. But his network didn't cover every musician in Los Angeles. One evening, at a party at singer Cyrus Faryar's house, Michelle met singer and musician Gene Clark, who had moved on from the Byrds back in January, and began seeing him covertly. Within days, it turned into a full-blown love affair and, once again, Michelle found herself dodging her beleaguered husband. Though he didn't yet know it, John faced a steep uphill battle but, beneath all the heartache and outrage, he still longed for his estranged wife and was ready for her to open up her heart and let this fool rush in.

As a wife, Michelle had proven to be a lot of things to John. She was headstrong, prideful, impulsive and defiant but perhaps her most important characteristic was being an incredible songwriting muse. John had already scored two major hits whose origins centered on her whims, and their recent separation put him back to work writing several more. Going back to his grade school days at Linton Hall, he sought healing writing poetry and, over time, transformed it into a million-dollar product in songwriting. Her affair with Denny proved no exception. With an idea already in place from months earlier, John quickly put pen to paper and crafted a simple lyric that would come alive in the studio. It was a first for John, writing in the other man's voice, and painted him as a total cad.

I'm in way over my head, now she thinks that I love her.
Because that's what I said, now I never think of her.

Although that certainly wasn't the case with Denny, it sure was enough to make him blanch but he was far too weak to object and had no ground on which to stand. John's stature, both figuratively and literally, was far too imposing, so he was at his mercy. John took full advantage of having the moral upper hand, but he did prove merciful to Denny, sharing a co-writing credit with him for simply inspiring his latest song, which, in a short time, would prove extremely lucrative. Over time, Denny would take credit for writing the melody, but with John writing every single band arrangement, that's highly questionable. As the song continued, John's lyrics prove just how conflicted the protagonist is. Even though he initially admits that he's stringing the girl along, he contradicts himself moments later.

But I really need that girl.

Don't know why I'm living a lie.

Even though the song maintains the paramour's perspective throughout, John still finds a moment to send Denny a simple message.

But it makes me feel so good to know.

She'll never leave me.

When they set out to record to "I Saw Her Again" in April, John's arranging chops were razor sharp, and he brought with him his most complex vocal arrangement yet with chords that took unusual twists and turns while the vocals hung tightly with them. Like two jets in aerobatic flight, the vocals swooped under and above and swirled around the rhythm, augmenting the melody beautifully, proving that John was among the best of contemporary composers. Starting off with a ghostly vocal chorale, their vocals were multi-tracked, giving them a richer, fuller sound. When Denny belts out "I saw her again last night," three seconds later, he sings with the desperate senses of a spurned lover that only he could muster. John's vocal interplay with Cass and Michelle were his most ambitious to date. On paper, the "ah's," "ooh's" and "dit-ditti-dit's" must've seemed bizarre to his bandmates but they perfectly accentuated Denny's impassioned lead, and Cass' backing vocals are particularly mirthful. Being very familiar with the song's stimulus, she took particular delight in John's pointed lyrics, putting extra oomph into her soaring contralto, almost as her only act of vengeance toward Denny and Michelle.

Lou and John designed "I Saw Her Again" specifically to be a chart-topper. Once again, the sessions convened at Western Recorders with the usual cast of musicians. Though the arrangement was designed with the Beatles in mind, Lou and the Wrecking Crew musicians were clearly inspired by their work with Phil Spector's latter-day Philles releases and, more recently, Brian

Wilson's *Pet Sounds* LP. Sessions for that album, on which most of them played, had recently wrapped up, with the lion's share taking place at Western, and John's latest song had much more in common with that sound than anything the Beatles had done up to that point. The strength of the song lay in John's lyrics and vocal arrangements with the overdubs being mostly complementary but, at times, excessive. Denny's vocals tend to nearly be drowned out in spots. Noted composer Jimmie Haskell arranged a swirling string arrangement that comes in around the 23-second mark. Along with Cass and Michelle's spirited vocals, the arrangement keeps pace throughout the song, breaking into a beautiful intermezzo closer to the song's ending, which was omitted from the initial single release but placed on the LP.

Perhaps what set the song apart and made it even more special was one of those beautiful mistakes that could never be planned but give a song so much character that it can't be omitted. After laying down the basic music track, they recorded Denny's lead and the others' backing vocals in the multitrack. Like most professionally recorded songs of that era, multiple takes were done. On one particular take, following the bridge, where Denny sings, for the final time, "Every time I see that girl, you know I want to lay down and die," after the rhythm stops and goes back to the top, "I saw her again last night," engineer Bones Howe punched in too early on the vocal track, in order to capture their vocal, and all of the Mamas & the Papas came in a bar too early. They had to redo that portion, so Bones rolled the vocal tape back to the punch-in point but didn't go far enough. Unbeknownst to him, the portion of Denny's vocal that came in too early remained. After finishing the take, they mixed what they had down and listened back. What they heard was Denny singing, "I saw her . . . I saw her again last night," with the first part being from the take where everybody came in too early. It created the effect that Denny sounded like he started at the wrong point, caught himself, and picked up at the right point, which made him sound anxious and perfectly matched the song's intensity and subject matter. It was a glorious mistake, and Lou loved it. He told Bones to leave it in, and it became a classic song with a classic flub that doesn't sound like a flub to the untrained ear.

The single was released on June 25, 1966, as the follow up to "Monday, Monday," and hit the *Billboard* charts at number 53 the following week and had a quick climb, reaching the Top 10 by July 23 and peaking at number five the following week. It was another innovative song, based on personal experience, that capitalized on their fresh sound but wasn't a carbon copy of their prior hit singles. John had another million seller that put more money in his pocket, making the bachelor pad even more ostentatious, and pissing their neighbors off mightily with nonstop parties and a constantly lit pool.

With the "I Saw Her Again" single being mixed and pressed, and with a number one single and a number one album, the Mamas & the Papas were a hot commodity, and demand for live performances was increasing daily. Dunhill executive and group manager Bobby Roberts was feeling the pressure to get them out on the road, but he knew the current group dynamic. The four could barely be in a room together, let alone go on tour. But there was a lot of money in touring, especially as a headliner, and with every passing weekend not performing in front of an audience, they were losing a lot of it. He pressed John to get everyone in gear. There were big advances being thrown at them, and they had to seize the opportunity.

John and the others had worked hard to get to this point, and the fruits of their labors were greater than any of them ever could have imagined. Only a year earlier they were living hand-to-mouth with barely a nickel to rub between them and now the world was their oyster and the disrupted love triangle was threatening it. Right before a rehearsal one afternoon, before Cass arrived, John attempted to try and sort everything out and he laid it all out for them.

"We'd better straighten all this out fast," he told Michelle and Denny. "There's plenty of pressure coming down on me to get us out on the road. Cass is going crazy because she's dying to do her thing onstage and Bobby Roberts is going crazy. He's got dozens of calls coming in for bookings and he can't commit to them because we can't work the road in close quarters."

Denny made it even plainer.

"OK, which is it going to be, him or me?"

It caught everybody off guard and rattled up the tension considerably. This was not going the way John had anticipated. Caught in the middle, Michelle was overcome.

"I can't make up my mind," she said. "I don't want to make up my mind. I don't want to talk about it," she exclaimed.

She burst into tears and stormed out, passing Cass, who was on her way in, and retreated to Lookout Mountain with no resolution. Naturally curious, Cass asked what that was all about, and Denny did his best to explain.

"You people are too civilized, it's sick," she yelled. "Like bartering, it won't work! None of you should be respected."

Cass stormed out too. It seemed like nothing would be resolved, and the Mamas & the Papas' touring life was in danger, which, in the competitive musical landscape of 1966, could seriously limit their continued success on the radio. The Byrds, the Lovin' Spoonful, Bob Dylan, and all their other major folk-rock competitors were constantly touring, keep their names on the lips of music fans not only in the major markets, but in strong smaller ones as well.

Traditionally, a rivalry between two men over one woman's affections can bring out the worst but, oddly enough, in this case, it served to make John and Denny closer, at least on the surface. Now that the four were swimming in money and could afford impulse purchases, the two Papas bought matching Triumph motorcycles to comfort their mutual heartaches. But, once again, for John, it served a dual purpose. Since the motorcycles were so loud, one would know if the other attempted to slip off and court Michelle. But it was a fool's errand. Unbeknownst to either of them, Michelle was in the throes of a passionate affair with Gene Clark and all their attempts to woo her back were in vain.

In many ways, Gene Clark was the combination of John and Denny's best qualities. His creativity, passion and songwriting were on par with John's. In two albums with the Byrds, he'd written, or co-written, over one-third of their original songs, including the B sides to their number one singles "Mr. Tambourine Man" and "Turn, Turn, Turn," earning him the ire of his jealous bandmates who were still finding their songwriting chops. While they were still poor and living communally, Gene was driving around in a Ferrari. By the time he met Michelle, he'd been out of the Byrds for several months, but they were still benefiting from him with their current single "Eight Miles High," a song he'd conceived but was commandeered by bandmates Jim McGuinn and David Crosby.

Looks-wise, he resembled Denny with his aquiline nose and Prince Valiant haircut, although he'd recently had it cropped a little tighter since his leaving the Byrds. And, like John and Denny, he had folk roots, playing alongside Barry McGuire in the New Christy Minstrels for six months before striking out on his own. But his haircut, songwriting skills, and folk background are where the comparisons end. Gene possessed a rugged handsomeness and brooding James Dean–like intensity, and his athletic, muscular physique not only set him apart from John and Denny but many of the singers of the time. Gene was built like a halfback, and, although he wasn't athletically inclined, his chiseled physique drew the bulk of feminine attention when he stood front and center, shaking the tambourine. In person, he could be intimidating and imposing even though he had a gentle demeanor. At a tour stop in Virginia Beach in 1965, fellow Byrds David Crosby and Jim McGuinn managed to piss off a couple locals when they launched some firecrackers that accidentally landed on their adjacent hotel balcony and exploded right next to them while they were drinking. The two climbed over the railing and chased after them with Crosby taking the bulk of their beating while attempting to shut and lock the sliding door. Hearing the melee, Gene came rushing into the room, shirtless, and, upon seeing him, the drunken rednecks immediately retreated to their room.

Standing next to Michelle, they looked like a Hollywood power couple, convoying around in her Jaguar XKE and his Ferrari, but they were anything but. Gene insisted that their relationship be kept as quiet as possible. They were never seen together publicly, and, although he and John had never met, they shared a musical kinship and he did not want to be known as a paramour. Most of their time together was spent at Gene's Laurel Canyon home at 2014 Rosilla Place, less than a half-mile away from John and Michelle's house, which was buttressed by a dead end so that anyone coming close to the house could be easily spotted. The guilt Gene felt sneaking around with Michelle was overwhelming for him at times. Combine that with the stress he was under with his new band, known as the Group, sure to be compared with the Byrds. It would cause him to wake up in the middle of the night in a panic, and, several times, after sleeping together, he would tell Michelle that this was all wrong and she had to leave.

"We shouldn't be doing this," he would tell her as he rushed her to the door.

Michelle, on the other hand, had become a pro at cheating on John, and it hardly weighed on her conscience at all. For Gene's sake, she made it seem like she was doing her best to keep it under wraps but would let her guard down from time to time or act out passive-aggressively toward her husband. She'd occasionally call him to inquire about band-related business, while Gene was over, and make little to no attempt to conceal the fact that another man was in their home. John was no dummy. He could sense something was up and was able to deduce, through either his own faculties or through friends, that she was having an affair with Gene, although he never confronted him.

John didn't take it lying down. Michelle's affair with Gene only brought him closer to Ann Marshall. They spent much of May and June in a love affair, rendezvousing at the legendary Sunset Tower Hotel in West Hollywood. Besides making love, the two basked in one another's company while taking in the sounds of summer 1966, including the Beach Boys' *Pet Sounds* album. Being the child of Hollywood aristocracy, she would regale John with stories of old Hollywood, including her father's torrid romance with Gloria Swanson. John also grew closer to Lou Adler, taking him on as not only a friend but a mentor. Lou's life got a little easier with the May 14 announcement that entertainment conglomerate ABC-Paramount had purchased Dunhill Records and Trousdale Publishing. John often hung out at his home in Palm Springs, working on songs for their second album and taking in Lou's sage advice, which bolstered his confidence by stressing his importance within the band dynamic and helped put the group's petty squabbling in its proper perspective.

Even though the band stress was still at a fever pitch, Lou and Bobby Roberts were able to convince the Mamas & the Papas to get out on the road, beginning with some concert packages along the East Coast in mid-May, opening up for Peter & Gordon at Newark Symphony Hall in Newark, New Jersey. From there, they headed south to the Bayfront Center in St. Petersburg, Florida, on May 27, where they shared a bill with Brian Hyland and several local bands. After that, the group headed back home for a three-night stand in early June at the Melodyland Theater in Anaheim, California, with Simon & Garfunkel as the opening act. Though there was still palpable tension within the group, the first night went over uneventfully, but, on the second show of the second night, Saturday, June 4, all hell broke loose. The simmering tension between John and Michelle finally boiled over with the catalyst being a bright, beaming ex-Byrd who brazenly walked into the venue and sat front and center.

Shortly before the Melodyland appearances, near the end of a rendezvous with Michelle, Gene mentioned that he'd like to see the Mamas & the Papas perform live, so she casually agreed to arrange for a ticket for him through

Bobby Roberts' secretary. It was a risky move that that seemed harmless at the time. Considering her reaction on the night of the show, Michelle surely knew John was wise to their affair. After a soft acoustic performance by Simon & Garfunkel that whetted the crowd's appetite, the Mamas & the Papas were announced. Walking onstage to rousing applause, Cass glanced at Michelle with a look of terror, pointing out Gene with a head bob. Michelle had confided to her about the affair, and though she resented Michelle for sleeping with Denny, the affair with Gene brought her relief because it kept her fellow Mama away from Denny and pissed off John.

They needed to act and fast. Hastily, they positioned themselves in front of the mic stands nearest Gene, forcing John and Denny to the opposite end of the stage. Things went smoothly for much of the concert in terms of the cover-up, but the performance was somewhat stressful. The accompanying band was distractingly loud, which drowned out the vocals and reduced both "California Dreamin'" and "Monday, Monday" to discordant cacophony, which surely grated on John's perfectionist nerves. Toward the end, Michelle, much more relaxed, began singing directly to Gene and blowing him kisses. Catching his estranged wife's over-emotive singing and following her line of sight, which landed directly on Gene, he became incensed and promptly lost his mind mid-song. He stopped performing altogether and leaned into his mic.

"Get the fuck over here!" he shouted over the crowd of 3,200 young adults, teenagers and their parents and catching everybody onstage off guard.

Michelle knew she was busted. She and Cass carefully switched places with John and Denny, passing each other uncomfortably onstage. With everybody repositioned, they did their best to carry on in front of the bewildered crowd. John was seething and now was near his wife's newest lover, who was grinning from ear to ear. It took all he had to resist swinging his guitar at his head. As the concert came to close, emotions were running high and a sense of dread came over three-quarters of the group. Nobody knew what John was going to do. Would he confront Gene, or would he go after Michelle, who was mentally preparing herself for a race to the door? He chose the latter and chased his bride off the stage, up the aisle, through the backstage area and into the parking lot where he finally managed to cut her off at the driver's side door of her Jaguar, grabbed her arm and shouted at her that she was fired.

"I don't think you have the authority to fire me," Michelle shouted back.

"Oh really?" he replied contrarily. Pulling her closer for emphasis, he shouted, "You wait and see. You're out of this group! You're never singing with this group again!"

Michelle broke free, jumped into her car, and tore out of the parking lot. Lou, who witnessed the entire spectacle, grabbed John and tried calming him down. They both got into John's Jaguar, along with Ann Marshall who, ironically, was also in attendance, and sped off to Lou's Palm Springs home at 120 mph. John needed to calm down and get away from everybody and everything that reminded him of Michelle. After a long heart-to-heart with Lou, in which he told him he couldn't continue with Michelle in the band, he popped some acid in hopes of forgetting her. In the haze of his acid trip, he made his decision. Michelle was indeed out, and he meant it. Unfortunately, with the pressure of a second album looming over them, it posed a challenge but, for the sake of his sanity, he was willing to take the risk and would put his plan into action immediately.

The Sunday, June 5, concert at Melodyland and subsequent gigs were canceled or rescheduled and John organized a meeting with Cass and Denny to discuss the incident with Michelle and the future of the group. He told them that his unrequited love for Michelle was driving him to the breaking point and that, for the sake of his sanity, he could no longer be around her. Finally, he let all his anger out at Denny, asking him why he set him up for this and that he had to know of the consequences.

"You had to know it would come down to this! Was it worth it?" John barked.

Denny was visibly angry and hurt by John's words but couldn't muster the courage to say anything. John made it clear, in no uncertain terms, that he wanted to continue making music in some fashion and that Michelle wouldn't be part of it. They could join him or stay with her.

"I'll quit, form another group or do something totally different," he told them. "One of us has got to go. I'm quitting, as of now, unless Michelle goes."

They agreed that Michelle was out. As far as the band's success was concerned, John was the goose that laid the golden egg and Michelle was just a pretty face that could be replaced. To pledge any loyalty to her, under these conditions, would be fruitless. It was particularly tough on Denny. He was still in love with her, but his love was also becoming unrequited. Ironically, he found himself in the same position he'd put Cass in these many years. To cope with all the tension and heartache, he found himself diving more into Crown Royal Canadian Whiskey and developing into a functioning alcoholic. The following day, John and the others approached Jay Lasker, the new president of Dunhill Records, and asked him to have the label's attorneys draw up a formal letter stating Michelle's official firing from the group. Though befuddled, he complied with their wishes. With several concert dates lined up and fast approaching, John went to work searching for her replacement. He didn't know it at the time, but she was a lot closer than he'd expected.

On the other side of the canyon, Michelle was unaware of the plans made against her by her bandmates, although, in the days following the incident at Melodyland, their silence would become deafening. She easily deduced that something was up and was going through mental gymnastics trying to figure out exactly what it was. John's words in the parking lot stuck with her and she began wrestling with whether or not he actually meant what he said or if he was just blowing smoke. And could he even fire her?

Immediately after their fight, she had fled to a party at Cyrus Faryar's house, where Gene awaited looking like the cat who swallowed the canary, although he acted very surprised.

"Gene, how could you do that?" Michelle asked.

He claimed ignorance but had to have known something went down after John's public meltdown. After all, Gene was no stranger to band fireworks. He just didn't know the extent of the damage. The fallout from Melodyland spelled the end of their affair but Michelle wouldn't learn that it also spelled the end of her tenure in the Mamas & the Papas until a few weeks later.

After a little time to cool off, John was back in Denny's house but was making plans to move to an apartment in Sunset Towers in August. With the dust still settling from the weekend, the nonstop partying subsided for a while, and a more somber mood filled the house. John always sought solace and did his best thinking in the heated pool and went for a dip one evening shortly after the incident, smoking grass and taking in the city lights and the laurel and jasmine that fragranced the night air. While he was relaxing, Denny came out jingling his motorcycle keys.

"I'm heading down to the Strip to see what's happening," he told John.

"Want some company?" John asked as he stepped out of the pool and began toweling himself off.

"Nah, it's cool," Denny replied. "I'd just as soon hang out alone."

John thought nothing of it. The firing of Michelle was hard on everybody and temperaments had naturally become muted and restrained as a result. After all, he'd laid it on Denny pretty hard, and his friend was caught in the middle of the breakup with his wife and felt like a total cad. But all this had lulled John into a false sense of security. Unbeknownst to John, Denny had been communicating with Michelle through covert phone calls and arranged to meet her outside the Whisky a Go Go in a few hours. By telling John he was essentially going out to clear his head, he was able to get around their motorcycle security code. In his 1986 autobiography *Papa John*, John Phillips sets up the rest of the story.

Denny roared off on the Triumph and sped down Woods Drive to the Strip. The drugged-out nightcrawlers all turned to look. He pulled up along the curb in front of the Whisky and spotted a lean blonde beauty in tight jeans. She recognized him right away and walked to him.

"Hop on," he said.

"Where to?" Michelle asked, mounting the rear cushion. She clasped her hands tightly across Denny's stomach. Her head snapped back as the cycle tore off. A purple felt sack of Crown Royal dangled from the handlebar. Denny gunned the Triumph with a vengeance all over L.A. through the cool night. He was restless and disturbed. The cycle climbed up the canyon and came to a stop in front of the small red house on Lookout Mountain. "Why are you taking me home so soon?" Michelle asked.

Denny got off and faced her. "Look, this whole thing is too fuckin' strange and wishy-washy. I got an idea. Just stay on the bike with me and let's split . . ."

"What?"

"Yeah, just split, get the fuck outta here, tonight. I got four, five hundred bucks in my pocket right now. Yes. That's what we should do. Whattya say?"

"Where do you think we're going to go?"

"Duluth, Memphis, the islands. What's the fucking difference? I don't care. I'll work in a gas station. We're in love, aren't we? I mean, we'll just run away from all this crap and start over, just the two of us. Raise a family together. Isn't this what it's been all about?"

Michelle was dumbfounded. She stared away through the trees, then tried to read Denny's intense eyes to see if this was a prank. "We're in love?" She was stupefied, shaking her head in bewilderment. "I think you're crazy," she muted solemnly.

"*I'm* crazy? You wanna keep sneakin' through the bushes and lying to John? I say fuck it. Let's just split."

"You're out of your mind, Denny. We agreed to stop it at the Green House, remember? We promised John."

"John can't work or sleep, Cass is crazed. I don't know where the fuck I stand. I thought you and I had something that . . ."

"I'll see you around, man," she said, getting off the bike. "I can't handle this anymore. Let's just cool it, okay?"

Denny watched her walk off toward the house. "Yeah, sure," he said. "Cool it."

Denny had made his stand and landed flat on his face. It was a bold declaration of his love: to leave everyone and everything behind, including fame, notoriety and riches, and run off back to anonymity. But, while he was searching for true love, Michelle, raised in the shadow of Tinseltown, wasn't interested, at least not his interpretation of it. She'd come too far and endured too much to throw independence, financial stability and the adoration of millions of fans away. And his timing was peculiar. Before the Melodyland incident, with their current single racing up the charts, they had finished most of the tracks for their second album and now, here was the lead singer urging her to leave it all and be with him. She'd find his out his motive a few days later.

In a letter addressed to Michelle Gilliam Phillips, dated June 28, 1966, from the Law Firm of Mitchell, Silberberg & Knupp, Dunhill's legal team, Michelle received her walking papers from the Mamas & the Papas, and it completely blindsided her. It read in part: *This letter is to advise you that the undersigned no longer desire to record or perform with you in the future. Moreover, the undersigned desire to terminate any business relationship with you that may have heretofore existed.*

The bottom righthand corner of the letter bore the signatures by John, Cass, and Denny. It went on for two more paragraphs, of mostly legalese, but she didn't need to read beyond the first two sentences to get the message. She was out and it was official, and it wasn't only John who wanted her gone. Over the next several days, she went through a range of emotions: anger, fear, loneliness, disbelief. She'd expected some sort of terse rebuke from John, but she could always work on him. After he calmed down, a few nights of passionate sex and stroking his ego could undo most of the damage. It had worked before. Cass and Denny's inclusion in the decision was the gut punch. This was treachery, as far as she was concerned, and John had doubled-down on what he'd declared outside Melodyland by involving them.

She finally convinced herself that this was a ruse designed to make her feel bad and repent. After a day or two of crying and mentally processing everything, she fled to New York with her old high school friend Cynthia Webb, a Whisky a Go Go dancer, who was heading to play a series of dates at the Apollo with singer Otis Redding. Cynthia invited Michelle, and it was just what she needed to try and forget her dilemma. But those few days could not erase the fact that she was out of the Mamas & the Papas and had no viable alternatives to maintain the lifestyle to which she'd become accustomed. When she got back in L.A., she finally consulted her attorney to see if she had any legal recourse. The lawyer advised that she get the three together and ask for a formal release.

The showdown took place at Western Recorders, most likely in early July, during their first sessions following a short trip to London, England, where the band took some time to get away and rehearse the songs for the second album. In order to eviscerate any tangible evidence of Michelle's involvement in the songs they'd already recorded, John decided all her vocal contributions would be erased, a process that began on July 5. After making her way to Western in the afternoon, she walked into the Studio 3 control room where Lou and engineer Bones Howe presided over the board. In the studio, John, Cass and Denny milled about, working through arrangements, as the session was only beginning, unaware of her presence for several minutes. There was another figure present in the studio too: a tall, lanky woman, a couple years older than her, with gaunt cheekbones and a chiseled jawline, holding her tambourine. It was Lou's girlfriend, Jill Gibson, a periphery figure in the L.A. pop scene for several years, particularly in the career of Jan & Dean. Michelle had most likely noticed her before, but she was not the focus of this particular trip. When Lou tried preventing her from entering the studio, John spotted the commotion and wasted no time coming over to confront her.

"What do you want?" he asked her incredulously.

"I want a release," she replied.

"You can go fuck yourself," he quickly replied, as he made his way back into the studio.

Brushing Lou aside, she followed him in, fully intent on continuing the argument that had been building up inside her for the better part of a month. The rest of the band sat idly by and witnessed the inevitable blowout. John continued and hit her right where it hurt her.

"Oh, and by the way, stop pestering Denny with your calls."

"You want *me* to stop pestering Denny?" she replied.

Dumbfounded by what she'd just heard, she turned toward Denny, sitting on a drum stool, already drunk on Crown Royal, and grinning a drunkard's grin.

"Denny is that right?" she asked.

Maintaining his grin, he took another swig from the bottle, and said nothing.

With a well of anger already built up inside her, she reached the boiling point. Clenching her right hand into a fist, she flew toward Denny and socked him right across his chin, knocking him back into the wall and partially off his stool. Lou intervened, attempting to defuse the situation and get her out of there. Cass just watched, a passive-aggressive way of not supporting the devil woman who stole her man. As Michelle opened the door that led to the hallway, she turned and uttered four words that, over time, would come back to haunt her.

"I'll bury you all!"

And with that, she was gone.

CHAPTER 18:
MAMA JILL & TWIN GABLES

By the time the sessions for the Mamas & the Papas' second album rolled around, the approach to manufacturing their unique sound was fully fleshed out. Beginning with "California Dreamin'" in late 1965, engineer Bones Howe created the blueprint, recording the male and female vocals on separate RCA DX-77 microphones into a 4-track Ampex 300 recorder. Bones set the microphones up so that John and Denny would be facing Cass and Michelle, allowing for more natural singing and greater rejection and laid them out on separate tracks in the recorder. The other two tracks would be filled with music. Afterward, a new set of vocals would be recorded, in the same key because of limited VSO capability, and laid them atop the first-pass vocals in the multitrack. Bones would then mix that session down and bounce it to a second Ampex 300 deck and double the vocals again, giving the final mix three layers of vocals, which resulted in a richer, fuller sound on record and in car speakers.

When Bones left the sessions in August, he was replaced by Henry Lewy, which made room for John Phillips to take total control, and he never relinquished it. When the group was set to record, Lou would book 12-hour sessions at Western, convening at 4:00 p.m. and ending at 4:00 a.m. but oftentimes going over. Always the consummate perfectionist, John ordered take after take after take until reaching the sound he'd heard in his head. His taskmaster efforts usually ended up with his bandmates passed out in the studio, and it was particularly hard on Michelle, who was the least experienced and weakest singer of the group.

There was a world of difference between the sessions for the second album and *If You Can Believe Your Eyes and Ears*. For the latter, the band had lived communally for the better part of a year, rehearsed relentlessly, were ambitious and always came to the studio together. Harmonizing became second nature. After Denny and Michelle's affair was exposed, getting the four of them together in the studio to lay down vocals proved much more difficult and, considering the circumstances, they weren't as tight as they had been. When John and Lou were finally able to wrangle them for four dates in late April, five songs were completed, and three others begun. Michelle's firing served to complicate matters by causing an indeterminate delay. It would take a few weeks to find her replacement, and an emotional John insisted that every trace of Michelle be removed from the previously completed tracks. That meant vocals had to be recut and remixed, which would take considerable time. It was a tall task, and, as John braced himself for a long audition process, Lou had a simpler solution.

In April, his close friend Jan Berry, the musically gifted half of the hit-making duo Jan & Dean, suffered severe head trauma and massive bodily injuries when he slammed his Corvette into a parked truck at the intersection of Sunset Boulevard and Whittier Drive at 80 mph. In a cruel twist of life imitating art, the crash site was only a short distance from the actual 90-degree curve that inspired their 1964 Top 10 car crash anthem "Dead Man's Curve." It left him in a coma in UCLA Medical Center's ICU for two months, emerging with severe brain damage, partial paralysis, and speech impairment, which caused him to have to relearn speaking and walking. A few months before the accident, weary of his infidelity, his girlfriend Jill Gibson ended their relationship and moved out of their 4,000-square-foot Bel Air home and into a small apartment on Glendon Avenue in Westwood. Jan's accident brought them back together as she'd often visit him at the hospital during his convalescence. Lou was another frequent visitor, playing him Laurel and Hardy movies in an effort to lift his spirits. Though he'd known Jill since his earliest days producing Jan & Dean, their relationship quickly became romantic. Lou's marriage to Shelley Fabares was essentially dead on arrival. Although they'd dated for two years before their wedding on June 7, 1964, at which Jan served as best man, the couple quickly proved a mismatch, and it wasn't long before Lou put himself back on the singles market. (*Note: They officially separated in January 1967 but wouldn't finalize their divorce until 1980.*) Lou and Jill kept their relationship as secret as possible, but it wasn't long before whispers and innuendo began spreading around the studio and at Dunhill's offices. Phil Sloan, a devoted friend of Jan's, refused to participate in any session in which she was involved, and many of the musicians, particularly drummer Hal Blaine, were pissed off over what they perceived as a betrayal.

On paper, Jill Gibson was a ready-made replacement for Michelle. She was an attractive, blonde ex-model who, despite her limited singing ability, had been involved in the music business for several years and, much like Michelle, had been romantically involved with an extremely talented musician. She was also a California girl, having grown up in the suburbs of Los Angeles, on the border of West L.A. and Santa Monica.

Born on June 18, 1942, in L.A., the youngest of two daughters to travel agent entrepreneurs John and Joyce Gibson, Jill expressed an interest in music at age 10 when she took up the violin in order to play in her grammar school orchestra. She attended University High School in West Los Angeles whose notable alumni included Judy Garland, Elizabeth Taylor and Roddy McDowell. During her tenure, she roamed the halls with Nancy Sinatra, her brother Frank Jr., future Beach Boy Bruce Johnston, Doors drummer John Densmore, singer/songwriter Randy Newman, producer Kim Fowley, Dean Torrence and Jan Berry. She and Jan began dating her junior year just as his act with Dean was taking off with their Top 10 hit "Baby Talk," which Lou co-produced. At 19, she became one of the first models for the embryonic Nina Blanchard Agency and appeared in advertisements for Max Factor, dressmaker Peggy Hunt and in photo shoots with iconic fashion model Peggy Moffett. She also became a fixture at Jan & Dean's sessions at Western and United Recording Studios, and her semi-bare back graced the picture sleeve of their 1960 single "We Go Together."

As their popularity unfolded, and Jan developed more as a creative arranger and songwriter, Jill became involved in his projects and sang on several album tracks. He put her together with Dean's then-girlfriend, Judy Lovejoy, as a female version of Jan & Dean, issuing one single on the Festoon label in 1962. When Judy & Jill petered out, Jan brought her into the creative process, recording several songs she coauthored, including "When It's Over," their 1965 number 27 hit "You Really Know How to Hurt a Guy" and its flip side "It's as Easy as 1, 2, 3," the latter of which she sang exclusively and released as a single on Imperial a year earlier. At the time of their breakup in late 1965, Jill was moving away from music and into the field of professional photography. In other words, she was available.

Her good looks, along with her singing and songwriting ability, made her a no-brainer to Lou and posed a simple solution to Dunhill's Mamas & Papas problem. John, still Lou's protégé, was open to the idea and trusted his judgment. Considering the circumstances, he was in no frame of mind to act rationally and having a tall, good-looking blonde replace Michelle would really stick it to her. All they needed to do was convince Jill, but when Lou approached her about being Michelle's replacement, she wasn't exactly bowled over by the offer. She was a fan of their music but didn't want to place herself in the middle of John's marital problems. Having endured her own relationship turmoil with Jan, a superstar and sex symbol in his own right, she was well aware of the strain the music industry could put on a relationship.

Although unsure, she nevertheless accompanied the group to New York City, where ABC Records held a reception in their honor in July. Almost a year to the day of racing out of there as ex-folk musicians in search of L.A. fame, the group was the toast of L'Etoile, in the Sherry-Netherland on 5th Avenue in Midtown Manhattan, surrounded by industry executives, including ABC records president Larry Newton, and old friends the Lovin' Spoonful and John's former Journeymen bandmate Dick Weissman. According to his account, cocaine was passed around, which quite possibly was John's first exposure to the stimulant that would later destroy him. In the intoxicating haze of this glitz and glam, John convinced Jill to join up by promising her that, even if he and Michelle did get back together, she wouldn't be allowed to rejoin the group and Jill would remain as her permanent replacement. With this assurance, she acquiesced and went along for the ride. There was also a promise that she would be able to write with John. After the reception, the group headed to London on a week-long part promotional tour, part-vacation with new Mama Jill.

For John, the trip to England served as an impetus to the 1967 Monterey Pop Festival in that it opened his eyes to the seriousness and possibilities of rock and roll. Their debut single "California Dreamin'" had only been released there in February, peaking at number 23 May, but the follow-up, "Monday, Monday," surpassed it in its chart debut, and was firmly placed in its highest chart position of number three when they arrived. Mamas & Papas fever was now international.

With royalties rolling in, the Mamas & the Papas were instantly wealthy, especially John, and their look had changed considerably. They were now well-groomed and on the cutting edge of fashion. Cass could dress up her self-consciousness in expensive gowns and muumuus and have her hair done several times a week. John looked the part of an English dandy with a Van Dyke beard, complete with handlebar mustache, and his hair now partially covered his ears. Denny more resembled St. Francis of Assisi, minus the tonsure, but with a full chinstrap beard and mustache. His hair covered his ears and all his brow, coming to a rest just above his eyebrows. They fit in rather well with their English counterparts, even presaging the facial hair era that lay just over the horizon. In 1966, long hair on males in normal society was still uncommon and frowned upon by parents, teachers, coaches and employers. In the world of rock and roll, it was quite the opposite. It showed you "got it" and that you were part of an exclusive club. Traditional pompadours were passé, and anyone who still wore one wasn't to be trusted. So, when Rolling Stones lead singer Mick Jagger saw a quartet of two women and two males, with long hair and shabby dress, walking around Harley House, the same luxury apartment building near the Regent's Park he and model girlfriend Chrissie Shrimpton lived in, he felt at ease knocking at their door.

"Ahh, so it really is you," Mick said excitedly to an amused John who opened the door.

"Yes, it is," John replied. "And it really is you. How did you know?"

Dunhill had rented the group the 4,000 square foot, six-bedroom penthouse flat at the gated Edwardian mansion with double height ceilings and a 525 square foot terrace. It placed them in the lap of luxury right in the center of the current cultural capital of the world. After introductions and small talk, Mick and Chrissie took the group, minus an ailing Cass, to Dolly's, the most exclusive of all the "in" clubs, located in the basement of the Scotch of St. James in Piccadilly Circus. Only the elite were allowed in and executives at RCA, European distributors of Dunhill Records, had the presence of mind to include them on the list. Here, they were introduced to several luminaries of the British invasion, including Beatle John Lennon, Rolling Stones bandmates

Keith Richards and Brian Jones and his girlfriend at the time, Italian-German model/actress Anita Pallenberg.

The musicians got comfortable and engaged in plenty of meaningful and witty banter over the course of the evening and, after a request from Denny for some weed, Lennon called up fellow Beatle Paul McCartney, who came across town, from Abbey Road Studios, with a fresh dime bag to pass around. When John Lennon and Denny got to talking, the witty Beatle asked Denny which of the Mamas whispered "John, John," in the middle of their version of his "I Call Your Name."

"Cass," Denny replied eagerly.

"The big woman," Lennon replied with a dash of poorly concealed disappointment.

Denny confirmed it was, indeed, the big woman. "She loves your ass," he told him.

"Well all right, then, where is she?" he asked.

After telling him she was in bed sick, the four piled into his paisley Rolls-Royce and sped back to Harley House to meet her and smoke up in a more private setting. They arrived in the early morning hours and everyone made themselves at home in the grandiose penthouse. McCartney began plucking the strings on the broken harpsichord in the 27-foot long reception room while Denny zipped over to Cass' room, telling her the man of her dreams was in the apartment. She was in no mood for jokes.

"John Lennon's downstairs," he told her in rapt amazement.

"Fuck off and leave me alone," she yelled back at him. "I don't feel good, you sonofabitch! Don't do that."

"I swear on my mother's life," he protested. "John Lennon and Paul McCartney are in the living room!"

As Denny continued trying to convince her, the distant chime of the antique harpsichord rang from the living room. Clearly, somebody was there. With a sense of incredulousness, she got dressed, made her way down the hall, and beheld a sight she could never have imagined. John Lennon and Paul McCartney, who only two years earlier seemed a million miles away on her television set in a cheap New York apartment, stood in her luxurious living room, anxious to meet her.

"Hello beautiful," Lennon said to a stunned Cass who gleefully made her way to the fireplace where the two conversed for what seemed like an eternity.

Everyone settled in, smoked up, played music, sang and conversed to the predawn hours with the lights turned down low. As McCartney plucked away at the harpsichord, he began playing an impromptu, unrehearsed song that bore his unique characteristics. The room got atmospheric as everyone took in this magical moment. Jill stood by the window watching as a cat meandered slowly toward their terrace from the streetlight below, finally settling on their doormat, wrapping itself up warmly as the song ended. It was a tender ending to a majestic night. Around 8:00 a.m., Lennon and McCartney departed in the former's Rolls-Royce, and everyone else passed out on their respective beds.

Not to be outdone by his Beatle bandmates, the next day was spent with George Harrison and his wife Patti Boyd at their deluxe bungalow Kinfauns in Esher, Surrey, for dinner. They were joined later by Paul McCartney, who just happened by, but the action was far more subdued this time around. After tea, they sat around on the floor passing joints and listening to tracks from their forthcoming *Revolver* album, which was in its mixing stages. Shortly before this meeting, final mixes on George's three contributions had been completed. Everybody was impressed with what they heard. *Revolver* was a step ahead of their last LP, *Rubber Soul*, and, as they would see in one year, a step toward their landmark *Sgt. Pepper's Lonely Hearts Club Band* album. In turn, John and Denny played them their latest record, "I Saw Her Again," scheduled to be released domestically in one month's time, which was also met with praise. McCartney's trained ear was able to deduce the flub.

Later that night, after the free-flowing exchanges of musical ideas and weed had been exhausted, they were escorted back to Harley House in Harrison's limousine and a few days later flew home to L.A. John was particularly buoyed and inspired by their experiences with rock royalty. It set his mind in motion. Perhaps he hadn't sacrificed any musical integrity by abandoning pure folk for rock and roll. In fact, it was quite the opposite. He'd only enhanced it. Rock and roll had no limits, which increased his musical acumen and it was evident in his meticulous approach to making records, much like it was for the Beatles. The trip had not only served to distract him from his separation from Michelle, but it also opened his eyes to rock and roll's potential as a legitimate and respected musical form. He would now hold his rock music ideas in the same regard as he did with his folk music and would soon seek to bring that same sensibility to the world.

Shortly after returning to L.A., the Mamas & the Papas embarked on a short tour that fulfilled concert cancellations following the Melodyland incident. It took them to parts of the Southwest, Midwest, and Rocky Mountains. Not only were they able to work out some new songs live, including "I Saw Her Again" and "Dancing in the Street," but it also allowed them to measure their audiences' reactions to new Mama Jill. Although they were arguably the hottest new act of 1966, fans were still getting to know them so there was hope that nobody would notice or take issue with Michelle no longer being in the band. Following her ouster, there was no press release or announcement in any trade publications or fan magazines, but they weren't necessarily hiding it.

From the seats, it would be difficult for the average fan to realize that it was somebody other than Michelle, especially once the adrenaline kicked in, but John made the mistake of actually drawing attention to it relatively quickly. Their first makeup date took place on Friday, July 1, at the Dallas Memorial Auditorium in Dallas, Texas, as the highlight of a Dick Clark Caravan of Stars package show that also featured Brian Hyland and the West Coast Pop Art Experimental Band. Running out to Eric's opening guitar licks of "Straight Shooter," the audience was ecstatic as the group launched into the first verse and sang over the screams and mayhem that had become so commonplace at teen concerts in the era of Beatlemania. At the end of the number, after motioning the crowd to quiet down, John introduced himself, Denny, and Cass to ecstatic applause. When he introduced "Mama" Jill as the newest member of the group, a collective gasp filled the auditorium. After several seconds of what must've seemed like an eternity, he was forced to respond to the many audible inquiries of "Where's Michelle?" offering that she was in Mexico taking a "much deserved vacation." In the haze of confusion and head-scratching, they launched into a clumsy, word-scrambled version of their latest hit, "I Saw Her Again," which began a 40-minute set.

They followed that show up with a date at the Omaha Civic Auditorium in Omaha, Nebraska, and another in San Francisco. Whether John continued introducing Jill as the newest Mama is unknown, but the music press did catch wind of the personnel change following the Dallas concert and reports quickly began to surface. Page one of the July 9 edition of *KRLA Beat* ran the headline "A Break-Up for the Mama's and Papa's," offering in the opening sentence that a "personality clash" between John and Michelle resulted in her "being replaced by another female musician." The secret was out.

Lou Adler took matters into his own hands by participating in a feature article that appeared in *KRLA Beat* two weeks later, which sounded like it could've been written by Dunhill's publicity department. Jill's alluring head shot took up one-third of the front page and sat atop a title that read "Brand New Mama." Page two featured a new black and white publicity shot of the group featuring Jill up front, back against the wall and coolly leaning over. The article boldly declared "Michelle's Out." Opening with a confirmation of Michelle's status within the band, the article then launched into an approximately 450-word article that mostly highlighted Jill's attributes with carefully chosen background facts, full of inaccuracies, that leaned heavily on quotes from Lou Adler. He describes her as a "very artistic and aesthetic person" who paints, loves flowers and has penned several hit songs for Jan & Dean. It closes by telling the readers that Jill has been accepted by the band, who hopes their fans will accept her as well.

Though it certainly painted a happy picture, it wasn't as seamless a transition as the article suggested. Michelle's role within the group had been underestimated by the others. Even though she wasn't a great singer and didn't write songs, their friendship and history together and the fact that she was John's wife was an afterthought that became glaring and caused each member to quietly miss her. Though Jill was a slightly better singer than Michelle, her deficiencies were more of a liability and not as easily forgiven. As sessions for their sophomore album continued into July and August, the uncomfortableness of breaking Jill in and finding a vocal symmetry never seemed to ebb. Cass and Denny could be seen exchanging noticeably frustrated glances as they recut vocals for songs on which Michelle had already sung. It was a frustrating process for John too. Although the casual listener most likely wouldn't notice any difference, his composer's ear could, and his well-oiled vocal machine had to tediously be taken apart and put back together again.

On the road, it wasn't any better. As word of Michelle's departure spread, fans increasingly voiced their displeasure. To make matters worse, the group hadn't worked out a viable set and were thin on new material. At a gig in Forest Hills Stadium in Queens, New York, on August 6, in front of a crowd of approximately 14,000, this combination caused a handful of disgruntled fans to stop the show. John tried to bamboozle the audience by having the group perform "Straight Shooter" twice to open the show and, only six songs in, in the middle of "Monday, Monday," nearly two dozen kids charged across the tennis courts and rushed the stage with several shouting, "Where's Michelle?" Four of them even managed to get on the stage, causing police to encircle it and remove them. John was visibly upset and even traded barbs before cutting the show short. The group retreated backstage and made their way out of the facility, leaving an angry crowd in their wake. The negativity rankled John, who was still in a highly emotional state, and his increasing drug use didn't help matters.

Back in L.A., Michelle decided she wanted back in the group and was going to make a considerable effort to get back in John's good graces. She began calling him regularly in late July to shamelessly, yet strategically, grovel. She knew that in order to rejoin the group she had to first get back to being his wife. Initially, John maintained a cool and hardened visage when met with her attempts, but it was a façade. Though he'd busied himself with Ann Marshall and others to satisfy his sexual and relationship needs, it was still Michelle he loved and her attempts at wooing him were long awaited and silently welcomed. But, keeping himself in check, he wouldn't be swayed easily and was resolved to stick with his decision to keep her out of the group. Sensing an opening, Michelle continued chipping away at his ego. The fact that he even took her calls was a breakthrough. After a few days, she got around to asking for her reinstatement.

"There is absolutely no way I can get you back into the group, Mitch," he told her over the phone. "I have irreversibly made it so much more palatable for Cass and Denny."

The day the group headed east, Michelle went to his lavish ground level apartment at Sunset Towers as he was packing and in desperation begged him to not only take her with them but to allow her to perform as well. Moving in closer, kissing and caressing him, she also asked him to take her back as his wife. John was not moved.

"Hey Mitch, I love you. I always have," he told her. "I just can't work with you, that's all."

The rejection was enough to drive Michelle to tears and she began crying hysterically, begging him not to do this.

"Please don't take Jill," she cried desperately. "Take me back, John. Please. I'll do anything!"

"Mitch," he said as he packed his bag, "I can't take you."

Walking out the front door and through the garden, he made his way to the awaiting limo in the circular Sunset Towers driveway. Michelle followed not far behind but all she could do was watch as he handed his luggage to the driver and climbed into the back of the limo, where Cass and Denny waited for him. She froze, not yet ready to confront all three. Their smiles and laughter were a crushing blow, and it wasn't lost on John. Though he maintained a cool exterior in the face of all this, it did have an emotional impact that came to the surface over their short August tour.

But the ideal that John strove for in Jill began to crumble on the road. After their disastrous appearance in Forest Hills they played another series of concerts in the Rocky Mountains, the Great Plains and the Southwest regions of the country and, although Jill could sing and it really made no difference to most of the audience who the fourth vocalist was, it did to John. Every cry of "Where's Michelle?" and every deficient note agitated him and made him miss his wife more and more. The Mamas & the Papas were more than just four singing voices; they represented a shared experience between friends. They were not a machine where a cog could simply be replaced with a new one. Michelle also had an edge to her that Jill didn't. She belonged to their sound, their presence, their jokes and to the little things, like their "Mugwumps" language. In other words, she was too organic to be replaced. Michelle liked smoking dope and taking LSD. Jill didn't. In fact, she had no interest in getting high and felt quite uncomfortable when John peer-pressured her into taking a hit before going onstage or popping pills before sessions. For three users who had a sacramental viewpoint when it came to drugs, her attitude was a real bringdown and a line of demarcation between hippie and establishment. No matter how much they dressed it up, Jill just wasn't a "Mama."

Back in Los Angeles, Michelle drowned her sorrows at the Whisky a Go Go, hanging out with owner Elmer Valentine and actor Steve McQueen. When she wasn't there, she was at home mentally debating with herself over her situation in solitude and working out strategies that might win John over, but it was all a waste of time. Time was the greatest healer in this case and, on the day of group's return to Los Angeles, Michelle received a phone call from John asking her to meet him at their Learjet at the airport. She got there in time to see it land and, for the first time since the spring, received a cheerful greeting from Cass and Denny as they got into their limo, which bolstered her spirits. She met John who invited her into his awaiting limo. Not much was spoken. There was no, "You're back in, baby," not even a sorry. The reaction of the crowds and the lack of chemistry with Jill forced John's hand. As their history together dictated, when John and Michelle got over a difficult hump, it was never spoken about and that was the case with her reinstatement. There was just a mutual understanding and they moved on from there. It may have covered the wound, but it didn't keep it from festering. John left the task of informing Jill to Lou, who for the most part took it in stride, but did remain bitter toward John for breaking his promises. The original four were back together again.

Now that Michelle was back in the group, John had to clean up the mess that their sophomore album had become. Over the course of her approximate two-month hiatus, John replaced her vocals with Jill Gibson's on "Even If I Could" and "Trip, Stumble and Fall" and recorded five new songs, "I Can't Wait," "Dancing Bear," "That Kind of Girl," "Did You Ever Want to Cry" and "Strange Young Girls." Untouched vocals that would appear on the album were "I Saw Her Again," "Words of Love" and "Once Was a Time I Thought." With an August 30 deadline looming over their heads, the Mamas & the Papas reworked two songs: a cover of Martha & the Vandellas' "Dancing in the Street" and the Richard Rodgers/Lorenz Hart standard "Here in My Arms," for which they repurposed the backing track for a John Phillips original, "No Salt on Her Tail." Doors keyboardist Ray Manzarek, a relative unknown at the time, was brought in in his first major studio assignment to overdub the Hammond B-3 for the track after John saw the group live at the Whisky a Go Go. They also recorded another Rodgers and Hart song, "My Heart Stood Still," which they would lip-synch on the March 2, 1967, edition of weekly anthology series *ABC Stage 67*, "Rodgers and Hart Today."

John also scrambled to replace Jill's vocals with Michelle's on "Strange Young Girls" and "That Kind of Girl," but ran out of time for the rest. The August 20 edition of *Billboard* listed their new album title as *Crashon Screamon All Fall Down*, slated for an August 30 release, and was previewed in the August 27 edition of *KRLA Beat*. The album even made it to the test pressing stage with several thousand slicks printed and distributed for trade advertising and record store promotion. Curiously, another shot considered that was taken by Guy Webster and slated for use in a billboard campaign on the Sunset Strip featured the original four in the window of an abandoned house in the desert between Phoenix and Los Angeles. The colorful photo featured Michelle crouched on the window ledge with the other three crowded behind her. At some point, between the test pressing of *Crashon Screamon All Fall Down* and Michelle's reinstatement in the group, the decision was made, most likely by John and Lou, to change the album to an eponymous title with a picture of Jill, in a similar position, superimposed over Michelle. When Michelle learned that not only was that photo being considered for the album, but for a Sunset Strip billboard as well, she went ballistic. Since rejoining the group, she'd been rather demure, attempting to patch up her marriage to John, and ate a lot of humble pie in order to reestablish her friendships within the group and not lead Denny on, but this move broke her silence.

"I have been taking a lot of shit here and this is the worst of all," she told John and Lou. "I don't know why it is so important, but it is. This is L.A. and it is my city."

Whether it was Michelle's confrontation or just common sense setting in, the picture was reverted back to its original form. When the album was released on October 22, it contained 12 songs: 10 originals written, or co-written, by John and two covers, "Dancing in the Street" and "My Heart Stood Still." Through the sessionography, it can be concluded that Michelle appeared on all but four songs, "Trip, Stumble and Fall," "Dancing Bear," "I Can't Wait" and the stereo LP mix of "Even If I Could." There simply just wasn't enough time to replace Jill's original vocals on the four remaining songs without causing a significant delay and, in 1966, with competition getting fiercer and the entertainment platforms getting larger and more complex, lost time could be a death knell. To coincide with the album release, Dunhill also issued a non-LP single, "Look Through My Window," a John Phillips original, which traces its origins back to Michelle's affair with Russ Titelman, but was a dud by their standards, only peaking at number 24.

Although the album lacks the cohesion and unbridled enthusiasm of their debut, it is an otherwise solid effort with vocal arrangements and production approaching the same level as the Beach Boys' *Pet Sounds*; not such a bold claim when you consider John's first-rate talent for blending vocals and the fact that the same musicians played on both albums. Both elements gave the album a Spectorian wall of sound, but it differentiated itself with John's fingerprint and Cass and Denny's powerful harmonies.

What it lacks in consistency, it makes up for in sound and is a red-hot example of summer 1966 that sits comfortably next to *Pet Sounds*, the Rolling Stones' *Aftermath*, the Beatles' *Revolver*, Simon & Garfunkel's *Sounds of Silence* and Bob Dylan's *Blonde on Blonde*. John's lyrics matched his ambitious vocal harmonies in a manner unheard of on the pop music scene but also shows him deviating from his comfort zone by incorporating organs, woodwinds and heavy reverb, proving that he was fully ensconced in the contemporary pop scene. The album also serves as a road map of his torrid relationship with Michelle beginning with the opening track "No Salt on Her Tail" where John reaches back to a line from an 18th-century Simple Simon nursery rhyme to indicate that he's setting his lover free.

This little bird she can fly away,
No salt on her tail, no cage to make her stay.

Though this song shows a more resigned, plaintive approach to his frustration, other songs like "Trip, Stumble and Fall," "I Can't Wait" and "That Kind of Girl" depict a more resolute protagonist eager to watch his wayward lover get her just desserts. John reaches perhaps the apex of his vocal prowess with beautifully complex arrangements on "Even If I Could" and "Strange Young Girls," which sounds like a late 60s update on baroque chamber choirs rounded off by an eerie guitar played through a rotating Leslie speaker. It gives the song a dark atmosphere that matches its lyrics about LSD youth culture. Another highlight, "Dancing Bear," reminiscent of a Broadway solo, featured a sensitive vocal from Denny atop a muted arrangement augmented by a woodwind section of flute, oboe, and bassoon. It told the story of all the things the singer wouldn't be and was as un–rock and roll and mature as the Beatles' "Yesterday."

The treasure that John and Lou initially overlooked was "Words of Love," which was pulled from the album as a follow-up single to "Look Through My Window" in late November and made a slow, but steady, upward climb to number five in January. Written while John lived with Denny, with lyrics inspired by Michelle's indifference to him during their separation, it was the first single to feature Cass on lead vocals and she shone. John's throwback tune, with a saloon piano, harkened back to the speakeasy days of Prohibition and it set well in the early days of Flower Power and it made Mama Cass a star and a household name. "Words of Love" perhaps more than any other John Phillips song inspired the late 1960s subgenre "sunshine pop," evident in songs by groups with female leads like the 5th Dimension and Spanky & Our Gang.

In the sixth-ever published *Crawdaddy Magazine*, launched a mere nine months earlier, reviewer Daniel Gannon referred to the album as a "strange and wondrous" animal, citing the strongest tracks as "Dancing Bear," "Strange Young Girls," "Even If I Could" and "Words of Love," which he referred to as the "best all-around cut." Gannon had high praise and expressed his appreciation for John's innovative, yet simple, arrangement talents.

"The principle of the sound is simple: the melody is stated by the male voices in the bass line, and in the intervals between phrases the upper voices sing a slightly ornamented version of the immediately preceding bass-line phrase," he wrote.

Reviews like this signified a new dawn in rock and roll and put John's arrangement level on par with Brian Wilson and Paul McCartney. The question was, could he keep pace?

With everything surrounding the Mamas & the Papas seemingly getting back to normal, minus Denny's now-unrequited love for Michelle, which drove him further into the bottle, they embarked on a short tour to promote the new album, and was their most aggressive one since their respective folk days. But it was a new day for all involved. Unlike the Hootenanny tour and even the national tours of their folk-rock predecessors only a year earlier, there would be no tour buses or seedy motels. The Mamas & the Papas arrived in style by a private Learjet and stayed in the finest of accommodations. The era of rock and roll excess was underway.

Beginning September 2, the group convened a nine-week tour that took them across the United States, beginning with the Carousel Theater in West Covina, California, and quickly made its way to the East Coast, covering larger venues in Washington, D.C., New York City and Baltimore, Maryland. Those dates were followed up by a scattershot itinerary of cities that ranged from Minneapolis to Chapel Hill, North Carolina, to Detroit followed by shows in Atlanta, Miami and Chicago and back to New York. It concluded at Moody Coliseum on the campus of Southern Methodist University in Dallas, Texas. The band was playing in front of audiences that ranged from 10,000 to 20,000 and were escorted by new road manager Peter Pilafian, roadie Tom Saunders, and bodyguard Terry Dean, who was employed specifically by Lou

Adler to minimize flare-ups between band members. It was mostly easy duty for him save for one scary moment when the group was forced to fly commercially following their October 23 gig in Atlanta.

For the first time since before the trip to the U.S. Virgin Islands, John and Michelle had gotten along like husband and wife. She had moved into his apartment in Sunset Towers, where their sex life was rekindled, and it sparked somewhat of a honeymoon period for them. On board the airplane, sitting on the tarmac at Atlanta Municipal Airport, the two sat next to each other, cozying up and canoodling as much as the passenger seats would allow. They began playfully drawing on each other's hands and wrists with a felt-tip pen, a playful pastime they'd engaged in on tour buses, but the sweet turned sour as Michelle started sketching a face on John's hand. Upon completion, John's demeanor quickly changed, and he turned indignant on the spot.

"You're fired!" he shouted at her.

Michelle was shocked by the reaction, or so she let on, and began asking him what on earth he was talking about.

"That face is Gene Clark's!" he asserted.

Michelle continued feigning shock and began to get up out of her seat.

"You know it is Gene Clark and I know it is Gene Clark, and you are fired!" he shouted.

Michelle had heard enough and began heading to the exit.

"Fine!" she shouted back. "Bye everybody."

Before she could make her way through the cabin door, she was grabbed from behind by Terry Dean, much to the shock of their fellow passengers, who strapped her in a seat away from John where she sobbed for the remainder of the flight. Terry tried his best to calm her down.

"Calm down," he told her. "John's just being hysterical. You and I know it."

It turned out to be a hiccup. Cooler heads prevailed and the group completed the tour then headed back to L.A. for some rest. The truth, however, was that Michelle did indeed draw Gene Clark's face on John's hand.

With a renewed interest in their marriage, John and Michelle made the conscious decision to use their sudden wealth to finally purchase a proper home. Since getting married in December 1962, they'd spent their entire marriage in rentals, and now that a spark had been rekindled, they made the logical move. Michelle was also feeling the call to motherhood and, though, deep down she knew she wouldn't stay married to John for the rest of her life, he was the only one she could imagine fathering her child. In addition to the coziness of finally having a home of their own, it would also keep them a safe distance away from the craziness they had manufactured in the heart of L.A. With a number one album, another one on its way to the Top 5, three Top 5 singles, including the number one "Monday, Monday," John's wealth was considerable, and he could afford to pay cash for a luxurious Los Angeles suburban home. And so, on a day in late autumn, John and Michelle went driving through Brentwood, Westwood and Bel Air in search of it.

Driving northwest on Sunset Boulevard in his Jaguar, John and Michelle entered the East Gate of Bel Air Road and continued at 25 mph northward up Bel Air Road, which was a world within a world and far removed from reality. John and Michelle stepped into a fairy tale made of mansions and movie stars, finely manicured lawns and hedges and entire staffs devoted to maintaining these enormous estates that could only be owned by a minority of wealthy people. It was the apex of capitalism, and something John and Michelle couldn't have even come close to imagining only a year earlier, sleeping on Jim and Vanessa's floor.

As they made their way through lower Bel Air, they passed gated mansion after gated mansion. When they came upon the Chartwell Estate on their right, perhaps the crème de la crème of Bel Air and the site of exterior shots for the *Beverly Hillbillies* TV show, Michelle noticed a for sale sign on an English Tudor across the street from its north gate and told John to stop. Even at 6'5", John could barely see over the gate, marked 783 Bel Air Road. It looked deserted, so they decided to hop the fence and what they discovered was a 5,400 square-foot fairy-tale English Tudor with twin roof peaks that looked like it could've been plucked from the English countryside. Michelle fell in love with it instantly.

"I want this house," she told John.

"You haven't seen inside," he replied.

They walked up to the front door and peered through its carved wood barred sidelights to see the dimly lit atrium where there hung an enormous and grandiose French crystal chandelier. Even though there was no furniture inside and dusty old drapes still adorned each window, John and Michelle could tell this was something special.

"This is the one I want," Michelle reiterated.

John could sense Michelle's excitement and, sensing a tangible spark in their reunion, he agreed. He loved it too. After getting in touch with the real estate agency handling the sale of the house, they learned the property was named Twin Gables and it once belonged to actress Jeanette MacDonald and her husband Gene Raymond, ironically perhaps the most conservative couple in the Golden Age of Hollywood. Raymond had presented it to her as a wedding present in 1937, 11 years after its construction had been completed. They left Twin Gables in 1963 when Jeanette fell ill with heart trouble and had to seek an arterial transplant at Methodist Hospital in Houston, Texas. The house was sold to their friend Bo Roos, business manager to many Hollywood stars, including John Wayne and Fred MacMurray. The asking price was between $225,000 and $250,000. John offered $150,000 with a $90,000 down payment. To their surprise, the offer was accepted. When they took an official tour of the grounds, the full grandeur of the home was opened to them.

The house sat on two acres of prime Hollywood Hills real estate overlooking Lower Bel Air, Santa Monica and the Pacific Ocean. The massive house contained four bedrooms, four bathrooms, a library and a wine cellar with a few bottles left over. Also included were the standard large formal dining room, a sitting room, a den, and a living room, complete with fireplace and 30-foot ceilings. A half level to the rear led to the kitchen. Adjacent to the living room was an actual English pub, with a gray slate floor and hand-carved wooden gargoyles, that had been disassembled and shipped over from England and reassembled brick by brick. The pièce de resistance, however, was the enormous cedar closet MacDonald had constructed to house her many dresses, gowns, lingerie, and thousands of accessories and accoutrements that befitted the crowned Queen of Hollywood 1939. Cedar wood is a natural deterrent for moths, the enemy of stored clothing. It encompassed an entire wing of the house and was composed of hundreds of drawers, layered in rows, in all shapes and sizes, labeled very orderly with hand-inscribed tape.

Outside the rear entrance stood a grape arbor that garnished a pathway that led to the pool and the guesthouse, which was a smaller-scale version of the main house. There was a rose garden also decked with an arbor, a fountain, and a finely manicured garden that resembled a Sicilian vineyard and set the tone for the entire grounds. It provided an inspirational setting for John's songwriting as he traversed the stone walkway, noodling on his guitar, high on acid and grass amid the azaleas and phlox that garnished the landscape. From their vantage point, they could see sailboats speckled on the horizon of the Pacific Ocean.

Despite the house's classic interior, John and Michelle set out immediately to make it their own, and that involved converting the library into a hippie-chic Indian hookah lounge with a six-foot high hookah, paisley silk curtains, and large throw pillows specially designed by Toni at Profile du Monde. They plopped a full-size pool table right in the center of the dining room and dined in the pub. Lou Adler gave them a housewarming gift of a couple of champion peacocks and two hens who poked and pecked about the yard, and ABC Records President Larry Newton gifted them with ten crates of fine artwork from his personal collection to decorate the walls.

Michelle went to work filling the house with high-end furniture and began perusing many local auctions, purchasing an antique grandfather clock, Tiffany lamps, antique silver and crystal, and a 250-piece set of Limoges china. John had a custom-made oversized bed constructed with a space mattress designed by NASA and, for the kitchen, they imported tiles from Guadalajara to give it the Mexican look that so dominated Michelle's childhood. They spent money faster than they made it and, with their seemingly unlimited funds, they also decorated their driveway with three vintage Rolls-Royces. The beach at St. John, the East Village apartment, and Harold the Bleak were now distant memories.

All the changes they made to the interior were de rigueur of the time, and very much reversible, but the cardinal sin they committed involved tearing out the cedar closet to begin construction of an in-home recording studio. John was in such a creative groove that he craved the ability to lay down everything from song ideas to finished tracks in the comfort of his own home. Interestingly enough, Bel Air zoning laws of the time forbade home recording studios, so John had to hire a contractor who swore to secrecy and did it under cover of darkness. One by one, they ripped out each beautiful and irreplaceable piece of cedar and tossed them into a pile outside. The custom-made closets and drawers would be replaced by a spacious soundproof studio, control room and sitting area that was only accessible through a secret panel. It would take over a year to complete and wouldn't be used until early 1968. As the new year of 1967 unfolded, great changes were afoot for the Mamas &

the Papas as they continued climbing up the mountains of success and excess. John's desire to evangelize rock and roll integrity continued to grow as well and, pretty soon, he would take on a massive undertaking that would put rock and roll on the world's stage like it never had been before that would both legitimize it to the general public and change it forever.

CHAPTER 19:
THE RIOT ON SUNSET STRIP DELIVERS

November 1966: The era of rock and roll excess is underway, and it's personified in the Mamas & the Papas, particularly on tour. The Beatles, the Rolling
Stones and the Byrds all showed signs of this and set roots but John Phillips
and his penchant for the finest and most excessive really gave it wings. Even
Bob Dylan's entourage couldn't match the Mamas & the Papas'. Friends,
family members, managers, personal assistants, ex-bandmates, drug dealers,
nutritionists, and many others went along for the ride with the group as they
Learjetted across the country.

The group lived dangerously. On board their private jets, they smoked
marijuana freely. Whenever an unsuspecting pilot or copilot queried what
that strange sweet and sour smell was, Denny would tell them they were
cheap French cigarettes, which always drew giggles from those in the know.
Even more dangerous was, with pot smoke wafting throughout the cabin,
occasionally a fun-loving pilot would consent to their request for parabolic
flight where the nose of the aircraft is lifted to a pitch angle of 45 degrees and,
once it hits its peak, the pilot pushes the stick forward until the nose of the
plane is pointed downward at a pitch angle of approximately 30 degrees. This
essentially puts the craft into freefall, giving the sensation of weightlessness
to all on board and causing those who aren't strapped in to gently float from
the floor to the ceiling and back. Passengers who are high get even more of
a thrill.

Offstage behavior mirrored that danger. Groupies were everywhere, and so many of the men in their party, minus John because of Michelle's presence, had their choice of female companionship with any of those who were willing to give. Drugs and alcohol were passed around liberally. Though the main drugs of choice were still marijuana and LSD, harder drugs like cocaine and heroin were on the periphery. There was always a wild party to be found before, during, and after the show at a hotel or restaurant with many in attendance acting wildly even after the group had to move on to the next city. At the St. Regis Hotel in New York, new tour manager Peter Pilafian was spotted walking on a ledge 30 stories above 55th Street. At another show in Phoenix, following the after-party at the Best Western, a hungover Eric Hord put their whole floor in a panic when he looked out the window after ordering room service and noticed dozens of police cars in the parking lot. After alerting Cass who, in turn, alerted the rest of the group, every illegal drug got frantically flushed down the toilet. When the Doctor called back downstairs, feigning concern over his breakfast, he inquired about the police activity and was told the hotel was hosting a police convention. Antisocial behavior and paranoia were creeping in.

From their onset, the Mamas & the Papas performed while stoned. It wasn't uncommon to see their limousines pull up to the venue with most or all of them rolling out completely out of their minds, with their opulence either being an inspiration or source of frustration for their opening acts and paying customers. After their concert at Fordham University in late 1966, opening act Webster's New World got booted off the tour by Lou Adler because their absolute onstage professionalism contrasted with the Mamas & the Papas' sloppy, stoned-out performance. It's a well-known music business faux pas to upstage the headliner.

But, even if their performances were occasionally sloppy and drove some attendees away, they were still the hottest act in the country both on radio and onstage, and it would benefit them profoundly in the coming months. The mere sight of the Mamas & the Papas onstage drove the mostly teenage crowds wild, drowning out inadequate stage sound systems, and those who got close to them often sought to grab, tear, and rip any memento they could from them. Perhaps the most important factor for John and Michelle in late 1966/early 1967 was that they were actually enjoying themselves for the first time in the group's professional tenure. With much of the drama from the last year and a half finally behind them, they were able to reconnect somewhat and enjoy their time on the road. Thanks to the healing hands of time, they were much more playful and emitted a sense of frivolity they hadn't experienced since the Virgin Islands. Denny and Cass were another matter. Though they were pleasant, the tightness that had bound them together in 1965 was gone forever. His unrequited love for Michelle caused him to remain in a state of perpetual drunkenness, and Cass' self-consciousness and equally unrequited love for Denny drove her to surround herself with new friends and opportunistic lovers. But there was still a bond between the four of them. Cass and Denny were always playing practical jokes on anybody and everybody in their caravan, their signature prank being pie-throwing, à la Soupy Sales. It often provoked an equal or more intense reaction. Moments before going out on the stage of the Hollywood Bowl, John and Denny got the best of her by dumping a full bucket of water over her head, completely destroying her makeup, soaking her outfit, drawing her ire and forcing her to sing onstage with her dress clinging to her body.

The Mamas & the Papas' approach to playing in front of their fans was very cavalier for 1967. They essentially only played on weekends and commanded a $20,000 price tag per show. John would cancel gigs whenever it struck his fancy and avoided touring in cold weather. They also weren't much for engaging with fans after the show was over. The most important thing was to get back to wherever they were staying and resume getting stoned and move on to the next town. Peter would often be sent to the upcoming venue early in the week to scour the underground system of tunnels that existed beneath most venues so the band could make an easy, hassle-free exit to their soundproof limo. It came in particularly handy when John made disparaging comments about the war in Vietnam during a concert at the War Memorial in Rochester, New York, and saw firsthand just how divisive the issue was becoming. When he refused to recant his statements, the stage manager pulled security, and the group was forced to get out of the arena on their own, getting the scare of their lives when rambunctious fans surrounded their limo and began rocking it back and forth.

But the middle-aged conservativism that permeated upstate New York and Middle America stood in stark contrast to the hippie youth culture on college campuses and major cities, particularly Los Angeles. Back home, as John and Michelle relaxed in their Bel Air home overlooking downtown L.A., distracted by parties, orgies and songwriting, six miles to the west, the rising tide of youth counterculture manifested itself in the organized protest of the early November 1966 announcement that the city of Los Angeles would purchase the underage club, Pandora's Box, where John began his music career nine years earlier, and demolish it. It was a double whammy for L.A. youth and the thriving Sunset Strip club scene as, concurrently, a 10:00 p.m. curfew was implemented unannounced by Los Angeles County Supervisor Ernest E. Debs, who was no friend to area youth. Anyone under the age of 21 found roaming Sunset Boulevard and surrounding West Hollywood areas past curfew would be found in violation and could be fined, lose driving privileges, face community service, or be taken into custody.

Unbeknownst to the young people who patronized the Strip regularly, Debs secretly desired to turn that fruitful area into a financial district complete with a new 14-mile stretch of freeway that connected Santa Monica with Laurel Canyon. But, in order to make this a reality, he had to quash the area's newfound popularity, which posed a considerable threat. But his plan was flawed from the beginning, as the Hollywood Hills stood in the way of any major construction, and the project was opposed by most of its residents. Nevertheless, his determination remained forceful and he urged no quarter be given to underage violators.

For the first few days of November 1966, hundreds of unsuspecting kids were intimidated or manhandled by the many area police officers who enforced this new mandate with great fervor. Dozens were whisked away to police stations and sat in makeshift waiting rooms, normally reserved for police line-ups, and waited for their anxious, angry parents to come and claim them. Not all parents sided with the curfew. Over the course of those several days, a steady stream of letters flowed into the City Council and Los Angeles Mayor Sam Yorty's office complaining of police harassment, describing the curfew as unrealistic and pointing out that, outside of the Sunset Strip clubs, the city provided no alternatives for evening youth activities. The kids simply wanted to see their favorite bands play. Complainants were given half-hearted responses, including a silly list of traditional youth activities offered by the city, including chess, archery and weight lifting, making it clear that they had no intention of promoting or capitalizing on this organic rock and roll phenomenon that naturally budded on the Strip.

Neither Debs nor the police could've anticipated the equal and opposite reaction that ensued in short order. A few unknown L.A. teens took matters into their own hands by organizing a peaceful protest outside of Pandora's Box on the evening of Saturday, November 12. They printed up a modest number of flyers and hit the streets, asking the proprietors of all the underage clubs, one by one, to post them in a high-traffic area. Fifth Estate club owner Al Mitchell took a liking to their initiative and pitched in $20 to print 2,000 more fliers, and went a step further by calling for a collection among the patrons and raised enough to print another 3,000. Soon, word got to KBLA disk jockey Humble Harve Miller who announced the gathering on his 9:00 to midnight program and urged participants to tread cautiously.

As the hour grew nearer, thousands of Los Angeles young people had flocked to the area. Several entertainers had come down to lend solidarity, including young Hollywood liberals Brandon de Wilde, Peter Fonda, Jack Nicholson and Bob Denver and singers Sonny & Cher, David Crosby, P. F. Sloan, and Buffalo Springfield co-founder Stephen Stills. When police got wind of the protest, they doubled down, dispatching an unusually large number of personnel to the scene to ensure they didn't have a repeat of the Watts uprising.

The gathering took on a much more ominous tone as squad cars cruised up and down the Sunset Strip and Crescent Heights Boulevard warning that anyone under the age of 18 found in the area after 10:00 p.m. would be arrested. It did nothing to dampen the enthusiasm. In fact, it had the opposite effect. It brought more protesters out, riled agitators up and made it a much more dangerous situation, especially considering that a good number of spectators and media who had made their way out to witness the spectacle firsthand, including former Beatles correspondent and current Byrds/Beach Boys publicist Derek Taylor. Signs were everywhere with messages protesting police brutality: "Ban the Billy Club," "Rights for Youth Too," and "Stop Blue Fascism" read some of them.

When 10:00 p.m. came, the LAPD began enforcing the curfew and taking into custody the most obvious in violation. Protestors began mobilizing, and marches began in earnest. Sunset Boulevard became clogged with the bodies walking arm in arm, picketing, and chanting. And the chants weren't limited to the teen curfew. Civil rights abuses and the war in Vietnam were also protested. As the crowd continued to grow larger, the police ceased enforcing the curfew, and orders were given to avoid any aggressive action and let the mob dissipate on its own. When three off-duty Marines got into a fender bender and assaulted the driver in the other vehicle, the fuse was lit. Their pushing and shoving with police had a domino effect and it spread through the crowd causing an all-out riot, and then growing tension finally spilled over. Fists were thrown, innocent people pushed, and vehicles forced to a dead stop were rocked back and forth.

When the riot squads were dispatched, battle lines were drawn. Protestors fruitlessly battled with nightstick-wielding police officers. Those dressed in riot gear formed "flying wedges" in an effort to push the crowds off the street and out of the area, but the tenacious kids would just retreat and regroup on another block throwing bottles, rocks, and anything they could get their hands on at the police. One group of teenage protestors commandeered a bus while another protestor, named Allan W. Gordon, tried setting another bus on fire by dropping lit matches into the gas tank. He was subsequently arrested. The riot on Sunset Strip went on for five hours. Dozens were arrested, and a larger number were taken to the hospital to treat cuts and bruises. Although the rioting eventually ended, the enthusiasm didn't. More protestors gathered the next night and throughout the month of November. All in all, 337 people were arrested in connection with the protest and rioting, Pandora's Box was successfully purchased by the city and razed, and the Board of Supervisors abolished all youth dance permits in unincorporated areas of Los Angeles by month's end. Although the adults may have won the battle, they would not win the war. 1960s teenagers had been emboldened by rock and roll and they demanded to hear it whenever and wherever they wanted.

A quick cash-in attempt was made by Hollywood by using the riots as the basis for the trashy exploitation flick *Riot on Sunset Strip*, starring aging former leading man Aldo Ray as a conflicted police captain confronted with volatile youth culture bursting at the seams for their voices to be heard. Boasting of itself as "the most shocking film of our generation," it was a dud. L.A. rock bands the Standells and the Chocolate Watchband provided a portion of the soundtrack, with the former performing the film's title track. Although it did provide the film with some entertainment, it was all quickly forgotten. A more enduring testament to the Strip and the riot was created by Michael Nesmith, whose fabricated television band, the Monkees, recorded his "Daily Nightly," filled with his unmistakable, enigmatic prose:

Passioned pastel neon lights light up the jeweled traveler
Who, lost in scenes of smoke-filled dreams find questions, but no answers.

Even more enduring was Stephen Stills' firsthand account of the evening of November 12, "For What It's Worth," which darkly portrays the police presence. Stills' lyrics got to the heart of the matter and further exacerbated the division between the nation's youth and authority.

There's battle lines being drawn. Nobody's right if everybody's wrong
Young people speaking their minds, getting so much resistance from behind.

Recorded three weeks later and rushed to radio stations and record stores before Christmas, "For What It's Worth" captured the beginning of the rise of youth counterculture and would bring Buffalo Springfield to prominence, appearing on every L.A.-based variety show from the *Hollywood Palace* to the *Smothers Brothers Comedy Hour* and performing it in an episode of the CBS crime drama *Mannix*. In a very short time, the song would be co-opted by the antiwar movement and become a testament to hippie resistance to the Vietnam War and the draft.

But the most enduring testament to the Sunset Strip curfew riots had its roots six months before the actual protests took place as the pushback from police and authorities against the rock and roll scene was beginning. In May 1966, pop artist Andy Warhol brought his Exploding Plastic Inevitable Show out to the Trip, a new club on Sunset Boulevard, for a residency. It featured his artwork, films and music by the New York-based avant-garde rock band the Velvet Underground & Nico, anchored by prolific singer/songwriter Lou Reed. Midway through their engagement, the police shut down the Trip for serving underage patrons and subsequently shut the up-and-coming club down temporarily. Similar targeting took place at the after-hours club Canter's and the restaurants Gee Gee's and Ben Frank's. Some music industry patrons took notice, and two in particular, Byrds manager Jim Dickson and Elektra Records talent scout Billy James, formed an advocacy group for their artists and their audience, which they dubbed Community Action for Facts and Freedom (CAFF).

Initially, the organization was media-based, promoting the positive qualities of young people and dispelling myths through the press and on radio, but after the riots in November, it sought to raise funds to subsidize the legal defense of many of those arrested. The first and only event to bolster their coffers was a benefit concert staged at the Valley Music Theater in Woodland Hills on February 22, 1967. With the help of local promoter Alan Pariser, the lineup featured Buffalo Springfield, the Doors, the Byrds, and Hugh Masakela as opening acts for Peter, Paul and Mary. With 3,000 enthusiastic young patrons attending the concert, it was a rousing success. The fever among the fans and the musicians was high and ambitions grew larger with Masakela urging Pariser to organize another one. The young impresario agreed and envisioned a larger setting with record company support and a television broadcast: an American version of Italy's Sanremo Festival. The cream of the music industry could gather and unveil new songs to an audience more than willing to listen. Jim Dickson lost interest when the idea of holding it in Tijuana was seriously considered and withdrew. He did, however, recommend Pariser to music agent Ben Shapiro, who had his hands in just about every form of entertainment. He organized the Monterey Folk Festivals in 1963 and 1964, booked artists like Bob Dylan and Miles Davis and conceived Woody Allen's directorial debut, *What's Up, Tiger Lily?*

Shapiro bought into the idea, formed a corporation and raised $50,000 to secure the Monterey Fairgrounds for June 16 and 17, 1967. He and Pariser immediately booked Ravi Shankar for $3,500 in order to look legitimate to the cream of the pop scene. He'd recently become a rock musician's musician after the Beatles began incorporating the sitar into their music. Then, they set their sights high. As esteemed as Shankar was, he was not going to get young kids hiking up north. The two hottest acts in rock and roll in 1967 were still the Beatles and the Rolling Stones, and that's who they wanted atop their bill. They set up a meeting with former Beatles correspondent Derek Taylor, who moved to Los Angeles in 1966 to set up his own press agency. He was the man who could get them in touch with both bands, but, unbeknownst to anyone at the time, the Beatles had played the final concert of their career in Candlestick Park back on August 29 and let Taylor know they weren't interested. The Rolling Stones' Mick Jagger and Keith Richards were in the throes of a legal nightmare after a drug bust at Richards' Redlands estate only a couple of weeks earlier, which put the kibosh on any immediate international touring. Pariser and Shapiro were disheartened, but Derek Taylor presented a more viable and local option. The Mamas & the Papas were the hottest act in showbiz and were a stone's throw away and, along with producer Lou Adler, were probably the only ones capable of financing such a grandiose operation and turn a profit. The trick now was to get them to buy into it.

While the riot and the fallout were going down in Los Angeles, the Mamas & the Papas couldn't have been any further away both figuratively and literally. Though residents of Los Angeles, none of them frequented the Sunset Strip with any sort of regularity and, while the curfew riots were underway, the group was fulfilling tour dates in New York and Texas. As soon as they returned, work began on their third album. From November 15 through 18, John was at Western Recorders laying down the backing tracks for a series of covers that would take up most of the first side of the album. The peace in John and Michelle's marriage made things at home easier but it also had a deleterious effect on his songwriting. He went into the sessions with essentially nothing and crafted new arrangements for the classic "Twist and Shout," hits for both the Isley Brothers and the Beatles, the Temptations' "My Girl," and the Shirelles' "Dedicated to the One I Love." Though the two former arrangements were rather pedestrian, John's arrangement for the third reinvented the song.

The song was suggested by Michelle at a recent group meeting to discuss what songs they were going to record for the next album. After running through most of the songs he'd written and stockpiled since saying goodbye to folk in 1965, John had a dearth of original music on hand. In an interview with *KRLA Beat* the previous summer, John spoke about his approach to songwriting and admitted that he only wrote spontaneously and had difficulty sitting down with the purpose of coming up with a song. With a deadline on the horizon, a series of covers was absolutely necessary, and everybody tossed out some ideas. Michelle's first suggestion was the Coasters' "I'm a Hog for You Baby," the B side of their 1959 number seven hit "Poison Ivy." It was a gritty and rocking R&B tune and as far off John's radar as a song could get seven years earlier. Neither he nor Cass had even heard of it. A few other suggestions were made in the Crystals' "He's a Rebel" and the Shirelles' "Will You Still Love Me Tomorrow," but John wasn't too familiar with either and struggled with arrangements. It was the Shirelles' follow-up hit that struck a chord with him.

Beginning life in late 1957 as a single for the R&B quintet the "5" Royales, "Dedicated to the One I Love" featured an impassioned vocal by Eugene Tanner and blistering guitar licks from its coauthor, Lowman Pauling. With a melody based off an obscure 1955 ballad by the Casanovas called "I Don't Want You to Go," the sentiment of the song was slightly more sensitive compared to the "5" Royales' usual material, but it rocked nonetheless. It was all at once soulful, gritty, melancholy and sweetened with plenty of doo-wop vocal elements. But with all it had going for it, it didn't chart anywhere.

In the spring of 1959, a teenage girl group from Newark, New Jersey, called the Shirelles appeared with the "5" Royales on a package show at the Howard Theater in Washington, D.C., where they witnessed the veteran quintet's performance of it. Captivated by the song, they learned it before heading back to New Jersey and performed it for their manager Florence Greenberg. Greenberg had just sold her Tiara record label to Decca and used the $4,000 profit to launch a new label called Scepter. She was keen to follow up on the girls' earlier success with the number one hit "Will You Still Love Me Tomorrow," and, after hearing them practice "Dedicated to the One I Love," with a few feminine touches added, she booked a session at Beltone Studios in the Brill Building and issued it as the label's third single in May 1959. It failed on its first run, but Greenberg was so confident that she reissued it in January 1961 and was rewarded with a number three hit in the *Billboard* pop charts.

In John Phillips' ear, he heard a platform to display the group's dynamic vocal interplay and put Michelle, the least gifted vocalist of them all, in the spotlight for the first time. Through the number of tempo changes, lyric rearrangements and a chord change to G major, John made the song completely his own. There were clever nuances, like Cass and Michelle singing "Life, can never be" on the same beat as the word "love" as Denny and John sang, "This is dedicated to the one I love" and a swirling, square dance–like musical interlude that proved even an R&B tune could fit well into the folk-rock mode.

With the basic music track completed by November 18, John summoned the rest of the group down to Western Recorders to lay down vocals and what they emerged with was their next single. Michelle's vulnerably soft introductory vocal, over John's gently picked twelve string, lulled the listener into a soft sense of security. John layered and staggered multiple takes to give a Wall of Sound touch of which even Phil Spector would be jealous. Thirty seconds later, the group joined in, with Cass' contralto seizing control until Denny joins her with the title line. As the band kicks into full gear, complete with saloon piano, Michelle's opening vocal is left in the dust as the song becomes a mid-tempo interchange between Cass, Denny, and musical arrangement but returns to softer territory with every reprise of "This is dedicated to the one I love."

It was a solid opener to what would become the *Deliver* album. As 1966 drew to a close, John set to fleshing out original material. From the onset, it was thin and not as impressive as his previous originals. "String Man" and "Free Advice" made good album filler but neither song was going to make the public forget about "California Dreamin'" or "Monday, Monday" nor were either strong enough to be issued as a single. There was hope in a song partially commissioned by Lou Adler and possibly inspired by John and Michelle's reunion with ex-Journeymen tenor Scott McKenzie at a show in Washington, D.C.

Since their last time together in 1965, at John and Michelle's East Village apartment, which he'd been subletting while they were in St. Thomas, Scott had been trying to ignite a solo career. Capitol Records retained him following the Journeymen's breakup and issued two singles under his name. The first, a strong cover of British singer Mike Hurst's "Look in Your Eyes" backed with Les Vandyke's "All I Want Is You," didn't chart. The second single, released eight months later, featured an odd pop arrangement of country singer Webb Pierce's 1953 number one hit "There Stands the Glass" backed with Scott's original "Wipe the Tears (From Your Eyes)." It solidified his fate at the label. It too went nowhere and shortly after he was released from his contract. Still in Greenwich Village, he teamed up with eccentric veteran folk singer Erik Darling who was retooling his trio, the Rooftop Singers, two and a half years removed from their international hit "Walk Right In." Along with original group member Bill Svanoe, Darling recruited Scott as well as Patricia Street and Susan Manchester in order to beef up their integrated sound and join the folk-rock craze. They called themselves Project X and issued two singles between November 1965 and February 1966 on Vanguard that were dead on arrival. The band collapsed, and all went their separate ways.

Scott retreated to Washington, D.C., and was wallowing around with no real direction when John reconnected with him in October 1966, and, for the first time in many years, both were happy to see each other. During this same trip, John was also able to reconnect with his mother, sister and several of his old Del Ray Locals buddies at a reunion held at the apartment of his ex-wife Susie, with whom Scott had had a brief affair. It was the first time John had seen any of them, including his children, since the Virgin Islands nearly two years earlier and, even though he hadn't sent Susie any child support despite his newfound wealth, the reunion was amicable. He even introduced her to marijuana and tried to convince her to move out to L.A. with the kids. Though that prospect didn't interest her, it piqued Scott's interest, and he joined the band for their last two dates before heading west with them and settling into one of John and Michelle's guest bungalows.

Shortly after returning to L.A., John put his musical clout to good use by steering Scott's career. It had become en vogue in the 1960s pop scene for popular artists to produce other artists and lend their expertise to honing their sound. Curtis Mayfield and Smokey Robinson both had considerable success doing it in the R&B field and, with the British Invasion entering year three, successful artist/songwriters like Paul McCartney and Mick Jagger were getting more involved in the producing and arranging of their respective bands' works and lending their talents to other artists. Jagger even produced a U.K. number one hit for Chris Farlowe who covered the Stones' original "Out of Time." A little closer to home, and perhaps more influential, was the Beach Boys' Brian Wilson, who had been writing and producing for other artists as far back as 1963. Being as talented an arranger as he was, John eagerly entered the fray to see what he could do to help Scott get his career back on track. Not long after getting back home, John introduced him to Lou and before he could even adjust to L.A.'s morning smog, Scott was booked for a recording session at Western for a one-off single on Epic Records with John producing. But, in an interesting twist of fate, the meeting with Lou, while designed to help Scott, actually set the Mamas & the Papas' next hit single in motion.

Lou Adler was the consummate musician's producer. Although he chewed up and spit out his fair share of artists along the way, he took a keen interest in the ones he admired and, up to that point, none had interested him more than the Mamas & the Papas who descended upon his life like a big paisley cloud less than two years earlier. Lou was always up on who was who in the music business and knew that Scott had served as John's tenor in the Journeymen. John, who had a penchant for storytelling, had grown exceptionally close with Lou and spent many an evening regaling him with tales of the Smoothies, the Elmwood Casino, Greenwich Village, and coming up in the rough-and-tumble folk scene of the early 60s. And the story of how the Mamas & the Papas came together on an island in the middle of the Caribbean was so fanciful that, if it was a Hollywood movie, nobody would believe it. There were a lot of pieces to put together, and Lou suggested that John do it in song. It seemed like a tall order at first, but one that might just help kick John out of his dry spell.

With the working title "Talkin' Mamas and Papas," a nod to folk music titles of days past, John set out to tell their story in a three-minute pop vignette. And, much like he did four years earlier with "California Dreamin'," he elicited Michelle's help in composing it. Neither were overwhelmed by the prospect when they actually sat down to write it. Autobiographical songs seemed to be their strong suit. They first came up with a series of rhymes and lyrics based on actual events but not in chronological order, which made their writing session much looser. When they were finished, they picked out the best verses and stitched them together in proper order. It was perhaps the best musical experience the couple would ever have together. Even though there was much pain in their history, time did heal many of the wounds and they had a ball writing it, laughing out loud regularly at lyrics that made it and those that didn't.

What they ended up with was a somewhat true but extremely clever account of how the quartet came together, which, even more amazingly, incorporated the movements made by many of their folk contemporaries around the same time. Interestingly, the song skipped the Journeymen experience altogether and began with John and Michelle's desire to shed their folk skin and find their true musical calling, which wasn't entirely true, at least in John's case. Then, in chronological order, the listener learns about Denny and Zal Yanovsky's surf group, Cass' unsuccessful attempt to become a nightclub singer in New York, Jim McGuinn and Barry McGuire both emigrating to L.A.'s music scene, the Mugwumps, Cass' unrequited love for Denny, Zal and John Sebastian breaking off to form the Lovin' Spoonful, the New Journeymen, McGuinn and McGuire having success in L.A., the decision to go to the Virgin Islands, Cass' late arrival, maxing out Marshall Brickman's American Express card, living on the beach in St. John and the ultimate decision to join McGuinn and McGuire in L.A. And all in 3:52! A few liberties were taken. Cass never actually planned to go to Swarthmore College nor did she hitchhike to New York, but it made a great rhyme. The only thing that gave Michelle pause was John's line, "And no one's getting fat except Mama Cass." Much like John thought of her line about going into a church in "California Dreamin'" four years earlier, Michelle assumed it was just a placeholder until he thought of something better, but John was resolute about this one. As self-conscious as Cass was about her weight, Michelle was not looking forward to presenting her with that one.

"This is art," John said in reply. "We can get away with anything, particularly the truth."

John had really begun zeroing in on Cass around this time. Her star was rising, and it rankled him considerably. Since the Flores Street incident, she had begun distancing herself from the group more and more. She withdrew to a three-bedroom English country revival on Woodrow Wilson Drive, overlooking the San Fernando Valley. Seeing her less and less was tough on Denny and Michelle, because they genuinely cared about her. On the contrary, she and John were never particularly close and there was a constant power struggle between her incredible voice and his creativity, but they knew that for the Mamas & the Papas to thrive, they needed each other. However, John considered his talents to be superior and, to keep her in her place, he could be unbelievably cruel by saying things like she smelled or telling her not to lose too much weight because her eyes would get too close together.

"You should have your own record label, Cass," John once said to her. "Fat Records. Then, the record label's ads could read, 'Another obese release from Fat.'"

Whatever pain John's sadism and cruelty caused Cass, she buried it and didn't allow it to break her bubbly façade. She enjoyed ticking him off in return and the best way for her to stick it to him was to sing that line with as much vim and vigor as she could muster. On the record, she belts it out so convincingly that it's as if she's singing about someone else. Fat jokes were nothing new to her. She'd heard them all her life and, now that she was famous, they only grew louder and wider. To a more fragile personality, it could've been deadly, but Cass' will and determination was fierce. It took a lot of hard work to get where she was, and she wasn't about to let that sidetrack her. Besides, she had some joyous news, which she'd been keeping to herself, to distract her from all the noise.

At a rehearsal around the New Year in John and Michelle's pub room, Cass excitedly broke the news that she was five months pregnant, which caught the other three off guard. Because of her build, her natural body size and a pregnant belly were indistinguishable, so nobody feigned surprise. Fittingly, John trampled all over her good news.

"Fine," he said. "When are you having the abortion?"

Michelle and Denny weren't particularly stunned at his brazenness. In fact, they looked at Cass for an answer, almost as if in agreement. Even though abortion was illegal in the state of California and would remain that way for another two years, it wasn't uncommon for women in the entertainment business to have an illegal abortion performed, especially those whose career was arching like hers. So, the question wasn't off the wall but her response sure was.

"No, no . . . I'm having it" she replied. "My doctor's actually surprised that I'm pregnant . . . woman my size don't usually get pregnant . . . and I may never get pregnant again."

It was a bold move in 1967 and even though the stigma of abortion was bad, single motherhood wasn't that far behind, and embracing it was unheard of. Cass' decision flew right in the face of social convention and helped set the tone for what happened after the 1960s, when single motherhood became quite common. But John's question had nothing to do with social stigma or life and death. He was concerned about her availability.

"How are you going to go on the road with us, Cass?" he asked quizzically.

"I'll go on the road," she told him. "I'll pull my weight, John Phillips. I'll be there."

Cass wouldn't reveal who the father was and kept that secret closely guarded for the rest of her life, not even revealing it to Denny or Michelle. And they were genuinely alarmed because she'd most recently been dating an unsavory character named Harrison Pickens "Pic" Dawson III, a drug dealer and general ne'er-do-well who was the son of a State Department official. Pic had been sent to the finest private schools on the eastern seaboard only to be kicked out of each one for his sociopathic behavior. His rugged exterior, James Dean–like demeanor and bad boy image was very appealing to Cass. The two of them first met during her short tenure at American University several years earlier but lost touch after her folk career began. Upon her success, he reconnected with her, moved into her basement and began a love affair fueled partially by her need for male companionship and his need for drugs. Rather than acquiesce to Michelle and Denny's desire to know who the father was, she added to their frustration and worry by referring to it as an "immaculate conception."

Sessions for the third album resumed on Monday, January 9, and several tracks were completed that week before heading out for concert dates in Berkeley and Sacramento. For "Talkin' Mamas and Papas," John brought with him his most elaborate arrangement yet. It was a clever one that started off with a 12-string guitar intro, to capture its folk essence, played dually by both John and Scott, before breaking into a Beatles-influenced pop arrangement designed for overdubs. And, much like John and Lou did with flautist Bud Shank for "California Dreamin'" over a year earlier, they called in multi-instrumentalist Jim Horn in the middle of the night to lay down an extended flute solo before the final verse.

Even though the Mamas & the Papas' personal lives were more in order than they had been for the previous two albums, the sessions for the third album were considerably darker. There was palpable tension in the air between John and some of the studio musicians. Whether it was the steady ingestion of LSD over the past two and a half years, success going to his head or a combination of the two, John was much more demanding and antagonistic, which wouldn't be so bad if he wasn't oftentimes inattentive and contradictory. He demanded perfection from the start. There was no room for error or for letting the musicians get a feel for the song at the beginning of each session. He wanted it laid down correctly from the start.

He particularly got into it with guitarist Phil Sloan and drummer Hal Blaine, the latter of whom was perhaps the most easygoing bandleader in all of pop music. As accomplished as Phil was as a songwriter, guitarist and artist, he was still 10 years younger than John, and the gratitude he initially had for him helping hone the sound of the Mamas & the Papas had turned into competitiveness and resentment.

"You fucking know nothing," he would tell Phil. "You don't tell me how to make a record!"

His clash with Hal Blaine was of a strictly professional nature where John inadvertently added and subtracted bars without telling any of the musicians, which caused everybody to get out of sync. After they finished one particular take and prepared for another, Hal wanted to make sure the change was noted and that everyone was on the same page.

"OK, John, are you going to add a bar?" he asked.

"I didn't add a bar there," John replied.

"John, you did," Hal retorted.

"I want to do it just the way I did it!" John exclaimed.

The tension was rising so, rather than press an artist, Hal simply made a note of it and resumed the session. After a couple of run-throughs, they started the next take and John changed it up again, throwing everyone off once more. John jumped up.

"OK Blaine," John yelled. "That was you that time!"

Hal practically leapt over his drums and charged after him but was restrained by Lou, Joe Osborn and Larry Knechtel, who also whisked John out of the room to the kitchen where they fed him several cups of coffee to shake him out of whatever drug-induced haze he was under. After John sobered up some and tensions cooled down, the two apologized and resumed the session.

Cass wasn't immune to John's wrath in the studio either. He considered her uncontrollable, unpredictable, and slipping away from his grasp, so whatever he could do to make her work harder and reach levels strenuous even for her vocal range pleased him. He would wear her out, almost purposely, with take after take and no clear explanation as to why after she questioned him. Even at times where she felt she'd nailed it, she would push through, even pregnant, until the session finished. John gave no quarter and she'd often make herself a target. The same studio habits that drove Tim Rose crazy had the same effect on John, and, even once she'd finish eating, she'd have to wait for the food to settle. It was maddening, not only for John, but for the musicians and the rest of the group. It was behavior like this and the nocturnal nature of the session that caused engineer Bones Howe to quit once and for all early into the sessions. For him, the good times were over.

They wrapped the sessions up near the end of January and the masters were sent to print for an early March release. Another fantastic Guy Webster photograph of the group, taken in late 1966, was chosen as the cover as they frolicked in John and Michelle's pool, conjuring up an image of their more carefree days in the U.S. Virgin Islands. In an existential sense, the picture sums up the existence of the Mamas & the Papas: four adults, fully clothed in a luxurious pool, looking their grungiest, behaving like kids half their age, drinking from the well of John's suspended hat as the water trickled out from various holes.

The album was titled *The Mamas & the Papas Deliver*, after Cass' pregnancy, and hit stores on March 7. It was a pleasant enough collection of songs that fit well into their canon but, next to their first two, was an overall lackluster effort with the most glaring omission being the lack of solid John Phillips originals. "Dedicated to the One I Love," issued as a single on Valentine's Day 1967, kicked off side one in glorious fashion and set high expectations for the listener. All but two songs on side one were covers, which was increasingly becoming passé in the latter-era British Invasion and folk-rock scenes.

"My Girl" was a bit of a misstep and an ill-suited follow-up, although it was salvaged by Denny's crisp vocal. John's over-arrangement made the song much more middle-of-the-road with their background vocals sounding more like the Anita Kerr Singers. "Sing for Your Supper," featuring a glorious lead by Cass, was a 1938 Richard Rodgers–Lorenz Hart song from their Broadway musical *The Boys from Syracuse* and was one of four songs recorded by the group for the *ABC Stage 67* production *Rodgers & Hart Today*, which aired five days before the album's release. If the song proved anything to the listener, it was that John Phillips had an incredible talent for making other songwriters' work sound like his own, but the song sounded dated compared to the others. The rock scene was progressing so quickly between 1966 and 1967 that many songs recorded only months before suffered the same fate. "Twist and Shout" was an attempt at repeating the success they had with "Do You Wanna Dance" on the first album, which took a fast, frenetic floor-shaker and turned it into a slow, dreamy dancer. This time, however, John's arrangement bore bad fruit. After the rocking versions put forth by the Isley Brothers and the Beatles, his version was awkward and misplaced. Denny sounds like he's drifting off to sleep as he's urging his partner to "shake it up baby, twist and shout."

The first original, and strongest track on the entire album, was John and Michelle's ode to their history now titled "Creeque Alley." Sometime between the end of the session and the album's pressing, it was changed to honor the alleyway in Charlotte Amalie, St. Thomas, where the Mamas & the Papas came together and was much better suited the song's tribute quality. The incredible lyrics, combined with John's magnificent arrangement, perfectly matched the album cover and would be parsed for decades by fans of the group and folk-rock in general. It would be the second single taken off the album in April and reached number five. Debates ensued about the correct pronunciation of "Creeque" and the song would irrevocably link the Mamas & the Papas with the Lovin' Spoonful, the Byrds, and Barry McGuire. Another solid John and Michelle collaboration "Free Advice" closed the first side.

The second side contained nothing but John originals and was much weaker in comparison. Beginning with the mid-tempo "Look Through My Window," first issued as the group's follow-up single to "Words of Love" five months earlier, the side cycles and sputters through five near misses and one dud. "Boys and Girls Together" and "Did You Ever Want to Cry" both feature far-too-subdued leads by Cass and aren't very memorable. "Frustration" is an incredible instrumental begging for lyrics and a shared lead by Denny and Cass and "John's Musical Box" is simply a recording of an actual musical box owned by John and Michelle and a complete throwaway. But the strength of "Dedicated to the One I Love" and "Creeque Alley" ensured massive sales and it peaked at number two in May, kept out of the top spot by *More of the Monkees*.

With the third album sessions out of the way and, with a short break between concert dates, the Mamas & the Papas were able to go to their separate corners and deescalate. Cass flew out to the East Coast and awaited her dilation in seclusion. Pregnancy did nothing to deter her from abusing drugs. She smoked marijuana regularly and took acid five times while pregnant. When she gave birth by C-section to her daughter Owen Vanessa Hendricks at Cooley-Dickinson Hospital in Northampton, Massachusetts, on April 26, 1967, she was under the influence of LSD. After a month-long convalescence following a complicated surgery, she returned to Los Angeles and settled into her new Hollywood home commingling regularly with assorted musicians, sordid drug addicts, and pushers.

Denny also retreated to a new house, a four-bedroom single family home on Appian Way in Laurel Canyon that once belonged to legendary silent film actress Mary Astor. There he spent most of his days in a drunken haze with his unrequited love for Michelle getting the better of him. In tribute to his alcoholism and fondness for Crown Royal, he had drapes custom made out of his numerous purple felt bags that came with the bottle. When he wasn't pining away for Michelle, he occupied his mind by throwing wild, uninhibited parties that never seemed to stop and engaged in lots of gratuitous sex. He had a constant stream of party guests and roommates moving in and out, including folk mentor Fred Neil and Barry McGuire, whose career had virtually nosedived after introducing the Mamas & the Papas to Lou Adler.

John and Michelle's marriage, on the outside, looked rejuvenated, but it was mostly superficial. They too retreated to their new home in Bel Air and became a Hollywood power couple, hosting lavish parties under the direction of their personal assistant Steve Brandt, a gossip columnist and friend to many a young film actor and director. The debaucherous gatherings served as the breeding grounds for terminal infidelity. The mansion was soon filled with the young Hollywood cognoscenti who were pushing the limits of traditional decency in film. Roman Polanski and his girlfriend Sharon Tate, power couple Roger Vadim and Jane Fonda, and notable actors Christian Marquand, Candice Bergen, and Marlon Brando could be seen breezing about the Phillips' grounds regularly. When Warren Beatty told John that he went to rival Washington Lee High School in Arlington, Virginia, the same years John was at George Washington, they became fast friends.

With Brandt in charge of the invitations and the catering, John handled the booze and the drugs and made sure plenty was on hand, especially their big three: LSD, marijuana, and amphetamines. He would take an entire brown jug filled with pills and spread them out across their full-size pool table. The green felt would become covered in multiple-colored bennies, free for the taking, and, in the Hollywood drug culture of the late 60s, nobody asked. They just popped. What made it even more dangerous is that, quite often, many of their guests brought their children. No regard or safety measures for them were even considered.

Despite the appearances of good times, the group had become so fractured personally that there was no going back. They hardly socialized with one another anymore and rehearsals were becoming fewer and fewer. The public didn't notice though. Despite the third album being their weakest offering yet, it shot to number two on the *Billboard* LP charts and "Dedicated to the One I Love" hit the same spot on the Hot 100 on March 25, and hit the same spot in the U.K. in May. The Mamas & the Papas were red hot and on the verge of blowing up, but resurgence was heading John and Michelle's way in the form of two guys just back from Monterey.

CHAPTER 20:
WE'RE HAVING A FESTIVAL

In late October 1963, Bob Dylan laid down a new song that was a commentary on the shift in the social fabric called "The Times They Are A-Changin'." Little did he know that the popular music field, of which he still laid on the periphery, was about to change drastically and in only a mere matter of months. He had no way of forecasting the onslaught of the British Invasion, the rise of Motown or the creation of folk-rock, but, when his song was released in mid-January 1964, and rose to the public consciousness following the arrival of the Beatles, Dylan served as a type of soothsayer in the minds of many of America's youth. For him, his times changed even more following the release of his full-band single "Like a Rolling Stone" in July 1965.

By the spring of 1967, the times began to change again for nearly every group that ignited the original changes three years earlier. It proved to be a year of transition. The styles and trends that had ignited John Phillips' rock and roll sensibilities two years earlier had either evaporated or altered completely and were replaced with musical experimentation that mirrored the rising use of drugs, particularly LSD. These new sounds, often filled with backward guitars, Vox Continental organs and sitars, were often combined with a youthful sense of social justice brought on by Bob Dylan's protest era and the rising outspokenness of young popular musicians and Hollywood actors. It was the fruit borne of "Eve of Destruction" and "For What It's Worth." The protest movement that shut down the Sunset Strip in Los

Angeles for several nights in November 1966 had infiltrated youth culture and filtered onto college campuses, focusing instead on free speech, the Vietnam War and the Civil Rights Movement. The music changed the times and the times changed the music and artists who stood on a firm foundation only a year earlier had to anticipate the flow or be trampled underfoot.

The British Invasion, which sealed the fate of so many of the American rock and roll and pop acts who preceded it, was fading by early 1967. American folk-rock acts, influenced by all facets of the Beatles, had staged a counterassault, and the pushback left weaker British artists like Gerry & the Pacemakers, Freddie & the Dreamers, Billy J. Kramer & the Dakotas and Herman's Hermits in its wake. Self-sustaining rock bands with mature, insightful lyrics and electrified folk arrangements were becoming more in vogue, and those who were unable to compete didn't last. The Beatles rewrote the script in February 1967 with their revolutionary double-sided hit "Strawberry Fields Forever" and "Penny Lane." The psychedelic nature of the A-side dealt a lethal blow to stronger British bands like the Animals, Manfred Mann, and the Searchers who'd built their success on non-original material. The Beatles' chief competitors, the Rolling Stones, were slow to respond due to their own legal and management issues but they would eventually come back stronger and revitalized. The Dave Clark Five, the Beatles' first rival in 1964 and 1965, was serving up a rocking version of Johnny Mercer's corny 1938 standard "You Must Have Been a Beautiful Baby" in spring 1967, cementing their last trip to the Top 40. The free ride for anything British was over.

The first wave of British Invasion counterrevolutionaries who were mentioned in the Mamas & the Papas' "Creeque Alley" were also facing hard times. After Gene Clark left the Byrds in January 1966, they began to sputter, only reaching the Top 15 one more time with his enigmatic six-stanza poem he called "Eight Miles High" that depicted the group's disastrous tour of England in August 1965. Lead guitarist and singer Jim McGuinn wrapped an improvisational 12-string Rickenbacker jam around the rhythm section largely based off relatively recent stylings offered by jazz saxophonist John Coltrane and sitar maestro Ravi Shankar, giving the song an ominous rhythm. But trouble followed the song shortly after its release in March 1966 when radio industry trade sheet called *Bill Gavin's Record Report* referred to the song's murky lyrics as "LSD talk" and stalled its trajectory to the top of the charts. After that, the group struggled to regain their footing, and a power struggle began to develop between outspoken rhythm guitarist and singer David Crosby and the team of band leader Jim McGuinn, who now went by Roger, and bassist Chris Hillman.

The Lovin' Spoonful were also victims of drug stigma but in reverse. Following an impressive run of hits that included their debut "Do You Believe in Magic," "Daydream," "Did You Ever Have to Make Up Your Mind" and the blockbuster number one "Summer in the City," all of which were written or co-written by John Sebastian, bandmate, Zal Yanovsky was growing restless. His whacky sense of humor lent itself to a cruel honesty and he often voiced his displeasure over the strength of John's songs and the boredom he felt playing to large audiences. A growing rift was forming between him and John Sebastian, but it may have been due more to Zal's growing insecurity following a May 1966 bust, along with bassist Steve Boone, for marijuana possession in San Francisco. Though the alpha male in the group, under the lamp of police interrogation, where he was threatened with deportation to Ontario, he wilted like a flower and bargained his way out by agreeing to turn in his dealer. When word leaked out, he became persona non grata in the counterculture and a liability to the band's status. He was fired in June 1967, but the damage was irreversible. One month later, a group calling itself the Defense Fund and Freedom League of the Brotherhood of Smoke took out a full-page ad in the left-wing *Los Angeles Free Press* recounting the incident, implicating Zal and Steve Boone and urged readers to destroy all their Lovin' Spoonful records and merchandise. It sealed their fate. They only reached the Top 40 once more.

By 1967, it seems the only folk refugee the public had a growing yen for was Bob Dylan. He'd been a major source of inspiration for all these artists but was missing in action. As the Mamas & the Papas, the Byrds and the Lovin' Spoonful were becoming household names, Dylan's full-band, electric singles and albums were just as hot. Beginning with "Subterranean Homesick Blues," which just grazed the Top 40 in April 1965, Dylan reeled off nine singles and three LPs in a year and a half that sounded fresh and original. With jangly guitars and a prevalent Hammond organ, over a strong rhythm section, he created a whimsical circus-like atmosphere where his word marathons made him the sardonic ringmaster. His impact was so well received that his back catalog and publishing demos became a treasure-trove for aspiring and established artists, and many became hits for his contemporaries. His follow-up single "Like a Rolling Stone" reached number two and broke the unwritten pop single two-and-a-half-minute rule by clocking in at an unprecedented 6:07. Four of his next eight singles hit the Top 40 and a crazy tour mirrored his records. With Canadian band the Hawks, in tow, Dylan toured the United States and England to a mix of new fans and disenchanted folkies who felt betrayed by their former guru's decision to enter the rock and roll arena, but, nevertheless, came to see him. Each concert was met with contrasting boos, cheers, laughter and hisses and, even though Dylan fostered all of this, he could never have predicted the toll it would take on his psyche. The tour ended in midsummer 1966, and with a network special, a book deal and another tour on the table, he retreated to his home in Woodstock, New York, with his new bride Sara Lowndes, for some rest. But, while following her home from manager Albert Grossman's house on his Triumph Tiger 100 motorcycle on July 29, 1966, he wiped out and was thrown off, breaking several vertebrae in his neck. He spent the next six to eight weeks recuperating in his home and wouldn't be heard from for another 17 months.

It seemed like nothing good was happening to the innovators of folk-rock. The Mamas & the Papas arrived on the scene the better part of a year after their predecessors. Were they next?

John took his music seriously. It was his lifeblood, and, because of his natural arranging ability, he held himself and his contemporaries to a high standard as a folk musician and now as a rock and roller. His praise and his criticism meant a lot to his circle of friends and, because of the strength of his impeccable arrangements of the Mamas & the Papas' records, he'd earned a very favorable reputation in the industry. On February 18, 1967, the Recording Academy published their annual list of Grammy Awards finalists for 1966 with "Monday, Monday" being nominated in four separate categories, including Record of the Year, Best Performance by a Vocal Group, Best Contemporary Rock and Roll Record and Best Contemporary Rock and Roll Record Group Performance, Vocal or Instrumental. It was unprecedented recognition by an academy, which traditionally held rock and roll in low esteem and, despite being the curators of popular music on an international level, paid little attention to the most important musical trend of the last 10+ years.

In its nine-year history to that point, the Grammys had been most interested in middle-of-the road, adult contemporary music, regularly giving awards to artists whose heydays were in the postwar, pre–rock and roll era of 1946 to 1954 and were shamefully out of touch with what was trending musically. Frank Sinatra and Henry Mancini routinely swept up at the awards in many of the popular music categories from 1959 to 1966. In fact, rock and roll wasn't even considered a category until the fourth annual ceremony held on May 29, 1962, with Chubby Checker's "Let's Twist Again" winning the award for Best Rock and Roll Recording. In the ensuing years, subsequent winners in that category included the Statler Brothers, Roger Miller (twice), both known mostly as country acts, and Petula Clark, who was about as rock and roll as Peggy Lee. Up until the awards ceremony for the year 1966, Elvis Presley had been nominated just three times, with no wins, and the Beatles six times with only one win for Best Performance by a Vocal Group for "A Hard Day's Night" in 1964.

The academy was still slowly coming around to rock and roll when the Mamas & the Papas were reeling off hit after hit, which is why their February 1967 announcement was historical. For the first time ever, there were more rock and roll artists nominated in a multitude of popular categories than there had been in all previous years combined. Besides the Mamas & the Papas, other relevant artists nominated were the Beatles, Sandy Posey, Nancy Sinatra, the Beach Boys, the Monkees, the Byrds, Dusty Springfield, and the Association. In addition to the four categories that the Mamas & the Papas occupied, rock and roll artists were nominated in seven others, including Album of the Year, Song of the Year, and Best Vocal Performance for both male and female.

The ceremony was held concurrently at the Beverly Hilton Hotel in Los Angeles and at the New York Hilton in New York City on March 2. John, Michelle, and Denny attended the former together. Cass chose to remain home because of her pregnancy. All dressed formally and, if it wasn't for their unconventional long hair, they wouldn't have stuck out at all. They weren't yet bold enough to tackle the dress code. John and Denny both wore dark double-breasted suits and bowties. John's hair was longer than ever, with an effective comb-over that covered up his ever-increasing baldness. With a full beard and mustache that highlighted his Native American cheekbones, it was his best look yet. Denny's hair, though still long, had been professionally quaffed with sideburns that ran at least an inch past his earlobes. Michelle looked stunning in a simple shirt dress that emphasized her bohemian simplicity. Her long, straight hair, with a part in the middle, looked rather unkempt compared to the bouffants and bubbles that dominated the ball room. But rather than mute her beauty, the chic hippie look only enhanced it and surely whet the sexual appetite of many of the bourbon-swilling, cigar-smoking music execs in attendance.

Though prestigious, the Grammys was still a few years away from being the grand event it eventually would become and wouldn't be broadcast live on network television for another three years. It had more of a variety show vibe than an Oscar-type awards show, and winners did not make speeches. Frank Sinatra, who took away five Grammys, including Record of the Year and Album of the Year, didn't even attend. Nevertheless, there were several notable presenters and performers, including Ray Charles, Eydie Gorme, Sammy Davis Jr., Peter Noone and the New Vaudeville Band who performed their number one hit "Winchester Cathedral," winner of Best Rock & Roll Recording. Clearly, the Mamas & the Papas were in uncharted territory, and there were plenty of shots taken at the rising counterculture they represented. Comedian Godfrey Cambridge made the first joke at their expense. "I guess you've heard the Mamas & the Papas are expecting a baby. They can hardly wait. It'll be the first time they really know which is the mama and which is the papa."

But whatever barbs may have stung were eased when the Mamas & the Papas were announced the winner of the Grammy for Best Rock & Roll Group Performance, Vocal or Instrumental for "Monday, Monday," beating out the Beach Boys' "Good Vibrations" and the Monkees' "Last Train to Clarksville." The song about the day of the week that Denny, Cass, and Michelle initially detested was arguably the first true rock and roll song to be recognized by the music industry as award worthy. It was a huge moment for John and one that he savored. It served to swell his head even more.

In mid-March, the group reconvened for two weeks in Oahu, Hawaii, where they played a couple of dates, including one before an electrical storm swept across the island. Upon their return, they took a hiatus for Cass' maternity. Denny retreated to his new Laurel Canyon home. John, with no sessions or concerts in sight, had plenty of time to get high and quench his ever-increasing, extramarital sexual appetite, or so he thought before Alan Pariser and Derek Taylor came a-knocking at their Bel Air mansion on the afternoon of April 4 with a proposal that would ultimately bring rock and roll to the level of respectability he desired. In a gesture of goodwill, they brought along "noted" Hollywood pot dealer David Wheeler and a gift of "Ice Pack," potent, high-grade marijuana packed in insulated ice bags. Ben Shapiro stayed behind, pacing nervously in his office.

After Michelle wrestled open the large oaken front door and welcomed them inside, introductions and pleasantries were exchanged. Nobody in the room had met before but John knew Derek by reputation. His mixture of proper British etiquette and hipster style belied his anxiety. Alan was the opposite. He was visibly edgy, which Derek feared might earn them an early departure. After what must've seemed like an eternity of awkwardness, John finally got down to business and asked them what brought them to his home.

"Well, John," Derek said. "We're having a festival and it wouldn't be one unless you chaps performed."

"Oh, I see," John responded with an ever-widening yet suspicious grin. "Who'd like coffee?"

All three unexpected guests nodded and moved from the foyer to the living room, engaging in idle chitchat about the carpets and Jeanette MacDonald as Michelle went off to brew the coffee. Since she represented one-quarter of the group, they waited for her before continuing the pitch. Upon her return, Derek resumed festival talk, telling them they had rented the fairgrounds in Monterey, California, a peninsula town of about 20,000 people, located about 325 miles northwest of L.A. and 120 miles south of San Francisco, for a weekend in mid-June. They wished to showcase the contemporary rock and roll scene in sort of a mini–Newport Folk Festival, with the Mama & the Papas serving as the grand finale. The payoff for their involvement was a cool $5,000. It slammed the brakes on an otherwise interesting conversation. John was unimpressed. That was chump change for them. For their concert in Denver alone, they were paid $60,000 in cash.

"You really have a nerve," Michelle barked back, telling them that price was laughable, especially considering what the gates receipts would be alone.

On the surface, it must've seemed a bit surreptitious to John and Michelle and Derek easily let her say what she was thinking and, throughout the entire exchange, maintained an uncomfortable grin. With a festival, surely other acts were being invited, which aroused John's curiosity and that's where he went first.

"Who else did you ask?" he inquired.

Alan did his best bullshit act and rattled off a list of no-names and Ravi Shankar, but John could see through it all. At this stage, they clearly had nobody, and no contracts signed. Michelle sensed it too and ratcheted up the tension another notch.

"You come here with no one signed and try to use John," she asserted incredulously in her best finishing school tone. "I think it's terrible."

Feeling like the proverbial turd in the punch bowl, Derek and Alan began fumbling around trying to find a way to exit as gracefully as possible. Desperately, Alan blurted out that Simon & Garfunkel were in town. It was a total gamble that risked blowing the whole thing. They hadn't even spoken to the duo, let alone invited them to participate in anything. John considered Paul Simon his creative equal, which gave him pause to think that perhaps there was something to this. The stakes had been raised. Alan placed his bet and had everyone's full attention. It was time for John to call, raise, or fold. He raised.

"I tell you what," John told them. "If they'll call me or I call them, and they agree and we both agree to do it together then it'll be cool. But that's the only way it'll happen, OK?"

With a sense of relief, they calmly bade John and Michelle farewell and then rushed off for the Beverley Wilshire, where Simon & Garfunkel were staying while playing a three-night stand at the Carousel in West Covina. It was a challenge for them but a win-win for John. His poker face had won out. He was completely sold on the idea but didn't want to tip his hand until after he'd talked with Lou about it. This potentially could be the answer to a question John had been wrestling with for months. How can he elevate rock and roll to the respectability of jazz? Over the phone, Lou told him he was crazy and to go back to bed. He had a lot going on at the time, forming a new record label called Ode with his Dunhill profits and getting it off the ground. But John's proposal nagged at him throughout the evening and in the middle of the night he called him back to talk turkey. John's intuition was confirmed.

Over at the Beverley Wilshire, Derek and Alan made an unsuccessful cold call to Simon & Garfunkel, but secured an appointment with them the following day, despite Shapiro's objections. He didn't trust when musicians banded together, and his mistrust would eventually seal his fate. After a round of ego-stroking and small talk, Derek brought up the festival idea to Paul and Art and mentioned the Mamas & the Papas' potential involvement. To his pleasant surprise, they were very agreeable and wished to speak with John about it.

"It sounds a gas and we've got some ideas," he told them as they piled into a limousine and headed back to the Phillips' residence.

When they arrived, Paul and Art immediately sought out John. There was plenty in common between them besides a few shared concert dates. All three had trod long, winding paths to stardom, beginning with various incarnations of 1950s pop music. Similarly, all three sharpened their skills through the folk scene and found stardom singing in harmony. Outside on John's grass, tossing a baseball back and forth, he and Paul discussed the possibilities of making it a weekend-long festival with nonstop music from worldwide artists who were on the cutting edge. Either inspired by a dream or Michelle's question of how we can afford to pay all these people to perform, John told everyone that this must be a nonprofit venture in order to get credible artists to participate. The idea appealed to Paul's liberal sensibilities, and he quickly seconded. This put Derek and Alan in an awkward position. Surely, they saw dollar signs disappearing before their eyes, but Derek dedicated his career to putting the artist first, and Alan was an heir to the Sweetheart Cup Company fortune, so both acquiesced. Ben Shapiro, on the other hand, was not so benevolent and, when word got back to him, he wasn't pleased. His warning had rung true.

With those parameters set, things began moving rapidly. On Thursday, April 6, John and Michelle convened an informal meeting at their home, which included Lou, Paul and Art, Columbia producer Terry Melcher, Lou's business manager Phil Turetsky, his attorney Abe Somer, Derek, Alan, David, and Ben Shapiro. The underlying purpose of the meeting was a takeover and Shapiro was either going to get on board with the nonprofit idea or get out. After several hours of deliberations, nothing got accomplished. They decided to break for the night, sleep on it, and reconvene the next evening. When that time came to pass, once again, nothing was accomplished. The only solution was to buy Shapiro out. He'd positioned himself masterfully. Stick with the charity and get next to nothing, hold out and get paid. His price for his interest, which included co-ownership of the festival dates, was $50,000, and they decided to split it five ways. John, Lou, Paul, Terry Melcher, and newest benefactor Johnny Rivers each ponied up $10,000, thus establishing the original board of governors whose interest would be repaid with the first profits.

Alan Pariser was retained and named a co-producer, not necessarily out of any sense of loyalty but because his name was on all the original paperwork.

With Shapiro out of the picture, the focus now became on who exactly they wanted to perform and who they didn't and whether invited acts would actually play for free. First out were the Dave Clark Five and Paul Revere & the Raiders. Although the board of governors certainly wanted to draw young fans, they didn't want them that young, which is also why the Monkees were eliminated. They were the hottest act in show business at the moment, and their potential invitation was a subject of considerable debate. They were ultimately withdrawn because they weren't considered legitimate by artists like John, Paul Simon, and the pop music elite. Quizzically, the Doors and the Young Rascals were also scratched from the list, and there were reasons for it. For the Doors, many in attendance thought they were extremely arrogant for a group with no hits, particularly their charismatic lead singer, Jim Morrison. The Young Rascals had a reputation of being a quartet of whiny New Yorkers who were very vocal about music industry cliques.

Another factor that possibly led to the Monkees' omission was the growing number of underground blues and folk-based psychedelic bands shaking things up in San Francisco and the inclusion of a manufactured pop group might be off-putting to them. These groups to the north were copious, had strange names, lived communally and most were unsigned by any major record labels. The two hottest, the Jefferson Airplane and the Grateful Dead, had recorded in RCA's L.A. studios over the fall and winter and left quite an impression on the producers and session personnel involved. The Airplane, in particular, were fronted by a dark-haired, wild-eyed ex–fashion model named Grace Slick who had a commanding voice and a powerful presence unlike any female singer who preceded her. The Grateful Dead had a reputation as a dirty, grungy, and a little bit dangerous band of suburban misfits who regularly spiked unsuspecting guests' drinks with LSD. When Warner Brothers label head Joe Smith ventured up to San Francisco to court them, he brought along two bodyguards. Both groups were a must for the festival.

Other musicians and music industry types would be invited to be on the board over the next week or so, including Byrds front man Jim McGuinn, guaranteeing the appearance of his group, and Motown singer Smokey Robinson, whose role would remain only titular. When politically cautious

Motown President Berry Gordy heard rumors about the antiestablishment nature of the festival, he forbade his artists from participating in it. Additional board members would accept invitations over the coming weeks, but membership was far from formal. No meetings were ever held. Being a festival board member simply meant a financial contribution and lending their name to create a formidable sphere of influence that would attract first-rate acts. A base of operations was quickly established at the vacated Club Renaissance on Sunset Boulevard in West Hollywood, and a staff was assembled that included Derek, Alan, Michelle, photographer and John's ex-lover Nurit Wilde and Peter Pilafian. Lou's girlfriend and Michelle's short-lived replacement, Jill Gibson, also helped work on some art concepts. Versatile musician Al Kooper, estranged from his group the Blues Project, joined the staff a few weeks later after coming to Los Angeles to recuperate from a nervous breakdown. Veteran promotional partners Lou Robin and Alan Tinkley were retained to handle all contracts. John and Lou jumped in with both feet and put their respective projects on the back burner to focus solely on the festival. Within a week or two they were jaunting back and forth to Monterey several times a week to try and persuade the mayor and city council members to let the festival take place and acquire all necessary permits.

The next, and perhaps biggest, member to join the board arrived unannounced. Beatle Paul McCartney had recently flown to the West Coast of the United States on April 3 for myriad reasons. His primary purpose was to surprise his girlfriend of four years, actress Jane Asher, on her 21 birthday. She was in Denver touring with the Old Vic's Theater Company's traveling production of *Romeo and Juliet*. Before that, however, he'd spent his first day in San Francisco checking out that nascent music scene whose reputation had stretched as far away as England. After hanging out with several members of the Jefferson Airplane at members Jack Casady and Marty Balin's shared apartment on Oak Street getting high and jamming, he left for Denver.

He flew back to Los Angeles on April 9, staying at the home of Derek Taylor, who very quickly took him to meet up with John and Michelle where he was filled in on their music festival plans. McCartney was keen on their idea, particularly introducing the newest, edgiest acts, and immediately suggested the Jimi Hendrix Experience and the Who, both of whom were tearing up the British club scene as well as the U.K. singles charts. He did, however, stop at any mention of the Beatles' physical involvement. Later that evening, along with Brian Wilson, McCartney arrived back at John and Michelle's place, where a wild party, filled with drugs, booze, countless naked people and John's eight-year-old daughter Laura, had broken out. A variety of musical instruments were brought out, and a jam ensued into the early hours of the morning. When the Beatle and the Beach Boy finally departed, the newly christened Monterey International Pop Festival, LLC, board of governors had their two newest members and a commitment from the Beach Boys to perform.

Two of the first acts to commit were secured by Lou in jazzy supper club singer Lou Rawls and unknown singer/songwriter Laura Nyro. Lou knew Rawls from his days working with Sam Cooke and had no trouble securing a commitment from him, as odd of a choice as he was. The 19-year-old Nyro had issued her debut album two months earlier on Verve Folkways, which featured her song "Stoney End." Lou loved it and recorded it with longtime session backup singers the Blossoms. It was released as the debut single to his new record label Ode in April. Lou showed his belief in Laura by giving her a prime evening slot.

Only a couple weeks into the festival planning, fugitive Rolling Stones manager Andrew Loog Oldham showed up on Lou's doorstep. Over the first half of 1967, he'd become estranged from his band following Jagger and Richards' drug arrest and his business manager Allen Klein's increasingly aggressive takeover of the band's management. He'd been warned that reckless Stones guitarist Brian Jones was next up in London Detective Sergeant Norman Pilcher's crosshairs and feared he'd follow him, as he too had acquired a nasty drug habit. Rather than guide his band through these choppy waters, he fled to the protective confines of old friend Lou Adler's Stone Canyon Road home. The two had befriended one another backstage at the filming of *The T.A.M.I. Show* in 1964.

What the Rolling Stones eventually viewed as a betrayal was a welcome addition to John, Lou, and the Monterey Pop Festival team. Andrew was happy to have something to distract him from his troubles and was quickly added to the festival's board of directors. He seconded McCartney's suggestion of Hendrix and the Who, and, since he had a working relationship with both artists' management, got in touch with Chas Chandler and Kit Lambert immediately. Another group he suggested that was making serious waves in the United Kingdom was Eric Clapton's new power trio Cream, but calls to manager Robert Stigwood went unanswered. Surprisingly, however, Mick Jagger did return his call and although the Rolling Stones couldn't commit to a performance, he accepted an invitation to join the board of governors.

Now that the festival's foundation was set and the infrastructure was being attended to by an able and anxious staff, it was time to travel to San Francisco and openly court many of the underground bands who'd caused many a music listener to turn on, tune in, and drop out of the AM Top 40. Their inclusion would bring the festival instant credibility for contemporary music buffs. John and Lou, along with Michelle and Andrew, arranged a meeting with *San Francisco Chronicle* music critic and scene advocate Ralph J. Gleason and local concert promoter Bill Graham in order to get several of the area groups on the bill. Gleason and Graham were two of the few trusted patriarchal figures to many of the local groups they were targeting, and Lou knew it was best to approach those two first and get their blessing before going to each band. The meeting went well, and Gleason and Graham consented, but the actual meetings with these groups weren't as smooth. They were very tribal, living communally in cultish enclaves in and around the Haight-Ashbury district, and had been taught not to trust anyone over 30. Each group had built up its own following playing in the various local clubs the Matrix, the Avalon Ballroom and Graham's own Fillmore. These clubs continued the vibe created by Ken Kesey's Acid Tests and were filled with sweaty young hippies, dancing carefree to their hometown bands who stood in front of a Joshua light show and underneath a cloud of green pot smoke.

John, Lou, and Andrew set their first meeting up with Grateful Dead managers Rock Scully and Danny Rifkin at the communal residence of a few of the members of the Jefferson Airplane. The problem for Lou and John was that these groups were antiestablishment. They didn't care about Lou Adler's clout or John's songwriting skills, which made them appear arrogant. Only a year earlier, they'd seen record labels from Los Angeles and slick A&R men set up shop in San Francisco, attempting to glom on to the colorful groups in order to sign the next big thing. Warner Brothers did an eight-month dance with the Dead before finally signing them on the band's terms near the end of 1966, and their relationship with A&R head Joe Smith was antagonistic from the start. The first thing they asked Lou was where the profits were going, which was a degree of audacity he'd never been experienced from an unknown artist. The San Francisco bands lived hand-to-mouth and wore it like a badge of honor and had suggestions as to who could benefit from the proceeds, including the free clinics throughout their city and the Diggers, a nonprofit, anarchistic community-action group that raised money to feed and nurse many of the homeless hippies in Haight-Ashbury free of charge. In their minds, anything out of L.A. was sly, slick, manufactured, and self-serving. John attempted to ease tension by talking in hip, contemporary lingo.

"What are you guys so paranoid about?" he asked. "You've got us all wrong. You're gonna dig this trip if you give it half a chance."

It only served to tick them off more, and rattling off the list of performers who would be there did nothing to sway them. The presence of the Rolling Stones' manager and the possibility of them performing didn't impress them either, or at least they pretended it didn't. When Scully and Rifkin questioned the gate prices, accommodations for attendees, and money paid to performers for expenses and the outrageousness of calling it a festival, nobody had any satisfactory answers. In their estimation, music was supposed to be free. The Grateful Dead associating John and Lou with the establishment blindsided them, and the meeting ended at an impasse. Scully and Rifkin spiked their drinks with LSD and sent them on their way. For now, it seemed like the San Francisco groups were out, but John and Lou weren't about to give up.

If John had proven anything over his past nine years in the music business, it was that he was an incredible taskmaster when he put his mind to it. When it came to organizing anything that involved entertainment, he had laser focus, an infectious tenacity and effectively mobilized people. From the Smoothies to the Mamas & the Papas, his success grew by leaps and bounds, and now his focus was the Monterey International Pop Festival. It consumed his every thought, and, in about a month's time, he took Ben Shapiro's weekend concert extravaganza, added a third day, organized an influential board of governors, got nearly a dozen of the hottest artists locked in, including the Who and Otis Redding, and organized a staff to cover every jot and tittle involved in making the festival a rousing success. With Lou's help, they successfully pitched the idea to ABC-TV which ponied up $400,000 for the TV rights and hired renowned filmmaker Donn Alan Pennebaker to shoot the concert footage. John and Lou also managed to fly back and forth between Los Angeles and Monterey three days out of each week to woo Monterey Mayor Minnie Coyle, city officials, and local police. For the first time in his life, John kept regular working hours.

But, if task-mastering was his strong suit, multitasking was his Achilles' heel, particularly when it came to writing new material for his band. Song-writing remained his breadwinner, and he had difficulty doing that when something like the festival or Michelle's infidelity occupied his mind. In an era where groups like the Beatles and the Beach Boys were releasing albums full of original songs, the last two albums from the Mamas & the Papas contained a total of six covers, and he hadn't even yet conceived anything new for their next one. There was no way that he could compose an album's worth of original songs in this maelstrom, but he did decide the festival needed a theme song and carved out time to write one.

San Francisco was weighing heavily on his mind. It was the most vibrant rock and roll atmosphere on the planet, and he yearned to be involved with it in some manner. The city's youth culture had changed quite considerably from when he was there only five years earlier and it would have a tremendous influence on his festival. John and the rest of the organizers badly wanted those vaunted bands to be a focal point of the concert and were in danger of featuring none of them. Most of the city's current rock groups had only been in existence for only a couple of years, with many founding members starting out in jug bands, a folk/bluegrass derivative that incorporated household items like washboards, spoons, and actual jugs. It was a brief local fad, but it brought together people like Jerry Garcia, Robert Hunter, Bob Weir, Ron McKernan, Jorma Kaukonen, and Country Joe McDonald but it, too, was eviscerated with the arrival of the Beatles.

Like their folk-rock contemporaries, the rock groups in San Francisco were mostly blues- and folk-based but much more insular than their L.A. rivals. What made them otherworldly was the community-wide tie to LSD via the Merry Pranksters and Ken Kesey, who'd been hosting his "Acid Tests" since 1965. Though based in Palo Alto, 40 miles south of San Francisco, the Pranksters hosted several tests in the greater San Francisco area throughout 1965, where participants would be fed LSD. The atmosphere was dark with live music, strobe lights, incense, fluorescent paint, and Kesey droning over a PA system, all designed to supplement the acid sensation. The Grateful Dead, then known as the Warlocks, got their start at Kesey's tests, standing on one end of the room and making unintelligible sounds with their instruments with hardly a soul paying them any attention.

The acid itself was mixed into Kool-Aid and served out of a big tub. Though these tests may have been supervised, they were crazy, wild, uninhibited and inebriated parties that had a profound effect on the youth in the area. Districts inhabited by college-age kids, like Haight-Ashbury, became awash in Day-Glo shirts and dresses and liquid light shows were a must at any indoor concert. Other more negative effects of LSD also became hallmarks of this new hippie subculture, including a lack of interest in personal hygiene and monogamous relationships, which, along with increasing use of the birth control pill, gave rise to the free love movement, which, in turn, gave rise to sexually transmitted diseases. Hair grew longer and more unkempt. Clothing may have been more colorful but also dirtier. All these characteristics were reflected in the music and the culture that surrounded the scene in San Francisco. But the place where this new LSD culture got its biggest exposure was on local stages, where bands and their followers, decked out in colorful striped shirts and various Wayfarer and Bolle sunglasses, created a surreal mood. Musicians who regularly used LSD could become captivated by the mere pluck of an electric guitar string and its feedback through an amplifier. At a week-long stand at the In Room in Belmont in September 1965, the Warlocks stretched Wilson Pickett's "In the Midnight Hour" into a 45-minute jam. They also electrified the jug band standard "Viola Lee Blues" into a showstopping electric jam that highlighted their sets for the next five years. By year's end, they changed their name to the Grateful Dead and start playing regularly at the Matrix, a club run by Jefferson Airplane singer Marty Balin. Their sound and set were coming together and featured much of what became their first album. They'd also managed to build a dedicated following, making them one of the top dogs among their peers.

By 1966, the Acid Tests had come to an end, with Ken Kesey becoming a fugitive from justice for drug possession and faking his own suicide. The music continued, however, moving to larger ballrooms, like the Avalon and the Fillmore. Local bands honed their sounds nightly in these vast turn-of-the-century dance halls. Though still not as refined as the groups in L.A., the insularity of the community allowed for its growth. The talented ones adapted those weird sounds and re-created them more palatably into long, extended jams that, by their end, had morphed into something else entirely more complex and satisfying. Not only the Grateful Dead but Jefferson Airplane, Quicksilver Messenger Service, and Big Brother & the Holding Company literally learned how to play as bands onstage. To skilled musical outsiders, like Steve Miller, who descended upon San Francisco in October 1966 from the much-more-disciplined Chicago club scene, it was absolute caterwauling, but it spread quickly and was soon perfected. Over the course of the next year, acid-drenched, Eastern-influenced hypnotic live jams became the hallmark of the San Francisco music scene.

The news media couldn't help but notice and be fascinated by this new youth movement, which coincided with growing Vietnam and free speech protests on college campuses nationwide, though they weren't necessarily one-in-the-same. The event that put "hippie" on the map was the Human Be-In at Golden Gate Park in San Francisco on January 14, 1967, which was organized by the underground newspaper the *San Francisco Oracle* in protest of the criminalizing of LSD in the state of California three months earlier. It brought together a who's who of the counterculture movement, including Allen Ginsberg, Ram Dass, Lawrence Ferlinghetti, Jerry Rubin, and acid guru Dr. Timothy Leary, who encouraged the over 20,000 in attendance to "tune in, turn on, drop out." It also featured music by the Grateful Dead, Jefferson Airplane, Quicksilver Messenger Service, Blue Cheer, and Big Brother & the Holding Company, now featuring Janis Joplin on lead vocals. The size of the crowd caught everybody off guard and gained plenty of media attention. TV and radio inadvertently helped to spread the hippie movement from coast to coast and engendered a nationwide pilgrimage of young people to San Francisco in the summer. It also caught the attention of John Phillips, who got a firsthand account of the gathering through road manager Peter Pilafian, who attended the event.

The San Francisco hippie movement was now nationwide. Various media outlets started predicting that, during the summer of 1967, over 100,000 young people would migrate to the area. In anticipation of this unique event, a group of San Francisco political activists, artists, and store owners in the Haight-Ashbury district united to form the Council for the Summer of Love to address issues such as homelessness, drugs, health issues, and outreach. John had seen this before, back in Greenwich Village in 1961, and how it unified many groups of social outcasts in a positive way. San Francisco was Mark 2 of this movement, and it was crucial that they get at least a couple of these groups on the bill. But the news of growing hordes of young travelers had its consequences. Officials of the city of Monterey were getting cold feet, particularly Mayor Minnie Coyle. She certainly didn't want drug-abusing hippies disrupting her small art community. Though a social liberal, her fears weren't based solely on their appearance, but also in logic. How on earth would a city of 20,000 people accommodate a tenfold increase in the population? Where would they sleep, eat, and go to the bathroom? And what would be left in their wake? John and Lou needed to get back up there quickly and put their cajoling skills into overdrive and resell the city on the festival. But, first things first. A song was on his mind.

With encouragement from Scott McKenzie, John began writing a song about this massive immigration to San Francisco and painted a peaceful picture that could serve as a promotional vehicle for the festival. Very quickly, John wrote the lyrics to "San Francisco (Be Sure to Wear Flowers in Your Hair)," which lauded this new generation of peace-seeking young people who had new ideas that were better than those of their preceding generations. In his song, they signified their peaceful nature by wearing flowers in their hair, and it wasn't a stretch. The song and its arrangement had massive hit potential, and its contemporary message of peace captured the zeitgeist of 1967. John quickly decided that Scott would record the song rather than the Mamas & the Papas. Time was of the essence. It was now late April, and only six weeks ahead of the festival. With Cass back east getting ready to have her baby and Denny on vacation in the Virgin Islands, they couldn't have recorded it in time if they wanted to. The lyrics and basic track were completed within a day at Western and Scott laid down his vocals the following day at Moonglow Records' recording studios in Hollywood. John was coming down from being strung out on bennies and slept through Scott's four takes. A promo mix was sent out the last weekend in April and was in stores by May 4. Full-page ads were taken out in both *Billboard* and *Cash Box* the following week, featuring portraits of Scott sporting a mustache. It cracked both charts on May 27, setting itself up to peak right at the start of the festival. Flower power had arrived.

For all intents and purposes, it seemed like John and Lou and the San Francisco groups were at an impasse, and convincing them to be part of this was going to be next to impossible. They were headstrong in their non-commercial philosophy and to them, beneath the fur hat and drug talk, John was just another untrustworthy L.A. operator looking to exploit them and their compatriots. But it was mostly just silly posturing that wasn't rooted in anything other than pride and machismo. In actuality, professional bands, their management and, most of all, their record labels want to broaden their base, get their music heard by new ears, and increase sales revenue.. Still, there was something noble about the Grateful Dead's steadfastness. They were looked at as leaders in that scene and yielded tremendous influence among their peers, and they knew it. Without San Francisco, the Monterey Pop Festival was in danger of just being another Dick Clark's Caravan of Stars. There needed to be an authentic antiestablishment element that only the Bay Area groups could provide, and the Dead knew it and exploited it. At this stage in their career, they were really nobodies from nowhere who'd barely played outside the protective confines of San Francisco. It was their mystique and their standing within their community that captivated John, Lou, and others and they used this as their bargaining chip.

For the moment, it seemed dark but, on April 21, their spirits were lifted when they received a telegram from Bill Graham, Jefferson Airplane's manager, confirming their appearance. The group had spent considerable time recording in L.A. and had recently appeared at a concert at the Cheetah in Venice with the Doors, which allowed John and Lou to court them on their turf. Graham was also a shrewd promoter who knew a good thing when he saw it. Looking at the growing concert bill, the decision to take part in it was a no-brainer. The fires were further stoked when their latest single "Somebody to Love" cracked the Top 100 on April 1 and was climbing steadily. Everyone knew this one was going to be big, and the Airplane would get a prime slot.

In a continuing effort to get the rest of the San Francisco contingent onboard, Paul Simon was dispatched to visit with the Grateful Dead and their managers Rock Scully and Danny Rifkin. It was a good chess move, as Paul had a little more musical integrity in their eyes than John and Lou. He was a rare breed of artist's artist who had radio appeal. Simon & Garfunkel were unique, self-sustaining American hitmakers who maintained pure folk integrity in a post-Beatles world. More importantly, Paul represented the integral shift in American popular songwriting. Songs like "The Sound of Silence," "Richard Cory," and "A Most Peculiar Man" spoke of existential pain, suffering and depression. Even his love songs, like "Kathy's Song" and "Homeward Bound," were deep-thinking and bore an influential adult approach.

They took Paul on a tour of Haight-Ashbury and made the five-minute walk to Hippie Hill in Golden Gate Park where nobody seemed to recognize him, and marijuana was smoked openly. At the Panhandle, toward the western end of the park, hippies undressed freely and swayed to the always-present music. And they were hairy. Many men wore big bushy mustaches and grew their hair down past their shoulders, making the Beatles mop tops from three years earlier seem like crew cuts. The whole scene was like a bohemian zombie land and unlike anything Paul had seen back in New York. After visiting the communal home of Big Brother & the Holding Company, they finally got down to business, telling Paul of their concerns over the L.A. suits running the festival, being exploited and the unanswered money trail. Paul shot straight with the Dead and argued common sense, urging them not to deprive their fans. They want to see their favorite bands. They don't care about legalities, how much somebody else is getting paid, and international rights. This is going to be the big, open-air concert event of the season. He complimented their integrity and told them he and Art were honored to play on the same stage with them. In the end, Paul made so much sense that they were forced to yield. They headed back to their home on Ashbury Street, where all but Paul and Pigpen toasted the occasion with Owsley Stanley's LSD.

When Paul phoned John to tell them they had reached a compromise, he was relieved, telling Paul he'd nominate him for a Nobel Peace Prize if he could. Starting on May 18, telegrams began pouring into the festival office from Big Brother & the Holding Company, Country Joe & the Fish, the Steve Miller Band, and Quicksilver Messenger Service all agreeing to perform. Not wanting to feel like the odd group out, the Grateful Dead confirmed two weeks later, the tipping point being the announcement of Otis Redding's performance. By the end of May, 28 groups were locked into the festival, all of whom agreed to perform for free, but an article that appeared in *Billboard* two weeks before the festival almost undid all their hard work.

On page one of the June 3 issue of *Billboard*, staff writer Eliot Tiegel hyped the upcoming three-day festival, describing it as a multimillion-dollar lineup of talent and estimated their collective services of all the artists somewhere in the $2 million range. Tiegel also broke the news that the event would be filmed and that Adler and Phillips "are holding the talks with film companies about shooting the event in color with the finished print to be sold to a TV network as a special." It was enough to get the Grateful Dead camp to scream "sellout." Calls were placed and threats of pulling out were issued. The Dead went so far as threatening to hold an "anti-festival" at nearby Army post Ford Ord with the other San Francisco bands and they held enough sway to make it come true. A damage-control meeting was called, and John, Lou, Derek Taylor, Andrew Oldham, and Paul Simon headed back up to San Francisco to sort things out with the group and their management. Things started out rough, with bassist Phil Lesh going on the offensive.

"Why do we get the impression you guys are going to film this thing and make umpteen double albums and sell it from here to Singapore?" he asked.

It was met with a collective sigh, but Lesh didn't relent.

"Let's say, for argument's sake, that you do film it. How many times is it going to be shown on TV?" he asked. "Why don't you just be honest about it now and we'll settle the whole thing up front?"

Once again, Lou and John put on their best soft hip-speak, assuring them that nobody was going to get ripped off and that this would bring the San Francisco and L.A. bands together peacefully.

"It's going to be magical, baby," Lou said. "Something you're going to want to tell your grandchildren about."

"Oh shit!" Lesh exclaimed. "Now I know we're gonna get screwed!"

With that, Lesh stormed out of the room. Once again, Paul Simon was the calming voice of reason.

"Who cares what these guys are up to?" he asked the Grateful Dead contingent still present. "Let's show them who we are."

Derek Taylor's presence was a calming one. In his incredibly diplomatic way, he convinced them that it's the artists and their integrity that were the most important thing to the organizers. Monterey would not be like a Dick Clark production where everybody gets exploited, ripped off, and kicked out the door. He reassured them that the concert was to push rock and roll into the level of respectability that jazz enjoys, and tremendous efforts have been made to set the precedent for future rock concerts. Derek and Paul's efforts to douse the flames were successful. They also reminded everybody in the room that the lion's share of the money would be used to benefit underprivileged children, the poor and unfortunate across the country. In an effort of goodwill, John and Lou also agreed to give the Diggers a sizable donation. By meeting's end, tempers had cooled off, and the show was still on.

With the San Francisco problem solved, John and Lou could now turn their focus to the officials of Monterey, who were still panicking over the numbers estimate and the reported presence of the Diggers, believing that young transients would trek to their city simply for free meals. News outlets, ratcheting up their coverage, were now predicting as many as 200,000 attendees, and Mayor Minnie Coyle was seriously considering revoking the permits. There just wasn't enough security and infrastructure to handle such a massive influx. John had to quell these concerns, and he did so by throwing on a suit and turning on the charm. Over a period of a few weeks, he met constantly with women's clubs and local Kiwanis, Elks, and Lions Clubs and motel owners, convincing them how beneficial this would be for their community. John and Lou even hosted a big luncheon to pitch the festival en masse, handing each attendee a copy of the festival's Articles of Incorporation, which stressed to the mostly liberal crowd that this was indeed a cultural event. He also assured them that the predictions were inflated and attendance by kids under age 18 would be minimal.

"The show is designed for those in the 19-to-35 age group," he told those gathered at the Mark Thomas Inn. "We have omitted acts that draw the real young kids and our publicity has solicited family groups."

Monterey Police Chief Marinello, a 33-year veteran of the force, was flatly opposed to the festival from the beginning but was won over by John's assurances that his entire force would be put to work and that they'd subsidize additional police from neighboring cities. He was perhaps even more appeased by Fort Ord's agreement to keep over 600 soldiers on anti-riot standby. Mayor Coyle was pleased to hear of additional allotted funds for sanitation and for city workers who helped at the festival. Every hotel and motel room in the greater area was reserved up front by the festival, which got all of them on board. John also played both sides against the middle by denying that any profits would not go to those in the "hippie underground" but only to scholarships and programs for those in need. Essentially, it was a great big promise by John and Lou that everyone would be on their best behavior, and it worked. All permits were granted.

The Mamas & the Papas had a couple distractions right before the start of the festival. The first was a Memorial Day performance at the Indianapolis 500 before the start of the race and the second was their second-ever performance on *The Ed Sullivan Show*, where they lip-synched to their latest hits,

"Creeque Alley," and "Dedicated to the One I Love." Neither reunion would serve as a warmup for Monterey Pop. All went back to their respective corners with John and Michelle gearing up for the grand spectacle and Denny and Cass paying it little to no attention.

In the week leading up to the Monterey International Pop Festival, the fever was high. Advertisements were everywhere, and articles were written about it in newspapers, fanzines and trade publications. The festival organization purchased radio advertisements from San Diego to Spokane and points east and DJs in all the major markets were hyping it up on their daily programs. Bumper stickers were handed out. On Sunset Boulevard in Los Angeles, a large fence wrap was purchased where the names of new groups seemed to be added daily. The curfew furor had died down considerably, and thousands upon thousands of young people got wrapped up in the hype. Plans were made, and rooms in the tiny community filled up quickly. Many people decided to go up with no plans of where to sleep or what they were going to eat. They just wanted to see and hear the music. The hippie migration was on, and Monterey Pop was going to be unlike anything the world had ever seen.

CHAPTER 21:
MUSIC, LOVE, & FLOWERS

On Friday, June 16, 1967, shortly before 9:00 p.m., John Phillips stood off-left of center stage in the arena on the Monterey Fairgrounds and took in the spectacle of the approximately 7,000 people who bought in to the hype and purchased tickets to witness the beginning of the first-ever international pop music festival. Another 20,000 milled about the 24 acres that surrounded the venue as the sounds of the gathering crowd and piped-in music filtered out onto the grounds. The weather cooperated, providing a cool, late-spring evening with the temperature in the low 50s, giving the night air a slight Northern California chill. The stage, hastily designed and constructed by veteran lighting engineer Chip Monck and volunteers, had its last nail driven into it only an hour before, signifying the vigorous 1,000 or so hours of hard work it took to get to this anticipated point. It was time to walk out and set into motion the 22 hours of music that would take place over the next two and a half days.

As John walked up to the microphone, he was greeted warmly by the crowd. He gave a quick thank-you to all the people who helped put this event together in such a short period of time. He reiterated the festival's theme of "Music, Love and Flowers," coined by Lou Adler, which also draped the apron of the stage in bright, bold script.

"The music will be here in a moment," he told those in attendance, including several hundred members of the press who'd come from around the globe. "And you got the flowers when you came in the door and we hope that everyone here will supply the love so we'll have a really good festival for everyone involved."

He was referring to the 150,000 Hawaiian orchids originally purchased to drop on the fairgrounds by helicopter but, because of high winds, were instead placed on each seat in the arena before each show. And flowers were indeed the main accessory of the event. Spectators had taken John's advice and wore them in their hair, on their clothes, and painted them on their faces. Looking out into the crowd, John couldn't help but notice their bright, brilliant colors that made it seem like a human flower garden. Everywhere, shirts, pants, blouses and skirts were colored or patterned in pinks, greens, yellows, purples and reds and many were adorned with beads. It was rock and roll, brought to you in Technicolor. As far as the love portion of John's greeting, it was still too early to tell, but things looked optimistic. He quickly introduced the first act and made his way offstage.

And then along came the Association. Through the lens of history, they seem like an odd choice to kick off this now-legendary festival and, for a countercultural event, they were incredibly mainstream. It's especially odd when considering that hotter, edgier groups like the Young Rascals and the Doors weren't even considered. But it isn't a stretch to say that a good many in the arena probably owned at least one Association record. Since their debut Valiant single in November 1965, they'd sold millions, including the number one hit "Cherish," and had been playing a bout of tug-of-war between hip and sappy, and sappy was winning. In late 1966, Warner Brothers Records purchased Valiant and the Association's contract, and, beginning with "Windy" in May 1967, their producer was former Mamas & Papas engineer Bones Howe. It was their second number one hit. Lou wanted Bones to be at the board mixing the Mamas & the Papas when they closed the festival on Sunday night, and, being fair-minded and loyal, he gave the opening slot to his old colleague's new band.

Out they strolled, overdressed for the occasion in a mixed bag of double-breasted and three-button suits and corduroy blazers, carrying their respective instruments, to a lukewarm crowd. They opened with a little schtick, engineered and narrated by bassist Brian Cole. In a sardonic critique of mass production and the music industry, Cole likened the group to an industrialized machine called the "Association Machine." After introducing each respective member by his euphemized instrument title, they motioned around the stage like robots until Cole reeled off the count, "1-2, 1-2 . . ." and began plucking the opening notes off their debut hit, "Along Comes Mary." Written by enigmatic L.A. songwriter Tandyn Almer, it was a word-packed, ambiguous part-tribute, part-lament to marijuana that had gone into the Top 10 the previous summer. Suddenly, they came alive and began swinging their bodies and guitars around their microphone stands as singer and rhythm guitarist Jim Yester passionately exclaimed the complex lyrics and never missed a beat. Square or not, these guys could play. It was a perfect start to the night and almost a knowing wink to light up and allow the sweet and sour aroma of marijuana to fill the arena, despite the heavy police presence. After several meetings with organizers and onsite medical personnel, Police Chief Frank Marinello agreed not to arrest anyone seen using drugs, unless it was overt or they were stirring up trouble. In stark contrast to the Sunset Strip riots, which spawned this event, patrolling police were actually a friendly sight, with flowers adorning their hats and motorcycles. Backstage, Alan Pariser and David Wheeler danced and hugged like teenagers, realizing their dream had come to fruition and was playing live right before them.

The rest of the Association's 30-minute set elicited a positive, rocking beginning. They did their job and get the crowd revved up, but momentum would stumble a few times before getting back on track later in the evening. Out next came unknown Canadian band the Paupers, crowbarred in by manager Albert Grossman in concession for his client Mike Bloomfield's hot new band, Electric Flag. In what would become a familiar theme for Monterey Pop, bassist Dennis Gerrard came out high out of his mind on LSD and his bass out of tune. Their set was a disaster. In very short order, Gerrard's amp blew up, guitarist Chuck Beal's Echoplex tape delay snapped, and his amp blew up as well. All the audience could hear were drums, rhythm guitar, and vocals. After six painful songs, they exited to scattered applause.

In a major style shift, next up was Lou Rawls, whose set mostly amounted to a soulful supper club performance of 1930s and 40s standards like "Autumn Leaves" and "On a Clear Day You Can See Forever" with well-rehearsed raps between nearly every song. He also performed his 1966 hit "Love Is a Hurtin' Thing" and his most recent one "Dead End Street." More importantly, he was the first of four black performers to grace the "Music, Love and Flowers" stage where African Americans also ended up being a minority. In the weeks leading up to it, one major critique of the Monterey Pop Festival was the lack of black performers, but the dearth wasn't out of malice or spite. The organizers were mostly a progressive, pro–Civil Rights Movement lot who, ironically, had been blackballed by Motown's owner Berry Gordy. That eliminated major acts like the Supremes, the Temptations, the Four Tops, board governor Smokey Robinson and his group, the Miracles, Martha & the Vandellas, the Marvelettes, Marvin Gaye and Stevie Wonder. Pop R&B chanteuse Dionne Warwick had also been invited but was unable to get out of her committed performance at the Fairmont Hotel in nearby San Francisco and the gospel-soul trio the Impressions, led by prolific and outspoken songwriter Curtis Mayfield, committed but never showed up. All in all, Rawls' set was enjoyable but forgettable.

The Paupers were a household name compared to the third act, British folk singer Beverley Kutner, who went simply by her first name. She was Paul Simon's current girlfriend, and he made sure she got some performance time. John allotted her time enough for three songs, and she was gone before anybody realized it. At this point, fans in the stands must've been wondering if this was the best they were going to get. Where were all those big names that adorned the advertisements? What about Buffalo Springfield and the Byrds? Anybody who left now probably felt completely justified.

And if the organizers thought act four, Johnny Rivers, was going to satisfy any grumblings, they had another thing coming. Though he'd been one of the hottest acts of 1965 and 1966, one year can make quite a difference in the dog-eat-dog world of pop music. With an all-star house band, including Wrecking Crew staples Hal Blaine on drums, Joe Osborn on bass, Mike Deasy on guitar and Gary Coleman on vibraphones, a hairier and fashionable Johnny came out on fire with the Beatles' "Help," which was off-putting to some. Also sitting in with the group on piano was Johnny's 20-year-old arranger, Jimmy Webb. They rocked through seven more numbers, including the hits "Memphis," "Mountain of Love" and "Baby I Need Your Loving," but all met with tragically light applause. Like the Association, he was an unappreciated hitmaker who, though dressed in hippie garb, was still a pompadour in a suit to current music snobs whose main act was stealing others' material. The era of writing your own hits was peaking, and Johnny mostly relied on others. After the finale of "Poor Side of Town," Johnny proudly exited stage left to minimal applause and headed backstage to the buffet of food and drugs.

The festival had lost its momentum. In front of the stage, malaise was creeping in and backstage, the tension was getting palpable. Simon & Garfunkel were the night's closers and Paul was pacing backstage sternly telling the bands before them not to go over their allotted time so he and Artie could play their complete set without violating the midnight performing curfew. So far, the Monterey Pop Festival was a dud and, if the highlight was going to be the Association, this whole thing would be better off forgotten. But that was all about to change.

One of the innovations Chip Monck provided at Monterey, which has been taken for granted at concerts ever since, was piping in music over the stage speakers between sets. He knew there was going to be at least 20 minutes of downtime between acts and the silence could be dangerous, leading people into getting into fights or threatening others' safety. Popular music distracted people through dancing and singing while the stage crew broke down previous sets and assembled new ones and sound-checked them, if possible. With this puzzling start to the festival, Monck's idea kept the peace as the penultimate group for the evening, Eric Burdon & the Animals, made their way to the stage.

The Animals were one of those groups that everybody liked. Since they first jumped on the scene in the summer of 1964 with their blistering, electric arrangement of the folk standard "The House of the Rising Sun," they issued hit after hit featuring Eric Burdon's passionate, masculine lead vocals coupled with Alan Price's ominous-sounding Vox Continental organ. They were instantly likable but a bit flawed. The five-man group had no strong songwriters and had to mostly rely on the rearrangement of old blues songs or compositions from Aldon Music songwriters. They struck gold with Barry Mann and Cynthia Weil's "We Gotta Get Out of This Place," a rearrangement of Nina Simone's "Don't Let Me Be Misunderstood," and "It's My Life," three eventual hippie anthems, but, by late 1966, their mojo had run out. Burdon's ego matched his vocals and isolated him from his bandmates, and the group's finances had been completely mismanaged, causing everyone to run scattershot.

The Animals that Burdon brought with him to Monterey had only been together for six months, but they were a tight musical unit, led by Vic Briggs on guitar, Barry Jenkins on drums, Danny McCulloch on bass and John Weider on rhythm guitar and electric violin. Although they'd been touring the

United States steadily since February, Burdon was edgy before going on and copped a couple hits of acid off John to calm his nerves. A few minutes later, as a chilly fog began rolling in, San Francisco promoter Chet Helms introduced them as a surprise from England, which garnered rousing applause.

When they walked out on stage, they looked like a band of scallywags in from the Barbary Coast. After a brief thank-you in Burdon's thick North East English accent, Vic Briggs launched into the *Dragnet*-inspired opening of "San Franciscan Nights," a tribute to the city's multicultural peace and love scene and their forthcoming single. They only played three additional songs, but they were all memorable. "Gin House Blues" was a bawdy, speakeasy Bessie Smith lament originally titled "Me and My Gin" that stretched out for six rocking minutes. They followed that up with a Bo Diddley–inspired eight-minute version of Donovan's "Hey Gyp (Dig the Slowness)." Burdon and the Animals brought heavy blues with them that served to tease the next day of the festival and it got the crowd rocking. But they saved the best for last.

After an awkward introduction of their final song, John Weider began slowly strumming his electric violin to an audience that was completely enraptured. Soon enough, Burdon augmented Weider with his tambourine while Vic Briggs eased in, lightly accompanying him to the familiar Eastern-influenced introduction of the Rolling Stones' "Paint It, Black." It surely captured the attention of Rolling Stones co-founder Brian Jones, who'd just stepped foot on the festival grounds. Only 36 days earlier, and on the same day bandmates Mick Jagger and Keith Richards were officially charged with drug possession stemming from their February arrest, police raided his Kensington apartment and arrested him and his friend Prince Stanislaus Klossowski for possession of hashish. Jones posted bail and kept a low profile before being officially charged on June 2. Despite all this, he was permitted to fly to the United States to attend the Monterey Pop Festival.

After the rhythm section fully kicked in, the new Animals broke into a hectic two-minute frenzy complemented by a Joshua light show playing behind them that featured strobe lights, hypnotic spirals, protozoan shapes, and a time-elapsed 8mm movie of a young blonde woman flashing a Mona Lisa smile. It represented an acid trip on film. As Briggs stood stoically staying in unison, Weider's curly Afro whipped from side to side as he sawed away on his gypsy violin only to bring it down as Burdon walked coolly in between them to his microphone and uttered the opening lines. The entire arena was fixed on him and sang along to the Stones' instant classic from a year earlier. The rest of the song assumed its familiar pace until around the 4:15 mark when Burdon slid into a stream-of-consciousness rap over soft musical accompaniment, which would become a feature on albums with his new crop of Animals. After approximately two minutes, he took it back to the bridge and the band brought it home, with Barry Jenkins leading the charge on drums at a rapid, steady pace, crashing to a delightful ending. Brian Jones leapt to his feet and led the excited applause. Burdon gave a quick thank-you and retreated to make way for the evening's finale, Simon & Garfunkel. Monterey had its first highlight.

It got a lot quieter when the folk-rock duo strolled out in turtlenecks around 20 minutes later with only Paul's acoustic guitar. They would not be accompanied by the house band. It wasn't atypical. Despite their albums being mostly full-band arrangements, Simon & Garfunkel concerts were surprisingly low budget. John Phillips introduced them as two very close friends and, at this stage, truer words couldn't have been spoken. Chip Monck, tripping on Owsley Stanley's Monterey Purple, a special LSD concoction made in honor of the festival, shone a bright red light on them throughout their performance, which made it look as if they were performing inside a submarine. Ever the consummate professionals, they forged through it as they kicked off with "Homeward Bound" and six more numbers, including their most notable hit, "The Sound of Silence," and their current one, "At the Zoo." More recognizable songs like "I Am a Rock" and "Scarborough Fair" were omitted in favor of the deep track "Benedictus" and the as-yet-unreleased "Punky's Dilemma." Their set lasted less than 30 minutes with the duo providing a soft, beautiful ending to the night. There was no trouble, no disturbances, no stoned-out hippie freaks breaking up the quiet art town. The naysayers were pleasantly surprised and, though it sputtered at times, the Association, Eric Burdon & the Animals and Simon & Garfunkel saved it and gave everybody in attendance a reason to stick around for day two.

When the sun shone on the Monterey Fairgrounds Saturday morning, the grand spectacle that was the festival was fully revealed. Located a stone's throw from the Pacific Coast Highway, the fairgrounds were easily accessible from the north or the south and were within walking distance of the Monterey Regional Airport and two miles from both the train station and the bus depot. Beginning in late April, brochures were printed up and distributed to record stores, head shops, and various other places where young music lovers gathered. It advised them of transportation, lodging, seating, weather advisories, and what clothes to wear along with a mail order ticket form. Every radio market within traveling distance was saturated with promos and advertisements, and the buzz got off to a fast start and remained steady. Prices ranged from $3.00 for the cheapest matinee seats to $6.50 for prime evening orchestra seating. And for $1.00, you could gain access to the fairgrounds and just mingle. The campaign worked. Thousands of kids from up and down the West Coast and many from as far east as Idaho, Utah, and Wyoming made the journey.

Since the fairgrounds first opened in 1936, the city had plenty of experience and infrastructure to handle weekend-long activities, particularly concert festivals. The Monterey Jazz Festival has been held there annually since 1958, and two folk festivals were held in 1963 and 1964, but this was something entirely different. Rock and roll music had developed a larger, more diverse and rowdier following by 1967 and, by all accounts, at least 100,000 people were expected. Bathroom facilities were expected to be adequate, and local Kiwanis and Lions clubs provided concessions like hot pastrami sandwiches and corn on the cob. Free food was provided by the Diggers out of San Francisco.

The 3,000 reserved motel and hotel units in the Monterey-Carmel-Pacific Grove-Seaside area were quickly booked and filled with performers and attendees with deeper pockets or a need for creature comforts. For instance, at one hotel, Henry Mancini's son could be found in the room adjacent to LSD millionaire Owsley Stanley's and Jefferson Airplane's. For those with no plan or more inclined to depend on Mother Nature, which was the majority, sleeping on the grass or under cars and trees was the preferred method of shelter at night. With dozens of colleges and universities in the general area, including Stanford, Cal-Berkeley, UC-Davis, Santa Clara, Cal State, and San Jose State, youthful hippie bohemia was everywhere. Beginning almost exactly a year earlier, young people all along the Northern California coast, from Big Sur to Mendocino, started living communally among nature in teepees and tents and were ripe for this type of hippie extravaganza. All sorts of caravans arrived from points north, south, and east, including cars, buses, and vans painted in all sorts of psychedelic imagery and filled with mattresses. In the spirit of tremendous benevolence, Peninsula College opened up its adjacent football field for attendees to pitch tents and sleeping bags. Beginning Friday night, it was a haven for free love, drug use, and jamming. The after-hours silence was often broken by screams and moans of people experiencing good and bad acid trips mixed with acoustic strumming and group singing. For those who experienced bad reactions to psychedelics or marijuana, the Bummer Tent was set up by Marin County residents Tom Law and his wife Lisa for assistance and to keep them out of sight of any patrolling police who might consider them troublemakers. It proved valuable when thousands of Owsley Stanley's Monterey Purple tablets were freely passed around, and many attendees experienced adverse reactions. Also on-site for similar purposes was local psychiatrist Dr. Charles Rosewald and a medical tent where Pebble Beach residents Doris Day and Kim Novak volunteered their services.

John had named Peter Pilafian a co-producer and put him in charge of the various vendors and booths that would supplement the festival. Over the course of several weeks, he lined up all sorts of merchants who fit the festival's vibe, including art galleries, boutiques, face painters, and florists as well as guitar and amplifier manufacturers. Throughout the weekend, hippies were able to shop for modestly priced clothing and accoutrements to enhance their new fashion sense. There was also a projection room and a display for the new Moog Series III modular synthesizer, which attracted many a professional musician in attendance. There was also an impromptu stage not far from the entrance to the main stage for jamming and seminars and a closed-circuit TV that broadcasted the performances. For those who brought children, there was even a children's playground and a babysitting service.

Peter was also in charge of the general artistic motif that surrounded festival, which drew much of its inspiration from the Human Be-In back in January. In addition to the aesthetics provided by many of the vendors, it also included a giant statue of Buddha similar to the one at the Human Be-In. Backstage, no expense was spared for the performers. Several local restaurants donated their services and there was a constant buffet of every type of food imaginable. There was also a cornucopia of drugs and booze, which were consumed openly and heavily by many. Performers about to go onstage were granted access to the dressing area beneath the stage. Local music supplier ABC Music Center, run by Monterey resident Mike Marotta and his family, provided the backline for the stage made up mostly of Fender

Dual Showman Amps, which gave the concert a sound like no other before it. While performing a soundcheck, Byrds guitarist David Crosby remarked, "Groovy! A nice sound system at last!" Interestingly, the weekend prior, the Byrds performed at another festival, the Fantasy Fair and Magical Mountain Music Festival, 14 miles north of San Francisco, sponsored by radio station KFRC. John and Lou scouted the festival and went over staging and the sound system with promotions director Mel Lawrence to make sure they absolutely nailed it for Monterey. Placed in charge of the elaborate Universal Audio 4-track, 12-position soundboard were noted San Francisco–area recording engineers Wally Heider and Bill Halverson, who despite limited or no time at all for soundchecks between performances, delivered an incredibly pleasing sound for both musicians and festival attendees.

During much of the festival, John could be found in the office near the stage juggling tasks in order to keep things running smoothly. And Saturday brought plenty of challenges. Rumors had swirled for weeks that the Beach Boys, who were scheduled to be the evening's closer, would not be performing at all, and the truth of the rumor was confirmed on the day of or just before the festival's start. Multiple reasons were given but the truth was that the Beach Boys would have been completely out of their element and they knew it. Although their records had progressed as brilliantly and progressively as the Beatles', their touring act still reflected their hot rods and surfboard era and the hippie crowd wanted nothing to do with "angling in Laguna in Cerro Azul" or "pink slips, daddy." As frustrating as that must've been, John had an ace in the hole in Otis Redding. The problem was, since confirming in early May, he and manager Phil Walden had been playing a game of phone tag and never connected. Otis and backing bands Booker T. & the M.G.'s and the Mar-Keys had been touring parts of Europe since March, and Walden had accompanied them. All John had was his word, given to Andrew Oldham, and a telegram confirming their appearance. It was going to be an interesting afternoon.

It was also going to be a bluesy one, as six of the eight afternoon performers were blues-based, beginning with relatively new L.A. group Canned Heat, led by their heavyset and properly nicknamed singer Bob "The Bear" Hite. They had just been signed to Liberty Records and had performed at the previous weekend's Fantasy Fair along with five other bands who also played Monterey. They were able to snag the day two opening spot after manager John

Hartmann cornered Derek Taylor, who offered it to them and made no bones about the pressure that they'd be under to make sure it got off to a rollicking start. Canned Heat wasn't intimidated. They loved to play and, for them, it was just another booking. And they didn't disappoint, opening with their debut single, Muddy Waters' "Rollin' and Tumblin'," issued a week earlier. The rest of their set was filled with traditional blues covers recorded for their soon-to-be-released first album, which Hite plugged between each number.

Nobody in the audience could've prepared themselves for what came next. There'd been so much hype surrounding the San Francisco bands who'd given John and Lou such a hard time over committing to the festival and now it was time to finally hear one of them. First up was Big Brother & the Holding Company, led by a young Texas woman named Janis Joplin. She'd come to San Francisco in 1963 with friend Chet Helms and hooked up with future Jefferson Airplane guitarist Jorma Kaukonen, with whom she began regularly performing blues songs at tiny clubs. In that same time, she'd also acquired a nasty amphetamine and heroin habit and began drinking Southern Comfort heavily. After a tumultuous two years, which included an arrest, a return to Texas, a failed engagement, and a return to San Francisco, she hooked back up with Helms who was now managing Big Brother & the Holding Company. Not initially bowled over by her singing, the hippie group nevertheless made her their co–lead singer in June 1966 and signed with Mainstream Records in September. They grew together quickly, but by the time Monterey came around, it was evident that Janis was outgrowing everybody.

In the metamorphosis that separated hard rock from rock and roll, Janis' rugged and emotive performance may be the harbinger. The band practiced the entire week leading up to the festival, and it showed. Janis sang with such a gritty, soulful, and passionate intensity, like a white Big Mama Thornton, that it shook the arena. Her backing vocals even salvaged the numbers guitarist Sam Andrew took lead as he was often off mic. They blazed through five numbers, including band staples "Down on Me" and "Ball and Chain," and when it was all over, everyone in the arena was on their feet. Monterey had its first iconic moment but, unfortunately, no film of it exists. In one of the dumbest moves in rock history, new band manager Jules Karpen exerted the same silly San Francisco bravado shown during the April negotiations with the Grateful Dead and absolutely insisted to John and film director D. A. Pennebaker that his group not be filmed. Too much exposure, he argued. The cameras were pointed down and, after their hair-raising performance, everyone involved knew they'd missed out on a highlight; that is, everyone but Albert Grossman, who was busy courting Janis to join his cadre of impressive clientele, which included Bob Dylan. The middle-aged, heavyset manager used this as an opportunity to flex his muscle and impress his potential new artist. It backfired. Janis was beside herself, coping by chugging from a mixture of codeine, cough syrup, and Southern Comfort. She wanted to be in the film but wasn't strong enough to assert herself.

Like so many of her fellow musicians, John had a soft spot for Janis and became her advocate. She came to him in tears, crying to him about her predicament. He insisted he'd find a spot for them to perform an encore on Sunday, and went to confront Karpen who deferred to Grossman. Grossman wasn't up for freebees. He said if Big Brother was going to do a repeat performance, they'd have to be paid. John, losing his peace and love demeanor, reverted to his old Day Ray local persona, took his hot coffee, and poured it over Grossman's head.

"I'll spend every dime I've got to sue you for being detrimental to her career, for misrepresenting yourself," he told the wet impresario.

Being the surly ballbuster who got pretty far being the top bully in an industry full of bullies, Grossman surely wanted to retaliate in kind, but, looking around him and seeing he was on John's turf, had no choice but to capitulate. Big Brother & the Holding Company would go on Sunday afternoon and perform two songs and would be filmed by Pennebaker and his crew. The question now was, could they bring the house down again?

While all this was transpiring, another San Francisco group, Country Joe & the Fish, led by ex-Navy air traffic controller Joe McDonald, were onstage mesmerizing the crowd with their heavy psychedelic meanderings. They were anything but the blues, which was probably a good move following Janis. This misfit group of ex–Berkeley Free Speech Movement activists expatriated to San Francisco in 1966 and signed with Vanguard Records. Together, they strongly represented another characteristic of the Bay area bands, sarcasm and cynicism, which was evident in two numbers they performed, "Not So Sweet Martha Lorraine" and their 1930s-style, anti-Vietnam novelty, "I-Feel-Like-I'm-Fixin'-To-Die Rag." The latter offered a tongue-in-cheek criticism of the dehumanization involved in the Vietnam War with acerbic lyrics that only an ex-serviceman could provide. The highlight, however, was their long, trippy instrumental, "Section 43," which perfectly set the LSD experience to music and enhanced the mood for those who were tripping on the grounds that sunny Saturday afternoon and even for those who weren't.

Grossman wasn't the only headache John had to deal with that afternoon. Sometime mid-afternoon, Monterey Police Chief Frank Marinello walked into the festival offices with a concerned look on his face and told John that he'd gotten word that a gang of Hells Angels were on their way to Monterey, and it could mean some serious trouble. Although the infamous motorcycle gang inadvertently helped the Mamas & the Papas find their name, nobody wanted them roaming around the grounds like a pack of hungry dogs.

On the West Coast, the Hells Angels had inserted themselves right inside the counterculture and were considered a threat by police everywhere. Hippie youth had an innate mistrust of authority in just about every capacity and the Hells Angels, through a mix of intimidation, fear and gruff coolness, often elected themselves security of their gatherings. Much of the time, it was a welcome marriage, but there could be a tentativeness to it, especially considering that some members of the motorcycle club were involved in criminal activities, including drug dealing, trafficking in stolen goods, and extortion. Their lifestyle also attracted ex-convicts, drifters, and tough guy wannabes. The festival was running peacefully and smoothly and John didn't want any motorcycle gangs disrupting the goodwill built up between them and city officials who still had the authority to pull the plug.

John, Chief Marinello, and a contingent of officers headed out to the city limits on Highway 1 and waited. Marinello made it clear to John that he couldn't prevent anyone from coming into the city, and that they could only get involved if they broke the law; ironic considering John was high on LSD at the time. When the Hells Angels arrived, it proved to be somewhat anticlimactic. All they really wanted was to see the show. John told the spokesman that he couldn't help them. They'd been sold out for weeks, and the entire peninsula was overcrowded and booked up. Seeking to find any avenue onto the fairgrounds, they offered to be security. With the extraordinary amount of police presence already there, mixing in the Hells Angels could prove disastrous. John told them thanks but no thanks. They had it covered. In a spirit of diplomacy, he told them that had they reached out sooner, they could've made arrangements. The Angels mounted their bikes and peacefully rode off. Potential disaster had been averted.

Back at the festival, former Blues Project front man Al Kooper, along with a makeshift band that featured Harvey Brooks on bass, took time away as Chip Monck's assistant to entertain the crowd. His short set was followed by the Butterfield Blues Band, Quicksilver Messenger Service, the Steve Miller Band, and Mike Bloomfield & the Electric Flag who closed out the afternoon. Things seemed to be running smoothly, but in the offices, John was still putting out fires and frantically going over potential no-show contingency plans since he still wasn't 100 percent sure of Otis Redding's arrival. It caused his mind to race. Even though Walden confirmed Redding's appearance, he was initially noncommittal and only agreed after conferring with mentor and Atlantic Records co-owner Jerry Wexler. Otis had performed to a lukewarm audience at the Fillmore in San Francisco a year earlier and was wary about playing to that scene again. He also wasn't eager to play to these people for free. John's anxiety grew. Only the scheduled pickup time at Monterey Regional Airport would tell.

An unwelcome distraction came in the form of a phone call from John's ex-wife. Susie tracked him down on the office phone and informed him that she was serving him with papers for back alimony and child support. Although he was making more money than he'd ever dreamed possible, John wasn't ponying up the $250 a month required by the court to properly take care of his children who were living hand to mouth back in Alexandria, Virginia. She told him she still had her job at the Pentagon but, even with overtime, she was barely making ends meet. Their 10-year-old son Jeffrey was also experiencing emotional problems, attributed to John being an absentee father by his school psychologist. By this time, the Mamas & the Papas were in every music publication and grocery store tabloid with articles about homes in Bel Air and Jaguars. With each article, she became more and more incensed. The publicity brought on by Monterey Pop was the last straw, so she placed the call and miraculously got him on the line. This was the last thing John wanted to hear in the midst of his triumphant moment, but, rather than be contentious, he went immediately went into damage control mode.

"Move out here," he interrupted. "When the festival's over, we'll make arrangements to move you all out here. It's ridiculous for us to go through this."

Whether he meant it or not, he'd convinced Susie, who hung up the phone in a much calmer mood. A few minutes later, he received another personal phone call. This time, it was their housekeeper on the other line. Their home had been burglarized. Somebody drove a truck up to the main entrance, walked right in and drove away with wads of cash John had stowed away and lots of musical equipment.

"Can't deal with it now," he told her. "Call the Bel Air police!"

Also, perhaps it had something to do with Susie's comments about their son Jeffrey or being the face of such a huge event, but for the first time in his life, John acted paternal. Owsley Stanley and his companions were still passing around his Monterey Purple LSD, and several people were freaking out. It was a particularly potent bad strain and, for first-timers, it was terribly powerful. Tripping on acid is always a crapshoot for experienced users anyway. Tom and Lisa Law's bummer tent was filling up, and on-site medics were trying to bring many down with Thorazine and there were plenty of cameramen and brownies on hand to capture these negative reactions and the last thing John, or anyone associated with the festival, wanted was negative publicity. Rock and roll already had a bad rap. There was no need to add to it. Also, several musicians were consuming it too, and that could negatively affect the onstage product. Something had to be done and since it would be impossible to take everyone's acid tablets away, the solution was to find Owsley. John sent out his backstage security detail, including his personal bodyguard and old Del Ray Local buddy Jimmy Shortt, to track him down and it didn't take long. They took him to John who questioned him about just how strong his acid was. He told him each tablet contained 1,000 micrograms of LSD. John flipped.

"You fucking asshole!" he screamed at him. "We've put months of hard work and hundreds of thousands of dollars into this and you're running around dosing kids on bad acid?"

He dragged Owsley to the medical tent so he could see the results of his handiwork but he was hardly moved. He'd been turning people of all ages on to acid since 1965, being the personal chemist of Ken Kesey, the Grateful Dead, and much of the San Francisco music scene. He'd witnessed all types of reactions on people of all ages and became pretty desensitized. Some of the kids in the tent, who were as young as 14 or 15, recognized Owsley and accused him of dosing them. Jimmy, who was a particularly large and powerful man, lifted Owsley up by his lapels and asked John what he should do with him.

"Throw him out!" he exclaimed.

With that and the other challenges behind him, or put on the back burner, John headed out to the Monterey Regional Airport to pick up his new Saturday evening closer, Otis Redding. At least, he hoped he'd be there. Unbeknownst to him, or anyone else for that matter, was that Booker T. & the M.G.'s and the Mar-Keys had arrived the day before and were holed up in their hotel rooms. Otis and Phil Walden flew separately out of Atlanta and arrived on time. John was relieved. He escorted everyone back to the fairgrounds and let them get settled in. What they beheld was a bizarre scene, particularly for nine guys from the South. The music was blistering, people were dancing freely in the open air. Acid-dazed stares and hippies, hippies, hippies. Even though Memphis was one of the more progressive Southern cities, it was nothing like this. Jerry Wexler also arrived around the same time and greeted Redding and Walden in the VIP section backstage. The 50-year-old mogul stood out among the young musicians and hipsters backstage, wearing a houndstooth flat cap and full salt and pepper goatee. He'd convinced Redding that this was going to be beneficial for his career but, after looking around at the flower power that was coming out of every nook and cranny of the grounds, he began having second thoughts.

"This really frightens me," he told Walden. "I'm afraid Otis is out of context here. This could be terrible."

The momentum that built up quickly between John's commandeering of the festival idea to June 16 was astounding. In only a couple of weeks, advertisements and announcements produced such a fever that it turned into the most anticipated social event on the West Coast. By the end of Saturday afternoon's performances, tens of thousands more people had arrived and were filling up the quiet peninsula town, making Mayor Minnie Coyle's and Police Chief Frank Marinello's fears appear a little more realistic. Fortunately for them, peace and order were maintained. And while it was a place for strangers to gather and become friends, it was also a site for reunions and nowhere was it more evident than backstage.

Although he was serving a function as John's bodyguard and childhood friend, Jimmy Shortt enjoyed cutting it up and acting more like his former delinquent self around his old buddy, even if the two couldn't look more opposite. John's hair was long and dirty while Jimmy wore his in a crewcut, looking as if he'd just stepped off Fort Ord. John gave him one of his hats so he wouldn't scare anyone away by his mere presence. John also got to reunite with his old San Francisco days buddy Tommy Smothers, who was on hand to introduce several of the acts. Tommy and his brother Dick were four months into a two-year run hosting a comedy variety show on CBS with humor and musical acts that appealed to the counterculture.

Michelle could be seen reminiscing with old Kingston Trio friends Nick Reynolds and John Stewart and her onetime replacement Jill Gibson. Cass arrived on Saturday with her sister, the aspiring singer Leah Cohen. Denny, however, was nowhere to be found, which was a cause of grave concern. They were set to be the festival's closers in about 30 hours and they couldn't do without their lead singer who was missing in action. Another headache for John was brewing.

There were plenty other nonperforming musicians moving around back-stage, including Monkees Micky Dolenz and Peter Tork, guitarist Mason Williams, Paul Revere & the Raiders bassist Phil Volk, and Merry-Go-Round drummer Joel Larson. Former Modern Folk Quartet singer Henry Diltz was underway in his new and more successful career as a staff photographer. Along with Atlantic Records' Jerry Wexler, plenty of other music moguls were on hand to witness this revolution, including Columbia Records president Clive Davis, Reprise Records head Mo Ostin and Elektra Records founder Jac Holzman. By festival's end, several offers were made on behalf of their respective labels to many of the unsigned bands.

But not everyone was elated to see each other. A much cooler reunion took place between Rolling Stones co-founder Brian Jones and the band's estranged manager Andrew Loog Oldham. The two had never liked one another almost from the instant they met four years earlier and now they found themselves in awkward company at Monterey. It was Andrew who fostered the power play of Mick and Keith versus Brian and now he found himself in their crosshairs as well. In one candid photograph taken of the two at Monterey, Andrew looks as if he's telling Brian to "beware the Ides of March."

Several Hollywood film and TV actors made the trip north. Candice Bergen, Dennis Hopper, Doug McClure, and Carol Wayne and her sister Nina could all seen hobnobbing with the musicians. Future film superstar Harrison Ford worked as a messenger for the festival offices, and there were plenty of other future stars in attendance. Aspiring actress Peggy Lipton, who would star in the TV series the *Mod Squad* two years later, 18-year-old Jackson Browne and eventual Van Halen front man Sammy Hagar were in the audience as well as a group of friends who, after the festival, would form the group Sweetwater. Two years later, they'd be the first band to perform at the Woodstock Festival in Bethel, New York. In the press office were Jann Wenner, who would publish the first edition of *Rolling Stone Magazine* within four months, and Robert Christgau, then writing for *Esquire*, who would eventually become one of his contributing editors. On what could be considered a scouting mission was Bob Dylan's longtime tour manager Victor Maymudes and a small film crew sent by the Beatles whose twofold mission was to document the festival for them and procure plenty of acid for John Lennon, as LSD had recently been criminalized in the United Kingdom.

It was quite a mixed bag, and all settled in to watch the evening's performances beginning with another San Francisco group, Moby Grape, led by former Jefferson Airplane drummer Skip Spence. This group was not as difficult to commit as their contemporaries as they were in the middle of an intense publicity campaign engineered by their eager label, Columbia Records, who happily agreed to volunteer their services. Two weeks earlier, they released five singles from their forthcoming debut LP in one day and took out full page ads in *Billboard* and *Cash Box*. It was about as un–San Francisco as a band from there could get and diminished what is otherwise a great debut album. With so many other San Francisco bands looking on, Moby Grape was tense, and it showed. They steamrolled through four songs and were out the door.

Up next was South African trumpeter Hugh Masakela and his sextet who lent his jazzy, African rhythms to contemporary songs like the Beatles' "Here, There and Everywhere" and Janis Ian's "Society's Child." Unfortunately, they came off as a complete bore and played for nearly an hour, pushing everything back and endangering the midnight curfew and potentially Otis Redding's set.

After breaking down the Masakela band's large set, the founding fathers of folk-rock, the Byrds, took the stage. They weren't all that different from the lineup who had led the counterattack to the British Invasion only two years ago. All they were missing was former co–lead singer Gene Clark, which, for John, was a good thing. After an introduction by guitar virtuoso Mike Bloomfield, they opened up with the B side to their final hit, the appropriately titled "Renaissance Fair," which recounted a colorful festival and featured beautiful three-way harmony between Jim McGuinn, David Crosby, and Chris Hillman that foreshadowed Crosby's sound with Stephen Stills and Graham Nash. But, onstage, they were anything but harmonic. Crosby was overpowering, singing so forcefully that it almost seemed like a power play.

Between numbers, Crosby rambled on like a maniac, introducing every single song while McGuinn and Hillman scowled at him from the shadows. He encouraged everyone in the world to take LSD by quoting a recent Paul McCartney interview in *Life Magazine*, elicited a conspiracy theory that the U.S. government was behind the JFK assassination, and announced they wouldn't be playing any of their big hits. The pièce de resistance of their awful performance was their version of "Hey Joe," which Crosby dedicated to Tim Rose and Jimi Hendrix. To call it a train wreck would be the understatement of the festival. They raced through it at top speed, missing notes, lyrics, and basic song structure. McGuinn's guitar was out of sync throughout the entire two-minute performance and his solo at the end was so discombobulated that it almost seems as if he was being self-destructive to undermine Crosby, who just shouted the song into the mic.

The crowd may not have known it, but they were witnessing the destruction of a band onstage. Relationships had been frayed since almost the beginning, and Hillman, who was hired to be their bassist in 1965, was asserting himself into the mix more and putting pressure on the already-paranoid Crosby. Four months after this performance, Crosby would be fired, and within 15 months, McGuinn would be the only original member remaining. Even a guest appearance by Hugh Masakela on trumpet to close the set with "So You Want to Be a Rock 'N' Roll Star" couldn't save their abysmal performance. To everyone's relief, they left the stage and made way for the relatively unknown Laura Nyro. Anyone who came specifically to see the Byrds surely left disappointed.

Nyro's performance did nothing to alleviate the bad taste in everyone's mouths. The 19-year-old singer/songwriter from the Bronx was like something from outer space, even to the stoned in attendance. She wore a dark dress and heavy mascara, and her face appeared ashen, almost like a vampire. Accompanied by the Hi Fashions, her songs matched her look. They were monster mixtures of folk, rock, doo-wop, and girl group, designed to appeal to everyone but appealing to no one at Monterey. Onstage, she was awkward and clumsy in only her second-ever public performance and, though it's been reported for years that she was booed off the stage, the crowd was mostly indifferent, using this time to get refreshments, go to the bathroom or just catch up with those around them. She ran offstage in tears to the arms of her friend, and manager-in-waiting, David Geffen and was consoled by Michelle, who took her into their limousine and drove her around the grounds in an effort to calm her down and reassure her of her talent. She did, however, make a positive impression on one very important audience member. 5th Dimension producer Bones Howe made note of two of her songs, "Stoned Soul Picnic" and "Wedding Bell Blues." There would be a happy ending for Laura Nyro.

Satisfaction finally arrived in the form of Jefferson Airplane, whose opening number "Somebody to Love" had just officially jumped into the Top 5 in *Billboard* and *Cash Box*. The magnificent blend of Marty Balin and Grace Slick was crowd-pleasing, and their hard-rocking rhythm section of Jack Casady and Spencer Dryden represented San Francisco well. Equally impressive were guitarists Paul Kantner and Jorma Kaukonen, whose ominous opening notes on his Gretsch summoned the darkly intriguing LSD anthem "White Rabbit." As their set went on, particularly their 10-minute plus closer, "The Ballad of You & Me & Pooneil," backstage Otis Redding's anxiety grew with each passing minute, unsure of how he'd go over with this crowd.

Jefferson Airplane's eight numbers pushed the evening past the midnight curfew, prompting an ass-kissing session from John Phillips to Chief Marinello, who agreed to let the final act go on, but the set would have to be reduced. Redding and Walden agreed to trim it down to five songs and, after what must've seemed forever, the stage was finally set up for them. Booker T. & the M.G.'s walked out into the chilly, damp night in matching chartreuse suits and began an abbreviated two-song set with the Mar-Keys. Typically, Redding had his own traveling band, but, at Wexler's insistence, he brought the M.G.'s, who played on his records, to support him.

Redding came out to their fanfare in a dark lime green suit with his name flashing on the screen behind him like a frantic heartbeat. He opened with Sam Cooke's "Shake" that transitioned right into the current number two hit in the United States, Aretha Franklin's "Respect." That's about as well as most of the audience knew Otis Redding. The song was actually written and originally recorded by him. In fact, his version hit the number 35 spot nationally in the summer of 1965 but nobody remembered it. Franklin turned it into a

woman's anthem in the dawn of the Sexual Revolution and it would forever
be associated with her. Though Redding rocked the R&B charts and was a
big name on the chitlin circuit, to most in attendance in Monterey, he wasn't
a name like James Brown or Wilson Pickett. He hadn't charted higher than
number 21 but that was all about to change. Everybody was up on their feet,
dancing to the infectious Memphis rhythm, and pushing closer and closer
to the stage, causing a slight crush. Marinello freaked, recognizing that this
could cause serious injury or even death. He found John and pulled him away
from the backline.

"That's it. We're closing you down," he told him. "They're out of their
chairs pushing forward. If they don't immediately get back in their seats, I'll
order fire, police, and sanitation to close the house down."

"You pull the plug, my man, and we got no sound, no light and a lot of kids
out there on a lot of drugs with nowhere to go but crazy," John yelled back.
"Then you really will have a problem."

Marinello agreed. He urged John to somehow get ahold of Redding and
get him to calm everybody down. John made his way to the rear of the stage
and poked his head out from near the drum kit and motioned to Redding to
come over. When he gracefully danced his way to him, John told him that he
had to get everybody back in their seats or they'd shut the whole thing down.
Redding nodded and made his way back to center stage. In the cool night air,
cold enough to see his breath, he spoke to the crowd, telling them to get back
into their seats and said those six words that have become synonymous with
Monterey Pop ever since.

"This is the love crowd, right?"

The crowd roared. "We all love each other, don't we?" he yelled back.

With a love platform, he launched into his next number and biggest crossover hit to date, the slow ballad "I've Been Loving You Too Long." It worked.
Everybody grooved and got back in order. Another disaster averted. Redding
had them in the palm of his hand, wrapping up with his version of the Rolling
Stones' "(I Can't Get No) Satisfaction" and his dramatic reworking of the old
1930s chestnut "Try a Little Tenderness."

Redding left an indelible mark on those in attendance. His performance
had matched Big Brother & the Holding Company's, and many in attendance
and across the nation would purchase Otis Redding LPs and 45s in the ensuing days, weeks, and months. He benefited tremendously from the Monterey

effect but, tragically, his biggest success wouldn't come until after his untimely death less than six months later when his Beechcraft H18 airplane plummeted into Lake Manona in Dane County, Wisconsin, also killing four members of the Stax/Volt band the Bar-Kays and the pilot. Released in January 1968, "(Sittin' on) The Dock of the Bay" would go to number one in mid-March, becoming both his signature tune and his swan song. But on that night, Otis Redding was fully alive and proved the counterculture could indeed shake!

Two nights in and the Monterey Pop Festival was living up to its billing. Even if it ended there, the performances by Big Brother & the Holding Company and Otis Redding were enough to make it a memorable occasion. On the docket there were still enough notable groups, including Buffalo Springfield and the Mamas & the Papas, to whet everyone's appetite, but it would be the performances of two groups who, at the time, had one U.S. hit between them that would make Monterey a cultural signpost, and nobody saw it coming.

CHAPTER 22:
BE SURE TO WEAR FLOWERS IN YOUR HAIR

The Monterey International Pop Festival was heading into its third day and was red hot. The media presence, which began as several hundred on opening night, had blossomed to over 1,100 people, giving the concert the most coverage of any event in rock and roll history. John's desire for rock music to receive the same level of cultural respectability as jazz and folk music was coming true right before his eyes. Word also spread up and down the West Coast that this was indeed happening, which caused several thousand stragglers who didn't buy into the initial hype to sojourn to an already-packed Monterey and catch what was left. Rumors abounded that the Beatles, who 23 days earlier had released their finest album yet, *Sgt. Pepper's Lonely Hearts Club Band*, were, in fact, on the fairgrounds and may make some kind of an appearance, fomenting a level of hysteria that created a potential danger.

But a little danger never deterred John Phillips. His professional career and personal life were fraught with it. It was only 22 months earlier that he, Michelle, and Denny, completely broke, loaded up a rented limousine and drove from New York to California in the hopes that a record label would sign them. Monterey co-governor Lou Adler took a chance in signing these dirty broke hippies and guided them to their rapid ascent atop the pop mountain, and Monterey was the fruit borne of that risk. They'd successfully walked the tightrope between the young people and the authorities, and they weren't going to let the exposure topple them.

The Grateful Dead didn't care about authorities and commandeered an unused portion of the backline and carted it off to the floral pavilion and then to the Peninsula College football field, where they staged informal concerts. Many of the musicians who'd already played the festival or were awaiting their turn made their way over there to play. The Dead and Quicksilver Messenger Service staged free concerts, and dream matchups were everywhere. Bob Weir and Paul Simon could be seen jamming with the Jimi Hendrix Experience and the Who's Pete Townshend sat in with Eric Burdon & the Animals on "House of the Rising Sun" around 4:00 Sunday morning. The performers and the fans did indeed supply the love and defused a potentially volatile situation. Everyone was in it together.

Back when John, Lou and others conceptualized the Monterey Pop Festival, two parts of the Mamas & the Papas machine were noticeably absent in Cass and Denny. Though Cass didn't feign any love for this festival project, she did have a built-in excuse in her weeks-old daughter Owen. She did manage to drop by the offices once or twice and made it to the festival on Saturday where, when she wasn't in the VIP section taking in performances, she held court backstage with her many musician friends and industry people.

Denny, on the other hand, was completely missing in action. He totally dropped out once the ball got rolling. Although still in love with Michelle, he'd taken up with a new woman, Linda Woodward, and took her and a couple of buddies to the Virgin Islands and stayed loaded on Crown Royal and marijuana for several weeks. Perhaps he was trying to recapture the magic. Though he had performed with them on *The Ed Sullivan Show* the weekend prior, he'd dropped out of sight and, as day three of the Monterey International Festival was beginning, there was no sign of him.

Another carryover from April was Ravi Shankar. When Ben Shapiro and Alan Pariser put their heads together for the concert, it was to be a pay-for-play event, and the first artist they reached out to was the sitar maestro who agreed to perform for a $5,000 fee. He was never approached about playing for free, and so his contract was honored. When asked about it by the press, he maintained that the money went solely to his music school in India. He was scheduled to be the only performer Sunday afternoon, which made his performance sort of a quasi-religious ceremony on the most sacred day in the Christian world.

Shankar was the most seasoned of all the musicians playing at Monterey, having studied various Indian musical instruments under Allaudin Khan beginning at age 14 in 1935. By age 18, his focus had shifted exclusively to the sitar and surbahar, and for the next six years he studied their classical music forms including ragas, dhrupad, dhamar, and khyal and joined the Indian People's Theater Association in Mumbai upon completion of his studies in 1944. Shankar made his first recordings five years later and performed for the first time in the United States in 1956 at a party thrown in his honor by jazz historian Marshall Stearns in New York City. He also began recording for the U.S.-based companies RCA Victor and World Pacific that same year.

His catapult as an influencer of Western music came less than 10 years later when Beatle George Harrison took an interest in the sitar while on the set of their movie *Help!* For a scene that took place in an Indian restaurant in London, Indian musicians were hired to add to the ambiance. After borrowing a Ravi Shankar album from Byrd David Crosby while on tour in the United States, Harrison bought a sitar and, after some rudimentary study, played it on John Lennon's "Norwegian Wood" during the *Rubber Soul* sessions six months later. The use of the sitar increased on their next album *Revolver*, although it's uncertain whether Harrison is playing it. Regardless, Harrison's interest started a trend. Upon hearing "Norwegian Wood," Rolling Stone Brian Jones took up the instrument and composed the famous introduction to Mick Jagger and Keith Richards' "Paint It, Black" in March 1966. After meeting Shankar following his concert in Bath in April 1966, Harrison arranged to travel to India in order to begin studying the instrument under his tutelage during the Beatles' hiatus from September to November.

When Shapiro and Pariser considered him in early 1967, his star among the counterculture was rising. A tidal wave of interest in the sitar coincided with the rise of psychedelic music, and soon Ravi Shankar could be heard in head shops and cafes across the United States and England. The instrument had also crossed over to pop hits, including "Turn Down Day" by the Cyrkle, "I Was Made to Love Her" by Stevie Wonder, and Scott McKenzie's "San Francisco (Be Sure to Wear Flowers in Your Hair)." His presence was anticipated by many in attendance on Sunday, June 18, particularly those sitting in the performers' section. He asked everyone in the arena to refrain from smoking and took the stage around 1:30. Along with tabla virtuoso Alla Rakha and Kamala Chakravarty on tamboura, he played in the cool, drizzly afternoon air for three hours, the first 45 minutes of which were spent tuning their instruments, although most people probably had no idea. Shankar was tense in the beginning, not knowing what to expect from the love crowd and annoyed at the steady stream of aircraft taking off and landing at the nearby airport.

When they finally got into "Raga Bhimpalasi" and settled in, playing raga after raga, the rain had stopped, and their glares toward the airplanes got shorter and shorter until they didn't hear them anymore and became enraptured in their music. As the intoxicating drone of their instruments continued on and on into the early afternoon, supplementing everyone's highs, they concluded with "Dhun in Dandra and Fast Teental," and, upon completion, received a standing ovation that lasted several minutes. Many of the musicians in attendance were so influenced by the sound that their next records included some form of Indian music, which would spread to fellow musicians who didn't even attend the Monterey Pop Festival. Animals guitarist Vic Briggs, who was already into Indian music, was so moved by Shankar's performance that, within three years, he'd leave the music industry behind, change his name to Vikram Singh Kalsa and began studying and teaching various forms of yoga and Sikh religious music.

It was a great start to the final day of the festival, and the good vibes were everywhere. Most of the crowd were settled in and feeling comfortable; everybody but John. As the Mamas and the Papas' performance grew ever nearer, he had cause for concern. There was still no sign of Denny.

At 7:15 p.m., the concert reconvened beginning with Al Kooper's old band the Blues Project out of Greenwich Village kicking off the final night. It was an awkward reunion, to say the least, between the three remaining original members and their former leader, now in the much humbler role of Chip Monck's lackey. The group was barely two years old when Kooper decided to leave, and the split was acrimonious. It didn't help matters when the group arrived in the middle of his impromptu set the day before, performing, of all things, a Blues Project song.

When they took the stage, they weren't overwhelming but nevertheless entertaining. It was beginning to become a trend with opening acts. They did, however, play an inspiring 10-minute version of one of their most beloved songs, a flute-led instrumental, "Flute Thing" from their second LP, *Projections*. With his flute miked up, Andy Kulberg led the free-form jazz masterpiece and proved that those East Coast boys were just as improvisational and avant-garde as the bands from San Francisco. They also managed a 10-minute reprise of the song Kooper had played the day before, "Wake Me, Shake Me."

Still no sign of Denny.

Another reprise took place right afterward when Big Brother & the Holding Company again took the stage and belted out two numbers, "Down on Me" and "Ball and Chain," for filming purposes. Janis Joplin was again center stage, dressed chicly, but far from the multicolored, feathery, flamboyant style she'd soon adopt. She and the band brought the house down and were now preserved on celluloid and were a sure bet to be in whatever TV special or film came out of this.

The group who followed up, the Group with No Name, could not have been any more anticlimactic following Big Brother's second blistering performance. Coming out onstage looking like made-for-TV hippies seen on *Dragnet*, the group went through four haphazard numbers that had no structure or cohesion before finally exiting stage left in utter frustration. Made up of John and Michelle's former neighbors, ex-Modern Folk Quartet singer Cyrus Faryar and his wife Renais, Association co-founder Jules Alexander, on hiatus from his band, bassist Dick Shirley, and drummer Frank Terry, John threw Cyrus a bone by putting him on the bill. He hadn't found much success since disbanding the MFQ and was trying to get something started. When they discovered John had sandwiched them between Big Brother's second performance and Buffalo Springfield, they were not overjoyed.

"God John . . . you put us on after this?" Renais asked.

The group died a quick death and were followed by another relatively short-lived, although much more talented, band, Buffalo Springfield, who helped foster the festival with singer/guitarist Stephen Stills' recollection of the Sunset Strip riots put to song, "For What It's Worth." It helped ignite the CAFF benefit concert, co-organized by Alan Pariser, where they also performed. But the Buffalo Springfield that performed at that concert was a much stronger unit than the one who took the stage at Monterey on Sunday night.

Although original bassist Bruce Palmer was deported before the CAFF performance, the forces of nature were Stills and Winnipeg, Ontario, native Neil Young. The band was a combustible mixture of personalities from the beginning, and the jostling for position proved troublesome. At some point, something had to give and that occurred when their label, Atco, decided to release Stills' "Bluebird" over Young's "Mr. Soul." Young called a group meeting, announced he was quitting and that was it. They couldn't even talk him in to waiting until after Monterey.

In his place stood the Byrds' David Crosby who, although was a better natural singer, could not duplicate what Young brought to the band. Ex–Daily Flash singer/guitarist Doug Hastings filled in on bass for Palmer who was in attendance but didn't perform. Their set reflected the change in personnel. It was weak, to say the least. Introduced by Stills' close friend, Monkee Peter Tork, they played six songs, including "For What It's Worth, "Rock and Roll Woman," and "Bluebird" but they were marred by Crosby's unfamiliarity with their arrangements. He played too fast and was out of sync with everybody else. There was a silver lining though. It was the first time Stills and Crosby performed together publicly, and their harmony showed significant promise. In one year's time, Crosby would be out of the Byrds, Buffalo Springfield would be extinct, and Stills and Crosby would be hanging out regularly with Mama Cass, who, in July 1968, would introduce them to her friend Graham Nash of the Hollies.

Nighttime had fallen and still no Denny.

They were now down to the final four performers and, for all of them, it was their samurai moment. Half of them would emerge victorious and set the stage for successful careers and their respective style-and-substance performances would leave an indelible mark that would make Monterey Pop the stuff of legend. The other half would not fare as well, and while one act wouldn't be fazed by a lackluster performance, for the other it signified the beginning of the end.

The two victorious groups were virtually unknown in the United States, but they were very familiar with each other and household names in England. The Jimi Hendrix Experience and the Who had made the British music public sit up and take notice over the last two years. The Who came out of the gates on fire with their first four singles all going Top 10. After a bit of a stumble during the first half of 1966, they got back to their hit making ways with "I'm a Boy" and "Happy Jack," the latter of which became their first U.S. hit and got them booked on some smaller gigs on the other side of the Atlantic. They were four powerful personalities, led by their moody, pugnacious lead guitarist and principal songwriter Pete Townshend, who was fast becoming one of the premier performers in England. The other three complemented him pro-foundly and gave the Who its four-pronged personality. On lead vocals was a blonde-haired, athletic ballast named Roger Daltrey, the stoic and confident John Entwistle on bass, and the mischievous and unpredictable Keith Moon on drums. Moon's boundless energy made the other three look like they were standing still. They entered the backstage performers' area like superstars and immediately rubbed John the wrong way, demanding a special introduction, a longer set, and to be the festival closer. They were denied all three and ush-ered into the dressing room under the stage where they stayed for much of the time leading up to their performance.

Jimi Hendrix was the complete opposite. He was even-keeled, confident, and cool, innate traits that were sharpened during his year of service with the premier light infantry 101st Airborne Division even though it didn't necessarily reflect in his conduct reports. After getting busted for car theft a second time, the young Hendrix plea bargained by choosing the Army over jail and immediately hated it. Though he completed basic training and was awarded his Screaming Eagle patch in January 1962, by the end of June, he'd grown completely disinterested in Army life. All he cared about was playing his guitar, which he started doing at age 15. He was honorably discharged because of "unsuitability" and began playing music professionally in 1963 with Army buddy Billy Cox. After their efforts fizzled, Hendrix spent the next three years as a touring guitarist for R&B artists like Sam Cooke, Wil-son Pickett, Ike & Tina Turner, the Isley Brothers, and Little Richard before forming his own band called Jimmy James & the Blue Flames in Greenwich Village, where his loud, grumbling guitar sound and theatrics were devised and refined. At a one-off gig playing guitar for Curtis Knight & the Squires, he was noticed by Keith Richards' girlfriend Linda Keith who introduced him to ex-Animals-guitarist-turned-manager Chas Chandler. Completely blown away by what he heard, Chandler whisked him away to England where they formed the Jimi Hendrix Experience with bassist Noel Redding and drummer Mitch Mitchell.

It was the dawn of the power trio era and the group made their wax debut in December 1966 with Hendrix's interpretation of Billy Roberts' "Hey Joe." Though typically performed as a frenetic fast-paced number, signifying the desperation of the song's protagonist, who shoots down his unfaithful lover and bolts for Mexico, Hendrix took the song to the ghetto by slowing it down, not unlike Tim Rose's version seven months earlier, and transformed Joe into a bitter, cold-as-ice killer who defiantly tells the song's narrator that he's heading down to Mexico where nobody can hang him for murdering his old lady.

"Hey Joe" was issued on Polydor Records and rose to number six in England. The follow-up, "Purple Haze," peaked at number three in the spring of 1967, and they came into Monterey with "The Wind Cries Mary" climbing into the U.K. Top 10. Jimi's U.S. debut of "Hey Joe" on Reprise was going nowhere but it only bolstered Jimi's resolve. He was eager to make his native country remember his name.

When Townshend and Hendrix met backstage, there was some competitive tension. The two were almost like gunfighters sizing each other up. They'd met once before, back in October when Chas Chandler introduced them upon asking Townshend for amplifier advice. Hendrix was about to start a series of legendary dates around London, where concertgoers would watch in awe as he played with his teeth, behind his back and with a style that was at once carefree, meticulous, and loud. Townshend became instantly jealous but nonetheless inspired to up his game. He made a point of staying sober to watch Jimi to make sure what he was seeing was real.

And Townshend influenced Hendrix in kind and began incorporating feedback, distortion, and theatrics into his act. At Monterey, their second meeting was peppered with a bit of tension as the Experience was slated to go on before the Who. A key to the Who's publicity maelstrom in England was that, at the end of their concerts, Townshend and Keith Moon would smash their instruments onstage. Hendrix had also taken to doing it, and Townshend was afraid of being shown up. Since most concertgoers at Monterey had never seen or heard of them, the shock value would be minimized if Hendrix did it first and they'd run the risk of looking like hacks.

Townshend went to John about swapping their place with Hendrix's but was refused. He told them there was a lighting schedule that had to be adhered to. Next, he tried Derek Taylor, who he knew from his time in London, but told him it was out of his hands. He suggested talking with Hendrix about it. Townshend tried, but Hendrix was pretty stoned and paid him little attention. He knew Townshend was jockeying for position and was unconcerned with his dilemma and paid more attention to picking away at his guitar. When Townshend got a little more abrasive, John intervened. He didn't want two of his final acts getting into a fistfight so, in the interest of the peace and love vibe of the festival, he suggested the rock and roll tradition of flipping a coin and the loser would go last. They both agreed. John flipped. Hendrix lost. The Who would go on after Buffalo Springfield. Everyone was alerted.

After an introduction by Eric Burdon, who warned the audience that this next group "will destroy you in more ways than one," the Who came out onstage the picture of the London mod scene with Roger Daltrey in a pink silk tablecloth, Pete Townshend in a lace ruffle shirt and pink floral frock coat, Keith Moon in a red mandarin jacket, and John Entwistle in a yellow and red jacket with an odd cartoon pattern. Their set and performance were unique to say the least, but they were pure rock and roll in its most contemporary form. Beginning with "Substitute" and followed by Eddie Cochran's 1958 hit "Summertime Blues," the group churned and burned through a combination of unique songs filled with Townshend's bizarre characters, including a masturbating adolescent, an old man constantly being picked on by children, and an unfaithful wife who has an affair with a train engineer. The latter was part of a nine-minute, six-movement rock opera, "A Quick One, While He's Away," from their 1966 LP *A Quick One*. But it was their closer that got everyone out of their seats. It had become their signature tune and another counterculture anthem and was called "My Generation." Daltrey sang it with his patented stutter that agitated parents and galvanized young listeners. Near the song's end, Daltrey began swinging his microphone over his head, while Townshend smashed his guitar into his amplifier. It was auto-destructive art, which Townshend had learned from Gustav Metzger, a pioneer of the movement who, in an effort to convey man's ability to destroy one another and the planet, painted with acid and other solutions in order to leave a permanent mark on the canvas. Townshend brought it to the rock and roll arena, purposely destroying his Rickenbacker at an early Who gig in 1964, and it didn't take long for their reputation to grow.

Three years later, the crowd at Monterey were both aghast and excited watching Townshend forcibly separate the body of his Fender Stratocaster from its neck. Ravi Shankar, who treated his instruments like sacraments, looked on in anguish and fled the grounds. Keith Moon ratcheted things up a notch by setting off smoke bombs and dismantling his drum kit. Sound technicians immediately began crisscrossing the stage, trying to protect the backline and the microphones. Lou Adler even ran out from the wings, scampering across the stage chasing Keith Moon's kick drum. The Who left a trail of destruction behind them and it looked like Townshend's words before launching into "My Generation" might've come true: "This is where it all ends." But it was far from over.

Amid the furor, good news had met John. Denny finally arrived.

Though stagehands did their best to clean up the splinters, shards of plastic, and broken guitar strings, the Grateful Dead took the stage in the ashes of the Who's performance and looked every bit like the grungy San Francisco band they were reported to be and the antithesis of Hollywood sheen. In fact, they were downright homely, albeit in a glorious rock and roll way. Leader Jerry Garcia looked magnificent in his dark green and blue-striped sweater, rainbow pants and thick, shaggy shoulder-length hair. His clean-shaven face and receding chin made him look bizarre, and the others looked equally as odd. Bassist Phil Lesh had manicured his previous pyramid hairstyle into a more manageable coiffure that better complemented his rather thin and wispy nose and jawline. On drums, Bill Kreutzmann resembled Prince Valiant in a striped T-shirt, and guitarist Bob Weir looked like a teenage girl. But the one who struck fear upon first sight was their stocky keyboardist, Ron "Pigpen" McKernan, who looked like he'd just stepped off his chopper and slipped onstage. He had dirty, long curly hair that flowed down to his chest and a big, bushy goatee complemented by a Native American headdress and just looked menacing, although he was, in fact, the shyest and sweetest member of the group.

But here they stood, the group who put John and Lou through the wringer and threatened to undermine the entire festival more than once. Now it was time to see what they were all about. They churned like a slow-moving locomotive through a 30-minute set in 40 minutes. Even though their career was relatively short at that point, the Dead were never bound by time before or after Monterey. They came up in the unlikeliest of manners, playing at weird hootenannies, at Ken Kesey's Acid Tests and in pizza parlors where the audience wasn't necessarily there for their music. It allowed them a semblance of freedom to stretch and improvise, which developed their unique bouncy, trippy sound over time. At Monterey, they were a bit out of their element, which caused them to be tighter than usual. Beginning with their debut album's closing number, a 14-minute version of "Viola Lee Blues," Jerry Garcia's meandering guitar picking sounded like a musical conversation between him and his bandmates. It easily became hypnotic as the band pushed further and further into a groove where the music drove them.

But it wouldn't be a true Dead performance without something weird happening. At the end of their opening number, Monkee Peter Tork came bursting onstage to awkwardly convey a message to fans outside the arena expecting to see the Beatles. Many fans who hadn't paid had begun climbing over walls and breaking down doors to get a glimpse of the Fab Four. It was a rumor started innocently enough by Johnny Rivers on Friday night when a couple police officers prevented his limousine from entering the backstage area. Johnny rolled down the window, pointed to his young arranger, Jimmy Webb, seated next to him and told the officer they had Paul McCartney in here. Webb had a cursory similarity to the Beatle, but it was enough to fool an unwitting cop who promptly allowed them through without question.

The presence of a Monkee on stage with the Grateful Dead perfectly encapsulated the most extreme of philosophical musical differences between L.A. musicians and the San Francisco groups, at least in the latter's estimation. It was the personification of manufactured versus organic. Phil Lesh did not take kindly to the interruption and, being one of the principal antiestablishment ballbusters in the band, couldn't help but heckle Tork, who, doing a favor for John and the organizers, pleaded with the teens not to vandalize the fairgrounds and destroy any goodwill built up between the hippies and the authorities. As Tork stuttered, stammered, and chuckled his way through his plea, Lesh took up the cause for those trying to get in and see the end of the festival.

"This is the last concert," Lesh said to Tork. "Why not let them in?"

Tork was completely thrown off guard by this and, being good-natured and nonconfrontational, took both sides of the argument, agreeing that, sure, they can come in but please don't do so by destroying public property. He further emphasized that the Beatles were not present.

"The Beatles aren't here!" Lesh yelled to the crowd. "But come on in anyway. If the Beatles were here, they'd probably want you to come in."

Tork was completely baffled by this interplay and began sounding like he'd rather be anywhere than where he was. Lesh had emasculated him in front of thousands of people and now he just looked like the big dummy he portrayed on TV. Perhaps busting into the middle of the Grateful Dead's set was not such a good idea. With as much dignity as he could muster, he pleaded once more as quickly as possible and got the hell out of there.

The Dead chugged through three more numbers and made their way offstage. It was probably their shortest concert since Magoo's Pizza Parlor in Palo Alto less two years earlier and, up to that point, their least gratifying. It was ironic that the San Francisco group with this much fanfare gave such an uninspired performance, especially considering how difficult they made their commitment. It was the beginning of a Grateful Dead tradition of blowing the big ones.

It was now time for the Jimi Hendrix Experience, and what an experience it would turn out to be for an unsuspecting audience. After a flattering intro-duction from Brian Jones, who called Hendrix the most exciting performer he'd ever heard, the Experience walked out looking more flowery than the Who. It was a British power trio thing. Hendrix himself looked like a psy-chedelic swashbuckler, dressed in red pants, a pinstriped orange ruffled shirt, and a black vest with matching bandana. The Seattle native couldn't be more excited, and he came across as being downright giddy playing in his native country and to a West Coast audience. And they were loud. The loudest group in the entire festival. After ripping through a Howlin' Wolf blues favor-ite, "Killing Floor," and the leadoff track to their as-yet-unreleased debut LP, "Foxy Lady," Hendrix engaged the crowd with plenty of "hey brother," "you dig" and "out of sight." After his greeting, they played a soulful, slowed-down rendition of Bob Dylan's "Like a Rolling Stone," giving it an Impressions-like melody and lulling the crowd into a groove.

The remainder of the set was an introduction to the new phase of rock and roll, including their debut and first U.K. hit "Hey Joe," which obliterated the Byrds' earlier mangled version. They also played their other two hits, "Purple Haze" and their most current, the cool "The Wind Cries Mary," as well as future album track "Can You See Me." Throughout it all, Hendrix was jovial, introducing his bandmates and telling the story several times of him not mak-ing it in the States and being accepted in England. Then, things got weird, or profound, depending on your point of view.

Hours earlier, after losing the coin toss to Pete Townshend, Jimi had extra time to strategize his own finale. Truth is, he'd already figured it out and had even tried it once before. Even though the Who had the market cornered on auto-destructive art onstage, Hendrix was looking to add it to his repertoire and even kick it up a notch so, back on March 31, on a package tour at the Astoria Theater in London, he conceived the idea of setting his guitar on fire at the end of their final number "Fire." As Jimi set his Stratocaster on the stage and walked toward the crowd in an effort to distract them, manager Chas Chandler ran out onstage with a bottle of lighter fluid and generously doused it on the body of Hendrix's guitar until it was completely soaked. Hendrix made his way back and struck a series of matches and rightly tossed them onto it and, before he knew it, was face-to-face with a four-foot tower of flames. Hendrix was able to finish the song on another guitar but was sent to the hospital where he was treated for minor burns.

This time, Hendrix was more careful. Earlier in the day, he and friend Jenni Dean-Harte drove around Monterey looking for a store that was open and carried lighter fluid. They managed to score some at a hardware store and Hendrix planted it onstage sometime before the Experience's performance. In the introduction of their finale, the acid had fully kicked in. Hendrix spoke a mile a minute, once again talking about being rejected by the United States and going to England and then made a vague statement about sacrificing something he really loved, which led those following along scratching their heads.

"We're going to do the English American combined anthem together. Don't get mad," he told the puzzled audience.

He then began making the most sublime feedback with his guitar and amp that quieted the whole arena before launching into the familiar opening chords of the Troggs' 1966 hit "Wild Thing." Hendrix was the coolest guy in the room with his long, lanky arms effortlessly working his guitar, eyes closed and swinging his head around, as though he was completely in tune with the music, while casually chewing on a piece of gum. His singing voice wasn't strong, but it didn't matter. He mostly spoke the sex-charged lyrics, giving them the proper enunciation.

Close to three minutes in, Hendrix began his solo by playing the melody to "Strangers in the Night," the Grammy winner for 1966 Song of the Year, with just his fingers on the frets. Was it a message to the music industry? Perhaps. Hendrix could duplicate Bert Kaempfert's melody with just his fingers. Could Kaempfert duplicate what Hendrix did? From there, it got wilder. After one more vocal refrain, Hendrix took a bow and walked over to the stacked dual speakers directly behind him creating feedback with his guitar while rapidly humping the speakers. From there, he turned right around to face the audience, dropped to his knees, stroked his guitar neck suggestively, unstrapped it and gently set it on the ground, all the while still playing it. It created an unearthly sound that no doubt had many in the audience wondering what they were seeing and hearing.

Redding and Mitchell kept the rhythm while Hendrix walked up and grabbed his stashed lighter fluid. Just offstage, John and Lou watched in amazement while next to them stood the much-less-impressed fire marshal, Jim Reynolds, who was already in a bad mood because somebody had already broken into his car and stolen his fire helmet and jacket. Sensing what was about to happen, John futilely attempted to distract Reynolds by pointing out how marvelous the crowd was. After Hendrix gave his Stratocaster a goodbye kiss, he struck a match and set it ablaze. Reynolds flipped out and began running toward him with a fire extinguisher. Lou grabbed his arm and pulled him back.

"It's OK. It's just part of the act," he told him.

This time around, it was a much more manageable fire for Hendrix, who summoned the flames like a witch doctor as soon as they started to rise. He then squirted more lighter fluid to make the flames rise higher then immediately grabbed the guitar by its neck and did his best Pete Townshend impression, swinging it like a baseball bat, knocking down two microphone stands while smashing it into the stage. With the fourth swing, he separated the body of the guitar from its neck and tossed it into the crowd, most of whom stood in shocked silence. The sacrifice was evident. The Jimi Hendrix Experience walked offstage, fully making their mark on America and they would go on to be one of the most influential rock groups in history. Pitied be the group who had to follow them, and it was none other than the Mamas & the Papas.

The Who and the Hendrix Experience performance aside, it was a tense day for the Mamas & the Papas as the reality of their performance grew nearer. Suddenly it dawned on John that they hadn't rehearsed, and, with Denny nowhere in sight for the first three or four hours of the festival, there was no plan B. How was it going to look if the foremost singing quartet in the music world, who were set to close this incredibly successful rock festival, was short a lead singer? No less unsettling was the notion that, even if he did show up, what were they going to sound like? It seems that John had spent all his energy managing everything associated with the festival except his own group. It was actually Cass who checked in with Denny to make sure he remembered Monterey.

"Don't worry, I'll be there," he told her.

On Sunday morning, June 18, his buddy Owen Orr came over to drive him up to Monterey. He asked Denny what time they had to be there.

"I don't know," he told him. "We're closing the show tonight."

"We got to get fucking going," Owen told him. "It's an eight-hour drive!"

Denny hadn't bothered to look at a map. He thought Monterey was only a couple hours north from Los Angeles. They dropped everything, jumped in Denny's Cadillac and took Highway 101 North. Ideally, it should only take five hours and change to make the 330-mile journey, but California traffic tacked on an extra three hours. As night fell and they entered the outskirts of Monterey, the enormity of the festival hit Denny as they crawled and snaked their way through traffic and headed toward the noise and had no idea what he was about to walk into.

The Who were in the process of smashing their instruments at the end of "My Generation." Drummer Keith Moon had just kicked over his bass drum and was making a victory sign before setting off his fireworks and making his way off the stage. Between the loudness, the smoke and the destruction, it looked like a riot more than a concert and Denny was baffled. He made his way backstage and found his bandmates who were relieved to finally see him and a little bit miffed that he pushed it this far, although nobody could stay mad at him for very long.

After catching up, getting briefed and taking in the scene backstage, Denny went into the dressing room underneath the stage to change into his psychedelic caftan. At some point after the Grateful Dead performance, the four managed to get together for rehearsal. They hadn't sung together regularly in three months and it showed. They ran through their standard concert numbers, "California Dreamin'," "Monday, Monday," "Got a Feelin'," and "I Call Your Name." Their latest hit, "Creeque Alley," which had peaked a couple weeks earlier at number five, was too complicated to even be considered. There was an attempt at a rehearsal for their previous hit, "Dedicated to the One I Love," but it was disrupted by Jimi Hendrix's performance, and, before they knew it, it was over. No more rehearsals. There'd be nothing new in the Mamas & the Papas' set. They had approximately 20 minutes to shake off the rust and finished their vocal warm-ups backstage among a crowd of people.

There also wasn't time for a soundcheck. The backing band made up of Dr. Eric Hord on guitar, Larry Knechtel on piano, Joe Osborn on bass and "Fast" Eddie Hoh on drums had to set up quickly and tune their instruments. Minutes later, the festival closers came running out to the looped opening chords of "Straight Shooter," Michelle shaking her tambourine and Cass her maracas. Denny looking bohemian in his colorful silk caftan and thin beard and John and Michelle looked hippie chic in outfits designed by Profile du Monde. Cass went basic in an understated, but no less designer, blue dress. And, to keep with the hippie ethos, both Michelle and Cass went makeup-less. John also displayed his signature look by coming out in a tall fur hat, which added about six inches to his already tall and lanky frame.

But their outfits were the best part of the Mamas & the Papas' performance that evening. From the moment they took the stage around midnight, they were out of tune. To make matters worse, the audience could only hear three of them. Michelle's microphone, perhaps courtesy of Jimi Hendrix's guitar sacrifice, was completely inaudible and his antics may have also obliterated the onstage monitor because the issue was never corrected until the third-from-the-last song in the set. John and Denny's microphones also remained too low throughout most of their set while Cass' was hot, which highlighted her vocal pitch being mostly out of tune. Their collective harmonizing never improved either, which is indicative of not being able to hear oneself.

For the audience, after taking in heavy doses of hard rock from Saturday on, the Mamas & the Papas' greatest hits package must've seemed dated, especially following the Who and Hendrix, and they played to a much smaller audience. Even some hippies had to go to work in a few hours and the crowd had thinned out. The myriad unknown groups who were well-received all week proved the audience didn't necessarily have to know all the songs. Other established acts like Simon & Garfunkel and the Animals left most of their older hits on the shelf and David Crosby straight-up announced the Byrds wouldn't be doing "Mr. Tambourine Man" and "Turn, Turn, Turn," because the times they were a-changin'. Still, however, live versions of "Dedicated to the One I Love" and "Creeque Alley" at least would've kept them current. If there was a highlight of their performance, it was Mama Cass' banter in between songs where she complimented Mike Bloomfield's performance, spoke lovingly about John Lennon, and praised the entire festival.

"We're going to have this festival every year," she told those still in attendance. "So you can stay if you want. I think I might."

After "I Call Your Name," John took to introducing the women to the audience. Mama Michelle, ever bashful whenever the spotlight shone on her, was referred to as their Mexican gypsy. Mama Cass was their psychedelic mushroom. Cass took the handoff and introduced the men. Still incapable of completely stifling her feelings for Denny, she introduced him as their sex symbol as well as rock and roll's answer to the Marshall Plan, in that he was a Canadian citizen who was now in the United States legally. For John, Cass was either caught up in the moment, truly proud of his accomplishments in staging the festival, or made a high art form out of bullshitting, because she went really over the top for his introduction, especially considering their history.

"And, last but certainly not least, on my extreme left, geographically if not to say politically, the gentleman who writes all of our original material and a good portion of the material that we steal. A fine man! A great musician! And a hell of an American, John Phillips! Chairman of the board!"

Cass had everybody rolling. John soaked it all in. It was the moment that all this had led up to: the Abstracts, the Smoothies, Michelle, New York, the Journeymen, the New Journeymen, the Virgin Islands, Los Angeles, California Dreamin', and now Monterey. It was public acknowledgment of his musical and his visionary genius, which was very gratifying for him. Amid the generous applause of those who remained, they eased into a most unharmonious version of "Monday, Monday," but Cass wasn't done. She had another big introduction planned and went into her own spoken-word rendition of "Creeque Alley" when she invited Scott McKenzie to join them onstage for a number. She talked about his connection to John via the Smoothies and the Journeymen and how, somewhere along the way, they lost him.

He came out clad in all white, including a long, Eastern-styled robe, to the bare-bones chords of John's festival song, "San Francisco (Be Sure to Wear Flowers in Your Hair)," and, if the Mamas & the Papas' performance was unimpressive thus far, it was about to get worse. Although he was in a better state of mind than he was during his Journeymen tenure, Scott was still a psychological mess and sheepishly walked onstage to the largest crowd he'd ever seen and began singing the reverse chord sequence of the melody and never got in sync. It was incredibly unsuccessful and only served to make them all look even less prepared. Mercifully, their best performance was their final one, the Martha & the Vandellas 1964 hit "Dancing in the Street," which sent everybody on their way.

"You're on your own babies because we're sure on ours," Cass told the crowd as she started singing "Calling out around the world . . ."

It was the perfect festival closer, as it served as both a Civil Rights and a hippie anthem, and sent everybody home. Chief Frank Marinello had already dismissed half of his police force, which opened up the potential for trouble, but the crowd, who was well-behaved the entire weekend, maintained their level heads. The party raged on though. The Who drove around town on the back of a flatbed truck, performing for the wayfarers. Motel Row resembled a line of college fraternities celebrating after a big football win on a Saturday night.

John and Michelle headed back to their room at the Highlands Inn in Carmel, where Michelle cried for over two hours. She wasn't happy with their performance, but she was also sad to see their beautiful creation come to an end and get back to normal life, which was anything but normal. It was a natural reaction to the end of months of hard work. She contributed the least to the Mamas & the Papas' sound, and her focus on Monterey gave her a sense of belonging that she'd never experienced within the group. She'd soon come to find out there her emotional outburst was partially due to another beautiful creation.

Denny and Cass piled into his big red Cadillac with a random group of friends and strangers, including his girlfriend Linda Woodward who grabbed a candle that had been lit on Friday and did her best to preserve the eternal flame with the top down. In the moment, the spirit of Monterey did take on somewhat religious overtones and the good vibes carried over into what is now known as the Summer of Love.

The narrative that would be put forward for years to come is that the Monterey Pop Festival served as the great rock and roll summit that brought together music factions from Los Angeles, San Francisco, England, Memphis, Chicago and parts of Asia and Africa, which served to dropkick the hippie philosophy into the forefront of Western culture and there's a lot of truth to it. Even though cultural issues like free speech, civil rights, and the Vietnam

War were paramount within the Monterey crowd, for three days, that was all put aside and love reigned even as short-haired, off-duty Army soldiers from Fort Ord milled about the fairgrounds.

But it wasn't all music, love and flowers for everyone, and the actions of the Grateful Dead and some in their entourage showed that a certain degree of animosity still existed. The idea of filming and recording the festival for future release always rubbed the Dead the wrong way, and it never completely dissipated. And even though the ill will died down during the festival, it reared its ugly head as they were heading to the stage for their performance on Sunday evening and John asked them to sign a release for broadcast rights. They refused. Near the end of the show, while many people were leaving or starting their respective after-parties, Dead managers Rock Scully and David Rifkin decided to get the last word in after noticing a stockpile of unused amplifiers loaned to the festival by Fender. Feeling like John and Lou hijacked the San Francisco groups for the sake of their own pockets, they concocted their evil scheme by approaching the two security guards assigned to guard it all with a commemorative toast. Little did they know of the Grateful Dead's penchant for spiking drinks with LSD and, sure enough, the whiskey bottles were laced. With those two freaking out, they borrowed their friends' van and began loading it to the brim with amps and made off with about $1 million worth of equipment, which they used to entertain the traveling bands of hippies visiting Haight-Ashbury over the next few weeks. Not wishing to go uncredited, they left a note that read, "Hope you dudes don't mind, but we've borrowed your gear for a few days. Reason is, the musicians that played on this equipment loved it so much that they wanted a chance to use it again. You'll get it back!"

Lou was justifiably upset. He was now on the hook for $1 million worth of equipment and wasn't anxious to tell the people at Fender that somebody managed to steal it. It took him several days, but he finally tracked Scully down and got him on the phone. He demanded that they return it at all at once and advised him that the police were already on the lookout for it. Always the hipster blessed with the gift of gab and funny retorts, Scully responded in that sardonic and cynical manner that only someone imbued in the San Francisco rock culture could.

"Why don't you come up and get it?" he told the fuming music mogul. "And be sure to wear flowers in your hair."

CHAPTER 23: SOMETHING ROTTEN IN THE STATE OF ENGLAND

The Monterey Pop Festival was a big part of a series of events that took place over the summer months of 1967. There's no official event that kicked off what is now known as the Summer of Love but many historians place it with the release of the Beatles' psychedelic masterpiece *Sgt. Pepper's Lonely Hearts Club Band* album on Friday, June 2, exactly two weeks before the start of the groundbreaking festival. It was a brilliant collection of songs, both trippy and simple, that sounded unlike anything they'd cut before and fit the uncommercial mold that was dominating the popular musical landscape. Songs like "A Day in the Life," "Within You, Without You," "Lucy in the Sky with Diamonds," and "With a Little Help from My Friends" redefined and reenergized not only the Beatles but also the music scene itself. None of the songs on the album were released as singles but several received significant radio play on the FM band in the United States. Though it had been around since 1933, FM was a relatively new medium as far as entertainment was concerned, and it attracted a new album rock format that competed with AM Top 40 in terms of listenership. It placed an exclamation point on the album movement started by artists the Beatles and the Beach Boys a couple of years earlier.

Monterey Pop benefited from perfect timing, providing a gathering place for like-minded youth ensconced in *Sgt. Pepper* and the culture that, through the reporting of mass media, quickly became a worldwide phenomenon. The good vibes that permeated the festival were evident in the number one hits that summer: "Groovin" by the Young Rascals, "Windy" by the Association, "Light My Fire" by the Doors, and "All You Need Is Love" by the Beatles.

After Monterey, the predictions of the mass migration to San Francisco came true. As soon as high school and college spring terms ended in late June, the streets in and around Haight-Ashbury became inundated with teenagers and young adults from all over the country and peace and love was indeed the order of the day for a little while. Hippie bastions began sprouting up in other cities around the world and became the overwhelming subculture on college campuses, especially in the United States. And, as with every man-made thing that appears holy and righteous, there was a soft, dark underbelly that countered that notion. Namely, it was hard drugs, and widespread use grew the heaviest back in San Francisco where the peace and love scene began. With thousands arriving daily with no place to stay, parks, sidewalks, bus stations and train depots began filling up with vagrant hippies, and opioid drugs like heroin and stimulants like crystal methamphetamines began spreading with cocaine following closely behind.

By midsummer, San Francisco was a circus. With all the publicity, bus companies began scheduling tours of Haight-Ashbury throughout the day, and gawking tourists would take in the spectacle, agitating the local hippies. Though well equipped with a free clinic and the Diggers providing meals, their charitable efforts had reached critical mass. For those who witnessed the phenomenon from its inception two years earlier, things got serious when two friendly neighborhood pot dealers were murdered within days of each other in August. With the scene flooding with middle- and upper-class high school and college age nomads looking to get high, drug turf wars became a life and death proposition. This unfortunate by-product spread its way across the country, especially south to Los Angeles where, over time, it became a blight on society. There, it manifested itself in the worst way in career criminal and sociopath Charles Manson, who was released from Terminal Island in San Pedro, California, for good behavior in March 1967. He'd served only six years of a 10-year sentence for violating probation from an earlier crime by attempting to cash a forged U.S. Treasury check. Venturing back out into society, he took advantage of several impressionable idealistic hippies and developed a cult of personality that was attractive to many young men and women who were eager to do his bidding. Very quickly it devolved into a steady diet of petty crime and sexual orgies, which, over time, blossomed into a local cult. Manson had bigger goals, however. As an aspiring musician who learned to play guitar in prison, he actively sought a path to rock stardom to feed his large ego, and a chance encounter with Beach Boys drummer Dennis Wilson helped him forge a dangerous one that trod upon a few in the Mamas & the Papas' circle.

John Phillips' Bel Air home embodied many of these negative aspects of the counterculture in the summer of 1967. Though John was not violent like Manson, his sexual appetite was voracious, and he surrounded himself with an admiring base of sycophants and groupies who provided drugs and sex at will. He'd also found that rock stardom that Manson was so desperately searching for, but his kingdom was beginning to crumble around him, and it was no more evident than at home. John was no longer timid about cheating on Michelle. He still did it behind her back but was starting to get careless. Over the course of her pregnancy, he cheated on her several times, including having sex with groupies inside the house while Michelle was sleeping. Pregnancy always had that effect on him and, as he had with his first wife Susie's pregnancies, he showed no interest in Michelle's unborn baby either. It made him feel trapped and isolated Michelle. The married half of the Mamas & the Papas were heading down an inevitable road.

In fact, the entire group was. After Monterey Pop, and the lack of any spark within the band, John had to come to grips with the fact that tensions were getting worse. Not only were he and Michelle slipping back to marital trouble, but Denny was deliberately avoiding them and slipping further and further into alcoholism. Cass was on a different plane entirely, surrounding herself with the likes of musician friends David Crosby and Joni Mitchell and her new boyfriend, Pic Dawson. In the months following her pregnancy, Cass was growing increasingly frustrated over the Mamas & the Papas' lack of touring. Since she didn't write songs, it was her main source of income and her funds were drying up. It was particularly troublesome because she had the biggest voice and personality and the most upside of the entire group. Pic and others, including manager Bobby Roberts, had been encouraging Cass to break off on her own for months and, with the lack of communication within the group, she was inching ever closer to crossing that threshold.

Once again, John defaulted to his chief method of coping with transitions and decided that the group would embark on another trip together, but this time to Mallorca, Spain. They'd depart after their Sullivan appearance and take a hiatus for an indefinite period of time in order to regroup and come back to the fourth album sessions recharged. In one way or another, he was going to try and rekindle that Virgin Islands magic. He would soon find out that magic moments can't be forced.

The negative realities of the current hippie trend that were unveiling themselves in San Francisco and elsewhere around the country were also present in the Mamas & the Papas' group dynamic and threatening to tear them apart. Monterey should've been a galvanizer but, for one reason or another, it didn't inspire them to get into the studio or beef up their tour schedule. They did have dates to fulfill and played the Public Auditorium in Cleveland on June 24, with the Buckinghams and Moby Grape, and on the East Coast in July where they played the Maple Leaf Garden in Toronto on July 1 and Carnegie Hall in New York City on July 13. They still maintained their "play when we want to play" mentality, which was having a deleterious effect on their popularity, but they'd all seemed to have reached a level of indifference when it came to reaching out to their fans and nobody showed it more than their leader. Because of John's songwriting royalties, he was rolling in dough and was ratcheting up his drug use with PCP, a stronger hallucinogenic that's addictive and can produce side effects like depersonalization and a temporary disturbance of a person's thought processes.

John was beginning to rest on his laurels as a hitmaker and it took new Dunhill president Jay Lasker to force the group back in the studio. It had been three months since the release of "Creeque Alley," which, by mid-July, had completely fallen out of the charts. John's ace in the hole was another biographical song he'd been toying around with since his days living with Denny in Laurel Canyon. "Twelve Thirty (Young Girls Are Coming to the Canyon)" somberly told the story of John's move from New York to Los Angeles and the positive effects of the change of scenery. It referenced the broken clock steeple attached to the defunct Jefferson Market Court building in Greenwich Village, which was visible from John and Michelle's old apartment at the Earle Hotel, and the revolving door of groupies at Denny's house on Woods Drive.

It was another personal song and showed him moving in a paradigm that matched with the dawning singer-songwriter era although his prolificacy didn't match that of a Neil Young or a Van Morrison. He'd originally planned on giving it to Scott McKenzie as his follow-up to "San Francisco" but, with the label pressuring him for material, kept it instead for the Mamas & the Papas' next single and it was cut rather quickly in their final session at Western. Always short of fresh material, the two-year-old "Straight Shooter," from their first album, was placed on the flip side. Released on August 26, it debuted at number 72 and certainly appeared it would follow the trajectory of their last two singles but ultimately stalled after peaking at number 20 in *Billboard* and number 15 in *Cash Box*. It was their worst showing since "Look Through My Window" back in October 1966 and, with John's creative coffers dry, it was a bad sign.

As Dunhill was preparing the new single for distribution, the Mamas & the Papas were preparing for one of the biggest shows of their career, headlining at the Hollywood Bowl on August 18 with Scott McKenzie and the Jimi Hendrix Experience as their openers. Mike Bloomfield's Electric Flag was also scheduled to perform but, for one reason or another, couldn't come to terms with the show's producers. It was supposed to be a microcosm of the Monterey Pop Festival, but the good vibes didn't carry over to the L.A. crowd. The Jimi Hendrix Experience, a month removed from the aborted foray as openers for the Monkees on their 1967 summer tour, received the same lackluster audience reception they'd experienced with Monkees fans. After smashing his guitar to pieces, he walked off the stage to a smattering of applause.

As disappointing as that certainly must've been to John, he had his own monkey on his back, namely, making up for the Mamas & the Papas' poor performance at Monterey. And he was ready. They had a few warmups since then and he was confident enough to make this a family affair. In the audience were his mother, his children, his sister, his nieces Patty and Nancy, his ex-wife and several friends, including Barry McGuire who helped spark this journey 23 months ago. John had put it out to the musicians and to the group that this was going to be their final live performance for an indefinite period.

By now, it was common knowledge that the Beatles would not be touring to support *Sgt. Pepper* or at all for the foreseeable future. The Rolling Stones' last concert was held in Athens, Greece, on April 17, 1967, and they wouldn't take a stage again until July 1969 as they dealt with legal troubles and internal power struggles. John placed his group on the same level and decided they too needed a respite. The difference was, both the Beatles and Stones had put in a solid three straight years of nonstop touring and issued a collective 12 albums, the likes of which changed pop music and culture. It allowed them a good amount of leeway with their fans and deeper pockets. The Mamas & the Papas only released three albums and toured intermittently, which didn't build up the kind of cachet that would allow them a similar grace period. It served as a death knell.

In Electric Flag's place was a string quartet booked by Lou Adler, who trudged over the broken pieces of Jimi Hendrix's guitar. If anything, they served to make the Mamas & the Papas much more anticipated and they came out to rousing applause. Like Monterey, they came out in silk hippiewear, custom-designed by Profile du Monde, and handed out Hawaiian orchids to the capacity crowd of 12,700. Cass even replicated the "one hell of an American" introduction for John Phillips. They played 12 songs and by all accounts, their performance at the Hollywood Bowl was much better than Monterey. The downtime even allowed for John and the band to create live arrangements for newer songs like "Dedicated to the One I Love," "Creeque Alley" and "Twelve Thirty." Richard Drew, of Pasadena's *Independent Star News*, wrote that this concert "will set a precedent for others to try and follow." It was high praise indeed, and one that the group should've been able to build upon, but they didn't. With that behind them, they prepared for a September trip to New York City for their third appearance on *The Ed Sullivan Show*.

In the meantime, instead of focusing on writing more songs for the Mamas & the Papas' fourth album, John was working on Scott McKenzie's follow-up to "San Francisco" and subsequent album. With "Twelve Thirty" commandeered for the group, John offered up another original, "Like an Old Time Movie." It was one of his best works to date sung from the point of view of a fed-up lover who has resigned himself to moving on. It was clearly about Michelle and most likely written during their separation a year earlier.

Don't come on so groovy
You do better mean
You're like an old time movie
One that I've already seen.

For the flip side, they recorded a Scott McKenzie original, "What's the Difference—Chapter II." The first version appeared as the flip to "San Francisco," but was overshadowed by the hit side. It was profound in its simplicity: a message song about here today, gone tomorrow that mirrored what exactly was going on with his friend's complicated group. Scott wrote it after the

Journeymen broke up four years earlier and it became a song that he kept on adding new verses to over the years. This second version wasn't as rushed and featured flute and strings overdubs. It complemented the A-side nicely and set the stage for his debut solo album, produced by John Phillips and Lou Adler.

Interestingly, the decision was made to record the remainder of the album in New York City the week leading into the Mamas & the Papas' September 24 appearance on *The Ed Sullivan Show*. Lou Adler had a strong relationship with Clive Davis, president of CBS Records, who distributed his Ode Records. He arranged for them to record at their new, state-of-the-art studios at 49 East 52nd Street, where they were joined by old friend Dick Weissman, making the session a Journeymen reunion. Although it sounded romantic, the culture within the New York recording studios differed tremendously from Los Angeles, and the two factions quickly began butting heads. Recording engineers in New York were under the auspices of the American Federation of Musicians, and union rules stated that sessions couldn't go beyond three hours without a break for the musicians and engineers. In Los Angeles, sessions were much more informal, and there were typically no scheduled breaks.

Things got off to a bad start at 52nd Street. Being a hands-on producer in Los Angeles, Lou Adler sat down at the board next to the engineer and began adjusting the pots, which was a violation of union rules. Only trained engineers could touch the equipment, and Lou was warned. When he violated that rule a second time, the session was shut down. Lou quickly placed a phone call to Clive Davis, in hopes of raining down holy fire on the engineer who dared to embarrass him, but he regretfully conveyed to him that even he was powerless against union rules. The sessions were then moved to Atlantic Records' recording facilities a dozen blocks east at 1841 Broadway where Scott, John and Dick were joined by session musicians Chuck Rainey on electric bass and noted jazz drummer Ted Sommer, giving the songs a fuller sound. Sessions began around 11:00 p.m. each night and ended around 4:00 a.m., which was unusual for New York, where studio recordings typically took place during regular business hours.

Six tracks were laid down, including two other John Phillips originals, "Twelve Thirty" and "Rooms." Tim Hardin's "Don't Make Promises" was also recorded, which Scott had been performing live at his recent concerts opening for the Mamas & the Papas. A second Hardin song, "Reason to Believe," Donovan's "Celeste," and the Lovin' Spoonful's "It's Not Time Now" were also recorded and shipped back to Los Angeles for Lou to mix and overdub. The rest of the album was filled out with songs that Scott previously recorded, including both sides of his hit singles and the A-side of his 1966 single "No, No, No, No, No," and would be Ode's debut LP in December.

Next up was the Mamas & the Papas' Sullivan appearance at CBS Studios at 1697 Broadway, which would turn out to be their final one. The group lip-synched to their current hit, "Twelve Thirty," after which they had a bizarre conversation with Sullivan in which he asked questions about why this type of singing is popular, to which they responded with short answers, including a rare response from Denny, and head nods. In the second half of the show they mimed a medley of "California Dreamin'," "I Call Your Name" and "Monday, Monday." The banter between the quartet and Sullivan got even weirder. With questions about the group's future being whispered among fans and questioned in the trades, John and Cass used this as an opportunity to announce the group was going on hiatus and going to Europe for a long vacation.

The plan was to travel by boat from New York to England, disembark for an extended publicity tour of England culminating in a triumphant perfor-mance at the Royal Albert Hall on October 31. That would be followed by a performance at the Olympia in Paris, and then it was off to the island of Mallorca, located off the east coast of Spain in the Mediterranean Sea, for some well-deserved rest, relaxation, and inspiration. Everybody agreed and were eager to spend a good period of time back in a warm climate, only this time around with fame and money. Lou even agreed to join them. He and girlfriend Jill Gibson would fly to London and meet up with them after Scott McKenzie's own publicity tour in support of his new single.

In true Mamas & Papas style, they forgot to make cruise reservations but were able to secure last-minute bookings on the SS *France* bound for Le Havre, France, after the shipping company, Compagnie Générale Maritime, reached out to them after hearing their announcement on the Sullivan show. Though Spain was their ultimate destination, on this trip, they'd only go as far as Southampton, England, where they'd be escorted to London by their friend, the Rolling Stones' manager Andrew Oldham.

Once again, the vacation would be a family affair, but on a smaller scale. Joining the group was Scott McKenzie, Cass' new boyfriend Leland Kiefer, road manager Peter Pilafian, and a few assistants. They made their way down to Pier 88 on the Manhattan Cruise Terminal on Friday, September 29, and boarded the ocean liner for a 2:00 p.m. departure. The journey across the Atlantic would take six days, and it got off to a good start. The ship's first port of call was Boston, where a roadie was sent ashore to score a pound of marijuana to last them through the trip. In England, they smoked hashish, not marijuana, and that prospect didn't sit well with John and the others.

From the onset, the group was treated like royalty. Although their bookings were last minute, they were given first-class accommodations. The *France* featured two grandiose dining rooms that required formal evening attire. The Mamas & the Papas and their entourage underdressed each evening and were never asked to adhere to the dress code. On one particular evening, John even wore a shoelace for a tie, drawing sneers and raised eyebrows from their blue-blooded shipmates. After dining on foie gras and caviar, they'd return to their staterooms and smoke grass and sip champagne under the crisp autumn moon, easily dispensing of their evidence in the ship's wake.

Everything was going groovy and reminiscent of the Virgin Islands trip until one of the *France*'s two fin stabilizers failed a couple days out from Southampton. Stabilizers are used to reduce ship motion while at sea and are solely for passenger comfort and nausea reduction. It occurred in the evening, while the group was enjoying a screening of the 1965 blockbuster film *Dr. Zhivago* in the ship's theater. As the *France* became noticeably rocky, affecting the picture on the screen, a crew member ran onstage and announced that one stabilizer had been lost and they might lose the other. Everyone was ordered back to their rooms and advised to don their life jackets and wait for further instructions.

John, and the others, who were high the entire trip, slipped and stumbled back to their cabins and obeyed orders as the smell of vomit wafted throughout the ship's corridors as it slammed to and fro among the waves. After Denny strapped two life jackets around Cass, who was freaking out and fearful of the worst, John lit up several joints to calm everybody down and they all got incredibly wasted, waking up a day later in much calmer waters.

After one more evening of fine dining, where the group managed to get dressed up in their finest Indian silks and received a standing ovation from their fellow passengers, everybody settled in as the ship neared Southampton and made its long docking process through the Solent strait and up the Southampton Water estuary. As they neared the cruise terminal, a purser made his way to their rooms and alerted them that a constable was waiting onshore to take Cass into custody and was ordered to seize all their passports. It was a sobering message, especially for a group hiding several ounces of marijuana, illegal in the United Kingdom since 1928, in the seams of their coats. As the blood rushed from John's face, he quietly ordered Cass to get rid of all the dope while he stalled the Customs and Immigration people. As he was still unaware of what the charge was, John's mind began racing as to what it could possibly be. Surely there was no way they could've known about the pot purchased back in Harvard Square, and why would they single out Cass?

As the minutes passed like hours, John grew increasingly anxious. He sent Michelle to find out what was keeping Cass. She went into her cabin and found her crouched above the floor of her bathroom in tears, ineffectively attempting to scoop of chunks of wet marijuana overflowing out of a backed-up toilet. Michelle took matters into her own hands by telling Cass to go join the others and went about systematically transferring the wet pot from one bathroom to the other, making Cass' mess practically invisible to the naked eye. When Cass returned, she told John and Denny that she had skipped out on a hotel bill back in the spring: the lavish Queen's Gate Terrace in London. She deduced that this is what the charge would be. John found this unbelievable, considering the money she had made with the band.

"I didn't, but a friend of mine probably did," she explained. "I gave him a couple of hundred pounds to pay the bill and I assumed he paid."

It was Pic Dawson, her sleazy, dope-dealing sometimes lover. As long as he was confined to Cass, they were forced to live with him, but now his actions were threatening the entire group. Michelle rejoined her sequestered friends in time to walk with them and the authorities down the gangplank, and the combustible mix of her stress and pregnancy hormones caused her to become enraged. As they reached the landing stage, the police placed Cass under arrest. Michelle, undaunted, pulled Cass toward the fleet of limousines dispatched by Andrew Oldham with officers on their heels. Lou and Jill arrived on the scene in one of the limos and the sight of Jill only served to intensify Michelle's anger. Though they were seen conversing cordially at the Monterey Pop Festival, Michelle still carried a lot of hurt from her temporary termination from the group. John took on the role of defense attorney and asked the arresting officers what the charges were. They advised him that this wasn't America, and they weren't required to inform Cass of the charges at this stage.

"If she doesn't know what she's being charged with, she's not going with you," John informed them as he motioned Cass and Michelle to a limo.

The police countered by parking their vehicles in their way, which resulted in a standoff. The Mamas & the Papas held their position inside the limo until the officer in charge called for a police matron. When she arrived, John and company were suitably intimidated. She was tall, larger than Cass and built like a rugby forward. She reached inside the limo, grabbed Cass' arm, and a tug-of-war ensued along with a lot of screaming and shouting. In the end, the matron, with assistance from six uniformed officers, won out. Michelle, still seething, jumped out of the limo and toward the matron and punched her right in the face.

"I'm coming back to book you for assault," the matron told her.

Michelle didn't budge. With her rage ratcheting up another notch, she made another run at the imposing matron. John held her back, but it wasn't easy. The last thing he wanted was half of his group sitting in a London slammer. As the police cars pulled away, they all collapsed to the pavement. The commotion was so hectic, none of them even realized their dope-dumping mission was successful. Nobody else was charged. Still enraged from the intrusion on their vacation, they did the only thing they could do, jump in their limos and follow Cass.

They took her to the Southampton police station, where she was charged with larceny. Hours later, she was curiously transferred to Scotland Yard in London, where she was strip-searched and held overnight. Since the hotel's complaint was a civil charge, no bail was set. Outside, word had gotten out and the media began surrounding police headquarters on Broadway in Victoria. John, Michelle, Denny, and Scott initiated a protest outside, making homemade "Free Mama Cass" signs. Fans had gotten wind of it and joined them in solidarity.

John, Michelle, Denny, Scott, Lou, Jill, and several other close friends and supporters filed into the courtroom to watch the arraignment. Cass wasn't the only one generating some heavy drama. In the spectator seating area, Michelle sat sobbing after instigating a fight with John over Jill's presence, which resulted in a screaming match in their limo on the way to the courthouse. Nevertheless, she sat down beside him while they waited for Cass to be escorted in. Lou and Jill sat across the aisle, and, when Lou glanced over at Michelle, she gave him the middle finger. Very casually, he got up and walked over to her.

"Michelle," he whispered to her, "You'd better think why you're so angry. You better just think about it."

He and Jill left the courtroom and, very shortly afterward, Cass was escorted in flanked by a bailiff and faced Magistrate Seymour Collins. It all proved extremely anticlimactic. Addressed as Cassandra Elliot and not her legal name, Ellen Naomi Cohen, the prosecution offered no evidence to support her skipping out on the hotel bill, or stealing keys or blankets, which forced the judge to throw out the case. He apologized to her on behalf of the court, telling her, "You leave this court without any stain on your character." Though it appeared to be just another witch hunt on a rock and roll star, the whole incident was much more duplicitous. Scotland Yard was really after the man who Cass trusted to pay the hotel bill, Pic Dawson. As the rock and roll community was growing larger and more international, so did his drug dealing, which put him on Interpol's radar. Whatever tactic they used to derive any information about Dawson out of Cass failed and she was released. Dawson drifted in and out of her life like allergies and she honestly could not say where he was. Getting back into her clothes and mustering up her dignity, she met up with her bandmates, friends, and fans and celebrated with a hash cookie she had kept in her purse, which she redeemed from a court officer. The police had no idea.

"Your London jails are wonderful," she quipped to a reporter outside Scotland Yard. "But there just weren't enough blankets in my cell last night. Believe me, one blanket doesn't go far around this chick!"

Everyone chuckled. It was as mirthful as a Beatles press conference circa 1964, and even though this incident appeared to unify the fractured group, it only served to widen the cracks on their façade. It all came to a head hours later at a party thrown to celebrate Cass' release at the Royal Garden Hotel where they were staying. Before the celebration commenced, everyone returned to their rooms to rest from this stressful experience. In the Phillips' room, Michelle still seemed overcome as she continued to cry, her emotions, no doubt, bolstered by being five months pregnant. John attempted to console her.

"What's the matter, honey," he asked.

"I think I'm in love with Lou Adler," she replied tearfully.

That was it for John. It seemed that any man he got close to, Michelle fell in love with, and it ended in bitter resentment. He grabbed his bag, left, and checked into a different hotel. But it wasn't wholly on Michelle this time around. John had taken little to no interest in her pregnancy and began slipping around behind her back, or so he thought. It's hard to deceive a deceiver. When she told John that she'd made special accommodations with the hospital to allow him in the delivery room, uncommon in those days, he was horrified.

"Surely I love you, Mitch, but I just couldn't be there," he told her.

Conversely, Lou was ecstatic that Michelle was pregnant. He bought clothes for the baby and had special maternity clothes made up. It naturally stirred up Michelle's resentment toward John and drew her closer to Lou. She decided the time was right to tell him about her feelings, and, in her hormone-filled state, walked to Lou and Jill's room. With Jill present, she began by telling him how annoyed she was by her presence on the trip, particularly since she had been her replacement. Seeing her constantly stirred up a bad memory of the hurtful letter from John, Denny, and Cass that terminated her employment. Lou certainly understood her feelings about that. What came next was a little more out of the blue.

"And second of all, I don't like that you're with her in the first place," she said. "Because I love you, very much, and I know that it's not fair for me to say this, but I don't want to see you with other women. Don't do it in my presence."

The Mamas & the Papas' psychodrama kept rolling along, and now Lou was tangled up in it. All he could do was stick his head in a bucket of ice he'd previously set aside to chill a bottle of champagne to try and defuse the situation with humor. Jill was noticeably put off by Michelle's gauche testimonial and they too checked out of the hotel shortly thereafter. Michelle's behavior had, once again, put a damper on everything and, although it seemed to be a capper on an already crazy day, the best was saved for last.

The group reconvened for a short press conference where Cass fielded questions from various reporters regarding her ordeal. She indicated strongly that they were all pretty shaken by the experience and decided to cut short their stay in London and head to Mallorca earlier than expected. Afterward, the Mamas & the Papas and their entourage headed to Cass' jail-release party at the Royal Garden with many London-based musicians and industry people in attendance, including Andrew Oldham and most of the Rolling Stones.

They all enjoyed rubbing elbows with their contemporaries and none more than Cass, so when she got an audience with Rolling Stones front man Mick Jagger, she began telling him about the whole nightmare. John overheard their conversation, sauntered over and rudely interrupted her mid-story.

"Mick, she's got it all wrong," he told him. "That's not how it was at all!"

It was particularly insulting for Cass. Not only was John's disruption done in front of one of her singing idols, and a global sex symbol, but Cass was pretty good at spinning a yarn. She'd had six years of talking to concertgoers from the stage while the musicians tuned up their instruments, and her savviness had become a cornerstone of Mamas & Papas' live shows. Whether it was his tone, his brashness, the stress from being jailed or simply 25 months of suppressed rage stemming from his verbal and nonverbal abuse, fat jokes, and/or dismissal of her talents, Cass finally exploded on John.

"FUCK YOU!" she screamed at him in front of everybody and stormed out of the room.

It was plain and simple and tame compared to other rock and roll fights, but it was significant for Cass. She'd never asserted herself to John like that before, and, though she didn't know it at the time, it was a turning point in her career. As she made her way into the lobby, she headed straight to Denny's room to vent and calm down. He had made a brief appearance at the party and then headed for the solace of his room and his Crown Royal bottle. And though he was a shadow of his former confident self, he was still her chief confidant in the group. Cass' knock woke him from a nap, and Denny was in a haze when he opened the door to a screaming Cass.

"Fuck him! I can't take any more of this shit!" she exclaimed. "That's it! You're on your own from now on! I quit!"

Denny quietly closed his door. He'd heard this tune before and figured it would all blow over by morning. But, this time, it didn't. Word of Michelle's declaration of love to Lou had spread, and it was further justification for Cass to split. She fled to new friend Graham Nash, who she first met a few months earlier while his group, the Hollies, were in Los Angeles, and stayed with him before heading on to Paris to deescalate.

On October 14, only 10 days after their announcements, the Mamas & the Papas' concerts at the Paris Olympia and the Royal Albert Hall at the end of the month were canceled. Local promoter Tito Burns, who booked the latter show, was highly miffed, calling the group's actions "unethical and unprofessional."

"If this is all they think of their British fans, they don't deserve to have any," he told *Disc and Music Echo*.

Amid all this group turmoil, a reporter from *Melody Maker* managed to track down Cass, who was still fuming over the whole incident and was quite open and honest with him.

"We thought that this trip could give the group some stimulation," she told him, "but this has not been so."

She continued by telling him that the group would never again work together in Europe but added that they were working on a new album. She further muddied the waters by adding that the group had done all they could and were just repeating themselves. To the outsider, the Mamas & the Papas certainly appeared to be over, but John didn't appear to take any of this seriously. In many ways, he too saw the writing on the wall and seemed to be at peace with it. In a *KRLA Beat* article published shortly before they left for England, he expressed his disenchantment with the music industry and with the product his group had been putting out lately.

"We're beginning to feel phony as artists," he told the reporter.

Unfazed by Cass' outburst and the whispers among fans and reporters, he stayed on in London for a few weeks, accompanying Scott McKenzie on his promotional tour for his new single. His old bandmate was treated like a hippie guru everywhere he went, which awakened some of the fear and paranoia that gripped him during his tenure with the Journeymen. Michelle was there too. After recognizing all the havoc she'd helped sow by looking around and seeing everybody except she and Scott had left the hotel, she groveled her way back into John's good graces and traveled with him, Peter Pilafian, Abe Somer, Ann Marshall, Scott, and his girlfriend to Paris and on to Belgium.

On a lark, all except Peter and Abe decided to take a side trip to Morocco after Michelle read a feature on Marrakesh in *Vogue*. It was a hip travel destination for many European musicians and bohemians and its timeless and exotic culture, not to mention looser drug laws, attracted them like a magnet. They spent several days dining, shopping the old-world marketplaces, getting high on hash and maajoun, and being treated like royalty at luxurious La Mamounia, where they occupied the King's Suite. The mazelike alleyways that wended throughout the city surely must've reminded them of St. Thomas, harkening back to a much happier time. Perhaps if Denny and Cass had joined them, it could've served as more of a galvanizer, but it wasn't meant to be. Both made their respective ways back to Los Angeles with the future of the Mamas & the Papas in doubt.

News of the split hit the British press within two weeks of the incident but wouldn't hit the United States until December. *KRLA Beat*, which was suffering financially and publishing less frequently, published a detailed time line of the events of October in their December 2 issue. Perhaps more intriguing was a prediction the same publication made in their end-of-year issue on December 31, 1966. "Longer-lived groups who will vanish include the Byrds and the Mamas & the Papas." For now, it seemed like that prediction had come true.

CHAPTER 24:
NOT SO SAFE IN MY GARDEN

After John and Michelle made their way home from the Mamas & the Papas' European trip, they settled back into their Bel Air mansion, where the party resumed. It, of course, included more sex and drugs, but it grew more excessive and dangerous. With the Mamas & the Papas group in shambles, things were about to get more raucous and disorganized as the finishing touches were being made on his home recording studio.

As John's success grew, so did his ego. Outside of Lou Adler, he couldn't take any constructive criticism or suggestions on how to improve upon his arrangements, and his erratic behavior and rock star entitlement, caused in part by his ever-increasing drug intake, had isolated him from many of the musicians and staff at Western Recorders. Rather than dignify their whispers and glances, he sought the protective isolation of his home, where the music, and not session fees and designated break times, would be the sole focus. There, he could also comfortably abuse his body and welcome the presence of drug dealers, sycophants, hippies, wanderers, and groupies without feeling judged.

John had planned this almost from the day he and Michelle moved in to 783 Bel Air Road. The idea was to completely gut Jeanette MacDonald's custom-made, abnormally large cedar closets on the second floor and fit in a fully functional studio and greenrom. And gut it they did! It was a crime against aesthetics as the closets were the grand spectacle of the house. The custom-made closet, originally constructed in the 1940s, consumed an entire wing of the second floor and portrayed old Hollywood opulence in all its grandeur. In order to create a suitable space for his pampered movie star bride, Gene Raymond lowered the cathedral ceiling above the living room to increase the square footage. Walking into the nearly 2,000 square foot area, the cedar smell, a natural moth repellent, was pleasantly overwhelming. The left side comprised an endless wall of cedar drawers of all shapes and sizes with several small enough to house a single pair of gloves to deep king-sized drawers where she could adequately stretch out her many designer ball gowns without fear of wrinkling or squashing. The right side contained additional drawers and a large hanging space for her many dresses and furs. Beyond that lay a large sitting area where MacDonald could comfortably try on her many outfits with friends or spend her quiet time. To add to the intrigue, the closet was only accessible through a secret panel, opened by the press of a button hidden underneath a nearby desk.

While Michelle's wardrobe was only a fraction of Jeanette MacDonald's, the closet stirred up her princess sensibilities and displayed the endless possibilities of things to come. It could've been another star in the crown of a young woman who grew up middle class only miles away, but, alas, it was not meant to be. Throughout the spring and summer of 1967, the costly, settled cedar was mercilessly ripped off the walls by contractors and tossed into a dumpster where their splintered, shattered remains were unceremoniously carried to a nearby landfill. Nothing was left for posterity, not even a brass handle.

While the demolition work was being done, John and Michelle waited on a variance from the City of Los Angeles' Department of City Planning that never arrived. As it turned out, it was illegal to build and maintain a commercial studio in a residential area, but John would not be deterred. When it came to his music career, he never met a "no" he couldn't find a way around and this was no exception. He worked out an agreement with his contractors to continue working illegally. Under the cover of night, they carried in all the flooring, wiring, soundproofing, and lighting required to erect a fully functional studio, and the biggest asset in all of this was Jeanette MacDonald's secret entranceway.

After the closet was gutted, a large waiting room was constructed and filled with couches, large designer pillows, and a coffee table that transformed into a craps table and a roulette wheel. They also brought in antique slot machines and music boxes to make it easier for visitors and session musicians to more enjoyably while away their downtime. At the end of that room was a walnut staircase that led to the Honest John Studio, which occupied the entire A-framed attic. The actual studio was clean and advanced. All the wiring was built into the walls and floors and covered over with wood paneling and floorboards. Inside the control room was a soundboard purchased from Western Recorders, which was in the process of being upgraded to higher-end boards built by Colin Sanders. He would go on to launch Solid State Logic, which would become one of the preeminent recording hardware manufacturers in the world.

John was always very magnanimous when it came to including his friends in his many ventures and placed perennial gofer Peter Pilafian in charge of wiring his new soundboard. Though Peter graduated from Cass Technical High School in Detroit, he was a novice when it came to audio engineering and it showed. There were several technical difficulties with the board that frustrated Lou Adler, who exclusively ran the board for the Mamas & the Papas sessions that took place there. Short circuits and blowouts weren't an uncommon occurrence.

The studio become operable in the spring of 1967, just before Monterey Pop, but wasn't fully functional until the New Year. One of the first things recorded there was the jingle effect at the beginning of Scott McKenzie's "San Francisco (Be Sure to Wear Flowers in Your Hair)." It was actually bells from a vintage toy truck John and Michelle owned that jingled when rolled. John also claims that, after the Monterey Pop Festival, he invited Ravi Shankar to stay at their home for a few days and recorded a few demos that have since been lost.

But, as the studio was unveiled and ready for use, the Mamas & the Papas were not. There hadn't been much communication between John and Michelle and the other two since their ill-fated trip to Europe in October, and, in John's mind, he'd moved on and the same could be said for Cass. John had purchased a movie camera and was preparing to enter the world of film with Lou Adler, spurred by the editing of the Monterey Pop Festival movie, and paid little-to-no attention to their next album, which was due soon. Throughout the fall and early winter, the party in Bel Air rolled on. Steve Brandt continued to coordinate wild galas that included many of their movie friends like Warren Beatty, Joan Collins, Roger Vadim and his wife Jane Fonda, Peter Sellers, director Roman Polanski and his model/actress wife Sharon Tate, who provided a perfect distraction from the 800-pound gorilla in the room. The Phillips were clearly going Hollywood. As the goose that laid the golden egg stood with his head on the chopping block, their personal life continued its tailspin into decadence and ruin. It would take a much more somber evening at 783 Bel Air Road to get John back on track, but before that could happen, the Mamas & the Papas reunited, not to sing or record but to take care of some financial business.

The year 1967 was a roller-coaster ride for the group, to say the least, and that's not including all the inner turmoil. It started out better than it finished in terms of chart success with "Dedicated to the One I Love" and "Creeque Alley" both going Top 5, followed by John and Michelle's engineering of the Monterey Pop Festival, but it ended with a whimper. Only two of their final three singles of the year crossed the Top 40 with "Twelve Thirty" peaking the highest at number 20. Their sole album, *Deliver,* hit number two in *Billboard* and number one in *Cash Box,* but they hadn't capitalized on that success by releasing anything subsequently. Still, on paper, the group appeared to be on a roll, and it was enough for them to call a meeting with Dunhill president Jay Lasker in order to restructure their contracts.

They didn't enter the meeting on the best of terms with the cantankerous label boss. The delay of their fourth album violated the terms of their initial contract and forced Dunhill to release a greatest hits package, forebodingly titled *Farewell to the First Golden Era.* Nevertheless, the name and hits still carried a lot of weight, and Lasker was eager to sign them. They were still the hottest act on the label. Since "Eve of Destruction," Barry McGuire had virtually dropped out of sight and P. F. Sloan, session musician Phil Sloan's singing alter ego, never really worked out as a performer. The Grass Roots' breakout hit "Let's Live for Today" hit the Top 10 in the summer of 1967 but they were still a year or more away from hitting their stride, as were newly signed Canadian rock band Steppenwolf, whose debut LP, which contained their monster hit "Born to Be Wild," wouldn't be released until January 1968. With all these question marks, the Mamas & the Papas still had the upper hand.

Their accountant sent Lasker a letter talking about how broke they were although it was really Denny and Cass who were suffering the most.

John's royalties were still lucrative, bringing in nearly $500,000 over the fall months of 1967, but he wanted to cash in before the whole group went up in flames. It was nicely worded but basically threatened no new product until they cut a new deal that increased their royalty rate. Lasker read between the lines and, over the course of several weeks, shaped a new deal through Abe Somer's law firm, Mitchell, Silberberg & Knupp. John also participated in the renegotiations and was rather cavalier about it. Mentally, he was moving on from the Mamas & the Papas but kept that sentiment very well hidden. He brought along Michelle to a few preliminary meetings but her aggressive demeanor, brought on partially by being in her third trimester, caused John to end her participation prematurely. The desired result was to get everybody more money and her contentious relationship with Jay Lasker threatened that.

In the end, a satisfactory contract was ironed out. Their royalty rate would double, and their future would be set on ABC/Dunhill. ABC was satisfied because it could happily include the Mamas & the Papas, as well as promises of future solo releases by Cass and Denny, as part of their aggressive 59 album rollout over the winter months of 1968. But, as it had been so many times in the group's short history, there was tension at the collective signing in the conference room at Mitchell, Silberberg & Knupp and it was brought on by one tiny little clause in the new contract that nearly got overlooked.

When Michelle arrived, she had a sneaking suspicion. The emotional turmoil she sustained during her temporary ouster from the group over a year earlier still lingered whenever they all got together, and it mixed with the natural infusion of hormones that takes place near the end of a typical pregnancy. Fueled by that and her contentious relationship with Jay Lasker, which led to her omission from subsequent meetings, she decided to read the terms of the contract before signing it. Everything seemed to be in order until she got to the clause about solo pursuits.

It stated that in the event that the Mamas & the Papas disband, John, Denny, and Cass were free to refer to themselves publicly, and on their prod-ucts, by the title of "Mama" or "Papa," respectively. Michelle was not given the same permission. Under no circumstance was she allowed to refer to her-self as "Mama" Michelle Phillips. It was incredibly insulting and exclusionary, and it pierced Michelle to the core.

"What the fuck is this?" she asked incredulously of everyone in the room.

She pointed to the offending clause and read it aloud. A lot of brow-furrowing and head-scratching ensued, particularly between John and Lou, but nobody laid claim to it. Michelle focused her gaze on Jay Lasker, the new president of ABC/Dunhill Records, with whom she'd clashed from the moment they met. Lasker was an old-school record exec who jumped into the world of pop music after serving in the Army during World War II. Starting off at Decca Records as a low-level sales rep, he worked his way up to Detroit branch manager by 1951 and VP of sales by 1956. Before teaming up with Lou Adler and his Dunhill partners in 1965, he'd been the inaugural sales VP at Frank Sinatra's Reprise Records in 1960 and later served in the same capacity at the independent Del-Fi, Kapp and Vee-Jay labels. In his time, he'd helped break Bill Haley & the Comets' "Rock Around the Clock" and the Beatles in America when Vee-Jay picked up the option to release their singles after Capitol passed in 1963. His gruff demeanor, combined with his two decades of experience, not to mention his alleged mob ties, made him an intimidating presence to even the most hardened of agents and artists, but Michelle would not be moved.

"What the fuck is this?" she asked again, this time looking straight at Jay.

Her countenance was hot as the tension of the last 27 months was now boiling over in the law offices of Mitchell, Silberberg & Knupp. Lasker personified every grief-stricken moment she'd experienced as a "Mama," which was now on the verge of being taken away from her. She hearkened back to Lasker referring to the group as "animals" to Lou not long after he'd signed them, her temporary firing from the group, the letter signed by her bandmates who "no longer desired to record or perform" with her, and the ramped-up demands put on the group by the label to push out more product since the acquisition by ABC.

She and Lasker stared at one another like two gunfighters in an Italian western, both seeking to blow the other off the face of the earth. Lasker had no love for Michelle either. She was a hard, outspoken negotiator who made the contract renegotiation tougher and less profitable for Dunhill, and she was also a woman playing hardball in a man's world. After about a minute he slammed his briefcase shut and stormed out of the conference room with Abe Somer chasing after him. When Abe returned alone, he told them Lasker was insulted by the way Michelle looked at him like he was a piece of shit and that he wasn't going to sign the contract.

After several days, things cooled off and the contract was signed. Everybody won. Dunhill had the Mamas & the Papas locked in and the group got their royalty rate doubled. Michelle was also able to retain the use of the name "Mama Michelle" should she decide to pursue a solo career. But it was time to get back to work. They were nearly a quarter of a year late on their fourth LP and, with only four songs in the can, it had to be finished quickly for a spring release.

Back in August 1967, before the shit hit the fan, during a burst of creativity and inspiration brought on by Honest John Studio, John was able to wrangle everybody to Bel Air and get to work on the next LP. But it was not an easy process for anyone involved. The whole group, except for Michelle, who was three months pregnant, were still self-medicated and getting worse. In fact, it was here that Cass revealed to Denny that she'd begun using heroin, which alarmed everybody, even John. The studio musicians not only had to put up with their drug-and-alcohol-infused moodiness and sloth but with a studio that wasn't yet fully finished and had plenty of technical challenges, not to mention a completely kooky atmosphere.

The musicians, notably Hal Blaine, Joe Osborn, Larry Knechtel, Eric Hord, and David Cohen, would arrive in the afternoon to set up the studio and get tuned up. Since construction was still ongoing, it aroused suspicion from many of the neighbors who routinely noticed construction company vehicles parked in the driveway and supplies and equipment being moved in and out with no noticeable work being done. As the complaints mounted, zoning inspectors were dispatched to look around but couldn't find anything. Everything took place behind the secret entranceway. To keep the masquerade going more efficiently, a bevy of musical instruments were set up in the hookah lounge so that whenever an inspector or a police officer knocked on the door, everyone could be notified by a bell that ran from the foyer to the studio that John had specially installed. When summoned, they'd immediately stop what they were doing and run downstairs to them and acted like they were practicing.

The technical staff, which was mostly Peter Pilafian, wasn't very adept at mixing. He'd also dressed very flamboyantly, often running around in capes, earning the nickname "Count Pilaf," which made his ineptitude even more frustrating to the seasoned veterans. Over the course of August and parts of

September, the group recorded three new songs, "Gemini Childe," "Midnight Voyage," and "Rooms," the latter of which featured guitarists John York, on the verge of replacing Chris Hillman in the Byrds, and Paul Downing. After the hiatus that lasted throughout October, November, and most of December, sessions resumed after Christmas. The session musicians who participated in the late summer/early fall sessions returned to the clandestine studio and, although it was more complete than the one they left, the ancillary distractions that made the atmosphere considerably more unprofessional than a commercial studio still lingered.

John and Michelle typically slept in until 4:00 or 5:00 in the afternoon most days and a big meal would be served up in the dining room by their housekeeper Esperanza. Peter Pilafian would usually arrive around the same time to clean the studio up from whatever took place the night before and set up the board while the session musicians gathered and began setting up with Cass and Denny arriving around 7:00 or 8:00. Lots of time was wasted and too often recording wouldn't even begin until around 10:00 p.m.

John's writer's block continued, and, just as he had done with the last two album sessions, he came in with next to nothing. In fact, he wrote most of the remaining album tracks during the actual recording sessions beginning with "Safe in My Garden," which was started on December 27 but not finished until early January. And, although the songs were much more mature and showed him moving in the direction of his contemporaries like Lennon and McCartney and Brian Wilson, nothing was standing out as being hit-worthy. It surely must've concerned him as Jay Lasker was demanding product to keep the Mamas & the Papas relevant and profitable and things weren't looking too good at the moment. That all changed on a rare quiet night at his Bel Air home when Michelle's father and his wife came over for dinner.

Much of the evening's conversation centered on music, and John was reminiscing about a song from his youth, which he'd been humming for several days, "Dream a Little Dream of Me." It was a song the group used often for vocal warmups and, with recording for the fourth LP underway, it was fresh on his mind. It had been recorded and released twice in 1931, first by Ozzie Nelson and His Orchestra, followed by a version by Wayne King and His Orchestra with vocals by Ernie Birchill that went to number one. The simple little ditty became a standard when Kate Smith sang it on her premier broadcast of *Kate Smith Sings* on NBC Radio on May 1, 1931, and on many subsequent shows, it became one of her signature songs.

As John picked and hummed it, Gil talked about knowing one of the song's writers, Fabian Andre, and how he, Michelle and Rusty stayed at his home in Mexico City in 1951. The two had become friends while Andre was living in Los Angeles in the 1940s and he kindly offered to put Gil and his two daughters up while he enrolled in Mexico City College to study sociology and psychology courtesy of the G.I. Bill.

Andre and co-songwriter Wilbur Schwandt wrote the melody while touring the Midwest with their band, the Midnight Serenaders, in 1930. Renowned songwriter Gus Kahn, who'd already written the standards "I'll See You in My Dreams," "It Had to Be You" and "Yes Sir, that's My Baby," composed the lyrics. After its initial burst of fame, the song lay dormant for many years, regaining a degree of popularity when the King Cole Trio revived it on their radio show in 1947. In 1950, seven versions were recorded, two of which charted, one by Frankie Laine and the other by Jack Owens and the melody was often used as incidental music in The Adventures of Ozzie and Harriet TV show.. This is most likely John's first interaction with the song as a high school freshman dialed into *Your Hit Parade*.

That same year, in Mexico City, Fabian Andre, who never replicated the success he had with "Dream a Little Dream of Me," received a modest financial boon with its new hit versions. He'd spent most of his time drinking and milling about the neighborhood of Colonia Cuauhtémoc, where he'd often visit and spend time playing piano for young Michelle and her sister who were guests in his home for three months while Gil got settled. Eventually, Gil moved his daughters, and new girlfriend, into a home in Colonia Roma, and Michelle never saw Andre again. His name became a distant recollection until her time in the Mamas & the Papas when she heard, erroneously, that he'd died falling down an elevator shaft in 1960. He'd died alone in his room of natural causes.

The song was right up Cass' alley and Gil suggested to John that they record it. Over the course of the next week to 10 days, John mentally filed it away as he wrote and recorded "For the Love of Ivy," a title given to him by ABC Pictures who were producing a movie of the same title featuring Sidney Poitier. It was a tedious attempt at an opus with stacked vocals, consonance and dissonance, radical chord changes, and a tribute to street corner doo-wop as

John incorporated the familiar refrain of the Moonglows' 1954 hit "Sincerely." Vocal sessions went on for the better part of a week, and John drove everybody crazy periodically recording overdubs throughout the month of January.

Perhaps as an effort to decompress, he snagged Cass on the evening of January 4 to make a run at "Dream a Little Dream of Me." Like so many stories in the Mamas & the Papas' history, the perspective differs on just how eager Cass was to record it. John said she was difficult, and he had to drag it out of her. Cass maintained that she loved the song and was pleasantly surprised at John's suggestion and happily sang it. It was most likely a mix of both.

Cass did indeed love the song. Back in her pre-Big 3 days, when she was seeking a career on Broadway, singing this style of song was essential, but perhaps it felt like another desperate attempt by John to fill out the album with more covers. In the pop world of 1968, self-sustaining artists were the rage. The Beatles, who over the span of the last six months put out the landmark *Sgt. Pepper* album followed less than six months later by the nearly as brilliant *Magical Mystery Tour*. In fact, they hadn't included a non-original song since their *Help!* album 28 months earlier. Similarly, standard-bearers like the Rolling Stones, Simon & Garfunkel, and the Jefferson Airplane had given up cover songs in favor of fresh, original material much to their success, with many others following suit. For those on the cutting edge of the pop music scene, covers were passé. John had entered the last two album's sessions with a lack of original material and was forced to resort to covers. So, perhaps, if Cass or any other band member was annoyed, it was because John was becoming a less and less prolific songwriter, which threatened their standing.

That could explain Cass opening the session with a negative attitude, which caught John's attention. The Beatles had the current number one with "Hello, Goodbye" and the rest of the Top 10 was filled with original gems written by either the artist themselves or professional songwriters and here she was dusting off an old standard that was more likely to attract her mother than kids listening to Cream and Janis Joplin. There was nothing noteworthy about the session other than John having Cass sing it while standing atop a piano. She channeled her best Ella Fitzgerald as John whittled the arrangement down from foxtrot to slow dancer. When she finished, it was just another session. There were more songs to record and more overdubbing to be done as she quietly contemplated her future with the group and her solo career. Most of the instrumentation was overdubbed in the coming weeks but, when it emerged, like he'd done a year earlier with "Dedicated to the One I Love," John put his imprint on it, so much so that it sounded like one of his originals.

Over the next week, John and the group polished off three more originals, "Safe in My Garden," "Too Late" and the 40 second throwaway, "The Right Somebody to Love," where Michelle mimics the singing of a prepubescent girl. Whether by design or not, they took the next six weeks off and though they had nine songs in the can, including "Twelve Thirty," it still wasn't enough to fill an entire album or placate Jay Lasker. But John had a built-in excuse. Michelle was in her ninth month of pregnancy and needed to rest. There would be time enough to finish the album afterward. There was little Lasker could do and if John did indeed use it to buy time, it wasn't because he'd suddenly turned into Father Knows Best. He had another female on his mind and it wasn't his wife or his soon-to-be-born daughter. This one stood about 5'4", wore a pixie hairdo, and was married to one of the most powerful men in show business.

When Bob Dylan issued his album *The Times They Are A-Changin'* in January 1964, the meaning behind the title track seemed symbolic; a mere suggestion at the postwar undercurrent sweeping up baby boomer youth most likely met with scoffs or was dismissed altogether by any self-sustaining adult who even condescended to listen to it. Exactly four years later, the song seemed completely prophetic. With the rise of the Beatles, who crashed North America 25 days after the release of Dylan's album, the passing of the Civil Rights Act, the escalation of the conflict in Vietnam, the free speech movement, women's rights and the rise in drug use, the cultural landscape had taken a wild turn that nobody could've anticipated even a year earlier.

There were several politicians and entertainers who became personifications of each of these facets. For the women's lib portion, one actress who unwittingly represented the much more independent role women were taking on in Western society was Mia Farrow, although that was never really her intent when she burst on the scene in the fall of 1964 in the ABC prime time soap opera *Peyton Place*. Only 19 years old, she portrayed Allison MacKenzie, the mixed-up illegitimate daughter of local clothier Constance MacKenzie. Farrow's performance perfectly encapsulated the demure, waifish protagonist often the center of controversy in the dramatic little town and involved in a romantic relationship with Rodney Harrington, the handsome eldest son of Leslie Harrington, the rich owner of the town's textile plant, and his wife Catherine. Naturally, the circumstances of Allison and Rodney's backgrounds make it impossible for them to be together openly, resulting in many an interesting plot point.

In reality, Mia was the eldest daughter of noted film writer and director John Farrow and leading actress Maureen O'Sullivan, best known for her role as Jane Parker in three Tarzan features that starred Johnny Weissmuller as the legendary king of the jungle. Her father, a native Australian who claimed to be a descendant of King Edward VII, had been in movies since the silent era when his screenplay for the *Wreck of the Hesperus* was picked up by DeMille Pictures. Nine years and approximately 20 screenplays later, he directed his first feature in *Tarzan Escapes*, which co-starred his future wife.

Although Mia and her dad had a tender father-daughter relationship, his infidelities made him emotionally unavailable and it only worsened when their eldest child, Michael, was tragically killed in an airplane crash while the entire family was away in Spain filming *John Paul Jones*, John Farrow's final film. The entire family, which was at one time very tight-knit, went into free fall. Less than four years later, just as Mia's own acting career was taking flight, her father died of a heart attack while estranged from her mother. All their issues remained unresolved.

Shortly after accepting her role on *Peyton Place*, Mia met legendary singer Frank Sinatra while visiting the set of his film *Von Ryan's Express* at the 20th Century Fox studio located near the set of her show. She was invited by one of the film's co-stars, Johnny Leyton, with whom she'd worked on the film *Guns at Batasi* a year earlier. After Sinatra sent a gaggle of his associates to inquire about her age, he personally invited her to accompany him to a private screening of his new release, *None but the Brave*.

A whirlwind romance ensued but was kept under wraps for months, although occasional speculation appeared in gossip columns. The nearly 30-year age difference would be hugely scandalous and fodder for the press. Only those closest to Sinatra knew. They finally announced their romance to the world at a charity event in Hollywood in midsummer 1965 and followed that up with a wedding nearly one year later, gasps and guffaws notwithstanding.

Despite their large age gap, there was genuine tenderness and love there, but it was doomed from the start. Much like Joe DiMaggio and Marilyn

Monroe, Sinatra desired Mia to be a more traditional housewife and be subject to his whims. It would be nothing for them to be in New York and Sinatra
suddenly decide he wanted to jaunt to Las Vegas. Mia would have to comply
and sit with the other wives when he drank, laughed and gambled with his
buddies. Mia wasn't particularly imbued with the new feminism that was
bubbling under the surface for women her age. It's more that she just wasn't
ready or bred for that.

The tipping point came after Mia accepted the role of a lifetime, the lead in
Roman Polanski's *Rosemary's Baby*, based on Ira Levin's current best-selling
horror novel. She'd portray Rosemary Woodhouse, a diminutive young Catholic housewife selected by a coven of witches to carry the devil's child. Even
though Sinatra had planned for Mia to abandon her career after their wedding, he nevertheless encouraged her to take the role. Inside, however, he was
seething. He desired her to co-star with him in his next feature, *The Detective*.
She had, after all, quit *Peyton Place* at his insistence. The great compromise
was that they'd film their respective films concurrently and figure out what
to do afterward. When filming for *Rosemary's Baby* fell behind while *The
Detective*'s stayed on schedule, Sinatra had enough. He had his attorney draw
up divorce papers that were delivered to her on set at Paramount Studios in
Hollywood. Mia meekly signed them, and they were never spoken of.

Though they maintained a cordial relationship, Mia was now free to
explore the Los Angeles social scene with people closer her age, which is
when she met John Phillips. They had mutual friends in Roman Polanski
and his wife Sharon Tate, and they'd often meet up at the various gatherings
in their respective neighborhoods of Bel Air and Brentwood, not to mention
the artistic hot spot of Laurel Canyon. Their friendship quickly escalated into
a romance. To complicate matters, Michelle had also gotten to know Mia
through Ann Marshall, and the two women had formed a legitimate friendship. The free love vibe of the day should've been enough to perpetuate their
romance but human emotion, as always, overrode everything. Michelle, near
the end of her pregnancy, got incredibly jealous and hurt. It should've been
a time that brought her and John closer together, but it instead pushed them
further apart, and for the final time.

Things subsided when Mia split for India with her sister Prudence to study
transcendental meditation under Maharishi Mahesh Yogi not long after the
New Year. Inspired by his liaisons with Mia, and her waifish personality, John

composed one final song for the Mamas & the Papas' fourth LP, "Meditation Mama," on which he sang solo for the first and only time in group history. John and Mia did have several sexual encounters, but the relationship was always noncommittal. John mostly used it as a weapon against Michelle. She'd been killing him with trysts for seven years, and now it was his time to fire back.

After the birth of John and Michelle's daughter, Chynna Gilliam, on February 12, 1968, the handwriting was on the wall. The couple took a few weeks in March to retreat to Palm Springs for a reset, but John brought Mia along with them, and the two split for Joshua Tree, a national park east of Los Angeles that had recently become a popular hippie hangout. For several months in 1968, John and Mia had a minor affair, going to parties, to the beach and hanging with Roman Polanski and Sharon Tate. When *Rosemary's Baby* was released in June 1968, John and Mia got a kick out of sneaking into various movie theaters to watch it.

After Michelle fully recovered from her pregnancy, she retaliated by having an affair with British film documentarian John Sheppard and traveled with him to the East Coast while he was filming the Doors. When their relationship soured, she called John from his sister's in Washington, D.C., telling him she wanted to come back home. Sensing her vulnerability, John pounced.

"I'm in love with Mia Farrow," he told her.

Unmoved, Michelle came back anyway and made a concerted effort to try and win John back, even asking him to choose between Mia and her, but it was ultimately an empty plea. It was motivated more by pride than by love. The marriage was all but over. There was no support between partners, only petty, childish head games designed to torpedo each other's respective affairs to force them back together temporarily. For the sake of Chynna, they soldiered on for the remainder of the year, which gave both enough time to plan their exit strategies.

John and Michelle weren't the only two in the Mamas & the Papas with romantic problems. Denny had isolated himself from the group and was heading for ruin. His alcoholism had overcome him. His finances were being drained and he'd surrounded himself with leeches who were taking advantage of his good nature. Although Cass had seemingly written him off as she watched him pathetically pine away for Michelle these last two and a half years, she still loved him and believed deep down there was a chance for them romantically. She'd effectively buried her emotions but seeing him harm himself brought them all out again. One night, not long after the sessions for the fourth album had ended, she ventured to his home one last time only to find him drunk and surrounded by spongers. When she managed to pull him away from everybody, she proposed to him, but it was a fool's errand. Denny just laughed and made a joke of it, and Cass left him for the final time. If anything, it was confirmation that it was time for her not only to move on from him but from the Mamas & the Papas as well.

On May 14, 1968, the Mamas & the Papas' fourth album dropped with the uninspired title *The Papas & the Mamas*, and it very much mirrored the gloomy state of John and Michelle's marriage. The album peaked at number 15 and carried with it an unfamiliar, somber tone whereas previous efforts had been rousing, jangly and much more upbeat. Songs like "Safe in My Garden," "Mansions," and "Too Late" reflected a darker side of John's music not present before that didn't resonate with the record-buying public. There were always gems, particularly the inclusion of "Twelve Thirty," "Gemini Childe" and "Rooms," and the real crowd-pleaser "Dream a Little Dream of Me." There was no promotion outside of ads in trade magazines and tabloids and no TV appearances or radio interviews, which kept the album off the radar of a public inundated with endless musical possibilities.

Despite its poor chart showing, the sparser arrangement and muted harmonies did show that John was in step with the times. The fire of the psychedelic era enkindled by the Byrds and perfected by the Beatles, which in turn influenced bands on both sides of the Atlantic, was effectively doused by Bob Dylan and the Hawks. While the Summer of Love was in full swing, Dylan and the Canadian band that backed him up on his 1966 tour, made up of Robbie Robertson, Garth Hudson, Rick Danko, and Richard Manuel, were holed up in the basement of the Hawks' shared rental home in West Saugerties, New York.

As the Beatles, the Stones, and the groups in San Francisco were pushing the limits of sonic dissonance, they rehearsed endlessly in a makeshift studio from June to October as Dylan was convalescing from his motorcycle accident. Beginning with mostly country, folk, and blues covers, the sessions eventually unfolded into a platform for dozens of new Dylan originals that reignited his own career and a spate of new cover material for other artists. In

October, Dylan headed to Nashville with a batch of songs he kept for himself that would form his eighth studio album, *John Wesley Harding*. Lyrically, the songs were a hybrid of the long, meandering and verbose song structures of the past and the more succinct lyrics that would come in his next few albums. Musically, however, the album was ridiculously simple, with only Dylan on acoustic guitar, Kenny Buttrey on drums, and Charlie McCoy on bass, with occasional steel guitar overdubs from Pete Drake to give a few songs a laid-back country feel. When it was released in late December 1967, it took critics and fans by surprise and though it didn't comport with what was going on at the time, it was a bold, confident reaction by the artist many had mimicked only two and a half years earlier.

The Hawks followed Dylan seven months later with their more muscle-packed take on Dylan's new style. Changing their name to the Band, they signed with Capitol Records and released the anti-psychedelic masterpiece *Music from Big Pink*, influencing the likes of Beatle George Harrison and Eric Clapton so much so that the latter actually sought the group out to ask to join them. Clapton was riding high with Cream, but the music of the Band proved so influential to him that he moved them away from musical experimentation to something more straightforward and heavier. Other power trios like the Jimi Hendrix Experience followed suit and several were formed using this new Cream blueprint.

But, perhaps this biggest endorsement of this new style ushered in by Bob Dylan would eventually come from the two biggest pop bands in the world, the Beatles and the Rolling Stones. On November 22, 1968, the Beatles would release their stripped-down, eponymous double LP, known affectionately as the *White Album*, and the Stones would return to form two weeks later with the release of *Beggars Banquet*. Both albums featured remarkable 180-degree turns from their psychedelic offerings of 1967.

Lost in all this was the Mamas & the Papas' latest LP. Based on some of the current musical trends, the album met much of the criteria, but the writing was on the wall. Since Monterey, and the rise of the San Francisco groups, and with many of the artists on the cutting edge getting harder and heavier, groups that relied on harmony were on the way out. The Beach Boys and the Four Seasons, who had managed to commingle with the Beatles and the Byrds in 1965 and 1966, had now reached a commercial low point. Others like the Association, the 5th Dimension, and Spanky & Our Gang were relegated to sunshine pop and could find no place among the rock and roll elite. Still, there were exceptions in artists like Buffalo Springfield and Simon & Garfunkel but, in April 1968, the former stood on the brink of collapse and the latter would do the same less than two years later after the release of their most successful album, *Bridge Over Troubled Water*. The Mamas & the Papas had no place to fit in and had become borderline square. It seemed that John was done in by his own music festival.

After the Mamas & the Papas' first single off the album, "Safe in My Garden," stiffed, Jay Lasker and executives at Dunhill saw the writing on the wall and were desperate to salvage something out of the group's long-overdue album. They couldn't rely on John anymore. His tank was empty. He was out of ideas and seemed more interested in abusing his body with drugs and sex. The answer lay in that charming little chestnut, "Dream a Little Dream of Me," he recorded with Cass back in January.

In their short career, the Mamas & the Papas made several TV appearances and a common denominator, outside of their incredible music, was Cass' charming personality. She was always the spokesperson of the group and displayed an effervescent and delightful personality. Coupled with her honey-sweet vocals and amazing range, Dunhill knew it had the makings of a solo star. Mama Cass! The decision was made to issue "Dream a Little Dream of Me" as the follow-up single only two weeks after "Safe in My Garden." Though it wasn't a John Phillips original, it was the strongest track on the album and was a natural contender for chart success. The problem for John was, when it was released as a single, the label read "Mama Cass featuring the Mamas & the Papas." He was incensed.

It was a double slap in the face for him. Not only was his original single abandoned so quickly but, since the beginning, he and Cass had been rivals. Brain versus voice. From their earliest association, he never wanted her in the group, and, despite her invaluable contributions that were essential to their success, the feeling always remained, even though he never came right out and said it. It was more than evident in his demeanor toward her, the snarky comments he'd make to and about her and his overworking of her in the studio. Now, Mama Cass was the label's focus, and she was all too willing to pick up the baton. She'd been looking for a graceful exit and John hand-delivered it to her.

"Dream a Little Dream of Me" hit number 12 in *Billboard* and number 10 in *Cash Box*, earning Cass a three-album deal as a solo artist on ABC/Dunhill and there was no looking back. Her newfound solo success officially spelled the end of the Mamas & the Papas although they hadn't fulfilled the stipulations in their contract. That would come back to haunt them later. A futile attempt to keep the band's name in the charts was attempted when "For the Love of Ivy" was released as a single in August. It peaked at number 81, effectively sealing their fate. There was no meeting, no announcement and no press conference. There really wasn't a need for any. As Cass went off to promote her single and record her debut album, Denny would sink further into alcoholism while John and Michelle would retreat to Bel Air, forced to recognize that their marriage was over.

In a story that's been told both by John and Michelle, in their respective autobiographies, one of the most remarkable features at 783 Bel Air Road was the marvelous crystal chandelier that hung in the foyer and was visible in the evening to passing motorists. It was lit by hundreds of bulbs and, over the course of their two-year residency, one by one, each began to blow out. After a while, it became very noticeable and embarrassing for Michelle, who'd often ask John to please get on a ladder and replace them. He always said he would, but he never did. As 1968 meandered through a blur into 1969, the last bulb finally blew out figuratively and literally. In January 1969, Michelle and Chynna moved out, leaving John alone to carry on the endless party, which he did willingly. As always, he surrounded himself with women and friends, sex and drugs to masquerade the disappointment that surely must've eaten away at him during those few sober moments of truth. When he wasn't stoned and did have to face them, he had to accept the fact that his beloved musical creation, the Mamas & the Papas, was over. What started with a dream ended with a dream.

CHAPTER 25:
A DREAM ENDS A DREAM

For pop music, the difference between when the Mamas & the Papas called it quits in 1968 and 1971 were like night and day. The seismic shifts that took place following the release of the Band's *Music from Big Pink* at the height of summer 1968 had a profound effect that shook up everyone from established artists to up-and-comers. The Beatles and the Rolling Stones put out perhaps their best efforts of the 1960s in *Abbey Road* and *Beggars Banquet*, respectively, and the Who redefined themselves with their celluloid rock opera *Tommy*. Their roller-coaster efforts inspired a new breed of British rock and rollers who would go on to redefine the genre again in David Bowie, Yes, King Crimson and Genesis among others.

In the United States, Bob Dylan flummoxed everybody again by putting out a country album recorded exclusively in Nashville called *Nashville Skyline,* and his unique career kept chugging along. The Mamas & the Papas' other folk-rock contemporaries didn't fare much better than they did. The Lovin' Spoonful of 1969 contained none of their friends from Greenwich Village. After Zal Yanovsky was unceremoniously dismissed in 1967, John Sebastian exited exactly one year later and bummed around between Los Angeles and Broadway writing songs for Murray Schisgal's musical *Jimmy Shine*. He'd eventually record a solo album that wouldn't be released until January 1970. Barry McGuire, who'd also spent time on Broadway as a cast member of *Hair*, was back in Los Angeles by 1969 with no record deal and delving deeper into drugs and leeching off Denny's generosity. The Byrds had essentially become Roger McGuinn and his hired hands, including guitar virtuoso Clarence White, but it was co-founder David Crosby who found the most success. After his firing from the band in October 1967, his friendship with Buffalo Springfield singer/guitarist Stephen Stills grew deeper. When his band called it quits in May 1968, the two commiserated together regularly and put their frustrations to good use by writing songs and recording demos. When Cass Elliot introduced them to newly minted ex-Hollie Graham Nash, a new type of power trio was born after David and Graham discovered they harmonized beautifully together. In May 1969, they released their self-titled debut and it rapidly became a million seller.

Up in San Francisco, the groups who put John and Lou through the wringer over the Monterey Pop Festival were sorting themselves out too. The cream that rose to the top were the Grateful Dead and Jefferson Airplane, although, by 1969, the latter was beginning to splinter. They too were influenced by *Music from Big Pink* as well as the Crosby, Stills & Nash debut, which allowed them to shed their psychedelic skins and craft simpler arrangements. Their contemporaries Quicksilver Messenger Service and Country Joe & the Fish struggled to find a nationwide audience and would fracture or disband altogether in the not-so-distant future. Big Brother & the Holding Company completely collapsed after Janis Joplin left for a successful solo career in December 1968.

All this change culminated in the Woodstock Music and Art Fair held in Bethel, New York, on 600 acres of local resident Max Yasgur's dairy farm property from August 15 to 18, 1969. It was greatly influenced by the Monterey Pop Festival and was billed as "3 Days of Peace & Music," although it didn't have the nonprofit motives of John Phillips' festival. In fact, he was reportedly offered a seat on the festival's board but turned it down because of its for-profit nature. Over the course of three days, 31 artists performed, including six who'd performed at Monterey as well as Janis Joplin and Jimi Hendrix in new iterations. David Crosby and Stephen Stills, who also performed with the Byrds and Buffalo Springfield at Monterey, came to Woodstock as performers with partner Graham Nash and their new addition, Buffalo Springfield co-founder Neil Young.

The festival was a huge success. With ticket sales varying from $18 to $24 and limited to New York City record stores, organizers anticipated a crowd of approximately 50,000 but, over the course of three days, an estimated 400,000 showed up. The sheer number of people made it impossible to police, so it became a free concert fairly early on. It prominently displayed everything good about the hippie cultural movement and became the singular event of the 1960s. There were dozens of popular bands offered a spot on the Wood-stock stage, but the Mamas & the Papas weren't among them. It seemed that, by August of 1969, they'd become a distant memory in the collective musical consciousness. In one year's time, the Beatles would be officially over and into their solo careers, and if the Rolling Stones of the 1960s scared parents, the 1970s iteration was downright frightening with their new balls-out, heavy rocking, hyper-sexualized approach to rock music.

In May 1971, *Rolling Stone* writer Ben Fong-Torres was dispatched to Cass Elliot's Hollywood Hills home where the Mamas & the Papas had gathered to talk about how they were getting back together to record their fifth album. Their motivation, however, wasn't out of a sense of obligation to their fans, but rather to avoid being sued collectively by Dunhill Records, which was now known as ABC/Dunhill, for $1 million over breach of contract. Though John had announced to the label in 1969 that the Mamas & the Papas were no more, they were still contractually obligated to provide their label one more original album. In the ensuing years, solo careers and life got in the way and that obligation slipped further and further into their memory banks and ABC/Dunhill had deluged the market with multiple greatest hits repackages. When they got together that spring, all four were now actual mamas and papas. Denny and girlfriend Linda Woodward's daughter Jessica was born in 1969 and John had recently become a father for the fourth time when his girlfriend, actress Genevieve Waite, gave birth to their son Tamerlane.

Cass, as usual, was the most quoted in the article and, out of the four, her participation was the most in doubt, which naturally made her the most sought-out interviewee. Over the past three years, she'd been the busiest of them all in the public eye. She hit the ground running after the breakup in 1968 when "Dream a Little Dream of Me" peaked just outside of the Top 10 in August 1968. Dunhill quickly got her into the studio to build an album around it. John Simon, who'd produced the Band's *Music from Big Pink*, *Cheap Thrills* by Big Brother & the Holding and Blood, Sweat & Tears' Feb-ruary debut *Child Is Father to the Man*, was her choice to produce it, and he excitedly accepted. Mama Cass was the hippie queen psychedelic mushroom who all the hip elite in Los Angeles swarmed, around and Dunhill gave them complete control.

But whatever magic Simon had conjured up on his earlier efforts didn't seem to rub off here. *Dream a Little Dream* was released on October 19, 1968, and it was an inauspicious debut. Recorded at Wally Heider's Los Angeles studio, it was another sort of family affair for Cass. In addition to many of the studio musicians who's played on most of the Mamas & the Papas' albums, friends Stephen Stills, John Sebastian, and Cyrus Faryar lent their hands as well. She also recorded original songs by the latter two, as well as one by Graham Nash, but they were essentially throwaways. The title track wasn't rerecorded but, instead, became awash in sound effects by John Simon that did nothing to enhance it. Unnecessary rain, thunder, overdubbed strings, and an obnoxious Top 40 DJ stepped all over the intro and the coda.

One single, John Hartford's "California Earthquake," was released as a single and got as high as number 67, which confirmed Cass' stumble out of the gate. But, if her debut seemed like a misstep, her next project was an absolute faceplant. Bobby Roberts continued to manage the four of them individually, and he and the label saw Cass as their new golden goose. Her star quality was unquestionable, and he managed to get her booked at Caesar's Palace for a three-week headliner beginning October 14, coinciding with the release of her album. She was a natural at contemporary camp and her logical next move was a Las Vegas show, which was unprecedented for somebody from the rock and roll side of things. The king of rock and roll, Elvis Presley, wouldn't make his Las Vegas debut until the following summer. At that time, the big Vegas shows were made up of the Rat Pack and singers with crossover appeal like Nancy Wilson and Tom Jones, which made the scene about as un-rock and roll as it could get. But at a rate of $40,000 a week, she couldn't refuse.

Although Cass made her name in folk and rock and roll, the Las Vegas show appealed to her inner-Broadway senses, which had stirred in her since her childhood, and she vowed to bring contemporary rock and hippie to Sin City. Her plans started out grandiose. She told *Rolling Stone* writer Jerry Hopkins that she wanted to have her band floating about the stage on a helium set and wanted high-profile musicians like Mike Bloomfield on guitar. She'd also been trying to distance herself from her Mama Cass moniker and insisted that she be billed as Cass Elliot. Head writer for the *Smothers Brothers Comedy*

Hour Mason Williams agreed to write the script for a $10,000 fee, and Harvey Brooks was hired as the bandleader. The planning stages were fun but then reality and fear began creeping in on Cass. As the weeks wore on, her procrastination undermined the expectations. While Mason was busy writing and Harvey was tightening up the band, Cass was nowhere to be found. In the few months leading up to the opening, Cass only attended a handful of rehearsals, which sounded alarm bells to the show's organizers. There'd be two shows a night and, for a show at Caesar's Palace, every move must be rehearsed to the hilt. Then the fear began to mingle with sickness. Cass had been crash-dieting ever since leaving the Mamas & the Papas and lost nearly 100 pounds in a very short period of time. Even though she'd been at the lowest weight of her adult life, it had a deleterious effect, often leaving her bedridden with stomach cramps and nausea.

Seeing the state that Cass was in two days before the show's debut left Bobby Roberts in a panic. She was out of step with the band, and her voice wasn't up to par. Bobby even flew John and Michelle in Sunday to coach her and build up her confidence, but it was no help. With a raging fever, Cass went out onstage after a heroin dose and bombed in front of a star-studded audience that included Sammy Davis Jr., Peter Lawford, and Jimi Hendrix. Her second show was so bad that Cass apologized to the audience in the middle of it after many had already walked out. The show was promptly canceled after one night, and another act was flown in to replace her. The reviews were brutal and, as Cass checked into a Beverly Hills hospital for an emergency tonsillectomy, the executives at Dunhill were left to figure out how to salvage their star's reputation.

After the dust settled, they came to realize it was disappointing but not a career killer. After all, Cass' audience wasn't Vegas regulars and most likely wouldn't pay any attention to negative reviews. They got her back in the studio to record her follow up album but this time under the auspices of their A&R man and hit-maker Steve Barri who'd worked on all the Mamas & the Papas albums recorded at Western. The goal was to get her back on the charts and they succeeded. *Bubblegum, Lemonade & . . . Something for Mama* was released on July 5, 1969, and produced the Top 40 hit "It's Getting Better." Though it only peaked in the 30s in both *Billboard* and *Cash Box*, the better move was getting her on television. In 1969, she appeared on the *Hollywood Palace*, *Philbin's People*, *This Is Tom Jones*, *American Bandstand*, the *John*

Davidson Show, and the *Tonight Show.* ABC even believed in her enough to give her a variety show pilot that aired a week before the release of her second album and even though it featured friends John Sebastian, Joni Mitchell, and Mary Travers as musical guests, it too was panned by the critics. Cass often appeared nervous, and the sketches, which starred comedian Buddy Hackett and husband/wife team Martin Landau and Barbara Bain from *Mission: Impossible,* were too corny even by the normally low variety show standards.

It didn't slow her down though. In the year before reuniting with John, Michelle, and Denny, Cass stormed television appearing on more variety shows and even filling in for Johnny Carson, co-hosting the *Mike Douglas Show,* and becoming a semi-regular on the *Carol Burnett Show.* On TV, her infectious personality shone brightly to a vast audience and appeared at ease in every setting, but there was a drawback. In nearly every comedy skit that she was in, her weight was often the brunt of the joke. Nevertheless, she'd become a fixture and her television career began drawing better reviews than her musical one.

In September 1969, she released another single, "Make Your Own Kind of Music," but, like its predecessor, it barely cracked the Top 40 in Billboard and peaked at number 25 in *Cash Box.* For someone who hung out regularly with Crosby, Stills & Nash, not to mention Eric Clapton, Joni Mitchell, and John Sebastian, her music was more in line with the 1910 Fruitgum Company. Her next musical project was a little more under the radar, but it helped reestablish some credibility. Through her friend Gram Parsons, she was introduced to former Traffic lead singer Dave Mason, who invited her to sing background vocals on his sophomore album for Blue Thumb. She happily agreed and even got to sing lead on one song, "Here We Go Again," which she co-wrote with Dave's bassist Bryan Garofalo. When the album was released in March 1971, it was credited to Dave Mason and Cass Elliot, making it the first release not to refer to her as Mama Cass, and was highly praised.

During this time, Cass' personal life was still complicated. She never revealed the identity of daughter Owen's father, and it would remain a tightly held secret for the next 40 years. In 2008, it was revealed that it was L.A. studio musician Chuck Day, who toured with the Mamas & the Papas in 1967 as their bassist. A relationship never developed, and she didn't even reveal to him that he was the father. Pic Dawson continued to be in and out of her life and, during her Vegas debacle, she was involved with another nefarious character in Billy Doyle who would refer to himself as her fiancé and thrived on a rumor that he once killed a man. Both men were drug dealers and remained a terrible influence in her life. Cass had twice attempted unsuccessfully to wean herself off heroin, which she had started using just before the sessions for the *Papas & the Mamas* album but, with them around, it was a losing proposition.

When the Mamas & the Papas got together in May 1971, she had been dating an American journalist named Donald von Widenman, who she'd first met in London two years earlier on a promotional jaunt for her latest single, "Move in a Little Closer, Baby." The self-professed baron had been living there for several years and made such an impression on Cass that she invited him to her rehearsal for *This Is Tom Jones*. She'd spent several weeks in London, gallivanting around town with her new beau, which developed into a love affair. When she went home to Los Angeles, the two kept in touch and the next time she ventured to London, she holidayed with him in the South of France. This time, however, he followed her home to L.A. and became a significant presence in her life.

Denny had been considerably less busy than Cass following the breakup of the Mamas & the Papas. His alcoholism hadn't gotten any better, even after the birth of his and Linda Woodward's daughter Jessica, and he laid around for months at a time with no desire to work, create, or be a part of something. It seemed everything was messed up in his professional life. His drive was lost, his finances were in shambles, and he clung to the hope that the Mamas & the Papas would get back together. Feeling the need for a change, he, Linda, and Barry McGuire split for Fort Lauderdale, Florida, after discovering an uncashed cashier's check for $10,000. Near the end of 1969, he learned his mother was terminally ill and spent much of his time in Halifax until she succumbed on December 19 at the relatively young age of 66. He'd rented out his home in Laurel Canyon and ended up staying with his neighbor and it was there that he heard from Dunhill President Jay Lasker who'd informed him he was suing him for breach of contract. One provision of Denny's revised contract was a solo record, and he showed no indications of making one. Not wanting to shell out money out of his own pocket, Denny assembled a group that included Eddy Fischer and Dr. Eric Hord on guitars, Gabe Lapano on piano, Bryan Garofalo on bass, Russ Kunkel on drums, and Buddy Emmons on pedal steel. Dunhill staff producer Bill Szymczyk, a couple years ahead of his career-defining work with the James Gang and the Eagles, was assigned to produce it and make sure it got done in a timely fashion.

What emerged was an enjoyable, low-key country-driven album made up of several Denny Doherty–Linda Woodward originals, an attempt at a Hank Williams standard that was essentially album filler, and a combination of two Beatles songs. It was released in February 1971 to little fanfare and received little to no promotion. Denny didn't do any sort of album tour and the only television appearance he made in support of it was a disastrous performance on the *Tonight Show with Johnny Carson* where he emerged drunk and began singing the wrong song in the wrong key. After that, he hung it up. His heart wasn't in it. He'd simply done the album in order not to get sued and three months later found himself right back in the same position with his former bandmates, telling Fong-Torres, "I couldn't get as involved by myself as with other people."

John and Michelle continued to ride the roller coaster that was their relationship even after their divorce was finalized in May 1969. They both moved on to temporary lovers and ran in the same Hollywood Hills circles but would always circle back to one another. After Michelle moved out of their Bel Air home, she quickly got involved in a relationship with French actor/director Christian Marquand and began taking acting classes at Justin Smith's Acting Studio determined to break into the movies. But now that the pressure was off to make the marriage work, she and John easily slept together on many occasions until finally they had a blowup at the Daisy on Rodeo Drive, which turned physical back at John's house. It left Michelle with a bloody nose and John with a sore groin.

A few weeks later, on a trip with Lou and Denny to the Bahamas for a record industry convention, John received a phone call from a friend in Los Angeles and who told him a woman in London was trying to reach him in regard to his daughter Chynna. John got the number and phoned her immediately. It turns out she was the nanny Michelle had left Chynna with while she and Marquand enjoyed a long weekend at the Hotel Mamounia in Marrakesh, Morocco. She told John shed hadn't heard from Michelle in days and was growing concerned as Chynna was developing a cough. John took the first plane he could to Heathrow and took their daughter to his mother's house in Los Angeles. When Michelle tracked him down, she was furious. She didn't believe the nanny story. She thought John seized the opportunity to hurt her by taking Chynna away from her and a couple days later showed up at his Bel Air home demanding he turn her over. John refused and told her she wasn't here. Michelle stormed off and got a court order stating that he must surrender her. Now he had no choice.

Incredibly, several weeks later, Michelle and John could be seen together at a party given by director Roman Polanski and his wife actress Sharon Tate at their home at 10050 Cielo Drive in Benedict Canyon. According to John, after the party, he and Michelle reconvened at Roger Vadim and Jane Fonda's house for an orgy that also included actor Warren Beatty.

John's drug use continued to escalate, and it was during this time that he began using cocaine regularly. Although he whiled away much of his time at parties of all types, he was in search of his next musical venture and wasn't entirely sure where he stood in terms of the contemporary pop music scene. Dunhill was interested in him maintaining his creativity and even offered him some creative control by forming his own label under their umbrella, which he called Warlock. He began writing songs and working on demos for a solo album in his home studio in January that continued throughout the end of the year. As usual, his songs were biographical and dealt with the people he was running with at the time. There were a couple about Michelle, one about his former lover Ann Marshall, but there was more to come and some of the characters who helped fill the album would enter his life in the spring and summer.

John felt a simpler and less conspicuous venture back into music was through film scoring, and he actively sought it out. He'd been running with a very Hollywood crowd and through his friend Mike McLean, an up-and-coming casting director who'd most recently worked on Franklin J. Schaffner's *Patton*, he was introduced to a young English actor/director named Michael Sarne. The two hit it off immediately and, in no time at all, became fast friends. Michael had recently been named director of the film version of Gore Vidal's 1968 worldwide best-selling novel *Myra Breckenridge* as well as one of its screenwriters. He immediately enlisted John to write some music for the film, to which he happily agreed.

Michael was a hot commodity in the world of film having directed the 1968 cult classic *Joanna* starring South African actress Genevieve Waite. Her performance captivated many moviegoers, including John. He got a chance to meet her when she flew in from Europe to audition for *Myra Breckenridge* in late June. Michael dispatched John to go retrieve her at the airport and he immediately fell for her. She had curly blonde hair, bright green eyes and upturned nose that drew John in, and he immediately got to flirting. Her Betty Boop voice matched her looks and on the drive to Hollywood tickled John with stories of ex-lovers. Genevieve sparked John's creative drive when she likened him and Michael to 19th century English romantic poets and best friends Lord Byron and Percy Shelley, which over the coming weeks and months conjured up ideas of a film or album or both.

Over their two weeks together, John and Genevieve fell in love and were inseparable up until she left for New York in July to begin work on her next film *Move*, co-starring Elliot Gould and Paula Prentiss and directed by Stuart Rosenberg. Over the remainder of the summer, John spent his days in a small bungalow on the lot of 20th Century Fox in Hollywood working on music for *Myra Breckenridge*, which entailed going over new songs with legendary actress Mae West. His nights were still a nonstop party with movie stars that took him through the vast, wealthy neighborhoods in the Hollywood Hills. Though he still owned his home in Bel Air, for the summer he moved into Michael Sarne's guesthouse and the two spent most evenings traipsing from one party to another until the unthinkable happened.

On the morning of August 9, 1969, after a night hanging out on the beach with ex–New Journeymen bandmate Marshall Brickman, Michael Sarne and a few other friends for the purposes of checking out phosphorescent plankton, John was awakened by an early morning phone call from *Los Angeles Times* gossip columnist Joyce Harber.

"Thank God you're alive," she told John, which aroused his attention.

When he inquired as to what she was talking about, she told him about a grisly murder that took place at Roman Polanski and Sharon Tate's Cielo Drive home. No victims had been announced yet by police, and Harber was doing her due diligence in order to get the scoop. Since John was a regular at all the hip gatherings, he was one of the first she called. He was blindsided, and his mind began to race. How could this be? Who were the victims? What should he do? Then he remembered getting a message from his answering service the night before. It was an invitation from Sharon Tate to a gathering at her home. Roman was away in Europe, and she wanted some company.

The only other name he remembered hearing was Jay Sebring, hairdresser to the stars, into whose business venture Sebring International John had recently invested $10,000.

There was nothing John could do except turn on the news. The Cielo Drive home was completely taped off and inundated with police. Hours later, the victims were confirmed as actress Sharon Tate, who was eight months pregnant, Jay Sebring, and Polanski's friend the aspiring screenwriter Wojciech Frykowski and his girlfriend Abigail Folger, heiress to the Folger's coffee fortune. Also found dead outside was random victim Steven Parent, who was visiting the property's caretaker. It left the community in a panic and cast a dark shadow over the hippie movement. Polanski was summoned from London, and he made the gut-wrenching journey home.

Just as everybody in the Hollywood Hills was trying to process this tragedy, they were once again awakened to the news of another gruesome murder. This time, the victims were a middle-aged couple who resided at 3301 Waverly Drive in the Los Feliz section of Los Angeles, approximately 10 miles east of the Polanski home. Supermarket executive Leno Labianca and his wife Rosemary were stabbed 16 and 41 times respectively. When news began to spread, a panic ensued that would quickly spread across the country. There was nothing that connected the Tate victims to the Labiancas and, overnight, big parties, small gatherings, and all other night activities ceased, and, in the coming days, gun sales increased. Nobody went out. Michelle left her home in Malibu, and she and Chynna moved back in with John in Bel Air until the dust settled.

Many of the Mamas & the Papas were friends or associates on some level with several of the Tate victims. Cass was brought in for questioning because the word "PIG" was written on a wall in Sharon Tate's blood and some believed that it actually spelled "PIC," as in Cass' on-again, off-again boyfriend Pic Dawson. They wanted to know where both he and Billy Doyle were as many in the department believed the murder was a possible drug deal gone bad. John was on the L.A. Sheriff's Office's long list of suspects after they learned Wojciech Frykowski had been at John's house days before the murder, demanding to be let in. Also, since he had business dealings with Jay Sebring, lost money could've been a motive. In an even longer shot, sheet music for "Straight Shooter" had been found on the piano at the residence. The police came to his house to question him about that night but ultimately cleared him. Roman Polanski also took up his own investigation and considered John a suspect. Earlier that year, he and Michelle had an affair that Polanski caught wind of, and he believed John may have done this as revenge. One night in early fall, at a party at Michael Sarne's, an enraged Polanski snuck up behind John, who was sitting on a couch, and held a cleaver to his throat demanding that he confess. John was able to calm him down and convince him that he didn't kill Sharon.

No other murders took place in the ensuing months and the city was on high alert until the LAPD announced warrants for several suspects and noted that several were already in custody. The ringleader was a 35-year-old drifter named Charles Manson who'd spent much of his life in prison for nonviolent crimes. In the early 1960s, while serving a 10-year sentence at McNeil Island, Washington, for check forgery, he began taking guitar lessons and, after being released in 1967, moved to Los Angeles in pursuit of a music career. He played in and around college campuses and public parks, and developed a small following, many of them young women, that eventually turned into a cult. They lived communally on a small portion of dairy farmer George Spahn's ranch in exchange for manual labor. Over several months, the cult devolved further and further in sex and drugs, and, by the end of 1968, had morphed into a doomsday cult where Manson preached of an imminent apocalyptic race war that Manson nicknamed "Helter Skelter" after the Beatles song released in November.

Manson, through the sexual assistance of many of his female followers, got in tight with Beach Boys drummer Dennis Wilson. He liked what he heard from Manson and offered to pass some demos he'd made along to some of his record industry friends, including Terry Melcher, son of Doris Day and producer of many artists, including the Byrds and Paul Revere & the Raiders. Melcher had tepid interest in his music but was more fascinated by Manson's hippie commune and considered filming a documentary about it. But, after witnessing some of Manson's disturbing behavior at the ranch, he cut all ties. Manson became enraged and convinced his cult members that Melcher must pay. One member, Tex Watson, told Manson that he had been to a party a Melcher's house. They did some recon, even going so far as to knock on the door and ask for Melcher but had been told he had moved. Nevertheless, they carried out the murders at Cielo Drive and Waverly Drive, and seven people who had nothing to do with Terry Melcher were killed.

It cast a pall on the whole hippie ethos, which was done in further by the Rolling Stones' Altamont Free Concert in December where the Hells Angels provided security and one member, Alan Passaro, stabbed audience member Meredith Hunter to death after he brandished a gun in front of the stage. It seemed the cutting edge of music was getting dangerous, but John couldn't have cared any less. He and Genevieve became an item when she returned from New York and in November, he finally recorded several of the new songs he'd written over the past year. His eponymous solo album was released in April 1970 and it became unofficially known as *John, the Wolfking of L.A.* after the nickname Genevieve gave him after seeing him walking around in his long fur coat and howling at the moon.

The album was a collection of mild, country-driven arrangements that were on par with what was going on around him in greater Los Angeles and, as usual, were filled with characters and the events of his life. Genevieve had become his newest muse and, after telling him how him she wished she could come back as a Rolling Stone, he wrote "Let It Bleed, Genevieve" in her honor. The album was recorded in his home studio with Wrecking Crew musicians Hal Blaine on drums, James Burton and Eric Hord on guitars, Joe Osborn on bass, Larry Knechtel on piano, and Buddy Emmons and Red Rhodes on pedal steel. The 11 songs displayed his continued departure from the classic sound of the Mamas & the Papas and compared better with what was being released by the Flying Burrito Brothers, Rick Nelson & the Stone Canyon Band, and Poco. John even had a surprise hit in "Mississippi," which rose to number 32 in *Billboard,* but the album charted at a dismal number 181.

He supported it several months after its release with a small club tour that took him to the Bitter End in New York, the Cellar Door in Washington, D.C., and the Troubadour and the Bitter End West in Los Angeles. He was accompanied by an L.A. group called Trees and brought along his old Smoothies bandmate Bill Cleary and Michael Sarne. John and Michael had managed to secure an investor for their Byron and Shelley project, which, although still unclear on exactly what it was, included Mick Jagger's new girlfriend Bianca Perez-Mora Macias and Jimi Hendrix in some sort of as-yet-undefined roles. They used some of those funds to bring along documentary filmmaker Albert Maysles, who'd filmed the Rolling Stones' 1969 U.S. tour and captured the stabbing of Meredith Hunter at Altamont on film, to record footage for it. The project ground to a halt when Jimi Hendrix died of asphyxiation due to aspiration of vomit in London on September 18, 1970. It was the beginning of a series of setbacks that plagued John the rest of his career.

The whole solo experience left him cold. He had come to the realization that he just didn't have the desire to be a solo star and could no longer write Top 10 hits. He continued his film scoring work with the MGM movie *Brewster McCloud*, which he and Lou co-produced and starred Bud Cort and Sally Kellerman but came away unsatisfied with that whole experience as well. Even producing the album of new Dunhill/Warlock signing Jamme couldn't move him.

"There's not enough money around to make me sit in a room and sing every day," he told Fong-Torres. "I'd rather lay around the beach and be broke."

John also learned that he was going to be a dad for the fourth time, which ratcheted up the stress and the need to maintain the cash flow. John wasn't there for Susie and Michelle during their pregnancies. Would Genevieve be any different?

Life seemed to be meandering along for all four members of the Mamas & the Papas, and none of them seemed to care whether they got together again or not. That is, until Dunhill Records forced them to care. Around the time John and Genevieve's son Tamerlane was born on March 4, 1971, the four Mamas & Papas received a telegram from Dunhill Records informing them that they were initiating a lawsuit against them in the amount of $1 million for not delivering their contractually obligated fifth album. Denny reached out to the others and they came to the consensus that there was nothing they could do but make one more record. Though they'd made a lot of money over the past five years, none were rich enough to brush off $250,000. After talking to Bobby Roberts and Jay Lasker, the deadline got extended to November. The label even got on board by sending a camera crew to record footage for a documentary, but that eventually got scrapped.

In May, they convened at Cass' house for rehearsals, and it was weird in the beginning. They were all thrust back into something they thought was over and left in their pasts. In the time between receiving the telegrams and rehearsal, John composed feverishly and came up with nine new songs and one leftover from the *Wolfking* album in "Lady Genevieve." Michelle arrived with an original as well. She had made the most recent headlines after divorcing actor Dennis Hopper after only eight days of marriage. They met while filming his chaotic movie *The Last Movie* in Peru and fell in love, or so Michelle thought. After their wedding on October 31, 1970, they moved into the D. H.

Lawrence Ranch north of Taos, New Mexico, where Hopper scared his new bride and Chynna to death shooting guns in the house. Hopper was stoned on peyote most of the time, and the tipping point came when he freaked out and chained Michelle to a chair believing she was a witch. After getting free, she waited until Hopper passed out and made a break for it with daughter in tow for the Los Alamos County Airport, where their plane buzzed Hopper's pickup truck after he tried in vain to prevent it from taking off. Not long after arriving in Los Angeles, her father took her to his attorney to draw up divorce papers, telling her that although it's embarrassing now, she won't regret it. By the time of the fifth album sessions, she'd rebounded with actor Jack Nicholson.

Her chaotic entrance into the movie business inspired her to write her first group offering, "I Wanna Be a Star," which told the story of a naïve young move starlet wannabe. Even though she wasn't a strong singer, John was always able to get the most out of her voice and worked his magic with this one. Her disastrous marriage also served as the inspiration for another John original called "Grasshopper." He wrote "Pacific Coast Highway" about a girl who frequented the Topanga Corral club the same time he did and "European Blueboy" was his tribute to Michael Sarne. "Pearl" was written about old friend Janis Joplin who died less than three weeks after Jimi Hendrix and "Snowqueen of Texas" was about cult fashion model and friend Deborah Dixon.

Sessions began a month later and this time were held at the Sound Factory. As expected, John took complete control and he threw everyone a few curveballs. Instead of using the same crew of musicians he'd used from *If You Can Believe Your Eyes and Ears* up until his *Wolfking* album, John wanted to go a little funkier and enlisted former Motown musicians Tony Newton, Louis Shelton, and Clarence McDonald on bass, guitar, and keyboards, respectively, pianist Joe Sample and guitarist David T. Walker from the Jazz Crusaders, veteran session musicians Earl Palmer and Ed Greene on drums, Gary Coleman on percussion, and Jim Horn on saxophone and flute. It was a total left turn and one that caught Denny, Cass, and Michelle by surprise. Also, noticeably absent were John's 12-string Gibson and Lou Adler. He'd repeated his earlier success at Ode after signing noted veteran hit songwriter Carole King and producing her hit album Tapestry, which was on its way to being certified platinum and a major cultural influence. This was going to be a new venture, a new sound, one that continued with the steps John had been making musically since *The Papas & the Mamas*.

The sessions went through the summer with overdub sessions wrapping up in October. The new musicians gave the Mamas & the Papas a noticeably jazzier sound that made its presence felt on "Pacific Coast Highway," "Shooting Star" and "European Blueboy," which opened with a steel drum. This assortment of mostly black musicians even fashioned a Motown-esque opening for the album closer "Blueberries for Breakfast," even though it didn't really match the song.

John spent all of September and October meticulously mixing the album. He experimented by recording each vocalist separately and stacking them in the multitrack to create the illusion of harmony. It was totally unnecessary, and he'd often run into problems. For instance, he would tell one of them to sing it a certain way and if it didn't blend, they'd have to come back into the studio and sing it in a way that matched better. Another thing he did, whether deliberately or not, was mix Cass right out of the album. John would often use Michelle's vocal to give Cass' a softer edge, but he mixed her down so much that Cass sounds like Michelle's harmony singer. It worked well was on songs "Step Out" and "Snowqueen of Texas," where Michelle's soft, subtle harmony matches Denny beautifully, but their signature sound was mostly absent, and it stood out like a sore thumb. John's songs sound like he didn't even write them with Cass in mind.

The album, *People Like Us* after the opening track that paints a romantic picture of the group, was released on November 6, 1971, and, although the announcement of the reunion garnered some good press, it didn't continue after the release. It was understandably a letdown for many fans, and critics panned it for what it wasn't. It didn't sound like "California Dreamin'" or "Monday, Monday" and they all wondered where Cass was. She was on the cover and you can hear her a little bit but, in their older songs, her distinguishable vocals provided energy and life to John's songs. He'd certainly crafted a great batch of songs that fit well in the growing Southern California soft rock movement but sabotaged it by omitting the main ingredients.

But for the Mamas & the Papas it was c'est la vie. They weren't going to be sued for $1 million, and that was the most important thing for them. Even clearer now was the fact that the Mamas & the Papas weren't going to get together again anytime soon. *People Like Us* barely cracked the Top 100 in the *Billboard* albums chart and the lone single "Step Out" didn't fare much better. Everyone went back to their respective corners, no longer a part of

ABC/Dunhill. Cass scored the best deal, signing a $1 million, four-album agreement with RCA Victor and continued to make the television rounds, but she would never have another charting hit again. Denny and John both signed considerably smaller deals with Columbia that only resulted in one single each. Michelle wasn't interested in a singing career but did land a big role in the 1973 crime drama *Dillinger* starring Warren Oates and Ben Johnson that kicked off a moderately successful movie and TV career for her.

The next time the Mamas & the Papas were in a room together was at a Chinese restaurant in downtown Los Angeles on January 31, 1972, where John and Genevieve got married. New chapters had begun for everyone. The four needed each other to get where they wanted to be, but it was unsustainable and although they could be in the same room with one another, they just couldn't work together. Maybe one day they could try it again. John summed up the Mamas & the Papas best in a line from the title track to their latest album. "Oh, what a dump, now it's a palace/Where a Dixie cup becomes a chalice."

EPILOGUE

On July 29, 1974, any chance of another reunion of the Mamas & the Papas shattered into pieces when Cass Elliot was found dead in her bed at Harry Nilsson's London apartment. It was a gut punch to the others. She was only 32 and had just wrapped up a two-week stand at the London Palladium showing no signs of slowing down. Nevertheless, she died in her sleep and was discovered the following afternoon by her tour manager George Caldwell. Even in death, her weight became a joke. London doctor Anthony Greenburgh, who'd been her personal physician while in London, was the first to examine her body and stated to a reporter at the *Daily Express* that it appeared that she choked on a ham sandwich she'd been eating while lying down. However, a few days later, after a thorough autopsy performed by Dr. Gavin Thurston, it was discovered her death was a result of "fatty myocardial degeneration due to obesity," also known as heart failure. Nevertheless, as of this writing, most people still believe Cass died choking on a ham sandwich.

It came as a complete shock to fans and to the general public and continued the string of rock and roll artists dying young. She was the seventh post-Monterey casualty, following Otis Redding, Jimi Hendrix, Janis Joplin, Alan Wilson of Canned Heat, Brian Cole of the Association, and Ron McKernan of the Grateful Dead and another in the 1960s music revolution that also included Doors lead singer Jim Morrison and Rolling Stones co-founder Brian Jones. But the shock was profound. Nobody had expected Cass to die so suddenly and it quickly became clear that less than three years after their final album, the Mamas & the Papas lost the key ingredient to their sound and would never be able to fully reunite again. Their collective heartbreak was captured in a photograph taken by Frank Edwards as John, Michelle, and Genevieve Waite made their way to her funeral.

Over the years, the surviving members of the Mamas & the Papas would only publicly reunite three times: the first time on an episode of Denny Doherty's 1978 television variety show *Denny's Sho*, the second at the Palomino in Los Angeles after John re-formed the Mamas & the Papas and the final time at their induction into the Rock and Roll Hall of Fame on January 12, 1998. Cass had worked hard to distance herself from her Mama Cass moniker. Her final album, released in September 1973, was a live performance from Mister Kelly's in Chicago titled *Don't Call Me Mama Anymore* after the tour of the same name. Now her death meant she could never be physically tied to it again.

The closest the public ever got to hearing the Mamas & the Papas reunite on wax was on Denny's second and final solo album *Waiting for a Song*, which was only released in England, Canada, and Brazil in 1974. Cass and Michelle recorded background vocals for a few songs at a session in Los Angeles. In fact, when Cass was found dead, in her room was found the liner notes she'd handwritten for the album. It was one of the last things she ever did. Denny mourned Cass the remainder of his life and, in interviews, would often talk with regret about how he acted toward her when she declared her love for him. He never again recorded anything that would be released in his lifetime, but he kept himself busy mostly with acting and performing. After he and Linda Woodward split up in the mid-1970s, he and his new wife Jeanette returned to Canada in 1978, eventually settling in Mississauga, Ontario, where he lived the rest of his life. It was there where he began his long road back to sobriety. The hometown hero was awarded with *Denny's Sho*, which ran for half a season on CBC before being canceled. He acted sporadically throughout the 1980s and 1990s before landing the role of Harbour Master for five seasons on the CBC children's show *Theodore Tugboat*, which also ran on PBS in the United States.

He and Jeannette had two more children, John and Emberley. Shortly after his wife Jeanette succumbed to ovarian cancer in 1998, he debuted his one-man autobiographical musical *Dream a Little Dream: The Nearly True Story of the Mamas & the Papas*, which garnered good reviews. The nearly two-hour performance was co-written by Denny and playwright Paul Ledoux, who first met while working on the rock gospel music *Fire* in Calgary in 1989. In December 2006, Denny went in for surgery following an abdominal aortic aneurysm and had to be put on dialysis. Eventually his kidneys shut down and he passed away on January 19, 2007. He was 66, the same age as his mother when she died.

Denny's life wasn't completely devoid of music after his final solo album in 1974. In 1980, he joined John Phillips' new version of the Mamas & the Papas and recorded and toured with them for three years before John abruptly ended the group after walking offstage in Las Vegas in August 1983, telling everyone, "I don't want to do this anymore." It was his first big public move after a drug trafficking arrest where he stared down the barrel of 45 years in federal prison, which put his last 10 years into perspective and got his name back in the tabloids.

John's life had always been filled with drama and drug use, but both ramped up considerably in the years following the *People Like Us* album. After recording an album's worth of songs for Columbia Records, which remained shelved for 35 years, John concentrated on a space project he'd been developing since watching the Apollo 11 moon landing on July 24, 1969. John called it *Space* and began writing songs for it though he had no idea what it would be. Using his Hollywood connections, he conceived it as a film project and got financial support from his new friend the real estate estate mogul Len Holzer but when that dried up, moved to New York with Genevieve to turn it into a Broadway show.

John poured his heart and soul into this project and was able to formulate a plot and wrote around 30 songs for *Space*. The protagonist was an astronaut named Ernie Hardy who leads a contingent of interplanetary dignitaries on a mission to the moon disarm a humanoid bomb that will destroy the universe planted by the evil Dr. Bomb. The whacky plot appealed to no Broadway backers, but luck came in the form of the perennially untraditional pop artist Andy Warhol, who offered his services after hearing about their bad luck from his old friend Genevieve. He infused a healthy dose of seed money. Eric Lang was cast as Ernie Hardy, and Harlan S. Foss won the role of Dr. Bomb. Genevieve was brought on to play the ditzy character Angel, John played the role of King Can, and Denny Doherty was brought in to play the president.

The production and rehearsals were a comedy of errors. The cost-cutting and turnover doomed it. Director Paul Morrissey was fired two weeks before the opening and John lost his role as King Can and was replaced by Denny who still maintained his role as President. When the show, renamed *Man on the Moon*, debuted at the tiny *Little Theater* on Broadway on January 29, 1975, to a star-studded audience including Warren Beatty, Kurt Vonnegut, Geraldo Rivera, and Yoko Ono, it seemed like Cass' Las Vegas show repeating itself. It was a total bomb and got mercilessly panned by critics. By February 1 the show was canceled, which sent John into a downward spiral and off to London the following year.

When he got kicked out of the cast of his own show, John coped by starting on heroin, first snorting it and then injecting it. In London, he hooked up with Mick Jagger and played him some songs from the ill-fated show as well as some new ones. Mick came away impressed and, within 10 days, began producing a new John Phillips album for Rolling Stones Records. At Olympic Sound Studios, John not only worked with Mick but also Keith Richards and former Rolling Stone Mick Taylor. Keith and John's collaboration resulted in a deeper dive for both into drugs. Keith turned him on to medicinal cocaine, and John became a bigger user than ever before, which caused the project to drag on, much to Mick's consternation.

The album never came to fruition even after Keith hooked up with John in New York in August 1977. The biggest inspiration John got from his trip to England was to start dealing drugs. Much like had back in the East Village in 1964 with the drugstore next to his apartment, John set up an elaborate drug dealing scheme with Sidney Korn and Alvin Brod, owners of K&B Drugs on the Upper East Side. John had always put incredible effort into nurturing his passions, and, in the late 1970s, his passion was injecting cocaine and heroin and supplementing his high with barbiturates. And, much like he was with his music, his energy was contagious. His addiction managed to spread to Genevieve, who conceived John's fifth child Bijou under the steady influence of marijuana and alcohol. His eldest son and daughter, the latter of which was starring in the hit CBS sitcom *One Day at a Time*, were both addicted to cocaine. Through his drug connections, he was able to get ahold of several books of empty New York State controlled prescription forms in triplicate. After forming trust and friendships with Korn and Brod, John strolled into K&B Drugs once a week with prescriptions he'd filled out himself and walked out with bags full of various amphetamines, depressants, and heavy painkillers like Percodan. He trafficked these drugs through various dealers he'd gotten to know since being in New York and for his own habits, he'd maintained fresh supplies of prescription Dilaudad, Desoxyn, and Methedrene.

Before long, the DEA caught wind of what was going on and put John and K&B under surveillance. When they dropped the net on the whole ring on July 31, 1980, John was arrested and charged with conspiracy to distribute narcotics. He pleaded not guilty and was released on $50,000 bail. His lawyers immediately checked him into Fair Oaks Hospital for drug rehabilitation. They knew the first step to reducing his sentence was to get him clean and sober. The second step was to become a model ex-junkie and use his celebrity status for antidrug messaging. The first people John worked on, while in treatment, were his eldest son and daughter. Mackenzie's addiction had recently cost her her role on *One Day at a Time* and she needed to make the rehab rounds too if she was ever going to work again.

After a couple delays, John was sentenced on April 7, 1981. He stepped into the courtroom clean for the first time in over 20 years. His first taste of marijuana in 1960 to trying LSD for the first time with Michelle, Denny, and Cass in 1964 to injecting himself with cocaine and heroin the first time in 1976 led to this moment, and he was scared to death. Judge Leonard B. Sand was lenient, handing him an eight-year suspended sentence. He was ordered to spend 30 days in Allenwood Federal Camp, a minimum-security prison facility in Allenwood, Pennsylvania, famous for housing several of the Watergate conspirators several years earlier.

During his time at Fair Oaks, John's love for making and performing music began making a comeback. Another loved one John recruited to come clean up was Denny Doherty, who was still battling alcoholism. While there, they conceived the idea of re-forming the Mamas & the Papas but this time with Mackenzie instead of Michelle. Denny suggested Elaine "Spanky" McFarland, from the late 1960s hitmakers Spanky & Our Gang, to fill Cass' shoes. She was equipped with a booming voice and had lived through the zeitgeist.

Even before John's sentencing, they began performing. By the end of 1981, they'd begun sessions for an album at Mediasound and Electric Ladyland Studios in New York. John's ear for pop hits had made a return too, and many of the tracks recorded during that time reflect the pop sensibilities of the early 1980s. But concert promoters didn't want new music from the Mamas

& the Papas. They wanted the old hits, and it frustrated John to the point of breaking up the group in 1983. He would eventually go on to re-form them with Scott McKenzie taking over for Denny in 1986. In the interim, John and Genevieve divorced, and he wrote his first hit in 18 years with "Kokomo." He'd recorded a demo in 1985 featuring a duel lead by Denny and Scott that Mike Love and Terry Melcher got their hands on. John's original version, co-written with Scott, was more of a bittersweet reminiscence of times past in the tropics where John would often go to get away from it all. Love and Melcher turned it more into an upbeat travelogue meant to inspire people to go to Kokomo. Released in July 1988 and featured in the hit Tom Cruise movie Cocktail, it was John's first number one hit since "Monday, Monday."

In the years afterward, John began to struggle with alcohol, and, like many recovering drug addicts, needed a substance to lean on. After receiving a liver transplant in 1992, because of his many years of abuse, pictures of John drinking alcoholic beverages at a bar in Palm Springs, California, were published in the *National Enquirer*. He continued touring with the Mamas & the Papas, gradually becoming comfortable with the oldies show stigma. Denny, Scott and Barry McGuire all took turns in the 1990s being a Papa and, by the late 1990s, women not even associated with their circle were performing as the Mamas. John and Scott even attempted a Journeymen studio reunion with Dick Weissman, but nothing came of it. In 1995, he married artist Farnaz Arrasteh and retired from performing three years later. He did keep writing songs and, in 2000, found himself back in New York City at Sound on Sound Studios recording tracks for his second solo album. It would eventually be titled *Phillips 66*, but John would not live to see it released. After falling off a stool and badly injuring his shoulder, he was taken to UCLA Medical Centre. When the pain didn't subside, doctors discovered he had a stomach virus that affected his kidneys. He'd been put on dialysis and was expected to be transferred to an occupational therapy center in Palm Springs, but his condition took a turn for the worse and he died on March 18, 2001, at the age of 65 of heart failure.

In the remaining days of his life, John was in and out of consciousness in the ICU and was visited by many family members and friends. One visitor was his ex-wife Michelle. The two last saw one another at their Rock and Roll Hall of Fame induction over three years earlier but they hadn't been on speaking terms since before John's arrest in 1980. Now it was really the end, and sorrow and some regret had overtaken her and she needed to say goodbye. It was now her time to rouse him from his sleep and she told him, "You made me the woman I am today."

In the years following the breakup of the Mamas & the Papas, Michelle would not have been so complimentary. She and John's relationship nosedived in 1979 when Michelle received temporary custody of his and Genevieve's son Tamerlane because of their crippling drug addictions. Losing their son to Mama Michelle was like a dagger to their hearts. Michelle was never addicted to drugs and had been relatively clean since her breakaway from John. They grew further and further apart after John's marriage to Genevieve but reunited in 1975 when he caught wind of Michelle's solo deal with A&M Records. He volunteered to produce it, to which Michelle relented although she had wanted David Anderle. But John was always able to get the best out of Michelle's voice and got off to a quick starting producing half of her debut single, a tribute to Lou Adler called "Aloha Louie" that they co-wrote. He was able to complete one more song that landed on the album, eventually titled *Victim of Romance* but then disappeared. His drug addiction stifled his creativity, and then he and Genevieve left for New York.

It was after their daughter Chynna visited John in New York in 1977 that she caught wind of just how badly he and Genevieve were addicted and that they used in front of Tamerlane. After going to see New York to bring Tamerlane back with her to California, Michelle and John's sister Rosie got a court order granting Rosie custody of Tamerlane but acknowledging that he'd stay with Michelle and her fiancé Bob Burch. After realizing she and John had lost their son, Genevieve became grief stricken and pressured John into figuring out some way to get him back. The scheme he hatched could only have been thought of by a junkie. They rented a place in Newport Beach, California, in 1979 to give the appearance that they were going to be there a while and made the family rounds to give the impression that everything was fine. A few days later, under the guise of having Tamerlane and Chynna sleep over their house, Genevieve made off to Las Vegas with Tamerlane in a rented limousine while John took Chynna shopping at the mall. When it was evident that Genevieve and Tamerlane weren't coming back, John feigned concern and, a few hours later, told Michelle he'd just heard from Genevieve and that they were at a hotel in Las Vegas and that he was on his way to retrieve them. But, to no one's surprise, he never returned.

He and Genevieve drove cross-country like bandits and hid out at a rented home in Old Greenwich, Connecticut, overlooking Long Island Sound. Michelle filed felonious kidnapping charges against them and both were arrested in mid-December. John and Genevieve's attorneys, however, were able to convince the judge that Michelle was acting out of bitterness, and they were granted custody of Tamerlane. Weeks later, John's mother died, and nearly eight months later, John was arrested for his drug trafficking and, in the ensuing months, prosecutors used Michelle as a character witness against John. Any hope of a reunion of the existing Mamas & Papas died there. In 1986, their war grew colder when both put out competing autobiographies. Not even the success of John and Michelle's daughter in the pop band Wilson Phillips, made up of her and Brian Wilson's daughters Carnie and Wendy could get them speaking.

In the ensuing years, Michelle lived a quiet life. She bore her second child, a son named Austin, with actor Grainger Hines and adopted a second son, Aron Wilson, in the late 1980s. In 1988, Cass' daughter Owen enlisted Michelle's help in finding out who her biological father was. When they found out it was Chuck Day, former touring bassist of the Mamas & the Papas, they kept it hidden and only revealed it after his death in 2008. Michelle also worked more directly for her former group by lobbying hard to get them inducted into the Rock and Roll Hall of Fame and ultimately succeeded. On January 12, 1998, John and Michelle put their differences aside temporarily and performed "California Dreamin' with Denny at the Waldorf-Astoria in New York City; 33 years and three-and-a-half miles from where they first sang together as the New Journeymen." It was the last time the three would sing together.

It seemed that even in death, John Phillips stirred up controversy. In September 2009, nearly nine years after his death, eldest daughter Mackenzie Phillips published her autobiography *High on Arrival*. In it, she revealed that in August 1979, the night before her wedding to Jeffrey Sessler, her father raped her after she passed out following a cocaine binge. She woke up to him on top of her engaging in sex. It was traumatizing to say the least, but, in her inebriated state, she hardly had the wherewithal to stop him. But it didn't end there. According to her, their relationship became consensual and occurred regularly over the next 10 years. She finally ended it after she became pregnant and had an abortion, which she says John financed.

It cast another dark cloud over the large interconnected Mamas & Papas family and put John's name back in the gutter. Many, including ex-wives Michelle and Genevieve and daughter Bijou, stated publicly that they did not believe Mackenzie's allegations, but daughter Chynna and Denny Doherty's daughter Jessica Woods stated that they did believe her, and that Denny was aware of John's dark secret and was horrified. Like every family, the offspring of the Mamas & the Papas deal with their issues, but most don't experience a bombshell of epic proportions like this. In the years since, the dust has settled and the family can be seen communicating and posting photographs together on social media and many relatives visit Chynna on her popular YouTube show *California Preachin'*, but how they feel about it is known only to them. It's been discussed, pondered, argued about and dissected every possible way, and the truth will probably never be known.

BIBLIOGRAPHY

"A Break-Up for the Mama's and Papa's?" *KRLA Beat* 2, no. 17, July 9, 1966, 1.

Carlin, Peter Ames. *Homeward Bound: The Life of Paul Simon*. New York: Henry Holt and Company, 2016.

Deck, Carol. "A Tale of Mama's and Papa's." *KRLA Beat* 2, no. 7, April 30, 1966, 4–5.

Doherty, Denny. *Of All the Things: The Complete ABC/Dunhill Masters*. Real Gone Music, RGM0673, 2018, CD Liner Notes.

Einarson, John. *Mr. Tambourine Man: The Life and Legacy of the Byrds' Gene Clark*. San Francisco: Backbeat Books, 2005.

"Exhaustion Helps Papa's Writing." *KRLA Beat* 2, no. 12, June 4, 1966, 6.

Fiegel, Eddi. *Dream a Little Dream of Me: The Life of Cass Elliot*. Chicago: Chicago Review Press, 2005.

Gould, Jonathan. *Otis Redding: An Unfinished Life*. New York: Crown Archetype, 2017.

Greenwald, Matthew. *Go Where You Wanna Go: The Oral History of the Mamas & the Papas*. New York: Cooper Square Press, 2002.

Halifax Three, The. *The Complete Halifax Three.* Collector's Choice Music CCM-298-2, 2002, CD Liner Notes.

Hall, Doug. *The Mamas & the Papas: California Dreamin'.* Kingston, Ontario: Quarry Music Books, 2000.

Journeymen, The. *Coming Attraction—Live!* Collector's Choice Music CCM-416-2, 2003, CD Liner Notes.

Journeymen, The. *The Journeymen.* Collector's Choice Music CCM-415-2, 2003, CD Liner Notes.

Journeymen, The. *New Directions in Folk Music.* Collector's Choice Music CCM-417, 2003, CD Liner Notes.

Kobashigawa, Kimi. "The Mamas and Papas." *KRLA Beat* 2, no. 2, March 26, 1966, 14.

Kubernik, Harvey, and Kenneth Kubernik. *A Perfect Haze: The Illustrated History of the Monterey International Pop Festival.* Solana Beach, CA: Santa Monica Press, LLC, 2011.

Linton Hall Cadet. *Linton Hall Military School Memories: One Cadet's Memoir.* Arlington, VA: Scrounge Press, 2014.

"Mamas, Papas Quit Pop." *KRLA Beat* 3, no. 16, October 21, 1967, 2, 4.

McCluskey III, Jamie. "Cass Meets John." *KRLA Beat* 2, no. 23, September 10, 1966, 10.

"Michelle—All-American Beauty." *16 Magazine,* August 1966, 16.

"Michelle's Out!" *KRLA Beat* 2, no.19, July 23, 1966, 2.

Oldham, Andrew Loog. *2Stoned.* London: Secker & Warburg, 2002.

Phillips, John. *Andy Warhol Presents "Man on the Moon": The John Phillips Space Musical.* Varese Sarabande 302 066 965 2, 2009, CD Liner Notes.

Phillips, John. *Jack of Diamonds.* Varese Sarabande 302 066 819 2, 2007, CD Liner Notes.

Phillips, John. *John Phillips (Wolfking of L.A.).* Varese Sarabande, 302 066 752 2, 2006, CD Liner Notes.

Phillips, John, and Jim Jerome. *Papa John: An Autobiography by John Phillips*. New York: Dell Publishing Co. Inc., 1986.

Phillips, Michelle. *California Dreamin': The True Story of the Mamas and the Papas*. New York: Warner Books Inc., 1986.

Priore, Dominic. *Riot on Sunset Strip: Rock 'n' Roll's Last Stand in Hollywood*. Revised edition. London: Jawbone Press, 2015.

Scully, Rock, and David Dalton. *Living with the Dead: Twenty Years on the Bus with Garcia and the Grateful Dead*. New York: Little, Brown and Company, 1996.

Sloan, P. F., and S. E. Feinberg. *What's Exactly the Matter with Me: Memoirs of a Life in Music*. London: Jawbone Press, 2014.

Thomas, Michael. "John Phillips: The Wolf King as Lord Byron." *Rolling Stone*, No. 70, November 12, 1970.

Townshend, Pete. *Who I Am: A Memoir*. New York: Harper, 2012.

Tuck, Mike. "Cass Goes to England 'to Get' Beatles' John." *KRLA Beat* 2, no. 16, July 2, 1966, 7.

Walker, Michael. *Laurel Canyon: The Inside Story of Rock-and-Roll's Legendary Neighborhood*. New York: Faber and Faber, Inc., 2006.

Webb, Jimmy. *The Cake and the Rain*. New York: St. Martin's Press, 2017.

Weissman, Dick, and Frank Jermance. *Navigating the Music Industry: Current Issues & Business Models*. Milwaukee, WI: Hal Leonard Corporation, 2003.

Weller, Sheila. "California Dreamgirl." *Vanity Fair*, No. 568, December 2007.

Wolliver, Robbie. *Hoot! A 25-Year History of the Greenwich Village Music Scene*. New York: St. Martin's Press, 1984.

INDEX

Note: Photo insert images are indicated by *p1, p2, p3,* etc.